A history of the Greek resistance in the
Second World War

Manchester University Press

Cultural History of Modern War

Series editors   Ana Carden-Coyne, Peter Gatrell, Max Jones,
Penny Summerfield and Bertrand Taithe

Already published

Carol Acton and Jane Potter   *Working in a world of hurt: trauma and resilience in the narratives of medical personnel in warzones*

Julie Anderson   *War, disability and rehabilitation in Britain: soul of a nation*

Lindsey Dodd   *French children under the Allied bombs, 1940–45: an oral history*

Rachel Duffett   *The stomach for fighting: food and the soldiers of the First World War*

Christine E. Hallett   *Containing trauma: nursing work in the First World War*

Jo Laycock   *Imagining Armenia: Orientalism, ambiguity and intervention*

Chris Millington   *From victory to Vichy: veterans in inter-war France*

Juliette Pattinson   *Behind enemy lines: gender, passing and the Special Operations Executive in the Second World War*

Chris Pearson   *Mobilizing nature: The environmental history of war and militarization in Modern France*

Jeffrey S. Reznick   *Healing the nation: soldiers and the culture of caregiving in Britain during the Great War*

Jeffrey S. Reznick   *John Galsworthy and disabled soldiers of the Great War: with an illustrated selection of his writings*

Michael Roper   *The secret battle: emotional survival in the Great War*

Penny Summerfield and Corinna Peniston-Bird   *Contesting home defence: men, women and the Home Guard in the Second World War*

Trudi Tate and Kate Kennedy (eds)   *The silent morning: culture and memory after the Armistice*

Spyros Tsoutsoumpis   *A history of the Greek resistance in the Second World War: the People's Armies*

Wendy Ugolini   *Experiencing war as the 'enemy other': Italian Scottish experience in World War II*

Laura Ugolini   *Civvies: middle-class men on the English Home Front, 1914–18*

Colette Wilson   *Paris and the Commune, 1871–78: the politics of forgetting*

http://www.arts.manchester.ac.uk/subjectareas/history/research/cchw/

A history of the Greek resistance in the Second World War

The People's Armies

~

SPYROS TSOUTSOUMPIS

Manchester University Press

Copyright © Spyros Tsoutsoumpis 2016

The right of Spyros Tsoutsoumpis to be identified as the author of this work has been asserted by him in accordance with the Copyright, Designs and Patents Act 1988.

Published by Manchester University Press
Altrincham Street, Manchester M1 7JA

www.manchesteruniversitypress.co.uk

British Library Cataloguing-in-Publication Data
A catalogue record for this book is available from the British Library

Library of Congress Cataloging-in-Publication Data applied for

ISBN   978 1 7849 9251 4   hardback
ISBN   978 1 5261 4349 5   paperback

First published by Manchester University Press in hardback 2016
This edition published 2019

The publisher has no responsibility for the persistence or accuracy of URLs for any external or third-party internet websites referred to in this book, and does not guarantee that any content on such websites is, or will remain, accurate or appropriate.

Typeset in Minion by
Servis Filmsetting Ltd, Stockport, Cheshire

Contents

Acknowledgements		*page* vi
Abbreviations		viii
	Introduction	1
1	The rise and origins of the People's Armies	13
2	Patriots and scoundrels: motivation and recruitment in the People's Armies	71
3	Not by bread alone: combat, everyday life and the formation of guerrilla identities	115
4	Cause, comrades and faith: morale in the guerrilla armies	155
5	A society at war: guerrilla governance and everyday life in Free Greece	201
	Conclusion	257
Select bibliography		265
Index		272

Acknowledgements

The writing of a book is seldom an individual venture, and this one is no exception. The book is based on my PhD dissertation undertaken at the University of Manchester, where I was fortunate to have Professor Penny Summerfield and Dr Max Jones as supervisors. Their generosity, insight and unfaltering patience played a crucial role in sustaining me through graduate school and the writing of this book. I also owe thanks to Professor Peter Gatrell and Dr Ana Carden-Coyne who provided valuable help and advice. Special thanks must go to Emma Brennan and everyone at Manchester University Press for their support and patience. Furthermore, I would like to thank the anonymous reviewers for their valuable suggestions and diligence.

Many thanks must also go to the archivists and librarians at ELIA, ASKI, GAK, DIS and the Liddell Hart Centre for Military Archives at King's College as well as the staff at the inter-library loan section at Manchester University Library for locating a host of arcane books and responding to endless queries. I would also like to recognise the kindness of the Liddell Hart Centre Trustees who gave me permission to quote from the Centre's collections.

I owe a particular debt to all the people who opened their homes and shared their memories with me in Igoumenitsa, Souli, Senitsa, Arta and Ioannina. Their warmth, hospitality and patience was immense as was their empathy for the people against whom they fought during this turbulent period. These discussions have provided me with profound insights and a deeper understanding of this period and the ordeal of the people who were caught in the midst of these events.

Last but certainly not least I want to thank my family for their patience, love, emotional and material support. I owe my interest in this tumultuous period to my paternal grandfather, Pilios, whose stories of the war and recollections of an Epirus that has now vanished first prompted me

Acknowledgements

to study history. Special thanks must also go to my mother Dimitra, my sister Natasha and my father Giannis, a voracious reader whose knowledge and personal experiences of the occupation and civil war have been immensely helpful. This book could not have been written without them.

I would like to dedicate this book to the memory of my grandparents, Pilios, Anastasia and Kostas and my aunt Rina whose narratives, experiences and memories have shaped this book in more ways than one.

Abbreviations

AMM	Allied Military Mission
ASKI	Arxeia Sighronis Koinonikis Istorias/Archives of Contemporary Social History
BMM	British Military Mission
DIS	Diefthnisi Istorias Stratou/Directorate for Army History
EAM	Ethniko Apeleftherotiko Metopo/National Liberation Front
EDES	Ethnikos Dimokratikos Ellinikos Sindesmos/Greek National Republican League
EDIA	Etairia Diasosis Istorikon Arheion/Society for the Preservation of Historical Archives
ELAS	Ellinikos Laikos Apeleftherotikos Stratos/Greek National Popular Liberation Army
ELIA	Elliniko Logotehniko kai Istoriko Arxeio/Greek Archive of Literature and History
EPON	Eniaia Panelladiki Organosi Neon/United Panhellenic Youth Association
GAK	Genika Arheia Kratous/General State Archives
GES	Geniko Epiteleio Stratou/General Army Staff
IAM	Istoriko Arheio Makedonias/Macedonian Historical Archive
IWM	Imperial War Museum
KKE	Kommunistiko Komma Ellados/Communist Party of Greece
LHCMA	Liddell Hart Centre for Military Archives
OSS	Office of Strategic Services
SOE	Special Operations Executive
TNA	The National Archives

Introduction

Between 1941 and 1944, Greece was the site of a bloody conflict in which Axis troops, collaborationist militias, guerrillas and British operatives fought each other in a small-scale war of attrition. The end of the war was followed by an even bloodier civil war that lasted for three years (1946–49). However, the conclusion of the civil war did not signal an end to the hostilities between the participants and their descendants. In the subsequent decades, memoirists, journalists, politicians and historians waged a long rearguard battle in newspaper columns, lecture halls and publishing houses.

The civil war yielded several by-products, the foremost of which was the outlawing of the left and the persecution of resistance veterans and their families. The period of the resistance was regarded by the state as a rehearsal for the civil war, a view reflected in the numerous historical works and memoirs published by right-wing resisters and British liaison officers who presented EAM/ELAS[1] as a Soviet puppet that aimed to pave the way for a left-wing dictatorship.[2] These views remained the orthodoxy until the 1970s, when a new generation of revisionist historians challenged this paradigm and 'suggested that at the least the nature of Communist control of EAM/ELAS needed further investigation and at worst the Anglo-American imperialism had strangled a genuinely popular radical movement'.[3] Despite their radical difference in opinion, these scholars did not divert from the focus or the methodology of their predecessors; most revisionist studies adopted a top-down approach and focused on two issues: why EAM/ELAS failed to seize power and who bore the responsibility for the outbreak of the civil war.[4]

The end of the Cold War facilitated a much more detached discussion of the period and heralded an impressive shift towards social history as scholars began to delve into areas that had either been neglected or considered taboo by their predecessors, such as the experiences of women and minorities; the Holocaust and the complicity of the Greek state in its perpetration; collaboration; reprisals; and memory.[5] Quite impressively, this flare-up of social history bypassed the people who were more often than not at the centre of these events: the guerrillas. The only systematic study of ELAS is Stefanos Sarafis, *ELAS: Greek Resistance Army*, a highly partisan work concerned with tactics and politics that was written in the 1940s to defend ELAS and its leadership from their detractors.[6]

Historians of the Greek resistance are by no means unique in this respect, since the history of the Second World War armed resistance movements has been ignored by most scholars of the period in Western Europe. This choice was largely shaped by political concerns. During the post-war period, the political successors of the resistance movements tried to distance themselves from the militant image they had espoused during the occupation. Instead, they favoured more pacific depictions that emphasised the partisans' sacrifice and identified the guerrilla as a victim of war and fascism.[7] Accordingly the resistance was presented as the collective venture of the whole nation and the militant rhetoric of wartime partisans was toned down.[8] These representations had a dual purpose: to create a more inclusive image of the resistance that would facilitate national reconciliation and enhance the political appeal of the left, and to deflect accusations from the far right that the movement was, in reality, a civil war waged by the left with the ultimate aim of snatching power. These concerns deterred many left-leaning scholars from discussing the experiences of the guerrilla fighters, since they were fearful that such studies would potentially undermine this narrative. The study of the armed resistance had an equally minimal appeal to more conservative scholars and traditional military historians who considered it at best a sideshow to the Allied war effort, and found its politics embarrassing.[9]

These concerns also shaped the narratives of a large number of veterans. The majority of personal testimonies contain very little on battle and its effects, while the references to joyful killing and the pleasures of fighting that are common in the personal testimonies of combatants in other conflicts are also conspicuously absent from the accounts of resistance veterans.[10] The persistence of such concerns is exemplified by the virulent reactions of veterans and pro-EAM historians during recent debates on wartime violence. Veterans and scholars not only denied that ELAS was implicated in any violent acts against civilians and stressed that resisters were above all the victims of violence, but they also insisted that any discussion of resistance violence leads to an unacceptable moral relativism that threatens to equate the resisters with their collaborationist rivals.[11] Nonetheless, this view of the guerrilla movement was not universally accepted. Radical students and splinter groups on the left criticised this approach and espoused a much more militant image of the resistance, one that idealised violence and stressed the political context of the movement.

The image of EDES[12] and its association with violence is less contested; EDES was, after all, created and headed by a professional soldier, while many of its leaders enrolled in the regular army during the post-war period, sometimes reaching prominent positions. However, the relationship of EDES with the past was also not entirely unproblematic. The association between the resistance, guerrilla warfare and the left led EDES veterans and apologists to downplay their ragged and aggressive wartime image, and stress that EDES, unlike its arch-rival, was a regular army comprising disciplined, conscious and patriotic volunteers. Such an account did not always sit well with some veterans, especially in the EDES heartland of western Epirus, where the deeds of the guerrillas and their wild masculinity continues to be celebrated in folk culture.[13]

The aim of this book is to address the discrepancy in the existing historiography and provide the first systematic study of the 'People's Armies' of ELAS and EDES during the occupation. Of course, these were not the only armed resistance groups to emerge during this period; however, ELAS and EDES far surpassed their rivals in terms of size, numerical strength and geographical expansion. Furthermore, even though ELAS exceeded EDES during the later stages of the resistance, numbers remained comparable, thereby enabling a balanced comparative study. However, this book is not a military history of the resistance, and those looking forward to an account of battles and tactics or an assessment of the commanders who led the 'People's Armies' into battle will be disappointed. Those who are searching for new political insights into the resistance and the causes of the civil war will also be let down. The book does not shun combat or politics; indeed, both feature quite extensively. However, as Richard Holmes noted, battle is merely 'the tip of the military iceberg'.[14] This book is a history that focuses on the rank and file of both organisations. It explores how the guerrillas of EDES and ELAS perceived the conflict and their role in it, and discusses how they dealt with the exertion of everyday life in the field, how they tried to overcome the fear and stress of combat, and how they behaved towards their rivals and the civilian population. ELAS and EDES had armed branches in many cities and towns, but this book is not interested in them. This is a study of rural resistance and the men involved.

The guerrilla groups have been often represented as political armies; consequently, studies have focused on militants and their attitudes. The influence of militants in the writing of resistance history is understandable, as such men were far more likely to write memoirs which discussions of the guerrilla groups would rely on; they would also provide information to the local historian, write in newspapers or volunteer for interviews with the historian who is looking for a more local flavour. Such men were also much more likely to be involved in the composition of the songs and plays used by scholars to delineate the guerrillas' profile and motivation.[15] Therefore, for most historians it is unthinkable that a guerrilla could be anything other than a militant. The focus on these men has shaped both the tone of many accounts and the questions asked by historians, who are, are as a rule, interested in the ideological beliefs of the guerrillas.

However, this approach presents several problems. First, it limits the historical inquiry to those who took the trouble to leave behind their version of events. Furthermore, it obscures the distinctions between different categories of men, since press-ganged recruits, defectors and enlisted men are far less likely to have left behind a record of their activities and motivation. At the same time, such accounts tend to tone down the more unsavoury aspects of the guerrilla's experience, such as desertion, looting, fear and violence against civilians. However, the men discussed in this book seldom feature in this category; indeed, the book holds that militants were a decided minority among the guerrillas, most of whom were moved to enlist for reasons that had little or nothing to do with ideology, and who remained defiantly opportunistic and apolitical to the end.

Locating the voice of these guerrillas is a challenging task. The documents generated by the resistance – reports, circulars, court-martial records – are an extremely rich resource that provides important insights into daily life in the guerrilla bands, discipline and morale, and relations between the guerrilla bands and the civilian population. However, the use of such documents is not without dangers, since the men who compiled them were frequently prone to exaggerate their own achievements and downplay those of their rivals. There is also a tendency to gloss over some aspects of everyday life, such as desertion and looting, that might potentially tarnish them in the eyes of their superiors and thwart their chances of promotion. Gendarmerie reports and the dispatches of civil servants and government agents also provide useful insights into life in Free Greece and civil–military relations, even though the profound political prejudices of these men and women mean that such reports must, like those of the resistance, be read carefully. Red Cross reports provide valuable and balanced insights into the political and economic situation in Free Greece and the effects of reprisals on the rural population. An equally important but rather underused source are the reports, dispatches and diaries of British liaison officers. Some scholars have cautioned against using such sources, pointing to the intense anti-communism of some of these officers.[16] However, for the most part these reports provide an accurate and insightful image of life in Free Greece and even though the political prejudices of many officers are often obvious, the information provided on the guerrilla groups is rarely tainted as a result.

Despite their drawbacks, personal testimonies, diaries and memoirs are of paramount importance in reconstructing the experiences of guerrillas. Unfortunately, surviving diaries and letters are few in number, and most were written by educated militants who often occupied senior positions in the People's Armies. This problem can be addressed through the use of memoirs and oral testimonies. However, these sources also present several problems: the erosion of memory over time often leads to distortions and omissions; more importantly, memory is influenced as much by present needs and the expectations of a prospective audience as by past experiences. To complicate matters further, memoirists are often 'motivated as much by the need to address feelings which date from the event itself as from the imagined expectations of [the] audience at the moment of telling'.[17] Politics are an equally important concern, since memoirists often distort their experiences in order to render them compatible with the prerequisites of a particular political agenda. These problems have led some historians of war to dismiss memoirs as a source.[18]

However, every type of source brings its own specific problems. Catherine Merridale argues that letters are also often written with a particular audience in mind. This leads writers to conform to readers' expectations and, thus, to consciously omit events they might regard as inappropriate.[19] This has led some scholars to suggest that memoirs provide a more accurate and balanced view of personal experiences; according to Michael Roper, 'retrospective accounts are generally more reflective about the emotional experience of war than the letter or diary', since at the time of experience, language had tended to function as a primitive vehicle for ejecting raw and intolerable sense impressions ... time was needed before a coherent narrative could be constructed ... the sensations conveyed in letters, by comparison with memoirs, were relatively undigested and are often now opaque to us, forcing us to read between the lines.[20]

Memoirs must be treated with caution, but dismissing them entirely deprives the historian of a crucial source, since they can often provide invaluable glimpses of the everyday lives and perceptions of the guerrillas.

Oral testimonies are no less important and have been used extensively in this book. Many of the oral testimonies used in this account were collected between 2006 and 2008 in Epirus in north-western Greece. Very few of the men and women I interviewed had occupied senior positions in either organisation. Most of them were rank-and-file members: farmers, herders, artisans who had spent their entire lives in their native villages before joining ELAS or EDES. Some of the interviewees were illiterate and a number of interviews were conducted only partially in Greek, as several of them were more comfortable talking in their native Arvanite and Vlach languages. Unlike militants, who tend to situate their narratives in a broader national framework, most of the men and women whom I interviewed situated their narratives in their community. Indeed, for many of them the war was almost a village affair and the events that mattered were not the ceasefire between EAM and EDES or the formation of the PEEA (Politiki Epitropi Ethnikes Apeleftherosis) government but rather a murder that took place in their village, a raid in which a number of houses were burned or the loss of a family member. Accordingly the civil war clashes are recalled not so much as a fight between two opposing sides but rather as a struggle between rival families. Indeed, very few of the people I interviewed presented their choices as ideological; family and want were the most common drivers, as many either joined along with a family member or chose to enlist after they were advised to do so by a relative. Politics are not entirely absent, yet they play a secondary role to material circumstances; food and the difficulties of acquiring it were recurring themes in most interviews. These themes are no less present in the oral testimonies which I located in the archives, or the valuable collections of oral testimonies published during the past decade by several authors which have also been extensively used.[21]

Despite their usefulness, oral testimonies do not present an 'authentic' version of events; indeed, many interviewees tacitly avoided touching sensitive issues such as atrocities or the involvement of a family member

Introduction

in activities which they thought to be dishonourable, and some quietly avoided issues which they thought could damage the reputation of their community or of fellow villagers. The passage of time has also played an important part in eroding and distorting their memory of events. Despite these considerable drawbacks, oral testimonies provide access to regions that are impenetrable through traditional sources and can open avenues for inquiry and re-examination in a way that other sources cannot. As Roderick Kedward argued, 'oral testimony, even fifty years after the event, suggests hypotheses, provides personal details, reveals local colour, facilitates insights, and preserves individuality in a way that historians of an under-documented area of history cannot easily afford to ignore'.[22]

The book will address five main issues. The first is the rise of the resistance and the People's Armies. The book is not interested so much in the creation or political origins of EAM and EDES, as this has been discussed thoroughly in several important studies.[23] Rather, it focuses on how the resistance groups managed to take root and develop in rural areas and provides a better understanding of the resistance's social basis and the motivation of activists. Historians saw the emergence of the resistance as an outcome of oppression and economic disaffection; the book challenges these views and suggests that closer attention must be paid to local dynamics and the importance of culture and kinship ties. The book also explores the importance of violence and the role of the much-maligned 'foreign factor' in the formation and expansion of the resistance armies.

The second issue is that of motivation. The guerrilla fighters have been casually represented as ideological volunteers; according to one historian, 'most people made a moral choice, ideology really counted and it is this that makes this period distinctive'.[24] The book challenges this widely held view and explores a broad spectrum of factors, including kinship and regional ties, coercion and want. It is indubitable that the earliest bands contained a significant number of men who were politically motivated; however, the majority of these men were seasoned activists of urban extraction. On the other hand, ideology played a much less important role for the peasant recruits, the majority of whom were prompted to enlist by much more mundane factors: hunger, kinship solidarity – many of the early band leaders relied on their kinship and regional networks for recruits – problems with the law, adventure and unemployment. Most of these men shared a common characteristic: they were volunteers who chose to enlist of their own accord. The onset of the civil war rapidly changed this, as more and more men enlisted either because they were coerced or because they believed that participation in an armed guerrilla band would guarantee their safety and that of their families in an increasingly sectarian political environment. However, political polarisation did not increase the importance of ideology; indeed, political motivation became less and less relevant, as evidenced by the increasing rate of defections as individuals changed their allegiances in search of revenge, rewards and security.

The book is no less interested in the daily lives and activities of the guerrillas, which are discussed in the third chapter. Fighting was the ultimate purpose of the guerrilla; however, we know very little of how guerrillas experienced combat and even less about their activities and daily lives when they were not engaged in fighting. This chapter follows the guerrillas from enlistment to combat in an effort to understand how men experienced their participation in the resistance and how these experiences shaped attitudes and identities both within the bands and towards civilians. Becoming a guerrilla entailed a complete break with and departure from civilian life and home for years; for some young men it was the first time they had left their home and family; others had experienced combat and long periods of separation during the last war. However, neither group had any knowledge or preparation for the life that lay ahead of them. Guerrillas had to learn, often in a brutal manner, how to survive in the countryside, live off the land, deal with the civilian population and conduct operations in a harsh and forbidding environment. Combat had a similar impact: the harshness and the personalised nature of irregular warfare stunned many guerrillas. However, most men were eventually able to overcome their reservations and many found combat a fascinating and often enjoyable experience. These experiences bred a particularly masculinist culture that celebrated endurance, physical strength and violence and denigrated non-combatants as unmanly. Such perceptions gradually created a rift between the guerrillas and the men and women in whose name they fought.

The fourth chapter discusses the issue of morale. Resistance historians have, as a rule, attributed the resilience of the guerrilla armies to the combatants' ideological beliefs. These beliefs were undoubtedly important; however, political ideology alone was seldom able to prepare the men for the realities of the battlefield or sustain them through the tribulations of everyday life, and not all men joined for ideological reasons or were interested in politics. The resistance organisations were aware both of the importance of ideology and of the deficiencies of their men in this regard, and made persistent efforts to indoctrinate the guerrillas. However, very

Introduction

few men developed the messianic beliefs described by some scholars and many remained indifferent to politics.

Group ties, leadership and ideas of honour played a much more important role in helping men to deal with the exertions of combat and everyday life. However, these were not enough to sustain them as the conflict became a brutal civil war and the guerrillas found themselves fighting against the much more determined and well-trained Wehrmacht troops. The guerrilla organisations responded to these challenges by adopting increasingly stern disciplinary measures. These actions were often sufficient to stem the tide of desertion and restore discipline; however, they also bred resentment among the guerrillas and undermined the ties of comradeship that had characterised the guerrilla bands up this point. Guerrillas became increasingly withdrawn and looked for solace to the supernatural. Religious practices and rituals played a part from the very beginning in the lives of the guerrillas. However, as the war dragged on their importance and intricacy increased among the demoralised guerrillas, who came to rely more and more on them for respite and to establish a semblance of control in a chaotic situation.

The final issue addressed in the fifth chapter is daily life and guerrilla governance in Free Greece. Scholars have, as a rule, argued that participation in EAM was 'catholic' and 'PanHellenic' and presented the rule of EAM/ELAS as a 'cosmogony' that challenged the peasantry's traditional mores and introduced them to new 'collectivities, where they learned how to strike and protest, to conduct propaganda, to make demands, to sacrifice themselves, to fight'.[25] However, such idealised depictions fail to capture both the variety of experiences within Free Greece and the variety of peasant responses. The guerrillas were aware of the importance of developing a parallel state structure that would provide the peasantry with collective goods and endow their organisations with a semblance of legitimacy. However, guerrillas and civilians often had very different ideas of their respective roles and responsibilities, especially when it came to thorny issues such as justice and taxation. Guerrilla impositions were far from the sole problem, as the resistance's civilian institutions were notoriously corrupt and the men chosen by EAM/ELAS and EDES to govern local societies were far more interested in advancing their personal agendas than in serving their communities.

Such tensions were exacerbated by the inability of the resistance to protect the peasants from the increasingly brutal German reprisals and the clashes between the various resistance groups that eventually led to the formation of several Axis-sponsored anti-guerrilla militias in the first half of 1944. Violence led to counter-violence which gradually transformed rural Greece into a Hobbesian dystopia where guerrillas, militiamen and civilians used their weapons to settle scores, persecute opponents and exterminate their political rivals. However, militant support and armed disobedience were ultimately two extreme positions located on the edges of a grey zone in which the boundaries between opposition and support were uncertain and constantly traversed. Peasants often supported some actions of the resistance while remaining steadfastly opposed to others. Furthermore, peasants were able to resist guerrilla impositions and retain their autonomy in subtler ways; foot-dragging, bribery and sabotage were important weapons in the countless small struggles fought between guerrillas and civilians in Free Greece. However, both support and opposition were often unrelated to ideology. Survival was the foremost concern of the peasants whose attitudes were ultimately shaped by local issues, and their foremost allegiance lay with their kin and locality.

Notes

1 EAM was the acronym for Ethniko Apeleftherotiko Metopo [the National Liberation Front]; ELAS, or Ellinikos Laikos Apeleftherotikos Stratos [the Greek National Liberation Army], was its military wing.
2 Alexander Kitroeff, 'Continuity and change in contemporary Greek historiography', *European History Quarterly* 19 (1989), pp. 269–98.
3 Mark Mazower, 'The Cold War and the appropriation of memory: Greece after liberation', in Istvan Deak, Jan T. Gross and Tony Judt (eds), *The Politics of Retribution in Europe* (Princeton, NJ: Princeton University Press, 2000), pp. 224–5.
4 Nikos Marantzidis and Giorgos Antoniou, 'The Axis occupation and civil war: changing trends in Greek historiography, 1941–2002', *Journal of Peace Research* 24 (2004), pp. 226–7.
5 Nikos Marantzidis, Stratos Dordanas, Nikos Zaikos and Giorgos Adoniou (eds), *To Olokaftoma stin Ellada kai ta Valkania* [The Holocaust in Greece and the Balkans] (Thessaloniki: Epikentro, 2011); Giorgos Margaritis, *Anepithimitoi simpatrioties* [Unwanted compatriots] (Athens: Vivliorama: 2005); Riki Van Boeschoten, *Anapoda hronia: silogiki mnimi kai istoria sto Ziaka Grevenon, 1900–1950* [Difficult years: collective memory and history in Ziakas Grevenon] (Athens: Plethron, 1997); Tasos Hatzianastasiou, *Andartes kai kapetanioi I ethniki antistasi kata tis Voulgariki katohis tis anatolikis Makedonias kai tis Thrakis, 1942–1944* [Guerrillas and kapetanioi, the national resistance to the Bulgarian occupation of eastern Macedonia

Introduction

and Thrace] (Thessalonica: Kiriakidis, 2003); Stratos Dordanas, *To aima to athoon: adipina ton Germanikon arhon katohis sti Makedonia 1941–1944* [The blood of the innocent: reprisals of the occupation authorities in Macedonia] (Athens: Estia, 2007); Stratos Dordanas, *Ellines enadion Ellinon: o kosmos ton tagmaton asfaleias stin katohiki Thessaloniki 1941–1944* [Greek against Greek: the world of the security battalions in occupied Thessaloniki] (Thessalonica: Epikentro, 2006); Tasoula Vervenioti, *To Diplo Vivlio* [The dual book] (Athens: Vivliorama, 2003).

6 Stefanos Sarafis, *ELAS: Greek Resistance Army* (London: Merlin Press, 1980).
7 Alessandro Portelli, 'Myth and morality in the history of the Italian resistance', *History Workshop Journal Issue* 74 (2012), pp. 211–23.
8 Tony Judt, 'The past is another country: myth and memory in post-war Europe', in Istvan Deak, Jan T. Gross and Tony Judt (eds), *The Politics of Retribution in Europe* (Princeton, NJ: Princeton University Press, 2000), pp. 298–300.
9 See, for instance, Basil Liddell Hart's classic study, *A History of the Second World War* (London: Pan, 2011).
10 Joanna Bourke, *An Intimate History of Killing: Face-to-Face Killing in Twentieth-Century Warfare* (London: Granta, 2000).
11 Stathis Kalyvas, 'Aristere via: mythoi kai pragmatikotita' [Left-wing violence: myths and reality], *Ta Nea* 17993 (2004), http://www.tovima.gr/politics/article/?aid=311312 (accessed 20 January 2015).
12 Ethnikos Dimokratikos Ellinikos Sindesmos [the National Republican League of Greece].
13 Songs about EDES, Zervas and the *oplarhigos*/leaders of the organisation are still a staple of folk music in much of Epirus. Kostas Ioannou, *Alithines Istories tis Katohes* [True stories from the occupation] (unpublished, personal collection), p. 9.
14 Richard Holmes, *Acts of War: The Behaviour of Men in Battle* (New York: Macmillan, 1985), p. 11.
15 Riki Van Boeschoten, *From Armatolik to People's Rule: Investigation into the Collective Memory of Rural Greece, 1750–1949* (Amsterdam: A.M. Hackett, 1991).
16 Ole Smith, 'The memoirs and reports of the British liaison officers in Greece', *Journal of the Hellenic Diaspora* 11 (1984), pp. 9–34.
17 Michael Roper, 'Re-remembering the soldier hero: the psychic and social construction of memory in personal narratives of the Great War', *History Workshop Journal* 50 (2000), p. 184.
18 James McPherson, *For Cause and Comrades: Why Men Fought in the Civil War* (New York: Oxford University Press, 1997), p. 11.
19 Catherine Merridale, 'Culture, ideology and combat in the Red Army, 1939–45', *Journal of Contemporary History* 41 (2006), p. 312.

20 Michael Roper, *The Secret Battle: Emotional Survival in the Great War* (Manchester: Manchester University Press, 2009), pp. 22-3.
21 Georgia Skopouli, *Sta aposkia tis istorias* [In the margins of history] (Athens: Rodakio 2013); Vasiliki Papagiannis, *Kravges tis mnimes, katohe, antistasi, emfilios* [Screams of memory, occupation, resistance, civil war] (Athens: Sokolis, 2002); Giannis Priovolos, *Mia alisida mnimes, Achaea kai voreia Peloponnisos, 1940-1949* [A chain of memories, Achaea and northern Peloponnesus] (Athens: Alfeios, 2007); Thanasis Mitsopoulos, *Ananminiseis agoniston tou Vermiou kai tou Kaimaktsalan tou Paikou kai tou Kilkis* [Recollections of fighters from Vermio, Kaimktsalan, Paikon and Kilkis] (Athens: self-published, 1995). Unless otherwise noted, all the translations from Greek publications, archival documents and oral interviews are my own. The interview quotations preserve the grammatical inconsistencies of the original speech.
22 Quoted in Margaret Collin Weitz, *Sisters in the Resistance* (London: John Wiley, 1998), p. 15.
23 John Louis Hondros, *Occupation and Resistance, the Greek Agony 1941-1944* (New York, 1983); Prokopis Papastratis, *British Policy towards Greece during the Second World War, 1941-1944* (Cambridge: Cambridge University Press, 1984); Andre Gerolymatos, *Guerrilla Warfare and Espionage in Greece 1940-1944* (New York: Pella, 1992).
24 Stathis Kalyvas, 'Sillogike mnime, dimosia istoria kai politiki orthotita: I dekaetia tou 1940 mesa apo treis istorikes egkiklopodies' [Collective memory, public history and political correctness: the civil war in three historical encyclopedias], in Giorgos Antoniou and Nikos Marantzides (eds), *I Epohe tis sighises* [The era of confusion] (Athens: Estia, 2008), p. 207.
25 Kalyvas, 'Sillogike mnime', pp. 227-8.

1

The rise and origins of the People's Armies

On 7 June 1942 a group of 12 armed men arrived in Domnista, a large village located in the uplands of Evrytania in central Greece. The presence of armed bands was far from uncommon in the mountains during this turbulent period; however, it soon became obvious that these men were not mere bandits. They did not demand food or money from the peasants and avoided the shops and the village café. The group was led by Thanasis Klaras, aka Ares Velouhiotes, a veteran communist cadre who later became one of the leaders of ELAS, the principal guerrilla organisation in occupied Greece. After taking some minutes to chat with the few men who lounged in the village's *kafeneio*, Velouhiotes called for the president and the parish priest whom he asked to gather all the inhabitants in the village piazza. Once the villagers gathered, he gave a brief speech on ELAS and its mission that culminated with the declaration of 'the commencement of the revolution against the occupiers and their local collaborators'.[1] Velouhiotes's speech has been justly seen as the opening salvo of the armed resistance struggle. Armed bands had appeared earlier in several areas of Greece; however, the majority had steered clear of inhabited areas and avoided clashing with the Axis troops. In the following weeks, this would change radically as ELAS leaders increasingly followed Velouhiotes's example. They made appearances in villages where they spoke about ELAS, recruited volunteers and proceeded to attack gendarmerie stations and Italian patrols.

The events that followed the declaration made by Velouhiotes have been covered extensively by scholars; however, much less is known about the intervening period between Greece's capitulation and the appearance of the guerrilla armies. This chapter will chart the course of the

People's Armies from the establishment of the first clandestine nuclei to the appearance of the guerrilla bands, and examine the processes that led to the creation of the armed resistance groups and facilitated their expansion in the countryside. The Greek resistance has been often represented as a spontaneous patriotic affair; however, this was not the case. Unlike the Yugoslav partisans, the Greek guerrillas did not appear in any strength in the mountains until mid-1942; moreover, free zones were established only in late spring 1943. What caused this delay? The brutality exhibited by German and Bulgarian troops in suppressing the first abortive attempts at resistance in northern Greece in late 1941 certainly played a major role in convincing the political world and the peasantry of the futility of resistance. No less important was the infighting between the different Venizelist and Royalist political factions that were unwilling to put to rest their pre-war feud.[2]

However, these were not the sole causes behind this delay. The capitulation of the country was followed by its division into zones of occupation – Italian, German and Bulgarian – and the unprecedented looting of the country's resources by the Axis forces. These events led to a profound economic crisis that culminated in a devastating famine, resulting in the loss of thousands of lives in the winter of 1941–42. Several scholars have suggested that the crisis acted as a catalyst to the radicalisation of the population and the consequent appearance of the guerrilla bands.[3] However, the crisis did not have a uniform impact in the countryside. Some areas suffered greatly, especially the central Pindus highlands, yet other regions remained largely unscathed, while in some areas the peasantry were able to profit heavily from speculation and black market trade. Nonetheless, even in the most sorely tried areas, want and violence did not galvanise the peasantry into action; indeed, there was often a detrimental effect on the efforts of resistance cadres to raise support. An EAM cadre from the region of Parnassida, a poor mountainous area in central Greece, noted: 'everyone lived in agony and fear, worried about the outcome of this situation, about how they will be able to secure the morrow's bread ... hunger and fear forced even the most well-meaning people to avoid me'.[4] During this period, armed resistance and outright collaboration were two extreme positions which few were willing to espouse. The majority of the population were concerned with survival and moved within a grey zone where the lines between collaboration and resistance, rampant opportunism and patriotic activity were often vague and sometimes entirely non-existent.

Fear and want were not the only factors that stalled the formation of the guerrilla groups. EAM/ELAS and EDES were urban movements with weak ties to the countryside, at least during their inception. The absence of such ties made the task of guerrillas and agitators often difficult and sometimes impossible, as peasants were seldom willing to risk their safety and well-being for the sake of outsiders. One ELAS cadre noted that peasants would listen sympathetically and provide encouraging words, 'but decline to make any commitments about the future', or to provide them with food and other necessities.[5] The importance of such ties has been largely overlooked by scholars, who have focused on the role of ideology and attributed EAM's success to its political programme.[6] Political ideas were, of course, of great importance; however, as Paul Staniland noted 'they need to be turned into durable organisations in very challenging and dangerous circumstances. Insurgent leaders are not unconstrained agents who are able to create whatever organizations they please.'[7] Indeed, what often determined the success or failure of a guerrilla band was neither the strength of its arguments nor the rhetorical prowess of its leaders but its ties to local communities and its ability to mobilise local support networks. The existence of such connections gave the resistance bands access to reliable information, provisions and a ready-made pool of recruits, and enabled them to form bonds of trust and cooperative links that would be impossible for outsiders. The profound importance of these ties becomes evident when we examine the membership of the first resistance bands and political organisations, which were more often than not built around the cadres' personal and familial networks.

However, such ties were not always in place and often the guerrillas had to form political organisations from the top down. The guerrillas strove to achieve this by dealing in the only currency available to them at the time – violence. They offered their services to local warring factions, hunted bandits and collaborators, and punished 'moral' transgressors such as petty thieves and prostitutes. Such services served to ingratiate the resistance in the local communities and even led some scholars to present the guerrillas as Robin Hood-type outlaws. Yet many of the guerrillas' victims were neither collaborators nor delinquents, but members of the local elites: political power brokers, village presidents, gendarmerie officers, landowners, professionals and schoolteachers. These people were not always targeted for political reasons; indeed, it seems that much of the violence during this turbulent period was rooted in local cleavages. However, violence served to reshape society in a series of ways; it exhibited the guerrillas' reach, deposed potential opponents and solidified the alliances between the guerrillas and local political factions.

Violence played a pivotal role in the establishment of the People's Armies; however, this was not the sole reason for the peasants' support of the guerrilla organisations. The military ventures of the guerrillas gradually endowed them with an aura of invulnerability and earned them the admiration of large segments of the population, particularly among the youth who began to join in increasing numbers. The arrival and establishment of the British Special Operations Executive (SOE) in late 1942 played an equally important role. The British helped ELAS and EDES to deal with the lack of funds and provisions that had stalled their development and had created tensions between the guerrillas and the peasantry. Furthermore, the presence of the SOE helped legitimise the guerrilla groups, particularly among the rural elites who had been awed by the violence used by ELAS, and enabled them to expand at an unprecedented rate from their lairs in the Pindos mountains and lay the foundations for the creation of 'Free Greece'.

State and society during the first year of the occupation

No sight could have provided the traveller with a more striking contrast to the wretchedness of Athens in the summer of 1942 than the rich plain of Pineia in western Peloponnesus. However, Giorgos Papas had not journeyed for leisure or to trade on the local black market, as many of his fellow passengers might have thought when they saw this elegantly dressed man boarding the train. It is also uncertain whether the beauty of the landscape caught his attention. Undoubtedly, Papas was a brave man, something that he had proved repeatedly during the recent war. However, like most resistance novices, he could not stop worrying about whether his presence or purpose – to raise a guerrilla band – had been betrayed to the Italian Carabinieri and the gendarmes who checked passengers' papers at every station they passed through.

A few weeks before this trip, Papas had created a small nationalist resistance organisation. Following long discussions, he and his fellow conspirators decided to travel in his native district of Ileia to assess the possibility of forming a guerrilla band. Papas's first contacts were his fellow veterans from the Albanian front – shepherds, farmers and peddlers who lived in the region's many villages. However, he was turned down successively by his contacts, one of whom briskly told him:

> you'd better leave us in peace Mr Giorgos ... we're all nice and quiet here and the Carabinieri do not lift a finger against us, in fact they treat us much

The rise and origins of the People's Armies

better than the gendarmes ... whatever might happen, those on top will have a good time and the poor people will foot the bill. We have fought enough. Let them do the fighting for us now.

This experience led Papas to presume that 'nothing can be done ... indeed the calm that predominates in the whole rural area makes a striking comparison to the nervousness and anxiety that predominates in Athens ... here it is as if nothing has happened. The slow rhythm of everyday life has not changed a bit.'[8]

Papas was not the only one to fail in such a venture. With the exception of a few large market towns like Aigion, Amaliada, Pirgos and the city of Patra, EAM had made very limited inroads into the northern Peloponnese. Moreover, the first ELAS bands did not appear in this region until late in the spring of 1943, almost a year after they had appeared on the opposite coast of Roumeli. Unfortunately, Papas does not elaborate further on the causes of these failures. Many historians have presented Greece as a country on the brink of revolt as a result of food shortages and Axis oppression.[9] However, Papas conveys a very different image in his diary; food was abundant, the Italians hardly ventured out of the towns and when they did, they were much more amenable than their Greek counterparts. Of course, this view must be understood within the context of Papas's experience of occupation in Athens; after all, he was not the first townsman to view the countryside as a haven of quiet and plenty. Smirni Maragou, a left-wing medical student who returned to her native island of Lefkada in the winter of 1941, was equally shocked by the serenity and the abundance of food in the coastal towns of western Greece. For example, in Nafpaktus:

> the people lived without the constant agony of hunger; we went to a tavern for dinner and there was plenty of fish, even lobster and shrimp, the fishermen next to us were drinking and eating merrily, filling the air with their laughter and their voices. They lived in their own little world hardly interested in what was going on elsewhere.[10]

Maragou and Papas might have formed a different image if they had ventured further inland to the mountain villages of Panahaikon and Vardousia; however, it is certain that the hunger that ravaged the cities and many of the islands was almost unknown in many parts of rural Greece. The image of Italian benevolence conveyed by Papas's acquaintance also provides an equally striking contrast with the images of Axis brutality and callousness common in wartime propaganda. Italian occupation was certainly far from benevolent, and the available testimonies of

Italian soldiers provide an often shocking image of the trail of theft, loot, rape and violence in areas such as Thessaly and western Macedonia.[11] However, the patterns of violence and the attitudes of the occupying troops differed widely; often, the troops pursued very different policies in adjoining regions. Italian occupation was characterised by extreme brutality in the area of Konitsa in Epirus, where search parties casually looted peasant houses and tortured returning veterans who were suspected of harbouring guns and ammunition.[12] Conversely, such incidents were almost unknown in the adjoining area of Zagori, where the Italian presence was limited to a few isolated guard posts. Here, relations with the local population were largely amicable.[13]

The Greek resistance groups, like their French counterparts, placed 'heavy emphasis on silence'.[14] EAM's manifesto urged people to adopt a posture of 'dignified detachment' and advised them to desist from socialising with or assisting the occupiers in any way, stressing that any kind of help was nothing short of betrayal.[15] However, as Richard Vinen noted in his history of occupied France, 'real encounters' with the occupation troops 'did not always fit into preconceived code of etiquette'.[16] The Italian encampment in Sparta was crammed with Greek peddlers, most of whom were very young, who traded food and cigarettes with soldiers seeking to supplemented their meagre rations by selling their equipment to the Greeks.[17] An unofficial market was established between Greeks and Italians in the Zagori villages, in which peasants sold and exchanged contraband with the help of Italian soldiers who casually frequented the taverns and cafés of large villages such as Papigo, where they socialised with the local Greeks.[18]

However, this uneasy coexistence was not always in place. The capitulation in April 1941 was followed by a period of upheaval and anarchy. The southward progress of the German army led thousands of civilians, police officers and civil servants to abandon their homes through fear of reprisals. In northern Greece, the state had effectively ceased to exist.[19] These refugees were joined by tens of thousands of soldiers who tried to return to their homes by every means possible, often discovering that their families had moved out in the frantic weeks following the German invasion. Social dislocation was far from the only problem. Civil servants who returned from the front found themselves without work, shopkeepers found their shops looted and farmers found their livestock depleted and tools damaged by retreating soldiers and locals alike. Some tried to reclaim their property using violence, others turned to family and political connections, while a large number of returning servicemen, like

Giorgos Lazanis, a schoolteacher from a village near Ioannina, abandoned all hope and 'let fate take care of us ... while we waited for some news that would show us which road to follow'.[20]

This power vacuum led many prominent intellectuals and politicians to lend their support to the collaborationist government of General Georgios Tsolakoglou.[21] In his post-war memoir, Tsolakoglou depicted himself as a covert resister and paralleled his activities to those of the Byzantine scholar Gennadios Scholarios, noting that he too 'worked for the resurrection of the nation under the pretext of subservience'.[22] Even though such ex post facto rationalisations must be taken with more than a pinch of salt, like other military and political leaders who collaborated in occupied Europe, Tsolakoglou believed that collaboration would enable him to defend better 'the national interest, sovereignty and unity' of the country.[23] Tsolakoglou was a dour, professional soldier who had few friends and was neither popular nor loved. However, for many citizens and most politicians, his government was the only thing preventing a descent into chaos and which might eventually enable them 'to salvage what could still be saved' from the wreckage of occupation.[24]

The Tsolakoglou administration had three main aims. The first was to protect the country's territorial integrity and prevent any loss of land; the second was to preserve the existing state structures and enforce law and order; and the third and most important was to relieve the effects of the looming famine. In December 1941, in an encyclical addressed to the heads of prefectures, village presidents and mayors of the country, Tsolokaglou noted that 'my mission is to save the people of our country from the immediate danger of famine and to retain the moral and spiritual foundations of our nation intact until the day the sun of peace will once again brighten the dark skies of Europe'.[25] However, the government failed to achieve most of its goals. The gendarmerie was unable to reinstate control in the countryside, while Tsolakoglou failed to dissuade the occupation authorities from supporting Bulgarian claims in northern Greece or to check the brutalities committed by occupation troops. Furthermore, despite its efforts, the government failed in its foremost task of alleviating the consequences of famine. During the winter of 1941–42, thousands of city dwellers perished as a result of famine and related diseases. These failures undermined the legitimacy of a government already damaged by a series of resignations and internal feuds. Three months after General Tsolakoglou's government was sworn in, one of his ministers noted in private that 'the government is limited to

Athens, Piraeus and their environs at most ... beyond this boundary no one takes it seriously'.[26]

Although the government endured for several more months, it is certain that neither the Tsolakoglou administration nor the pre-war politicians who were unwilling to put the Venizelist–Royalist feud to rest presented a viable political alternative capable of rallying the people's loyalties. Essentially, this power vacuum gave birth to EAM and EDES. However, neither organisation was able to build a strong following until mid-1942. In the first year of the war, survival rather than revolt was the foremost concern of the bewildered citizenry of Athens, Thessaloniki and other major cities. A diarist described the situation in Athens as follows:

> nothing is important save the issue of food ... we have become desensitised to everything else, and this feeling becomes more and more intense. Now we really understand what seemed incomprehensible beforehand – the indifference that soldiers show towards those who fall dead or wounded next to them. The instinct of self-preservation silences all other voices.[27]

This sense of helplessness and social disintegration was equally apparent in many of the smaller towns and cities across Greece. A report from Macedonia in the summer of 1942 noted:

> the living conditions of the urban population are very harsh, particularly of the poorer classes who are deprived of everything ... and have already started selling their properties, houses, shops ... the people have been seized by panic, they do not care to protest and show no signs of anger against those who deprive them of their life blood but are willing to forego everything to ensure their daily bread.[28]

However, the situation in the countryside was often very different; indeed, the Axis presence was hardly felt in many mountainous communities of the interior. For example Tsamantas, a mountain town with 2,000 inhabitants nestled high in the Mourgana mountains near the Greco-Albanian border, was visited twice by occupation troops – during the Italian invasion in the autumn of 1940 and in June 1944 when the Wehrmacht laid waste to a number of villages in the area. During the four intervening years, the entire area of Mourgana, comprising 16 villages with 20,000 inhabitants, was completely free from Axis interference.[29] The Axis presence was more intense in the mountainous areas of Voion and Grevena in south-western Macedonia, where the Italian authorities used excessive violence in their search for arms during the summer of 1942.[30] However, this was not the case in the adjoining area of Florina, where the German authorities and the local representatives of the Greek state managed to form an uneasy alliance until the summer of 1943.[31]

The Axis presence was also thin in the mountain ranges of central and southern Pindus, the birthplace of the guerrilla movement. In the mountain village of Mirofilon in western Thessaly, the peasants 'were not harmed or ill-treated either by the Italians or by the Germans whom they saw only twice throughout the occupation. The Italians made a lukewarm effort to collect hidden guns and the peasants gave them a couple of old shotguns, they did not bother us any other time.'[32] The Axis presence was equally scarce on the other side of the Pindus mountain in the areas of Tzoumerka, Valtos and Radovizi, where the Italian troops made a single excursion in search of weapons in June 1941. However, their search was limited to large villages like Theodoriana, where they 'did not use any violence' and departed after replenishing their canteens with ouzo, never to appear again.[33] Even in Crete, where the concentration of German troops was higher than in any other area of Greece, German troops were seldom seen outside the island's cities and towns. Indeed, some peasants did not see a single German soldier for the duration of the occupation.[34]

The most significant problems faced by peasants during the first two years of the occupation were unemployment and food scarcity. The food crisis, which had been looming since the summer of 1941, resulted in a devastating famine that claimed thousands of lives in the urban centres. The countryside was less affected, though it was far from unscathed. Many rural communities relied on seasonal migration to the cities and the productive lowland areas. Peasants from the area of Tzoumerka in Epirus supplemented their income by working in the tobacco factories of Agrinion, the rice fields of Xiromero and Mesolongi and the olive groves of Magnesia, while travelling artisan-carpenters from Mourgana and stonemasons from Konitsa and Voion in western Macedonia travelled annually to the lowland communities of western Greece, Epirus and Macedonia in search of work. The breakup of the country into occupation zones governed by separate authorities stalled the movement of people and created financial and social havoc in hundreds of communities. This situation was further aggravated by the return of thousands of migrants escaping the famine gripping urban centres. The arrival of these men and women placed additional strain on the resources of many communities.[35]

These changes were felt particularly in the northern provinces of Epirus and western Macedonia, as these two regions relied almost exclusively on seasonal work and immigrant remittances. In these areas, unemployment led hundreds of peasants to cross the border into Albania and Yugoslavia in order to find work in the areas of Vourkos, Koritsa and Bitola. Many became vagrants who travelled the length of the border, sometimes working, at other times stealing or begging.[36] In many highland areas, wood and scrubland were burned and transformed into corn fields, while new crops were planted, like tobacco, which were low maintenance and had high monetary value, often yielding excellent results. For instance, in Zagori, the harvest of 1942 was the most successful in living memory.[37]

However, the rural economy was ultimately sustained by the black market, both in making produce available and in providing work for thousands of individuals. For many Greeks, the term 'black market' evokes images of urban degradation; accordingly, the stereotypical black marketeer is imagined as an affluent merchant or businessman with Axis connections, plying his trade in the slums of Athens. However, such images owe more to post-war representations than wartime realities. The black market involved a huge number of individuals who operated across Greece, bartering, selling and buying produce. As Violetta Hionidou noted in her pertinent study of famine in occupied Greece, 'it seems to have been almost impossible for people to survive the occupation without having made some kind of black market transaction, either as buyers or as sellers of goods'.[38]

Black marketeers varied widely in age and social occupation. Some were very young, such as Panagiotis Vihas, an 18-year-old boy from the mountain hamlet of Ktistades in Arta, who began his career in 1941 selling dairy products. After he had amassed a small amount of capital, Vihas began buying fabric and sewing equipment from the city of Arta. He resold this to the villages of the area at a handsome profit. Later, he turned to smuggling tobacco before deciding to settle down as a cobbler. These were good years for Vihas, who recalled several decades later that 'business was golden'.[39] Others were older men, like Giannis Peronis, a mason from the village of Pirsogianni who described himself as a 'faux black marketeer'. Unable to find work as a mason, Peronis turned to peddling raki, tobacco and fabrics to the Muslim peasants of Thesprotia, and turned his profits to olive oil which he later sold for gold to his fellow villagers.[40] Others, like Panagiotis Kostoulas, a merchant from the small town of Pogoniani in Epirus, were involved in more complex operations and wielded great influence on both sides of the border. An avid gambler who was always escorted by two bodyguards, Kostoulas ran a multinational operation that included Albanian producers, Vlach muleteers, Greek distributors and Italian customs guards.[41]

However, individual peddlers lacked his connections. These men and women relied on their small networks of relatives and friends who helped them evade the authorities and locate suitable buyers. Peddlers who crossed from the highlands of Mourgana to the lowlands of Albania could rely on men such as L. Mitsis, a shepherd who fled to Albania before the war after committing a murder. Mitsis arranged passage for travellers, provided them with information about potential buyers and sellers and, when necessary, equipped them with weapons.[42] Matthaios Tzouvalas, a peddler from the highland village of Vouno in Arcadia, relied on his personal and familial network. The base for Tzouvalas's operation was the village of Magoula in Sparta, the home of his younger son's godfather and fellow fighter in the Asia Minor campaign, Panagiotis Athaniotis, who put Tzouvalas in contact with local merchants and farmers, and provided information that enabled him to avoid unwanted attention from the authorities.[43]

In addition to food and tobacco, guns and military apparel were also sold. There was great demand for guns in the pastoral villages of central Pindus. In the areas of Radovizi and Agrapha, a serviceable rifle could fetch 30 kilos of maize or five gold sovereigns. Prices were even higher in Macedonia since guns had to be smuggled from the plain of Thessaly through the German and Italian occupation zones. Gun running had no patriotic connotations. Gun runners from Epirus sold to individual peasants, ELAS and EDES guerrillas, Albanian nationalists and Vlach legionaries alike. This trade persisted well into 1944, with guerrillas replacing the peddlers.[44]

The black market has often been associated with collaborationism. However, the lines between collaboration and resistance, activism and profiteering were muddled; frequently, profiteering and activism went hand-in-hand for men like Giannis Ladas, who doubled as an EPON activist,[45] or Labros Sabanis, a 19-year-old carpenter and EAM member from the Macedonian village of Nestorio. Like many men in his community, Sabanis was trilingual; he spoke Greek, Albanian and Macedonian, and like most of his fellow villagers he relied on the lowland communities of western and southern Macedonia for work. However, the division of the area into different occupation zones made work both scarce and dangerous, and led him to try his hand in the black market and smuggling. His first venture was unsuccessful, since his wares were confiscated by the Italian financial police. Sabanis tried to retrieve his merchandise with the help of an acquaintance who collaborated with the Italians. The man agreed to help him despite their political differences (Sabanis was a

KKE [Kommounistiko Komma Ellados – Communist Party of Greece] sympathiser), and assured the Italian authorities that the Sabanis family were 'good, law-abiding people'. Nonetheless, his efforts bore no fruit.[46] Following this failure, Sabanis turned his attention across the border. In 1942 he moved to Albania. This transition was not easy; however, his cultural knowledge enabled him to divert attention. Sabanis and his companion spoke only Albanian, donned Albanian attire and underlined their common heritage in their encounters with locals. They also took care to placate Italian soldiers by using fascist gestures. Sabanis's companion pinned a small picture of Mussolini to their chests. This was a boom year for Sabanis; he notes 'we were employed for the whole of 1942 ... and to be honest we had a really good time'.[47] However, his success was ended abruptly following the appearance of the Albanian resistance groups, which rendered southern Albania a particularly dangerous place. Consequently, he was forced to make yet another career change, this time by enlisting in ELAS.[48]

Sabanis's ability to perform different ethnic identities, alongside his eagerness to work with the occupation authorities and their native partners, not only denotes the fluidity of identities in the border areas several decades after their incorporation to Greece, but also serves to problematise the resistance/collaboration dichotomy used by scholars to analyse this turbulent period. Sabanis's successive transformation from travelling artisan to smuggler and then, in 1943, to ELAS guerrilla demonstrates the perilous nature of these categories. Indeed, while some of his actions – using the help of a known collaborator and donning fascist symbols – can be defined as forms of collaboration, they can just as easily be read as forms of resistance, since he used these stratagems to subvert the expectations of the occupying forces. Like thousands of women and men during this period, Sabanis lived and moved within a grey zone where the boundaries between resistance and collaboration were often unclear and where choices were dictated by everyday necessity, fear and want, rather than political ideologies.

Sabanis's situation was far from unique. Peasants in the ethnically mixed areas of northern Greece had few qualms about rotating between different factions, changing their allegiance as soon as a more suitable party appeared. Thus, peasants from the small Albanian speaking village of Belkameni in Macedonia successively sought the support of pro-Albanian notables, Vlach autonomists and even members of the local pro-Bulgarian faction, who actually castigated them for their opportunism.[49] Such attitudes were not confined to this area. In the first two years of the occupation, peasants in the Voion and Grevena areas oscillated between the pro-Romanian and pro-Greek factions, with hundreds declaring their Romanian ethnicity in the winter of 1942 only to retract their decision after the appearance of ELAS several months later. Such attitudes were not restricted to local peasants.[50] During the grim winter of 1941–42, a large number of men and women from southern Greece who resided in Macedonia opted for Bulgarian nationality in order to receive monetary and material help.[51]

In many cases, black market trade and intensive farming more than compensated for the economic crisis that ensued after the collapse. In some areas, the first two years of the occupation were the best in living memory. The black market brought a reversal of countryside–city relations. For the first time, peasants were able to dictate terms to cities, while the sleepy provincial market towns that had withered away in the pre-war period, such as Plaisivitsa and Pogoniani in Epirus, were suddenly turned into hubs of economic activity that attracted a motley crowd of merchants, smugglers and unemployed labourers.[52] A report from central Macedonia noted that while the bourgeoisie and the working class suffered, 'this is the best period ever for the peasants'.[53] Farmers on the rich plains of Thessaly and Boeotia, long the butt of jokes for the nearby townspeople, saw their fortunes change as they were able not only to repay loans that had crushed them for years, but also to build new houses and buy animals and equipment. In a world where everything had become reversed, townspeople were openly abused by peasants as beggars and sloths.[54]

This dramatic reversal of power between town and countryside was depicted vividly in the provincial press and personal testimonies, which described bitterly the sudden rise of the peasants whom they criticised for their lack of empathy towards their famished urban brethren. A parish priest in the town of Arta noted in his diary,

> Since September 1941 … the district of Arta is being swarmed on a daily basis by people who travel from all over Greece to procure food. Arta was nicknamed 'Little Canada' … the black market is rampant. Maize was sold for 24 drachmas per oka and now costs 1,200, beans from 50 drachmas to 1,600, meat from 50 to 1,200 … the peasants are taking advantage of the poorer classes … who sell for a few scraps their clothes and anything else they have of value to them.[55]

Stories about peasant gluttony and wealth became a staple for wartime newspapers whose readership saw the countryside as a lotus land whose prosperity was matched only by the avarice of its inhabitants.[56] Rural social and regional hierarchies were also deeply affected. Ioannis Nikolaidis, a schoolteacher from Zagori, described vividly the collapse of the old hierarchies in his native district. In Zagori, the local elite comprised civil servants, teachers and merchants. These men and women lived between the villages in which their families resided and the provincial capital of Ioannina where they worked. On 'peaceful days [they] returned during the village feast day to demonstrate their wealth', often spending hundreds of pounds. However, the war halted this and they were forced 'to limit their expenses to the most elementary needs such as bread' and 'become beggars for a few pounds of corn in the lowland villages'.[57] The men who took their place were shepherds, peddlers and farmers, the people who produced and trafficked in food and other necessary commodities, many of whom came from the 'primitive' and uncouth lowlands. The collapse of these local elites resulted in the gradual disintegration of social standards, as individuals and families turned against each other in order to gain access to resources or protect their properties. 'We were rudely awakened,' noted Nikolaidis,

> we discovered that human dignity is the cheapest commodity. Compassion was rare and everyone looked for an alibi to justify their lack of humanity. As time went by so did our souls empty and crude self-interest took over, turning society into a wild jungle. Friendships were tried, human relations deteriorated … and social hierarchies were turned upside down … a more brutal transformation of human relations … could not have happened.[58]

Smuggling and the peddling of illegal goods were hardly novel activities. During the pre-war period, many peasants used these methods to sell surplus produce and acquire products such as salt, tobacco, spirits and guns that were much more expensive in the formal markets, while smugglers were idealised for their ingenuity, cunning and defiance of authority. This was especially the case in border areas. However, the occupation changed both the extent and scope of these activities, since the black market effectively replaced the legal economy and involved tens of thousands of individuals, from provincial schoolteachers to respected professionals. Hardship and want strengthened the bonds of kinship but undermined all other societal ties and customs. The latter became less and less important as society was degraded to a Hobbesian dystopia, whereby everyone was regarded as a potential antagonist or enemy. Highland villagers turned against their lowland brethren, townsmen against peasants, producers against merchants; meanwhile success or even survival above the poverty line provoked envy and discontent. Matthaios Tzouvalas's activities drew the ire of his neighbours and set in motion a series of events that landed his family in an ELAS prison camp and himself in the security battalions.[59] Resentment seeped into many rural communities and slowly dismantled their social fabric, leading to the destabilisation of society, as families and individuals looked increasingly to their own for survival and expressed little concern for collective ventures of any kind.

This situation is exemplified by the lack of protest over food scarcity. Food riots were extremely rare beyond the cities. Moreover, while the peasants did their utmost to hoard and hide their produce from government agents, very few communities reacted violently. Many political activists were left puzzled by the peasants' passivity. Riots were rare in areas such as Agrapha and Tzoumerka, which had suffered greatly from hunger and had a long history of violence and brigandage, as well as in the productive lowlands of western Greece and Peloponnesus.[60] Anti-government actions were mostly limited to a number of ethnic Macedonian villages and some working-class communities, such as Limni and Kymi in southern Euboea. Here, the locals attacked gendarmes and smashed the shops of well-known speculators. However, such actions found no imitators among the rural population of the island, who felt no attachment to such communities and were less willing to risk their precarious well-being.[61]

Peasants, kinsmen, cadres: the formation of the resistance networks

The political effects of this social and economic crisis cannot be easily estimated. Some scholars suggest that an analogy can be made between economic crisis and political mobilisation, while others stress the importance of social culture. In his study *Paradosi Antarsias kai Laikos Politismos*, Stathis Damianakos argued that communities and groups with a tradition of defying the state's authority were more likely to support the resistance's activities than the 'tame', usually lowland communities that lacked a similar culture.[62] However, the reality was often much more complex. Few areas were more affected than the Agrapha region of western Thessaly. A mountainous province of 32,000 inhabitants scattered across 50 villages and hamlets, Agrapha remained largely autonomous during the Ottoman period before playing a pivotal role in the 1821 revolt and the irredentist struggles that followed the liberation. The endemic poverty and inaccessibility of the terrain also provided fertile ground for brigandage, rustling and smuggling well into the

1930s.⁶³ Pastoral activities remained the mainstay of the area's economy until the 1920s, while agriculture played a less important role since arable land was scarce and few families owned more than a few acres, which were often widely interspersed and unproductive. However, the gradual decline of pastoralism led to significant realignments in the local economy. Many families began to rely on seasonal emigration to the lowlands to supplement their income. Each autumn, hundreds of peasants travelled to the lowlands of Acarnania and Magnesia to work in the olive harvest, while an equally large number worked as seasonal labourers in the plains of western Thessaly and the towns of Agrinion and Karditsa. However, these activities were barely adequate for thousands of families who depended on state-subsidised corn to survive the winter.

This situation worsened considerably during 1941–42. The poor olive and corn harvest led to a rapid increase in prices and a decrease in the demand for labour. Those who were fortunate enough to find jobs were paid in kind. The unusually harsh winter of 1941–42 led to a massive loss of livestock, and even those who were lucky enough to salvage a few animals sold them or exchanged them for corn; in most cases, a sheep fetched 8–10 kilos of corn. The elderly, children, pensioners, civil servants and those who were unable to barter suffered immensely. During this grim winter, 35 men and women died from hunger and related diseases in the regional capital of Mouzaki, while many perished in the region's villages. A Red Cross committee visiting the area in the winter of 1942 noted: 'the provisioning situation in the highlands is tragic. The animal stock was depleted during the last winter ... at the moment 50% own no animal stock, 40% own between 1–10 animals and only 10% owns sufficient stock ... 70% of the highland population lacks almost everything and survives on herbs and dandelions.'⁶⁴

However, this situation did not push the local population towards revolt; indeed, neither EAM nor EDES managed to gain a foothold in this region throughout the occupation. Until early 1943 EAM had managed to attract only a number of delinquents, petty thieves and convicts led by an infamous rustler named Giorgos Bakogiannis-Karaiskakis from the village of Boukovitsa, while an EAM a report written by a local cadre a year and a half later underlined that 'EAM's writ runs thin'.⁶⁵ The resistance organisations were no more successful in other poor mountain areas, such as the Tzoumerka and Valtos ranges in Epirus and AetoloAkarnania. Giorgos Agoros, a cavalry officer and later commander of the EDES 3/40 regiment who tried to create a resistance organisation in his home region of Tzoumerka, met with a mixture of indifference and hostility. Agoros noted in his diary that 'national feeling is far from present' among the peasantry, which he attributed to 'the officers and intellectuals who viewed any national effort as premature and promoted an anti-guerrilla attitude', in addition to 'the hunger and want affecting the whole area'.[66] The situation was similar in the area of Valtos, an arid semi-mountainous province 100 kilometres south of Tzoumerka. Mimis Karras, an EDES member who was sent by General Napoleon Zervas to pave the way for the creation of resistance bands, reported to his associates in October 1942 that 'the peasants are without fighting spirit and show no willingness for the struggle'. According to Mihalis Miridakis, Zervas's bodyguard and confidant, this assessment 'was certainly unpleasant but was nonetheless a correct and precise description of the reality'.[67]

The base of the resistance during this period was not the 'untamed' highlands but rather the sleepy, law-abiding market towns and farming communities dotted across lowland Greece. The first ELAS bands in Epirus appeared in the basin of Kalamas, an area whose beauty and affluence were immortalised in Byron's *Childe Harold*. EAM's great influence in the area's principal villages of Protopapa and Zitsa earned them the nickname of 'Little Moscow' later during the occupation.[68] The influence of EAM was equally great in the prosperous market town of Thesprotiko, also in Epirus.[69] The first EAM nuclei in Thessaly were formed in the market towns of Tsaritsani and Rapsani, which also provided the first recruits for the region's ELAS.[70] Similarly in Peloponnesus, EAM first gained a foothold in the rich plains of Olympia and Triphylia. EAM had a particularly strong presence in the market towns of the area like Gargalianoi, 'the red town' of Messinia, which furnished more than 100 guerrillas for the regular and the reserve ELAS.[71]

Why did the resistance develop in these areas? Political tradition played a very important role. The land reform of 1925 transformed the majority of peasants into small proprietors who were largely hostile to the idea of socialism. Such attitudes were even more pronounced in the conservative mountain villages where 'communists were seen as lepers'.[72] Anecdotal evidence about peasant attitudes to communism are both plentiful and telling. An ELAS guerrilla from Roumeli recalled in his memoir how, before the war, village women used to cross themselves and spit on encountering their village's sole leftist, a practice associated traditionally with defence against evil spirits.[73] An EAM cadre from the highland area of Hasia in Thessaly noted, 'there were no communists in our region … we thought that a communist cannot be a decent human being; we were told that they were atheists who killed priests, demolished churches and confiscated people's properties and much more'.[74] Such attitudes were no doubt helped by the eccentricity and uncouthness of many rural cadres who possessed little of the discipline and sophistication of their urban brethren. Anti-clericalism was the foremost characteristic of rural leftists. An EAM cadre from Peloponnesus recalled 'the purpose of all the lessons was to prove that there is no God. Was that really all there was to communism? Instead of learning about social issues, about the programme of communism, everything started and finished with this.'[75] In many provincial towns, left-wing cadres congregated every Sunday outside the metropolitan church to engage in lengthy and often violent arguments with churchgoers, whom they tried to dissuade from attending the service.

In most cases, rural communism was the product of marginalisation, eccentricity and a desire to shock and impress. However, areas such as Zitsa, Protopapa and Tsaritsani had a much more serious tradition of political radicalism that can be traced back to the early twentieth century and the struggles over the division of rural estates.[76] Towns like Gargalianoi in Messenia and Amaliada in Ileia also had a small but active left-wing presence that consisted mostly of students, civil servants and professionals. The availability of cadres was not the sole criterion for the nurturing of EAM activities in these places. EAM was aware that these populous and affluent communities were in a much better position than the impoverished mountain villages to support and furnish recruits for the resistance bands. More importantly, syndicalism and returning emigrants from the United States and the major Greek cities – where former peasants were exposed to radical politics and new ideas about culture, society and gender relations – had introduced a new ethos to these areas. Protopapas was noted for the absence of violence and crimes that were common in these areas, such as rustling, smuggling and honour killings, as well as for the solidarity between the inhabitants.[77] Thesprotiko was noted for the progressiveness of its inhabitants and their active social life, enriched by theatrical performances and open-air serenades performed by the small local philharmonic and youth groups. These activities owed much to the presence of a large number of educationalists – Thesprotiko was the seat of the sole Gymnasium in the predominantly rural area of Louros – and the presence of many professionals and university graduates.[78] The social characteristics of these communities rendered EAM's modernist and egalitarian programme much more appealing than it was to those in most rural areas whose way of life was entrenched in tradition.

However, radical ideas were more often than not introduced from the top down by men belonging to the village elite. In Protopapas, these men were Periklis Zikas, a doctor, his brother Anastasios, an agronomist, and the teachers Takis Papalazos and Sotiris Tzalas. According to a local historian, 'this was a powerful group who determined the electoral attitudes in the village'.[79] Yet support for the ideas propagated by these men was not always due to ideological affinity. Peasants followed the lead of men like Zikas because of their personal prestige, out of a sense of obligation (Zikas was one of the few doctors in the area who showed genuine concern and was willing to help the peasantry) and finally out of a sense of familial solidarity.[80] Padelis Moutoulas's study of EAM in Ileia also underscores the importance of kinship in the formation of early resistance networks. According to Moutoulas, 'the first [EAM] circles are formed around the family'; in the market town of Amaliada, the first EAM network was constructed by communist veteran Nikos Belogiannis with the help of his high-school friends Theodoros Fragogiannopoulos and Lakis Agalos and their extended families. Fragogiannopoulos brought to EAM his father Sotiris and his siblings Mimis, Vittoria and Vaso, while Agalos recruited his brothers Leonidas, Spiros and Dionisis; Belogiannis's sister Orsa and his wife Eleni completed the first EAM nucleus in the town.[81]

Kinship and regional affiliations played a role of even greater significance in the smaller communities, as Pavlos Mihelioudakis came to realise. A 21-year-old undergraduate from the city of Chanea, Mihelioudakis was tasked with creating a resistance committee in the village of Askifou, a large village perched high in the Sfakia mountains. However, Mihelioudakis was ill prepared for the task. After a long and arduous trip, he reached Askifou. Lacking any local connections, he went around the village asking for shelter and 'after a lot of deliberation I was finally allowed to rest in a peasant home'. The next day, Mihelioudakis was able to find the village schoolteacher with whose help he managed to assemble a number of men in the village church. He asked them to provide a catalogue of the weapons available in the village and form a resistance committee. The assembled peasants declined firmly and Mihelioudakis was advised politely but sternly to return home; 'this was an arrogant move that ended up in a fiasco … the locals could not take seriously a 21-year-old boy like me'. The efforts of Mihelioudakis to set up a resistance nucleus in the village of Kastelli reached a similar conclusion several days later.[82] Harilois Vagias, a 25-year-old schoolteacher who tried to organise an EAM committee in the village of Skoulikaria in Arta, was equally unsuccessful. Vagias was accosted by peasants who were incensed that an outsider was attempting to create such an organisation in their village, 'and recruited the children unbeknownst to the parents, the parents unbeknownst to the children, kinsman unbeknownst to kinsman'. Vagias was accused of acting behind the peasants' backs 'like a snitch' and was warned by the village's headman, H. Tribos, a rich sheep farmer, 'to go away, go to hell and organise your own village'.[83]

Kinship connections enabled the resistance to overcome the peasants' traditional suspicions towards outsiders and make inroads into areas that were otherwise impenetrable. The areas of Fanari and Zalogo in the prefecture of Preveza present a characteristic case. These two regions were inhabited primarily by farmers and transhumant shepherds who voted predominantly for the Liberal Party before the war. The local prefect noted in a report on the political situation that 'there is no communist presence in the region' and estimated that the Liberal Party influenced over 70 per cent of the peasantry.[84] The locals' dislike for left-wing ideas was influenced undoubtedly by the region's long history of ethnic animosities between Greek and Albanian Muslim peasants, and its conservative ethos. The Orthodox Church and village headmen exercised a great influence on the peasantry of this poor and lawless area, where rustling and feuds were endemic well into the 1930s. The first entreaties of EAM were met with indifference; 'we were hopelessly behind in the rural areas', noted a local cadre, 'with the exception of Palioroforos, Louros and Stefani … the rest of our region's villages were unorganised until the summer of 1942'.[85]

However, a basis was built eventually, with some of the villages such as Kriopigi and Ano Rahi transformed into 'Little Moscows'. EAM's penetration of the area succeeded through the use of kinship and regional networks. A very significant role was played in this respect by Mihalis Ntousias, a politics graduate who was employed in the national bank at the time. Ntousias's family came from the village of Kriopigi, where they were affluent farmers, 'nikokiraioi', whose good name and prestige were also enhanced by the presence of several priests and educated men among their members. Furthermore, Ntousias managed to build his own extensive personal networks by acting before the war as the secretary of the local Liberal MP Giorgos Havinis. In the summer of 1942, he was despatched to organise the Zalogo region.[86]

Ntousias began organising the region from his own village. This choice was made both because of the village's central location but also because 'what weighed … was that all my close relatives lived in the village – all the villagers were related to me – but these would be willing to help in any possible way and undertake any task'.[87] Ntousias's first recruits were his brother Iraklis and his nephews Kostas Ntousias, a farmer, Pantelis Ntousias, a teacher, and Lazaros Tzimas, an engineer. Pantelis Ntousias was an invaluable asset to the local EAM; as a schoolteacher, he enjoyed the respect of most locals, many of whom had been his students. In such rural societies, the teacher 'was considered omniscient';[88] he was the community scribe, writing and reading letters for the largely illiterate peasants, providing support in legal issues and helping peasants deal with the twin locusts of gendarme and tax collector. Teachers also acted as doctors; a medical encyclopaedia was often the most prized possession of rural teachers. Pantelis Ntousias and Lazaros Tzimas had extensive connections and were able to put Ntousias in contact with several valuable recruits, such as high-school graduate Theofilos Tsoutsis. Ntousias then proceeded to the villages of Ano and Kato Despotikon, where 'I had several relatives and friends and therefore I had no difficulties in creating the committees'. The EAM committees in both communities were staffed and run by the Siskas clan, among whom Ntousias counted several cousins.[89]

In the following weeks Ntousias also organised the villages of Ekklisia, Polivriso and Mirsini. His efforts were facilitated by the presence of several Jehovah's witnesses, particularly in Mirsini. Such families traditionally met with hostility from the state, and therefore they reacted enthusiastically to Ntousias's prompts. Theofilos Tsoutsis also brought some unexpected allies. Tsoutsis had extensive family connections in the villages of the Fanari, a very conservative Albanian-speaking area. Tsoutsis was able to build an EAM committee in the village of Kanalaki with the help of his cousin, Hristos Kirgios, the village's schoolteacher. Moreover, he was helped in the village of Tsouknida by his cousin, Grigoris Ioannou, aka Tsouknidas, an infamous bandit who began his career by murdering a Muslim peddler in late 1941, and his clan.[90]

This pattern of development was common across Greece. A study of occupation in western Macedonia underlined that during the first phase of the resistance (1941–42), the 'pillars' of EAM's activities were 'the kinship and regional networks'.[91] The first EAM nucleus in the 'Little Moscow' of Meskla, a mountain village in western Crete, was structured similarly around the extended families of Bolourdakis and Tsamantakis,[92] while the first EAM nucleus in the 'red' village of Agios Sillas, also in Crete, was structured around the pastoral Samareitis clan, comprising Stylianos Samareitis and his four sons.[93] Family connections played an equally important role in the formation of EAM in the Messinian village of Kalliroi. EAM was introduced to the village by Thanasis Koutris, who had been a professional revolutionary since the early 1930s. His first recruit was his brother, Panagiotes, who brought along his fellow student, Dimitris Kanellopoulos. They were soon followed by the Kanellopoulos brothers, Kostas and Vasilis, and other members included brothers Othonas and Dimitris Driveliaris.[94] It is indicative that none of these men were peasants. Thanasis Koutris came from a prosperous peasant family and had studied law in Athens, while the Kanellopoulos family was one of the richer families of the upper Messini region; according to a local historian, they employed more than forty workers during harvest.[95] Othonas Driveliaris was a law school graduate. These men were assisted either directly or indirectly by other members of their families, among them Kanellopoulos's two sisters, and Koutris's younger brother, Thanasi, and his sister, Maria.[96] Regional and kinship ties played an equal role further south in the Mani peninsula where some of the first EAM nuclei in the villages of Agrilia and Paliros and the Oitilon area were formed around the extended families of activists.[97]

In many areas, the work of the resistance was further facilitated by the return to the villages of rural migrants and students. Many of these men and women had already been radicalised by the experience of hunger and violence in the urban centres. While only a small number, comprising largely students and civil servants, had been active in the resistance, the tales of resistance activities and the literature some brought with them paved the way for the appearance and acceptance of such a movement in the countryside. An EAM cadre from Ioannina noted:

> the course of events was accelerated by the arrival of a number of civil servants. They were afraid to stay in the towns ... and had come to the village for greater safety ... those who came from the cities spoke mostly about EAM, without necessarily being EAM members. This created an atmosphere that facilitated initiation.[98]

Nevertheless, kinship was not a guarantor of success. Some were unwilling to risk life and limb to serve an ideology for which they had little understanding or affinity, while others were bemused by their kinsmen's ideas. Maria Hatzi, the wife of a senior EAM cadre in Sarantaporo, a large community located in western Thessaly, found both EAM's programme and her husband's beliefs nonsensical: 'my husband used to read a lot, I am not quite sure what he read, I am illiterate ... I was thinking maybe I'll call a priest to read him some exorcisms ... I thought that he had really lost his mind.'[99] Equally, the appeal of power and prestige often trampled kinship solidarity and led relatives to join opposing camps. For instance, in the village of Popovo in Epirus, the Mouselimis clan furnished both the local EAM *ipefthinos* (the *ipefthinos* served as village president and all-round administrator; he was the senior EAM cadre and de facto ruler of the village) and an EDES leader. In the adjoining village of Koukoulioi, brothers Fotis Oikonomou, a teacher, and Kostas Oikonomou, a lawyer, occupied leading roles in EDES and ELAS, respectively. Fotis became an EDES enlightenment officer, and Kostas an ELAS *kapetanios* (a generic title given to the civilians who ran and recruited the ELAS bands).[100] Similarly, in the mountain town of Sirrako, the EAM *ipefthinos* and the president of the EDES committee for national struggle were cousins.[101] More dramatic was the case of the Maniate Petroulas and Stefanopoulos clans: several members were shot as German collaborators, while others who had fought for ELAS during the occupation were massacred by right-wing paramilitaries during the civil war.[102]

Kinship solidarity played an imperative role in the formation of networks; however, as they became involved increasingly in resistance activities, the men and women who joined initially out of affection for their kinsmen discovered new sources of motivation and a sense of pride in their ability to exercise political agency. The changes, yielded by EAM participation, were not always profound. The activities of Ntousias and his kinsmen were limited to providing help to travelling agitators and attending clandestine meetings in which they read EAM texts and newspapers. EAM activities in the community of Agnada, a mountain town of approximately 2,000 inhabitants in Epirus, were also limited to clandestine meetings where cadres discussed EAM's manifesto, listened to the radio and discussed news of the war.[103] Other organisations were more active. In the Evrytanian villages of Klitsos, Fourna, Mikro Horio and Megalo Horio EAM cadres created soup kitchens, helped run schools and raised self-defence committees.[104] EAM's popularity in the small village of Foiniki in Epirus was also undoubtedly helped by the local cadres' initiative in creating a soup kitchen and distributing food to children and the poor.[105]

These activities reshaped the cadres' attitudes and social relations within the villages. Slowly but steadily, EAM members built a society within a society; 'they isolated themselves, they spent their days taking long walks and stopped any discussion when an outsider approached, in the cafés they sat separately from the rest chatting quietly'.[106] These attitudes were criticised by some cadres who attacked them for acting like members of a sect rather than political activists; however, they also

A history of the Greek resistance

denote the emergence of a new consciousness among these men and women. Activists saw themselves as a select minority whose actions were destined to change the course of history. Delivering messages, providing food and shelter to fugitives, attending clandestine meetings and discussions might have done little to hinder the Axis dominance; however, they provided hundreds of men and women with their first chance for autonomous political and social action, and a powerful sense of belonging. This activism redefined the meaning and importance of political participation and gave resisters a strong sense of their importance as historical actors. Ntousias noted in his memoir, 'I felt that I lived in one of these unique moments in history that give us the chance to determine the course of events rather than letting others determining our fate. We all felt that with our actions we made history.'[107] This almost messianic sense of mission was demonstrated in the religious imagery employed by activists to describe their tasks. Gerasimos Priftis, a Corfiote civil servant who served as an EAM liaison in the area of Souli, described himself as 'an apostle of EAM' who, like his biblical counterparts, used to 'seize [his] staff and roam the villages' preaching EAM's gospel.[108]

Activism also led to an impressive realignment of political allegiances. Like many of his fellow villagers in the highland community of Katouna in Lefkada, Alexandros Logothetis viewed the left with suspicion and hostility. However, he did not fail to support his sons Poseidonas and Nikos, both of whom were KKE members. Logothetis was not a passive supporter; he provided food and shelter to fugitives, delivered messages and hosted meetings, often taking considerable risks. By 1943 he had joined both EAM and KKE. Kinship played an important role in Logothetis's choice, but it cannot explain his engagement and vigorous activity.[109] For neophytes like Logothetis, participation offered a sense of exhilaration, self-confidence and 'pleasure in agency'.[110] Historians have often described the resisters as martyrs and stressed their willingness to engage in sacrifice and self-denial. Despite such virtues being common among resisters, they were not the only or even the central feature of wartime activism. Resister narratives convey a profound sense of vibrancy, vigour and pride in their task. For many activists, participation in the resistance struggle had its own emotional rewards that were not dependent on the outcome. An EAM cadre from Epirus described his feelings during this period as those of 'enthusiasm, a sense of duty … but also pleasure'.[111] The same terms were used by a Macedonian resister to describe his experiences:

they gave me leaflets and I distributed them in shops, houses, wherever I had access to … whenever … a meeting was held at the shop I was on guard duty at the door … I realised that everything I was doing drew me closer and closer to danger, but the thought that we did all this to liberate the country from the foreigners made me ecstatic, it filled me with a secret joy that I was not left out of this struggle to cast out the invader.[112]

The majority of the men and women who joined EAM were motivated initially by affection for their loved ones and a feeling of family solidarity. However, as individuals became more invested and active in the day-to-day clandestine and organisational activities, the terms and understanding of participation changed. Involvement in these activities broke the repetitive patterns of everyday life, undermined traditional peasant fatalism and enabled participants to see themselves as historical actors for the first time. Indeed, for many of those who joined the resistance during these first two dangerous years, the joy of participation was one of the foremost motivators for and factors in the stunning success of EAM.

Regional and familial ties played an equally important part in the formation of EDES, the second largest resistance organisation formed during this period. EDES has been described variably as a mercenary organisation comprising the poorest peasants whose sole aim was to gain a few gold sovereigns, and as a 'traditional' organisation that lacked ideology and was backed by the more conservative segments of rural society who enlisted out of opposition to EAM's modernist programme. However, both definitions are problematic.[113] Unlike EAM, EDES began as a strictly regional venture. Along with the wide availability of primary sources, this makes possible a much better understanding of the process of its formation.

EDES had been in existence for almost a year before its founder, Colonel Napoleon Zervas, decided to proceed to form guerrilla bands in the summer of 1942. However, EDES was faced with several important obstacles; in contrast to EAM, which could rely on KKE cadres and a large number of fellow travellers around the country, EDES lacked any political basis and funds. Nominally at least, EDES belonged to the Venizelist/Liberal faction; however, the Liberal Party had been in disarray for several years, while some of its most important leaders such as Ioannis Mazarakis and Georgos Kafantaris were opposed to any military resistance and distrusted Zervas. Unlike KKE, the Liberal Party relied on an elaborate patronage system based on the provincial party bosses: landowners, professionals and military officers. Accordingly, peasant allegiances were primarily to their patrons, whom they often followed when they defected to a different faction. Zervas was aware that without the support of these men he would be unable to establish a basis, since he lacked the financial means, prestige and military muscle necessary to attract supporters. He noted characteristically in his memoir: 'guerrilla warfare is not unlike parliamentary elections, if you fail to win the backing of the local brokers you are destined to fail'.[114]

The first EDES base was the highland village of Stathas in western Greece. Zervas chose to establish his headquarters there for two reasons: the first was its position near the Ionian coastline and the strategic route that united Peloponnesus with mainland Greece; the second was that Zervas was related to Dimitrios Iskos, the scion of a historic local family who exercised great influence in the region. Zervas hoped that Iskos would help raise recruits among the peasantry and influence the area's conservative villagers and party brokers in his favour.

However, this plan backfired. The arrival of EDES was not seen positively by the predominantly royalist local elites who saw Zervas, a veteran supporter of the Liberal Party, as a threat to the local balance of power and were afraid that the presence of guerrilla groups might lead to reprisals against the peasants. In September 1942 the regional Orthodox metropolitan summoned the region's political and military elite to a clandestine meeting in the town of Mesolongi, where it was decided that EDES should be opposed by any means necessary. In late September 1942 Captain Ioannis Skilodimos was despatched to announce the decision to Zervas and Iskos. Zervas was defiant; however, he and his men became increasingly afraid that they would be murdered by Skilodimos's and Stratos's henchmen.[115] Eventually, Iskos caved in to the pressure and withdrew his support from Zervas, who was forced to leave Stathas. Zervas and his companions were livid, and some even suggested murdering Iskos, though they finally decided against it.[116] As one of Zervas's lieutenants later wrote, 'this was no magnanimity; Zervas could not afford to bloody the ground as we say here, because there could be a blowback. Iskos came from a significant family and had many followers.'[117]

Zervas's obstinacy led the local elites to take a further step by organising anti-guerrilla bands under Athanasios Karapanos and Evgenios Stratos, the scions of this region's most influential and prominent monarchist families. The first group, financed and armed by the Italians, was fielded in December 1942. These groups operated mostly in the lowlands of northern Acarnania and recruited from the local criminal element and the political clients of the Stratos family. The impact of these groups was important since they closed the area's more productive regions to EDES and deprived it of a crucial source of supplies.[118]

Subsequently, Zervas relocated further north; however, this move did not improve his situation. EDES's sole wireless and provisions were stolen by royalist agents and there was even an attempt on Zervas's life. He relocated again to the highland pastures of Sidekno where he was protected by Dimitris Magganas, a rich shepherd. This was the bleakest time for Zervas, who noted in his diary: 'I have never been so sad or desperate in my life, all the hopes that I have invested in Iskos are crushed … I haven't been able to find a single true patriot until now.'[119] During this period, Zervas took a crucial decision to relocate to the nearby area of Arta. Once again, he turned to the local elites for help. On 22 September 1942 Zervas and his entourage crossed the border to Arta and set up camp in the area of Kokkini Vrisi near the village of Megalohari. Following extensive negotiations, he was finally able to meet with several community leaders from the area; Grigoris Kossevakis, a rich landowner and veteran paramilitary leader of the Balkan wars from the village of Megalohari; Giorgos Matzoukis, a retired infantry major and aide of Zervas in the 1920s; Lazaros Tribos, a rich pastoralist from the village of Skoulikaria; and doctors Papahristou and Kosmas, who hailed from Megalohari and Mesopirgos, respectively.[120]

Zervas's appeal to these community leaders met with a mixed response. Matzoukis was negative; as a professional soldier he disliked guerrillas and was afraid that EDES activities would result in reprisals against the villages. Tribos was more positive, however, as was Kossevakis who decided to give Zervas his full backing. Zervas also found an unexpected ally in Spiros Karabinas, the 60-year-old headman of the village of Kleidi who enlisted in EDES along with several of his relatives.[121] The decision of these men to support EDES had several causes. EDES's presence was seen as a financial boon since it was believed widely that Zervas had the backing of the British. Patriotism and a strong sense of family and local pride also played a very important role. Nikiforos Kossevakis, Grigoris's son, prompted his fellow villagers to support EDES by reminding them that 'our village has the great honour to lead the national resistance struggle just like our forefathers did during the 1854, 1866 and 1878 uprisings against the Turks'.[122]

Furthermore, community leaders such as Kossevakis saw EDES as a prospective weapon in ongoing communal struggles. Megalalohari and the broader upper Radovizi region had been the Kossevakis family fiefdom since the late nineteenth century. Kossevakis's father, Sotiris, served as mayor of the area for 22 consecutive years. In 1910 Grigoris Kossevakis ran for MP; he was not elected but managed to secure a prestigious civil service position courtesy of his political allies. In 1912 Kossevakis returned to his home village to raise a band of 43 men with whom he fought in the Balkan wars and the northern Epirus struggle. His brothers Giannis, a professional soldier, and Nikos, a lawyer, also fought with great distinction. Kossevakis ran again for MP in 1926 and 1930 with two different parties; however, he was not elected, despite garnering the support of his fellow villagers. He succeeded his father as mayor and spent more than a decade in this position.[123] However, the success and affluence of the family created deep antipathies. Kossevakis had been feuding for years with the inhabitants of the nearby village of Miliana, who claimed that his estate belonged originally to their community, and with his fellow villagers who resented the family's dominance of communal affairs. In this respect, the support shown towards EDES was a conscious move designed to raise the profile of the Kossevakis clan in the ongoing struggles, and deter its antagonists from making a direct challenge to its power.[124]

Kossevakis's help was invaluable; he and his family provided housing, food and recruits and influenced many of the notables in the area to assist EDES. Kossevakis also enabled EDES to expand to the formerly impenetrable Valtos, where he counted among his relatives the powerful Iskos and Rokofilos families and Dr Stylianos Houtas, who had already created a small guerrilla band in the region. However, his help came at a high price, and while it gave EDES a new lease of life, it really created as many problems as it solved. Scheming notables were not the sole problem of EDES. The local EAM was unhappy with its presence and had begun a smear campaign against EDES and Zervas personally. EAM defamed Zervas as crypto-collaborator and claimed that he intended to establish a military dictatorship led by General Plastiras.[125] On 26 September 1942 Zervas met the local EAM representatives who handed over a series of demands. EAM was willing to cooperate with EDES as long as EDES provided all the funds, used EAM's structures for all its operations, and did not recruit any separate bands but used existing EAM members for all military operations. Finally, EAM asked that the non-local officers who accompanied Zervas return to Athens. Zervas did not accept these terms, noting angrily in his diary: 'these people want to turn me into their stooge otherwise they clearly hint that they will turn against me'.[126]

These were not the only problems confronting EDES. The local peas-

The rise and origins of the People's Armies

antry had a generally hostile attitude and were fearful that the presence of guerrillas would lead to reprisals, and even those who had enlisted by December 1942 were motivated primarily by the promise of monetary compensation. The limited financial resources were also running low; help promised by the Allies had not materialised and even Zervas's closest confidants, such as Iosif Papadakis, had begun to lose heart; 'we are desperate and disillusioned,' noted Papadakis, 'because we toil to no end'.[127] However, while Zervas and his comrades understood the peasants' fear and avarice (they lived, after all, in one of the country's poorest areas), they were furious with the attitude of the notables, whose continual demands for money and extortionate prices for supplies had almost bankrupted EDES. Zervas noted in early October: 'The Kossevakis have rebelled, because I haven't given them a blank cheque. It is hard to comprehend these predatory attitudes ... everyone is constantly demanding [money] but no one is willing to give anything in return while they charge an extortionate price for everything they supply.'[128]

EAM was far less dependent on notables; however, it too had to overcome peasant fears. Nikos Papanikolaou, a teacher in the highland village of Mirofilo in Thessaly, was aware of the presence of EAM and EDES in the lowland areas. He advised his fellow villagers to avoid joining either, as he was fearful that it might lead to internal divisions and violence; 'we were very reserved towards the resistance organisations, we were afraid of enmities and desired to remain united'.[129] Such attitudes were not uncommon. EAM and EDES appeared almost simultaneously in the highland town of Tsamadas in Epirus; most of the first recruits were professionals, merchants and graduates who agreed tacitly to avoid political strife and shelter each other in the case of clashes breaking out between the two organisations: 'here, our neighbourhood Thana supported EAM, the other *mahala* [village quarter, Varda] EDES ... they joined them and they agreed when EAM appears we will protect you and when EDES shows up you will protect us, now most of the villagers were illiterate, they couldn't understand many things, they couldn't understand why they'll need protecting'.[130] It was also not unusual for peasants to pledge support or give donations to more than one organisation. Stathis Kostantinides, a rich peasant from the village of Kleitos on the Kozani plain, gave money and supplies to both EAM and PAO (Panellinos Apeleftherotiki Organosi), a local nationalist organisation, for much of 1942, while rich pastoralists such as the Giounanis, a Sarakatsani clan in eastern Macedonia, funded the local EAM, the bandit gangs that operated in the area and a number of local Bulgarian officials.[131]

Such attitudes were not condemned by the peasantry, as they admired men like Giounanis for their cunning and ability to manipulate the powerful for their own ends. Opportunism was ingrained deeply in Greek political culture, especially in the poor mountainous villages of the interior where life was fraught with insecurity. In these regions, politics were dictated by want, fear and the pursuit of honour, and villagers thought little of abandoning a weak or incompetent patron for a more powerful one. Such attitudes were even more pronounced among pastoralists who took pride in their ability to outwit the law and play the gendarme and the bandit against each other. Peasants responded to the appearance of the resistance organisations in the same way: they evaded commitment, proclaimed allegiance to all passing parties and took care not to overly expose themselves by allying with anyone. However, the advent of the first guerrilla bands would soon render such tactics obsolete and present the peasant communities with a series of stark choices.

Silver and lead: ELAS, EDES and the politics of violence

ELAS was created on 2 February 1942; however, the first bands did not appear until June 1942. The first EDES bands were fielded in October of the same year. However, these were not the first armed groups to appear in the mountains of Greece. In Macedonia, ELAS was preceded by Eleftheria, an organisation created by Communist Party members and liberal army officers. Eleftheria fielded three armed bands in the areas of Serres and Kilkis during late summer of 1941. These guerrilla groups were able to score some small successes initially; however, the Wehrmacht's response was swift and brutal. The German forces chased out the bands and destroyed the villages of Ano and Kato Kerdilia, Abelofito, Keidon and Kleisto, executing 281 men. A brief uprising in the western Macedonian village of Mesovounon had equally catastrophic results; the village was razed to the ground and 142 villagers were executed.[132]

No more successful was the uprising that took place in the area of Drama on 28 September 1941. After a few brief successes the area was flooded with Bulgarian troops and irregulars who burned and plundered residences and killed civilians across the Drama prefecture. More than 1,000 civilians were executed while thousands fled in panic to German occupied Macedonia in order to escape Bulgarian reprisals.[133] The 'Lenin Tsardakas' band in Thessaly met a similarly untimely end. The band was formed by veteran trade unionist and KKE cadre Dimitris Tsardakas and was named after his younger son who had been executed by the Italians.

Tsardakas and his men pursued collaborators, clashed with Italian patrols and sheltered stranded commonwealth soldiers. However, they lacked both the infrastructure and the support for this venture. In the autumn of 1941 Tsardakas and his men surrendered to the Italian authorities, who had arrested their families and threatened reprisals unless they laid down their arms. Tsardakas, his son Kostas and another 30 guerrillas were led to the firing squad.[134]

The failure of these efforts can be attributed to several factors; the lack of central coordination, the severity of reprisals and the lack of infrastructure were the most obvious. However, another factor must be considered: the lack of experience and lack of ties with the local population. Men like Tsardakas were brave, but they had ventured into an area for which they had little aptitude or knowledge. Other bands were able to survive much longer by drawing from a tradition of guerrilla warfare and a militarist culture unique to their areas. We can distinguish three areas where such groups were present from early on: Crete, eastern Macedonia and Epirus.

Irregulars organised by local leaders and armed by the British played an important part in the Battle of Crete. Several bands who participated in the clashes were able to escape and regroup in the island's interior highlands in the autumn of 1941. These bands were led by men such as Adam Krasanakis, Manolis Badouvas, Vasilis Paterakis and Giorgis Petrakis. The majority of the band leaders were affluent middle-aged men, with extensive connections to the Liberal/Venizelist faction. Petrakis dominated the olive oil trade in the island, while Krasanakis and Paterakis owned thousands of sheep in the island's uplands. Many of these men were also experienced guerrilla fighters: Krasanakis had served for two years as a volunteer in the Balkan wars; Paterakis, who was 30 years old at the time, had taken part in the 1935 Venizelist coup and was known for his love of guns and his violent temperament; Badouvas had spent several years as a rustler and bandit in the mountains of eastern Crete and was a veteran of the Asia Minor campaign. These bands recruited primarily from their leaders' extended families – Krasanakis's band comprised his brothers, sons and 17 'first nephews', while Paterakis counted among his men 32 members of his extended family.[135]

Such armed bands also abounded in the ethnically mixed areas of northern Greece. The events at Drama led a number of men to seek shelter in the mountainous areas and form bands for self-protection. Their numbers were later swelled by fugitives from justice and youths attempting to avoid conscription into the Bulgarian labour battalions.

A history of the Greek resistance

Most of these men came from Turkophone Pontic Greek communities and were often led by local notables who had served as guerrilla leaders during the 1919–22 Greco-Turkish war.[136] Ethnic turmoil between Muslim and Greek peasants also led scores of men from the prefecture of Thesprotia in Epirus to form bands. This area had a long tradition of guerrilla warfare and was the site of violent ethnic conflict between the Albanian Muslim minority and the Greek- and Albanian-speaking Orthodox Christian communities between 1912 and 1917.[137] The arrival of the Italian authorities in April 1941 led to a renewed outbreak of ethnic violence. The first armed band was formed in the autumn of 1941 by Vasilis Baloumis, an illiterate shepherd whose bravery and marksmanship rendered him the undisputed leader of the area's bands. Baloumis's band consisted of fellow villagers, relatives and outlaws such as Miltiades Vasileiou, a rustler, and Markos Oikonomidis, who was on the run after murdering a fellow villager. This band was not unique: by early 1942 two more had appeared in the region, the first led by Kostas Georgiou, a shepherd from the village of Prodromi, and the other by Thanasis Bakas, a rural guard from the village of Senitsa. Like their Cretan counterparts, these bands relied on transhumant pastoralists, most of them Vlachs, for food, information and sometimes manpower.[138]

The first ELAS bands emerged in the summer of 1942. The background of these pioneers differed significantly from those who made up the independent bands. The first ELAS band that appeared in the uplands of western Roumeli in December 1942 was led by Kapetan Stathas, aka Kostas Tsaklatiras, a KKE cadre and candidate in the last pre-war elections, and comprised militant workers from the city of Agrinion,[139] a social group that also figured prominently in the first ELAS band to emerge from the Lekani mountain range in eastern Macedonia, led by veteran KKE member and tobacco worker Nikos Romtsos.[140] The situation was similar in Epirus where the first recruits to the Pakos-Exarhos band, which operated in the summer of 1942 in the lower Kalamas valley of Epirus, were KKE activists from the 'red' village of Zitsa.[141]

The strong political motivations of these men had a positive impact on the discipline, cohesion and combat-worthiness of the bands; however, determination and bravery were not enough. The independent bands were able to survive thanks to their leaders' experience of guerrilla warfare, knowledge of the terrain and ties with local communities that provided them with funds, provisions and information and, when necessary, recruits. Unlike them, the first ELAS bands often had no ties to the local peasantry and little knowledge of the area in which they operated.

Such difficulties could often be overcome with the help of local political cadres; nonetheless, despite the frantic efforts of EAM, there remained entire regions where the organisation was completely unknown as late as the spring of 1943. In such regions, the infrastructure of the organisation had to be constructed from scratch by the guerrillas. For instance, in the uplands of the prefecture of Arta, 'the political organisation was extremely weak, therefore it not only lacked the necessary means to help the guerrillas but it had to be actually created by the guerrillas in the villages'.[142]

The guerrillas of the 3/40 regiment that operated in Arta were not successful in this task, and remained little more than fugitives who operated clandestinely amid a hostile and indifferent peasantry until the appearance of the British Military Mission in the area. Other bands were even less fortunate. The profound lack of support from the peasants who often refused to sell them food and the unwillingness of the locals to enlist led the first band that was fielded by ELAS in Ileia in March 1943 to dissolve within two weeks. A second attempt to field a band in the same region a month later also ended in failure, with the guerrillas returning to the towns a week after they had set off for the mountains.[143] Nikos Romtsos's band fared no better. Romtsos and his men were shunned by the local peasantry who 'avoided cooperating with us'; hungry and isolated, the guerrillas were forced to retreat even further into the mountains until the band was eventually destroyed after a string of betrayals.[144] The reception of the ELAS guerrillas was equally frigid in the Almyros plain in Magnesia; when the band of Giannis Douatzis entered the village of Achilleion, 'we tried to wake the village with our songs, however, the peasants were too afraid to come out of their homes and we were obliged to drag them out by force'.[145] According to Douatzis, 'our organisation [EAM] has no influence whatsoever here'.[146] The situation was similar in the nearby region of Fthiotida, where in many cases peasants refused outright to provide food and information and 'threw the guerrillas out of their houses',[147] and on the island of Euboea, where Douatzis was despatched to raise a band in June 1943. Despite the guerrillas' entreaties, the peasants not only refused to provide them with food or shelter but in some cases even abandoned their villages to avoid contact with them: 'when they caught sight of us the peasants became terrified, some of them even fled the village'.[148]

Such attitudes were even more pronounced in central and eastern Macedonia, where the memory of the 1941 events had dampened the willingness of the peasantry. The remnants of the Odysseas Androutsos band took refuge in the Krousa mountains and desisted from any military activities until March 1943 when they moved further west. Guerrilla activity in the area of Kilkis did not resume until April 1943.[149] The situation was equally forbidding in the nearby districts of Pella and Serres where, after two failed attempts, ELAS was finally able to create a basis in the Paikon area after a group of 40 guerrillas 'invaded' from Free Greece.[150] The situation was even worse in the areas of Drama where, after a string of betrayals, the four ELAS bands that operated in the region were picked off one by one. Consequently, many of the demoralised guerrillas turned to brigandage and joined the gang of a notorious local brigand, Kapetan Valsami, 'eating, drinking and robbing without exception'.[151]

How can such attitudes be explained? The lack of ties played an important role, but it was not the only problem. Peasants might have sympathised with the guerrillas, especially when they were local to their district, and there would have been few objections to their patriotic goals. Nevertheless, as a study of partisan warfare in Eastern Europe underlined, 'in the eyes of the occupied population, the partisans' practical impact upon everyday life was more directly important than the partisans' long-term aims'.[152] Peasants did not lack patriotism; however, their foremost concern was the safety and well-being of their families. Consequently, many resented the presence of resistance forces in their communities, since it placed an often unbearable strain on their resources and could potentially result in reprisals. The dishevelled appearance of many guerrillas, most of whom were dressed in civilian clothes and carried antique weapons, and their constant demands for food also did little to help their cause or inspire trust. Many peasants saw the guerrillas as no different from the numerous groups of lawless men who operated in the highlands; 'when the first guerrillas appeared', noted an EAM cadre from Epirus,

> several people taunted and mocked them ... they'd say that the only reason they took up arms is to live at the expense of the peasants, that they are loafers, vagabonds and thieves, others said 'do you expect these shoeless, these people who used rope to make slings for their rifles to bring us freedom?' These and many other accusations circulated when the first guerrillas appeared.[153]

The difficulties encountered by the first bands made the guerrilla organisations acutely aware of the need to convince the peasantry that their presence would be beneficial to their communities. The guerrillas tried to achieve this by using the only currency at their disposal – violence. In the spring of 1943 the ELAS GHQ commissioned a pamphlet entitled 'The guerrilla of EAM-ELAS', the purpose of which was to serve as a roadmap for ELAS commanders. The anonymous author emphasised the importance of proper behaviour *vis-à-vis* the peasantry and the need to gain their confidence by protecting their properties from predators. The pamphlet underlined that the guerrillas must appear as the 'guardian angels of their properties and the sweat of their brow', and assist the peasantry in their everyday toils:

> the purposes of guerrilla warfare are not limited in this [warfare] but are extended into the field of the urgent practical needs of our people ... and follow faithfully the activities of EAM in the cities. [ELAS] does not only fight for freedom but also for the bread and the livelihood of the rural masses ... thus the guerrillas of ELAS protect the people from brigandage, re-establish the law, restore justice.[154]

The guerrillas took swift and often brutal measures against brigands, rustlers and anti-social elements; by early 1943 several large brigand groups in Epirus, Roumeli and Thessaly had been scattered and many notorious brigands had been shot, while theft, rustling and murders were also significantly decreased. Such activities bolstered the guerrillas' prestige among the peasantry. Often rural communities, exasperated by the lack of law and order and the indifference of the state, asked ELAS for help, pledging their allegiance in exchange for the guerrillas' assistance. 'Several murders took place after the gendarmes moved out from our village in early May', noted a magistrate from a Maniate village in mid-1943; 'the situation had become really dangerous, the villagers conferred and the majority decided to ask ELAS to take over the village, they proceeded to do so and the local authorities were abolished'.[155] The suppression of criminality played an equally important role in the development of EDES. The success of EDES in expanding its rule beyond the province of Radovizi was no doubt thanks to the activity of men like Alexandros Papadopoulos, a contractor from the highland village of Anogi, who managed to suppress within a few weeks the numerous bandit gangs that had pestered the area since late 1941.[156]

Bandits were not the sole target; traitors and collaborators of every ilk were targeted by the resistance organisations. Collaboration did not always have a political rationale. An EAM cadre from Laconia ascribed the 'profound' outbreak of denunciations in the first half of 1942, during which 'daughters denounced their fathers and sisters betrayed their brothers for harbouring British soldiers, for owning guns and for a myriad other reasons', to 'personal hatreds and petty differences'.[157] However, many peasants did not confine themselves to denouncing their personal enemies. Men like Nikos Maratheas, a rich landowner from the village of Neo Monastiri, took advantage of their connections with the Italians to enrich themselves through black marketeering and extortion. Maratheas provided a cut of his black market gains to the local Italian commanders in exchange for their help with troublesome tenants and business rivals. When several of his tenants raided his warehouse, Maratheas appealed to his backers, who responded by murdering 11 peasants and setting fire to 40 residences. The ELAS response was swift and brutal. A group of ELAS raided the estate of Maratheas, set it ablaze and shot him on the spot.[158] ELAS and EDES also targeted women and, in some cases, men who had had sexual relations with occupying troops; 'sexual collaborators' were often treated with extreme brutality. Hundreds of women had their hair cropped, some were branded with knives and irons, while others were executed after being subjected to torture by the guerrillas.[159]

Such actions earned ELAS and EDES the acquiescence of many peasants; however, callousness and brutality were often exhibited by the guerrillas. For example, Nikos Maratheas's 11-year-old son was abducted, tortured and raped by ELAS, before being murdered. This led some peasants to view them as no better than the men they set out to punish, especially when those being attacked were older, respected men. The brutality exhibited by the guerrillas in this case was far from rare. In the summer of 1943, 25-year-old Giorgis Psarakos, a veteran of the Albanian campaign from the village of Lapanagoi in the uplands of northern Peloponnesus, was tortured and then shot by a group of ELAS guerrillas for reporting a theft to the local Carabinieri station. The same band a few days before had executed a 16-year-old boy for stealing a ewe.[160] The vigilante justice of ELAS and EDES may have appealed to the guerrillas' self-perception as the protectors of the peasantry, but the guerrillas and the peasants often had very different conceptions of justice. Rustling and revenge killings were not seen as amoral or criminal acts by most peasants. Moreover, the men and, more rarely, women who engaged in such acts were regarded as heroic figures and few peasants would accept that a man who stole or killed to defend his honour was a criminal.[161]

Even when peasants benefited from the resistance's actions they did not necessarily respond by providing support to the guerrillas. ELAS's anti-rustling campaigns and eradication of banditry were of particular help to the Sarakatsani and the Vlach pastoralists in Epirus and central

Greece. However, neither group demonstrated any support for the left and very few men from either community enlisted in ELAS.[162] Moreover, the secretive and often gruesome nature of the guerrillas' executions often raised suspicions of foul play. Giorgios Agoros noted in his diary that

> unfortunately, every anti-communist who is targeted by ELAS is first denounced as a traitor. There are many traitors, however, the way EAM chooses to act is not beneficial to the national struggle, they do not ask the opinion of those who are not enlisted in EAM, they do not follow proper procedure, but execute these men secretively therefore leaving many peasants to wonder if the deceased were really guilty.[163]

The violence employed by the resistance bands during these chaotic years has been represented in widely divergent terms. Some pro-EAM historians argue that those shot by ELAS were traitors, while others admit that ELAS may have been guilty of victimising innocents. However, they insist that these were mostly anti-social elements and petty thieves who were targeted in accordance with the villagers' sentiments.[164] Conversely, anti-communist historiography presents all the victims of ELAS as heroic *ethnikofornes*, patriots who were executed because of their political beliefs.[165] Determining the patterns, causes and effects of violence in this period is a daunting task, partly because of the lack of sources and partly because of its highly localised and piecemeal nature. However, comparison of testimonies from different areas allows a more nuanced understanding of the motives, aims and repercussions of guerrilla violence during this period.

The ELAS bands who appeared in the highlands of Grevena and Kozani in the winter of 1942–43 were a far cry from the idealised partisans of many post-war histories. While their alleged purpose was to eliminate banditry and treachery, the criteria they used to define the perpetrators of such actions were vague. The most important of these bands was led by Filos G or Seftelos, a veteran communist of Pontic Greek extraction, and was made up of hardened leftists like Vasilis Dalianis, a stonemason, shepherds and farmers, most of whom came from the uplands of Grevena. Filos G was admired by the guerrillas for his bravery and 'superhuman endurance of hardship';[166] however, one of his men noted that 'he would torture citizens on the slightest pretext'.[167] This savage temper meant that his subordinates and the peasants followed him more out of fear than respect; a local schoolteacher noted that wherever Filos G and his band appeared 'there was fear and trembling'.[168]

The campaign of Filos G began in the village of Kivotos, a small community in the countryside of Grevena where several refugee families had settled in the early 1920s. The first action of the guerrillas was to seize Elias Phasas, the village schoolteacher, and beat him savagely in front of the assembled villagers. After the beating, Phasas was shot by the guerrillas under the pretext that he was spreading anti-EAM propaganda. The second person arrested was Nikolaos Tsaktsaras, who was denounced as a rustler by some of his fellow villagers; he was more fortunate in receiving 40 lashes from the guerrillas, which left him unconscious but alive. After the guerrillas were finished with Tsaktsaras, Filos G 'proclaimed the dictatorship of the proletariat' to the peasants who had assembled to witness the torture of their compatriot. The notables of the village of Spilaion were more fortunate. ELAS disbanded the small resistance group created by G. Vittos and Hristos Rammos to protect the peasants from Italian soldiers and Vlach autonomists, and tried the two men along with the village's priest, teacher and president for treason, even though their true crime was forming a band independent of ELAS. However, they were forced to exonerate them under pressure from their fellow villagers. The president of the village of Mirsini, Alexandros Tsalikidis, was less fortunate. He was executed as a reactionary and his body was left exposed; the same fate befell the president of Kokkinia who was shot following a savage beating.[169]

Filos G was also responsible for the beating of Spiros Papadimitriou, a forestry officer, and his girlfriend who was the schoolteacher of Ziakas. They were stripped and publicly lashed for offending public morality, while a tax collector was beaten almost to death for serving the collaborationist government.[170] The next victim was a peasant woman from Louvri, who was accused of having relations with Italian soldiers; she was beaten in front of the assembled villagers and later led to the village of Tsotili, where she was shot along with two women and their father. The former were accused of having relations with Italian soldiers and the latter was condemned for allowing this.[171] Such violence was far from uncommon in the uplands of Macedonia or, indeed, in the rest of Greece. In the lower Kalamas region of Ioannina ten men and women were executed by ELAS, and an uncertified number of civilians were beaten between July and December 1942.[172] Moreover, 11 men and women were executed in Arta by ELAS on a variety of charges and three women were beaten and had the letter Π, which stood for 'porni' (whore), carved into their foreheads and cheeks.[173]

Treason and relations with the enemy were not the only causes of violence; peasants who refused to hand military material or weapons to the guerrillas in the Othris uplands of Thessaly were 'quickly convinced to do so by the shepherd staff of Achilleas', the henchman of the local band who used a shepherd's staff to bastinado uncooperative civilians.[174] Such 'convincing' led to serious injury or even death, as in the village of Stenoma in Evrytania where a peasant 'was beaten to death for failing to deliver his weapon' after he was denounced by a fellow villager.[175] The emergence of ELAS in the area of lower Olympus was marked by a series of beatings, murders and executions of village presidents, gendarmes and rural guards. In mid-1942 the village presidents of Magoula, Giannota and Paliokastro were murdered by ELAS guerrillas.[176] The president of the village of Skamnos was more fortunate; after the guerrillas announced the beginning of the struggle to the assembled peasantry, he was delivered to Nikos Vidras, a former rustler, who proceeded to beat him unconscious.[177] Some of the executions were particularly gruesome. In mid-1942 the rural guard Panagiotis Pournaras, who had been denounced as an associate of the Vlach legion,[178] was arrested by ELAS and handed over to local peasants who proceeded to stone him to death.[179] A gendarme who enlisted in ELAS and was accused by his comrades of being a covert reactionary was killed in the village of Krania 'and was left in the middle of the road for several days as an example, so that the people would look at him and become afraid and terrorised'.[180]

The situation differed little in western Thessaly. The first ELAS band that appeared in the area of Aspropotamos, a mountainous region located between the prefectures of Trikala and Arta, arrested and beat the president of Armatoliko who was denounced by a fellow villager for diverting Red Cross supplies. The prisoner was transferred to the adjoining village of Aetos, a much larger community, where the intention was to execute him publicly; however, he was released after the Aetos elders intervened in his favour.[181] The same band led by Fontas Oikonomou, a young schoolteacher from the village of Tsaritsani, administered a public beating to an elderly retired officer in the adjoining community of Mesohora who had protested against the guerrillas' requisitioning policies. Also arrested was the community's president, Kostas Baroutas, an affluent merchant and veteran of the 1940 war, along with two other local men who, like Baroutas, were described by the guerrillas as reactionaries.[182]

The appearance of ELAS in the prefecture of Katerini was also marked by a series of executions and beatings. In early 1943 ELAS executed three gendarmerie officers in the environs of Katerini – Elias Thomadakis and Nikos Kotsopoulos, who served in the Panteleimonas station, and Elias

Sotiropoulos, who served in the station of Kolindros.[183] The arrival of ELAS in central Macedonia was also marked by a spate of murders, abductions and beatings of civil servants and gendarmes. On 29 October 1943 the commanding officer of the Drimos gendarmerie station was abducted by ELAS guerrillas. On 23 November the guerrillas abducted several gendarmes from the Nea Halkidona, Loudia and Halastra stations; on 6 November another gendarmerie officer was abducted from the village of Lavro in the Lagadas area; on 15 November 1943 Dimitris Dimitras, a tax-collector, was arrested by ELAS; on 29 November ELAS executed gendarmerie officer Nikolaos Pergadis in the village of Legadia; while on the 19th of the same month, the secretary of the Volvi village was abducted and murdered by ELAS guerrillas.[184]

Violence cut across geographical and social lines; it affected mountain villages and lowland towns alike, while village presidents, gendarmerie officers and rich landowners were targeted alongside housewives, poor farmers and shepherds. The breadth and extent of violence underscores that it was neither a marginal phenomenon nor the work of a few fanatics. Simultaneously, its random and haphazard nature challenges the view that violence was a carefully coordinated affair. It has often been suggested that the violence was initiated from above. However, the partisan bands, especially in the early period when the bulk of guerrillas were urban activists and working-class men, were outsiders to the areas in which they operated. Guerrilla bands relied on local cadres and sympathisers for information and intelligence. An ELAS guerrilla from Peloponnesus noted characteristically:

> as a guerrilla I've done a lot of [bad] things but not with my own initiative … the organisations, the *ipefthinos*, but also others, our own people in the villages and the towns gave us information and our commanders told us, go and arrest this one and bring him here for an interrogation or do not bring him up here but kill him where you find him.[185]

While the political motivation of such people and the guilt of many of those who were targeted by ELAS and EDES must not be overlooked, many were motivated by personal grudges and it was often difficult to separate private vendetta from political action.

Village presidents, rural guards and gendarmes found themselves in a particularly precarious situation, since their position and responsibilities gave rise to fierce enmities; the failure of a president to intervene in favour of a fellow villager in a court of law, a fine or an arrest for illegal felling created grudges that lingered for years. The appearance of the guerrillas was used by many to settle personal scores; enmities that had remained dormant for years came to the surface and were settled with violence. One ELAS guerrilla noted that 'the majority of denunciations were done for personal reasons and antipathies and were carefully planned to eliminate their rivals'.[186] Frequently, guerrillas found themselves embroiled in a maelstrom of accusations and counter-accusations that they were seldom able to navigate, especially since they could not verify the information and intelligence that local cadres provided them with.

The case of Thimios Tzallas, a rich farmer and president of Kosmira, a hamlet in the Lakka Souli region of Epirus, demonstrates the intersection between communal politics, financial rivalries and wartime violence. The Tzallas family has dominated the political and economic life of the village for several decades. However, Tzallas's affluence and accomplishments had set him at odds with several local families who in 1935 attempted to assassinate him. The attempt failed, although his would-be assassins were never arrested.[187] Violence resumed in the village in 1942 when his rivals torched Tzallas's home. The motives of the perpetrators are not entirely clear. Political rivalries played an important role, but economic reasons might also have been important since the region had become a hub for competing smuggling and black market networks. Tzallas's miraculous escape did not dampen the spirits of his rivals, who a few weeks later denounced him as a collaborator to a local EDES band. Tzallas was arrested and badly beaten by his captors but was released after he managed to convince the guerrillas that the accusations were unfounded. However, this was not the end of it. His detractors appealed to a different EDES band who, according to one source, received a bribe from Tzallas's opponents and arrested him again. Tzallas managed to escape his captors again despite being seriously injured and fled to EAM territory, where he promptly joined ELAS.[188]

Sometimes the causes of violence were even more intricate; for instance, in the village of Ligaria in Pangaio, a local EAM cadre and a gendarme were pursuing the same woman. Desperate to get rid of his rival, the cadre denounced his rival to an ELAS band, who arrested and murdered him.[189] Panagiotis Kostoulas, a rich merchant in Pogoni, was beaten half to death after he was denounced by a local EAM cadre who had a lost a bet to him.[190] Property issues, differences over land and pasture and professional rivalries were no less important. Rivalries over pasture and water access between the Dritsos and Tokas clans in the village of Samoniva in Epirus resulted in a series of murders after the two families denounced each other to the resistance authorities as smugglers and collaborators. The first victim of this feud was Tassis Dritsos; his assassin was a local EDES band leader who received a hefty sum to make sure that Dritsos would not escape alive. The Dritsos clan retaliated a few months later with the help of Tassis's brother-in-law, Tsilis Mastoras, an ELAS band leader who executed his killer, his wife and his son-in-law as Italian collaborators.[191]

Such cases were not uncommon and the ferocity of denunciation and violence shocked even seasoned guerrillas like Giannis Douatzis, who noted to an audience of EAM cadres in mid-1943 that 'the people were terrified' by the violence unleashed by ELAS on the island of Euboea. He stated

> I have already made myself clear in the meeting we held two nights ago when I said that we are people's fighters and not murderers … as I understand, both our people and the peasants have misunderstood badly our mission and aims since they are bent on killing anyone who has even exchanged a few words with an Italian.[192]

However, Douatzis's efforts did not put an end to the violence. Indeed, when he and his band visited the village of Theologos where some thefts had been reported by the local committee, the peasants 'immediately began to accuse and betray each other, presenting us with a ton of cases which they asked us to solve'. Douatzis refused to take any measures against any of the accused and abandoned the village in disgust.[193]

However, wartime violence was not a simple continuation of pre-war feuds. In most cases violence only broke out after the appearance of the guerrilla bands, which gave the peasants the means and the opportunity to settle their personal scores. Furthermore, despite its local roots, violence had a clear political rationale: 'to generate compliance via deterrence … and shape the behaviour of a targeted audience by altering the expected value of particular actions'.[194] Feuds were conducted clandestinely and followed a carefully scripted scenario; however, wartime violence had a public, almost theatrical character. Most of the beatings and executions took place in central locations, usually the village piazza, and were attended by hundreds of peasants. For instance, a miller accused of theft in the Epirote village of Kanalaki was publicly beaten in the village piazza by the local ELAS *kapetanios* who shouted to the peasants 'that's what happens to those who defy ELAS'.[195] Giorgis Psarakos, according to a local EAM cadre, was tortured for more than ten hours in the village school before he was dragged out and shot as a warning to his compatriots: 'he was swollen by the beating, one of the guerrillas stepped out and said, "Do you see this man? He is a traitor to our homeland and we are going to execute him and whoever one of you wants to he can follow him right now"'.[196] Similarly, after ELAS arrested Giorgos Simintzis, a gendarmerie officer in the village of Dovra in Zagori, they dragged him into the village piazza where they took turns in beating him in front of a crowd of villagers, before they finished him off with a shot in the back of the head.[197] Even when executions were not performed in public, the victims were left exposed in public areas, often with an explanatory note pinned to their bodies.[198] Two men accused of collaborating with the Italian authorities in the Feneos area of northern Peloponnesus were stabbed to death by ELAS guerrillas, who were ordered to leave their bodies exposed on a public road. A guerrilla who took part in these executions noted that 'we killed them [this way] to strike terror, so people would say "these people [the guerrillas] are butchers"'.[199]

The effect of these actions was unmistakable. Violence generated a climate of fear and suspicion among the peasantry which slowly eroded the social and kinship ties that bonded communities, thereby enabling the resistance bands to dictate their terms to the local populations who complied out of fear that they would be the next to be denounced and subjected to violence. After the first execution took place in the village of Krania, many peasants relocated to cottages or huts in the countryside away from the village:

> they did not want to meet other people in the village. They came here to arrange any pending affairs and then they disappeared again. We were very cautious, you didn't know who to trust and you were afraid that you'll be denounced by the people you least suspected, social gatherings seized and the life of the people became much more private.[200]

The same sense of fear enveloped the area of western Zagori following the murder of Simintzis. According to EAM cadre Kostas Nikolaidis,

> the setting of everyday life was changed. The killing ... prompted an array of emotional reactions, the majority of which remained hidden in the souls of the inhabitants notwithstanding their negative or positive view of the man who was executed ... there was no room for ... approving or disapproving what happened because nobody knew what the future held.[201]

The reappearance of the men who had executed Siminztis a few days later terminated this uncertainty but also demonstrated the powerful impact of this act on friend and foe alike. The speech of Nikos Ntemiris, the *kapetanios* of this band, was followed by thunderous applause; 'many of those [who applauded] disagreed with what happened in Dovra ... they all applauded nonetheless, some out of conviction and others out of the need to show that they did not oppose [the guerrillas]'.[202] The brutal execution and torture of three collaborators in the village of Oxineia had an equally galvanising effect on the peasantry. An ELAS veteran who witnessed the execution noted that 'they undressed them and tortured them nude in front of everyone'. Although few doubted the men's guilt, many peasants were stunned by the guerrillas' brutality, 'but who would dare to intervene, the fear was great'.[203] Nonetheless, the guerrillas' unexpected success and the brutal show of power convinced most peasants of the futility of defection:

> we had to serve the guerrillas ... they had the guns and saying no was not an option. We all became organised, men and women, some in EAM, others to reserve ELAS, others to EPON ... and almost everyone to KKE fearful that we would otherwise be branded as reactionaries.[204]

Violence reshaped the relationship between the peasantry and the guerrillas in other ways as well. The military activities of the early bands were rather lukewarm, since most bands devoted their energy until late autumn of 1942 to disarming gendarmerie stations and hunting bandits. However meagre these activities, they endowed the guerrilla bands with a mystique and captured the imagination of the peasantry. The beating of the president of Skamnos and the disarming of the local gendarmerie station gave the band of Nikos Xinos a sudden and impressive reputation among the peasants of the Elassona area: 'news of our appearance ... spread like wildfire in the whole prefecture of Elassona, many exaggerated our strength, some even said that our group was two hundred strong'.[205]

This was not unusual. 1942 was the annus mirabilis of the resistance, a 'time of tall tales'[206] according to Leandros Vranousis, when the mere presence of the guerrillas was to many a wonder by itself. 'People ... let their imaginations run wild and made up all kinds of grandiose scenarios that inflated the guerrillas' heroics', noted Vranousis:

> tales were spreading by word of mouth and the people, carried away by their very need and desire, inflated even the slightest achievement of the guerrillas. They imagined them as superhuman ... and ruthless punishers ... often they said the hills are black with the guerrillas or I heard that Ares was seen yesterday with thousands of riders and foot soldiers or that Zervas crossed to Valtos with a multitude.[207]

Indeed, for many the very presence of the guerrillas meant that these men were supported by powerful backers; 'they said they must know what they were doing, else how could they become outlaws and defy the occupier and his strength'.[208] Many guerrilla leaders carefully cultivated this view by presenting themselves as regular army officers or by exaggerating the extent and breadth of their activities.

Moreover, the clashes led to a realignment in the relations between the local elites and the guerrilla organisations, particularly EDES. In contrast to ELAS, which had been active since mid-summer 1942, EDES did not fight the occupation army until late autumn. The results of these first clashes were not impressive and the failure of EDES to prevent the raiding parties from setting fire to the villages of Megalohari and Skoulikaria led many peasants to turn against the guerrillas. However, the inability of the Italians to dislodge EDES, the impressive successes of some band leaders and the extraordinary bravery of Zervas raised significantly the prestige of EDES, especially among younger peasants, many of whom rushed to enlist as a result.[209]

These clashes also liberated EDES from the grip of local elites who, following the mishaps of Skoulikaria and Megalohari, had turned against EDES. Zervas reacted violently, knowing that he would be backed by the men who fought alongside him and their leaders like Karabinas, who distinguished themselves in these first clashes and gained a leading position in local society by virtue of their military feats. Zervas attacked personally and manhandled Lazaros Tribos, who protested over his tactics, and almost came to blows with Nikiforos Kossevakis. In his memoir, Kossevakis attributed these moves to Zervas's pettiness and jealousy; however, it seems that these were well-calculated acts whose purpose was to establish Zervas as the undisputed authority in the region.[210] These clashes finally enabled Zervas to gain a foothold and begin distancing himself from his backers, as he noted years later in his memoir: 'when a guerrilla movement takes roots and its leader becomes a legend and a song, then the role of the local notables gradually decreases and can be potentially diminished'.[211] These successes emboldened Zervas to take even more drastic measures: EDES forces seized and shot four peasants in the villages of Skoulikaria and Megalohari, whom they accused of collaborating, and arrested several notables who were accused of subverting its military efforts. These accusations were unfounded; however, the executions of these men had a huge impact on the local peasantry, since they demonstrated that collaboration or neutrality towards the Italians was not an option. Furthermore, the failure of the local notables to intervene in order to save the lives of these men exhibited clearly that EDES had the upper hand in the region.[212]

The heightening of military activities coincided with, and to a large extent resulted from, another major development for the resistance – the appearance of the Special Operations Executive (SOE). Historians on both sides have shrouded the SOE in myth; for the left, the British operatives were agents of the City of London and British imperialism whose sole purpose was to undermine the creation of a free socialist Greece.[213] Conversely, right-wing authors described the SOE as a nest of crypto-leftists whose abundant money and material enabled ELAS and other left-wing organisations across Europe to evolve from an assortment of gangsters and fanatics into a powerful organisation.[214]

The first SOE mission, consisting of a dozen men led by Brigadier Edmund Myers, was dispatched to central Greece in the autumn of 1942. Their purpose was to cut the flow of supplies from Greece to the Middle East by sabotaging the Athens–Thessaloniki railway lines. Despite significant problems and delays, the saboteurs were able to carry out their mission with the help of ELAS and EDES. This success convinced the Middle East Command that the guerrilla organisations had the potential to cause significant damage to the Axis. Between January and May 1943 over fifty operatives were despatched to Greece to serve as advisors, trainers and liaison to individual guerrilla commands. The SOE also began to provide the guerrilla forces with arms, uniforms and provisions on an increased scale.[215]

British help enabled EDES to expand dramatically and increase its forces from a mere 300 in January to more than 1,500 in March and 5,000 in September 1943.[216] The resistance, of course, did not owe its existence to the SOE, and it is certain that the guerrillas would have been able to survive without the SOE's help; however, it is very uncertain whether they would have been able to expand beyond the heartland of central Pindus. The weapons and funds provided by the SOE (according to an ELAS estimate the SOE provided them with over 100,000 gold sovereigns and made twenty weapon drops between March and September 1943) allowed the rapid expansion of the resistance into areas such as Peloponnesus, which remained closed until the arrival of the SOE.[217]

Peloponnesus was one of the more problematic areas for both EDES, which failed in its effort to raise bands in the prefecture of Achaea, and ELAS, whose development was also hindered by the staunch conservatism of the peasantry. This was particularly the case in the fiercely conservative areas of Messenia and Laconia, where EAM was a byword for communism among the peasants and the extremism of its local leadership had managed to scare off the middle classes and the regular officers; 'we had a group of 32 officers … Kostas [Blanas] spoke to these men about the proletarian revolution which led many of them to react'. Unable to find recruits for the bands or extract financial help from the citizenry, ELAS remained until the spring of 1943 a conglomeration of badly armed irregulars led by amateurs and composed of a mixture of petty criminals, eccentrics and political activists. The arrival of the SOE in the area presented a great opportunity that was used magisterially by the ELAS leadership. They managed to cut off the SOE operatives from the nationalist bands that operated in the area and surround them with their own men: 'we convinced the British that we must provide them with a guerrilla escort for their protection. They accepted and we gave them the most conscientious of our lads who were ordered to attend to them and to be on their best behaviour.'[218] ELAS's courtship bore fruit quickly, as the enthused British operatives promised its leaders that they would 'turn Peloponnesus into a true arsenal'. Indeed, within a few weeks they had made 'four drops and we were able to equip the guerrillas'.[219]

However, these were not the only benefits to accrue from the presence of the SOE. One of the foremost reasons for the failure of EAM/ELAS to attract support in the region was the widely held belief that they were merely a facade for the KKE. The British presence helped to convince the local royalist peasantry that ELAS was not necessarily a communist mole and provided ELAS with an aura of respectability that helped it to soothe the worries of many of its middle-class backers and attract support from the upper strata of rural society: 'some people from the prefectural EAM committee had begun to have doubts. These were the manager of the agrarian bank and the manager of some civil service in Laconia. I brought them into contact with the British, they were pleased and were actually enthused for seeing a representative of Britain.' ELAS followed a similar tactic in Arcadia and Ileia, and in two months up to September 1943 it had managed to increase its forces from a few dozen men to over 500, disperse the scattered nationalist bands and impose its control on Peloponnesus.[220] British funding, which was estimated by Major Nicholas Hammond to amount to 55,000 gold sovereigns between April and October 1943, enabled ELAS to unify the scattered guerrilla bands that operated in the highlands of western Macedonia in the spring of 1943, numbering between 250 and 300 men, and create a well-armed force of approximately 1,000 by August 1943, as well as raising bands in the adjoining areas of central Macedonia.[221] The arrival of the British

Military Mission also enabled ELAS to expand considerably in the areas of Arta and Preveza in Epirus, where it increased its forces from 60 men in April 1943 to 800 three months later.[222]

In June 1942 ELAS and EDES had fewer than 200 men across Greece. One year later, they had managed to create a free area that stretched from Cape Maleas to the Greco-Albanian border. How was this achieved? Scholars have suggested a range of factors: ideology, patriotism, Axis violence and oppression and the economic crisis. However, these factors often had the opposite effect to that expected; antagonism over limited resources and the fear of violence fragmented ties, inverted social hierarchies and led to a profound social demobilisation as communities and individuals strove to survive. The resistance activists managed to overcome these obstacles by mobilising regional, kinship and ethnic networks. These ties played a pivotal role in the creation and establishment of the first groups in the countryside as they helped the resistance agitators to overcome traditional peasant prejudices. EAM and EDES nuclei during this period were more often structured around the activists' extended families.

However, as the occupation evolved, new motivations became apparent. Participation in clandestine activities endowed many activists with a powerful, almost messianic, sense of their mission and purpose. Moreover, the activities of the guerrilla groups created a mystique around the guerrillas and their abilities, which convinced many peasants to offer their support. The arrival of the BMM played an equally important role. The British presence not only helped the resistance bands to expand but also endowed them with a much-needed aura of respectability which helped them to overcome the reservations of the peasantry and the local elites, who until then had viewed them as little better than bandits. Nonetheless, what ultimately facilitated the meteoric rise of the resistance was neither the provisioning of collective goods nor the admittedly vigorous efforts of an activist minority. Rather, it was the calculated and often brutal campaign of selective violence against representatives of the previous regime and local elites that pushed those who were undecided to support the resistance. Indeed, it was abundantly clear to the peasantry that those who failed to support the guerrillas ran a far greater risk than those who chose to do so.

Notes

1 Dionysis Haritopoulos, *Ares o arhigos ton atakton* [Ares, leader of the irregulars] (Athens: Topos, 2009), pp. 66–7.

The rise and origins of the People's Armies

2 Since 1912 the political life of Greece had been dominated by two political parties, the pro-royalist 'Laiko Komma' and the anti-monarchist Liberal Party, also known as 'Venizeliko' after its founder Eleftherios Venizelos. The rivalry between the liberal and the royalist factions dated back to the disagreement between liberal premier Eleftherios Venizelos and King Constantine I during the First World War. Venizelos insisted on Greece's participation on the side of the Entente while the king was in favour of neutrality. This dispute led to the liberal coup of 1916 and the eventual dethronement of the king. These events resulted in a prolonged feud between the two factions and a series of coups between 1922 and 1936. This rivalry perpetuated in the following years and afflicted the political life of Greece well into the occupation. The animosity between the two factions thwarted any efforts towards a combined anti-Axis front and opened the way for the eventual dominance of EAM.

3 Giorgos Margaritis, *Apo tin itta stin exegersi: Ellada anoixi 1941–fthinoporo 1942* [From defeat to revolution: Greece spring 1941–autumn 1942] (Athens: Politis, 1993).

4 Giorgos Houliaras (Pericles), *O Dromos einai asotos* [The long and winding road] (Athens: Oionos, 2006), p. 78.

5 Giannis Katsantonis, *Polemontas tous kataktites* [Fighting the occupiers] (Athens: Sinhrone Epoxe, 1979), p. 19.

6 Riki Van Boeschoten, *Anápoda Chrónia: Syllogiki Mnimi Kai Istoría Sto Ziaka Grevenon, 1900–1950* [Years of turmoil: collective memory and history in Ziakas Grevenon] (Athens: Plethron, 1997).

7 Paul Staniland, *Networks of Rebellion: Explaining Insurgent Cohesion and Collapse* (Ithaca, NY: Cornell University Press, 2014), p. 4.

8 Ellikiko Logotehniko kai Istoriko Arheio (henceforth ELIA)/The Triantafillakou Archive/Box 2/File 3/Giorgos Papas, diary, unpublished, ELIA Library, p. 136.

9 Mazower, *Inside Hitler's Greece*, chs 10–13.

10 Smirni Maragou, *I Lefkada sti dine tis katohes kai tou Emfiliou* [Lefkada in the maelstrom of the resistance and the civil war] (Athens: Elliniki Evroekdotiki, 1989), p. 177.

11 Romolo Galiberti, *Tripies botes, apo tin Merarxia Pinerolo stous andartes* [Torn boots, from the Pinorolo division to the ELAS guerrillas] (Athens: Filistor, 1998).

12 ELIA/Arheio Voulgarikis Katohes [Archive of the Bulgarian occupation] (henceforth AVK)/Diafora ipomnemata ektheseis tin apo tis katareuseos mexri simera diadramatisthedon en to nomo Kastorias kai Voiou gegonota, p. 10.

13 Ioannis Nikolaidis, *Ta hronia pou perasan, anamnseis* [The years that passed, memories], vol. 2: *1941–1967* (Ioannina: self-published, 1994), pp. 13–14.

14 Richard Vinen, *Unfree French: Life under the Occupation* (London: Penguin, 2006), p. 113.

15 Richard Clogg, *Greece 1940–1949: Occupation, Resistance, Civil War* (New York and London: Palgrave, 2002), p. 96.
16 Vinen, *Unfree French*, p. 113.
17 Haralabos Pieroutsakos, *Ena aetopoulo thematai* [An Aetopoulo remembers] (Athens: Proskinio, 2000), p. 63.
18 Kostantinos Diamantis, *Mnimes, polemos kai katohe: Papigo 1940–1944* [Memories, resistance and civil war: Papigo] (Ioannina: self-published: 2006), p. 47.
19 ELIA/AVK/Peri ton energeion kai protheseon Mousoulmanon Thesprotias; Athanasios Hrisohou, *I katohe en Makedonia, I drasi tis Voulgarikes Propagandas 1941–1944* [The occupation in Macedonia, the activities of the Bulgarian propaganda] (Thessaloniki: Etairia Makedonikon Spoudon, 1950), vol. 1, pp. 16–19.
20 Alexandros Lazanis, *Anamniseis apo to metopo tou 1940 kai tis katohes* [Recollections from the 1940 war and the occupation] (Ioannina: Dodoni, 2007), p. 45.
21 Hristoforos Hristides, *Hronia katohes 1941–1944: Martiries imerologiou* [The years of the occupation 1941–1944: testimonies from a diary] (Athens: n.p., 1971), pp. 21–2.
22 Georgios Tsolakoglou, *Apomnimonefmata* [Memoirs] (Athens: Akropolis, 1959), p. 159.
23 Yves Durand, 'Collaboration French-style: a European perspective', in Sarah Fishman (ed.), *France at War: Vichy and the Historians* (Oxford: Berg, 2000), p. 69.
24 Hristides, *Hronia katohes*, p. 5.
25 Tsolakoglou, *Apomnimonefmata*, p. 172.
26 Hristides, *Hronia katohes*, pp. 93–4.
27 Hristides, *Hronia katohes*, p. 172.
28 ELIA/AVK/Septemvres-Dekemvres 1942/Apospasma Deltiou Pliroforion minos Augoustou 1942.
29 Hristos Tseris, personal interview, Ioannina, 2008; Pinelopi Vezdrevani, personal interview, Igoumenitsa, 2009.
30 Hristos Vittos, *Ta Grevena stin katohe kai sto adartiko: Istorike Meleti Dekaetias 1940–1950* [Grevena during the occupation and the civil war: a historical study of the 1940–1950 decade] (n.p., 2000), pp. 149–60.
31 Athanasios Kallianiotis, 'Oi prosfiges sti Ditiki Makedonia 1941–1946' [The refugees in Western Macedonia 1941–1946], PhD dissertation, University of Thessaloniki, 2007, pp. 113–25.
32 Dimitris Papanikolaou, *Enas daskalos thimatai* [A schoolteacher remembers] (Athens, n.p., 1985), p. 26.
33 Rigas Georgios Skoutelas, *Ta Theodoriana Artas* [Theodoriana village in Arta] (Athens: self-published, 2006), pp. 159–60.
34 Antones Sanoudakes, Athanasias Psaroulaki and Giorgis Dafermos,

Ta limeria tou ELAS [The hideouts of ELAS] (Athens: Knossos, 1993), p. 41.
35 Dimosthenis Efthmiou, *Kastania I geneteira* [Kastania my birthplace] (Arta: self-published, 1993), p. 154; Skopouli, *Sta aposkia tis istorias*, pp. 202–3; Aristofane Tsaka, *Trilogia* [Trilogy] (Athens: self-published, 1988), p. 357.
36 Skopouli, *Sta aposkia tis istorias*, pp. 213–14.
37 Diamantis, *Mnimes*, p. 47.
38 Violetta Hionidou, *Famine and Death in Occupied Greece, 1941–1944* (Cambridge: Cambridge University Press, 2006), p. 98.
39 Skopouli, *Sta aposkia tis istorias*, pp. 74–5.
40 Skopouli, *Sta apostia tis istorias*, pp. 168–9.
41 Kostantinos Kostoulas, *Katohikes istories tou Pogoniou* [Stories from Pogoni during the occupation] (Athens: Elikranon, 2013), pp. 219–21.
42 Fotis Mitsis, *Orosima mis poreias* [Landmarks of a life] (Athens: self-published, 2006), pp. 49–50.
43 Giorgos M. Tzouvalas, *Anazitontas tin alitheia stis pliges pou anoixe o katohikos emfilios* [Seeking the truth in the wounds opened by the civil war during the occupation] (Athens: Etairia Meletis Ellinikis Istorias, 2009).
44 Apostolos Papakostas, memoir, unpublished, Skoufas Library Arta, pp. 35–41.
45 Skopouli, *Sta aposkia tis istorias*, p. 232. EPON, the United Panhellenic Association of Greece, was EAM's youth organisation.
46 Labros Sabanis, *Anamniseis apo tin ethniki antistasi kai ton emfilio* [Memories from the resistance and the civil war] (Athens: Metaihmio, 2007), pp. 28, 33.
47 Sabanis, *Anamniseis*, p. 36.
48 Sabanis, *Anamniseis*, p. 37.
49 Kitsos Giagiorgos, *Belkameni, ekato hronia zoi* [Belkameni, one hundred years of life] (Athens: self-published, 2000), pp. 164–5.
50 Stavros Theodosiadis, *I Pindos omilei: I ethniki antistasis 1941–1944* [Pindus speaks, the national resistance] (Kozane: Institouto Vivliou kai Anagnosis Kozanis, 2000), p. 74.
51 Hrisohou, *I katohe en Makedonia*, pp. 146–8.
52 Nikolaos Ziagos, *Ethniki antistase kai Aglikos imperialismos* [National resistance and English imperialism] (Athens: self-published, 1979), vol. 1, p. 78; Kostoulas, *Katohikes istories*, p. 219.
53 ELIA/AVK/Septemvres-Dekemvres 1942/Apospasma Deltiou Pliroforion minos Augoustou 1942.
54 Dimitris Dimitriou, *Antartis sta vouna tis Roumelis* [A guerrilla in the mountains of Roumeli] (Athens: self-published, 1965), vol. 1, p. 121.
55 Harilaos Vagias, *I Arta tis katohes* [Arta during the occupation] (Arta: n.p., 2004), pp. 137–8.

A history of the Greek resistance

56 Miltiades Malainos, *To simeiomatario tou Vlasi Roumeli* [The notebook of Vlasi Roumeli] (Athens: Zabra, 1960), pp. 183–4.
57 Nikolaidis, *Ta hronia*, p. 26.
58 Nikolaidis, *Ta hronia*, p. 25.
59 Tzouvalas, *Anazitontas tin alitehia*, pp. 90–1.
60 Gerasimos Maltezos, *EAM–ELAS, anamniseis kai zitimata stratigikis kai taktikis* [EAM–ELAS, memories and questions of tactics and strategy] (Volos: self-published, 1987), pp. 60–1; Priovolos, *Mia alisida mnimes*, p. 29.
61 Nikolaos Anagnostopoulos, *I Euboea ipo katohe* [Euboea during the occupation] (Athens: n.p., 1950), vol. 1, pp. 233–5.
62 Stathis Damianakos, *Paradosi antarsias kai laikos politismos* [Tradition of revolt and folk culture] (Athens: Plethron, 1987).
63 For a general discussion of the region and its history, see Stavraki Eleftheria and Fotis Krikzonis, *Agrafa: Odoiporiko sto hrono* [Agrapha: a journey into time] (Athens: self-published, 2008).
64 *Anagennisis* (newspaper, Trikala) 5 June 1942; *Anagennisis* 24 July 1942.
65 ELIA/Arheio EAM Palama Karditsas [the EAM archive of Palama and Karditsa] (henceforth AEPK)/Organotiki katastasi tou mina Iouliou/eparhiake epitropi mouzakiou.
66 Diefthinsi Istorias Stratou [Directorate for Army History] (henceforth DIS)/Arheio Georgiou Agorou [the Archive of Georgios Agoros] (henceforth AGA)/Diary, unpublished, DIS Library, p. 9.
67 DIS/Arheio Mihail Miridaki [the Archive of Mihalis Miridakis]/908A/Oi protoi antartes stin Ellada, p. 31.
68 Ziagos, *Ethniki antistase*, vol. 2, pp. 301–3.
69 Mihalis Ntousias, *EAM Zalogou, ELAS Souliou* [The EAM of Zalogo, the ELAS of Souli] (Athens: self-published, 1987), p. 54.
70 Lazaros Arseniou, *I Thessalia stin antistasi* [Thessaly during the resistance] (Larisa: ELLA, 1999), pp. 98–9, 112–13.
71 Pantelis Moutoulas, *Peloponnisos 1940–1945* (Athens: Vivliorama, 2004), p. 127; Kostas Bougas, *Matomenes mnimes, 1940–1945* [Bloody memories] (Athens: Pelasgos, 2009), pp. 41–2.
72 Papakostas, memoir, p. 47.
73 Hristos Giannakopoulos, *Anamniseis enos anthipolohagou tou ELAS* [Recollections of an ELAS lieutenant] (Athens: Epikairotita, 1994), p. 45.
74 Dimitris Raptis, *Apomnimonefmata, foteines kai mavres selides mia epohes* [Recollections, dark and bright pages of an era] (Athens: self-published, 2001), p. 8.
75 Moutoulas, *Peloponnisos*, p. 143.
76 Evangelos Vekris, *Protopapas, istoria kai paradosi* [Protopapas, history and tradition] (Ioannina: self-published, 2008), pp. 130–3.
77 Vekris, *Protopapas*, pp. 179–81.

78 http://www.rizospastis.gr/story.do?id=5316245 (accessed 5 January 2014); Ntousias, *EAM Zalogou*, pp. 54–6.
79 Vekris, *Protopapas*, p. 133.
80 Vekris, *Protopapas*, p. 179.
81 Moutoulas, *Peloponnisos*, p. 48.
82 ELIA/Arheio Proforikon Martirion ERT [ERT oral testimonies archive] (henceforth APME)/Pavlos Mihelioudakis.
83 Papakostas, memoir, pp. 48–9.
84 http://www.venizelosarchives.gr/rec.asp?id=24460 (accessed 5 January 2014).
85 Ntousias, *EAM Zalogou*, p. 55.
86 Ntousias, *EAM Zalogou*, p. 84.
87 Ntousias, *EAM Zalogou*, p. 85.
88 Giannis Simentzis, *Sta monopatia tis zois* [In the paths of life] (Athens: n.p., 1986), p. 18.
89 Ntousias, *EAM Zalogou*, pp. 85–6, 56.
90 Ntousias, *EAM Zalogou*, pp. 54–6, 62.
91 Kallianiotis, 'Oi prosfiges', p. 108.
92 Etairia Diasosis Istorikon Arheion (henceforth EDIA)/Arheio Nikolaou Tsamantaski [The archive of Nikolaos Tsamantakis]/I Antistasi sta Meskla [The resistance at Meskla], pp. 1–4.
93 Antonis Sanoudakis-Sanoudos, *Ta Matomena hronia* [Bloody years] (Athens: Taxideftis, 2014), pp. 1–10.
94 Moutoulas, *Peloponnisos*, pp. 190–3.
95 Grigoris Kribas, *I ethniki antistasi stin Messinia kai stous giro nomous* [The national resistance in Messinia and the adjoining districts] (Kalamata: n.p., n.d.), p. 45.
96 Moutoulas, *Peloponnisos*, pp. 194–6.
97 Ioannis Karakatsanis, 'I Mani ston Polemo' [Mani during the war], PhD dissertation, University of Athens, 2010, pp. 37–44.
98 Nikolaidis, *Ta hronia*, p. 35.
99 Papagiannis, *Kravges tis mnimes*, p. 274.
100 Mihalis Bolosis, personal interview, Igoumenitsa, 2007.
101 Skopouli, *Sta aposkia tis istorias*, p. 256.
102 Karakatsanis, 'I Mani', appendix, pp. 145, 271, 471–2.
103 Stefanos Filos, *Agnanta Artas* [The village of Agnanta in Arta] (Athens: self-published, 1989), p. 114.
104 *Mnimi kai Hreos, Afieroma sto Mikro Horio Evrytanias stin period tis katohes kai tis ethnikes antistases* [A tribute to Mikro Horia Evrytanis during the occupation and the national resistance] (Athens: n.p., 1983), pp. 54–8.
105 Panagiotis Mitsis, *Thimamai … apo ta paidika mou hronia, tin ethniki antistasi, tous diogmous, ton emfilio, tin politiki prosfigia, ton epanapatrismo* [I remember … my childhood, national resistance, persecution, civil war,

political exile, the return to the homeland] (Igoumenitsa: self-published, 2008), pp. 40-4.
106 Nikolaidis, *Ta hronia*, p. 35.
107 Ntousias, *EAM Zalogou*, p. 97.
108 ELIA/APME/Gerasimos Priftis.
109 Poseidonas Logothetis, *To hreos, mnimes kai martiries, 1940-1945* [The debt, memories and testimonies, 1940-1945] (Athens: Stohastis, 1992), p. 26.
110 For a detailed discussion of this term, see the brilliant study by Elisabeth Jean Wood, *Insurgent Collective Action and Civil War in El Salvador* (Cambridge: Cambridge University Press, 2003), ch. 1.
111 Elias Reggas, autobiography, unpublished, personal archive, p. 131.
112 Mitsopoulos, *Ananminiseis agoniston*, pp. 164-5.
113 Mazower, *Inside Hitler's Greece*, p. 138.
114 Napoleon Zervas, *Apomnimonefmata* [Recollections] (Athens: Metron, 2002), p. 151.
115 Genika Arheia tou Kratous-Kentriki Ipiresia [National State Archives] (henceforth GAK)/Arheio Mihail Miridaki [the Archive of Mihaili Miridaki] (henceforth AMM)/Small collections/Box 197/15, p. 11.
116 Iosif Papadakis, *To Imerologio enos agonisti* [The diary of a fighter] (Chania: self-published, 2009), pp. 26--27.
117 ELIA/APME/Apostolos Papakostas.
118 GAK/AMM/15, p. 11.
119 Napoleon Zervas, diary, unpublished, Skoufas Library Arta, p. 11.
120 Papadakis, *To Imerologio*, p. 27.
121 ELIA/APME/Apostolos Papakostas.
122 Nikiforos Kossevakis, *I triti alitheia* [The third truth] (Athens: Aggira, 2001), p. 201.
123 http://www.gnomiartas.gr/afierwmata/item/2103-kossi?tmpl=component&print=1 (accessed 10 January 2015).
124 Kossevakis, *I triti alitheia*, pp. 190-1.
125 Zervas, diary, p. 26.
126 Zervas, diary, p. 29.
127 Papadakis, *To Imerologio*, p. 21.
128 Zervas, diary, p. 44.
129 Papanikolaou, *Enas daskalos*, p. 33.
130 Pinelopi Vezdrevani, interview.
131 Kostantinos Kostantinides, *Stathis Kostantinides Hasilas, enas alliotikos kapetanios I katohe kai o emfilios polemos stin Ditiki Makedonia* [Stathis Kostantinides Hasilas, a different *kapetanios*, the occupation and the civil war in Western Macedonia] (Thessaloniki: Kiriakidis, 2010), p. 65; Nikos Hatzinikolaou, *Taragmena hronia sto Nesto, katohe-antistasi-emfilios* [Troubled years at Nestos, occupation, resistance, civil war] (Thasos: self-published, 2008), p. 68.

132 Hrisohou, *I katohe en Makedonia*, pp. 22–3.
133 Hrisohou, *I katohe en Makedonia*, pp. 28–32.
134 Arseniou, *I Thessalia*, pp. 99–101.
135 Antoni Sanoudaki, *Kapetan Adami Krasanaki, vimata lefterias* [Kapetan Adami Krasanaki, steps of freedom] (Athens: Knossos, 1981), pp. 35, 24; Antonis Sanoudakis, *Anexartitoi antartes, kapetan Vasili Pateraki* [Independent guerrillas, kapetan Vasili Pateraki] (Athens: Knossos, 1988), pp. 8–11, 124–5.
136 Tasos Hatzianastasiou, *Antartes kai Kapetanioi I ethniki antistasi kata tis Voulgarikes katohes tis anatolikes Makedonias kai tis Thrakes* [Guerrillas and *kapetanioi*, the national resistance against the Bulgarian occupation of eastern Macedonia and Thrace] (Thessaloniki: Kiriakidis, 2003), pp. 129–30.
137 For a general discussion of this issue, see Eleftheria Manta, *Oi Mousoulmanoi Tsamides tis Ipeirou* [The Muslim Chams of Epirus] (Thessaloniki: IMXA, 2004).
138 ELIA/APME/Gerasimos Priftis; Spirou Papamokou, *I Selliane, xthes kai simera* [Selliane, yesterday and tomorrow] (Athens: self-published, 1997), pp. 190–3.
139 Thanasis Kakogiannis, *Mnimes kai selides tis ethnikis antistasis, Agrinio-Ditiki Sterea Ellada* [Recollections and pages from the national resistance, Agrinion-Western Central Greece] (Athens: Kostarakis, 1997), p. 140.
140 Hatzinikolaou, *Taragmena hronia*, pp. 35, 103–7.
141 Ziagos, *Ethniki antistase*, vol. 2, pp. 188–91.
142 DIS/Arheio Dimitiriou Nikolopoulou [the Archive of Dimitrios Nikolopoulos] (henceforth ADN)/File 2/Ekthesi pros ton kathodigitiko pirina tou kommatos tis VII merarhias/20/12/44.
143 Pantelis Moutoulas, 'To EAM stin Ileia, I sigrotisi tis laikis igemonias 1941–1944' [EAM in Ileia, the construction of popular hegemony], PhD dissertation, Panteion University, 2012, pp. 109–15.
144 Hatzinikolaou, *Taragmena hronia*, p. 35.
145 Giannis K. Douatzis, *Imerologio kapetan Othri* [The diary of Kapetan Othri] (Athens: Aixmi, 1983), p. 230.
146 Douatzis, *Imerologio*, p. 230.
147 Zervas, diary, p. 72.
148 Douatzis, *Imerologio*, p. 284.
149 Kostas Tsanaklidis, *To 13 sidagma tou ELAS* [The 13th regiment of ELAS] (Thessaloniki: self-published, 1990), pp. 51–3, 63.
150 Istoriko Arheio Makedonia [Macedonian Historical Archive] (henceforth IAM)/Box 141/Istoria tou Apeleftherotikou kinimatos stin perioxi tou 30 sidagmatos, p. 1.
151 Hatzinikolaou, *Taragmena hronia*, pp. 46–7, 50.
152 Ben Shepherd and Juliette Pattinson (eds), *War in a Twilight World: Partisan*

and *Anti-Partisan Warfare in Eastern Europe, 1939–45* (London: Palgrave, 2010), p. 3.
153 Reggas, autobiography, p. 143.
154 Arheio Sinhrones Koinonikis Istorias (henceforth ASKI)/Arheio KKE [KKE Archive] (henceforth AKKE)/Box 493/File-30/1/58.
155 GAK/Arheio Emmanuel Tsouderou [the Archive of Emmanuel Tsouderos] (henceforth AET)/Apostoli A/File/2/Deltio Pliroforion iparithmon1/12.
156 Spiros Ioannou, *Agnostes istories tis katohes* [Unknown tales from the occupation], unpublished, personal collection, pp. 2–3.
157 ASKI/AKKE/Box 427/File-26/8/38, pp. 14, 16.
158 Dimitri Sakka, *To anthropino ktinos sto kairo tou emfiliou* [The human beast during the civil war] (Athens: Paraskinio, 2011), pp. 19–22.
159 Vagias, *I Arta tis katohes*, pp. 148–9.
160 Priovolos, *Mia alisida mnimes*, pp. 67, 82.
161 Ntousias, *EAM Zalogou*, p. 126.
162 Ntousias, *EAM Zalogou*, pp. 131–8.
163 DIS/AGA/Agoros, Diary, p. 11.
164 Margaritis, *Apo tin itta*, pp. 207–8.
165 Trifonas Papathanasiou, *I mavri vivlos tou EAM* [The black book of EAM] (Athens: Eleftheri Skepsis, 2011).
166 Dimitris Zigouras, *Ena megalo taxidi, ethniki antistasi, emfilios polemos, politiki prosfigia* [A long journey, national resistance, civil war, political exile] (Athens: Themelio, 2012), p. 91.
167 Andreas Tsiatas, *Anamniseis apo tin antistasi 1941–1944* [Memories of the resistance] (Athens: Ziti, 2009), p. 102.
168 ELIA/Arheio proforikis istorias [Oral History Archive] (henceforth OTA)/Giorgos Kosmatopoulos.
169 Vittos, *Ta Grevena*, pp. 196–216.
170 Zigouras, *Ena megalo taxidi*, pp. 92–3.
171 Tsiatas, *Anamniseis*, pp. 76–7.
172 Ziagos, *Ethniki antistase*, vol. 2, pp. 302–6.
173 Vagias, *I Arta tis katohes*, p. 148; Maltezos, *EAM-ELAS*, p. 149.
174 Douatzis, *Imerologio*, pp. 206–7.
175 Stelios Katsogiannos, *I Agnosti alitheia gia ton ELAS* [The secret truth about ELAS] (Athens: self-published, 1994), p. 43.
176 Ioannis Fakis, *Enthimimata zois* [Recollections of a lifetime] (Athens: self-published, 2012), p. 129.
177 Kallianiotis, 'Oi prosfiges', p. 182.
178 The Vlach Legion was a fringe collaborationist group that operated in parts of western Macedonia and Thessaly between 1941 and 1943. Its members were primarily drawn from the Vlach communities of these regions.
179 Fakis, *Enthimimata zois*, p. 131.
180 Fakis, *Enthimimata zois*, pp. 132–3.

181 http://www.dovroi.gr/index.php?categoryid=3 (accessed 5 January 2015).
182 Kostas Baroutas, *Mesohora, istoria, oikonomia, koinonia* [Mesohora, history, economy, society] (Athens: Erodotos, 1998), pp. 99–100.
183 Kostantinos Antoniou, *Istoria Horofilakes* [History of the gendarmerie] (Athens: n.p., 1967), vol. 3, p. 1660.
184 GAK/AET/Apostoli A/File 2/Makedonia/Antartikti Drasis kata ton Noemvrion toy 1943.
185 Priovolos, *Mia alisida mnimes*, p. 151.
186 Katsogiannos, *I Agnosti*, p. 53.
187 'Gegonota kai Sholia' [Comments and events], *Thesprotikos Agon* (newspaper, Paramithia), 21 November 1935.
188 Giorgou Dimitriadi, *Perpatontas sta agathotopia* [A walk in the badlands] (Athens: self-published, 1978), pp. 112–16.
189 ASKI/AKKE/Box 410/File-23/2.
190 Kostoulas, *Katohikes istories*, p. 128.
191 Giorgos Dimitriou, personal interview, Igoumenitsa, 2008; Kostas Tsipis, personal interview, Tsaggari-Souli, 2008; Dimitrios Ntritsos, personal interview, Koristiani-Souli, 2008.
192 Douatzis, *Imerologio*, pp. 290–1.
193 Douatzis, *Imerologio*, pp. 305–6.
194 Stathis N. Kalyvas, 'The paradox of terrorism in civil war', *Journal of Ethics* 8 (2004), pp. 100, 102.
195 Ntousias, *EAM Zalogou*, p. 130.
196 Priovolos, *Mia alisida mnimes*, p. 67.
197 Diamantis, *Mnimes*, p. 64.
198 ASKI/AKKE/Box 418/File-24/2/102.
199 Priovolos, *Mia alisida mnimes*, p. 61.
200 Fakis, *Enthimimata zois*, p. 132.
201 Nikolaidis, *Ta hronia*, p. 37.
202 Nikolaidis, *Ta hronia*, p. 38.
203 Mihalis Kosviras, *Apo to vouno ston amvona* [From the mountain to the pulpit] (Athens: Taxideftis, 2009), p. 110.
204 Kosviras, *Apo to vouno*, p. 114.
205 ASKI/AKKE/Box 429/File-26/4/13.
206 ASKI/Arheio Leandrou Vranousi [Leandros Vranousis Archive] (henceforth ALV)/Katohe kai Antistase stin Ipeiro, p. 8.
207 ASKI/ALV/Katohe kai Antistase stin Ipeiro, p. 8.
208 Nikolaidis, *Ta hronia*, p. 27.
209 Kossevakis, *I triti alitheia*, p. 138; ELIA/APME/Apostolos Papakostas.
210 Kossevakis, *I triti alitheia*, pp. 164–5, 136.
211 Zervas, *Apomnimonefmata*, p. 151.
212 Giorgos Papas, *Anamesa stous protagonistes* [Among the protagonists] (Athens: self-published, 2004), p. 85; Kossyvakis, *I triti alitheia*, pp. 100, 104.

213 See Dominique Eudes, *The Kapetanios, Partisans and Civil War in Greece, 1943–1949* (London: NLB, 1972).
214 John Keegan, 'When Britain turned terrorist', *Sunday Telegraph*, 9 February 1993.
215 For a summary of the SOE's role and activities in occupied Greece during this period, see Edmund Myers, *Greek Entanglement* (Gloucester: Sutton, 1985).
216 Lars Baerentzen (ed.), *British Reports on Greece* (Copenhagen: Museum Tusculanum Press, 1982), p. 78.
217 Imperial War Museum (henceforth IWM)/Nicholas Hammond oral testimony.
218 ASKI/AKKE/Box 418/File-24/2/90, p. 2.
219 ASKI/AKKE/Box 418/File-24/2/90, p. 2.
220 ASKI/AKKE/Box 418/File-24/2/90, p. 2.
221 IWM/Nicholas Hammond oral testimony.
222 DIS/AGA/File 12/Ekthesi Drasis tou 3/40 sintagmatos, p. 5.

2

Patriots and scoundrels: motivation and recruitment in the People's Armies

On 27 August 1942 a small column of armed men entered the village of Skamno in the prefecture of Ellasona. Some peasants may have mistaken this group for one of the many bands of desperadoes roaming the area's uplands during this troubled period; however, as they drew closer, the sight of the standard bearer carrying the Greek flag and the familiar sound of 'ta roda ta triantafilla', a popular patriotic song dating back to the Balkan wars, made clear that these men were something entirely different: guerrillas.[1] They were Nikos Xinos, a farmer, Lefteris Papastergiou, a ceramics maker, Mitsios Papas, a tobacco worker, Antonis Karamitsios, a farmer, Kostas Kipouros, a carpenter, Xenophon Papanikolaou, a farmer, and Vasilis Oikonomou, a ticket collector; all of them had been Communist Party members or fellow travellers before the war and five of them had attended the prestigious local gymnasium, which was unusual for men from this background. The other members of the band were Nikos Balalas, a farmer, Thomas Kapsalis, a labourer, both of whom had been active in the KKE before the war; Nikos Vidras, a rustler from the village of Polineri in Grevena; Giannis Kourkoulas, a gendarme from Corfu; Vasilis Barbarousis, a bandit from the village of Livadi in Olympus; and the three *papoudes* or grandpas, Thanasis Manikas, Panagiotis and Dionisis, the first from the Vlach village of Vlasti in western Macedonia and the others from Litohoron. Manikas and his comrades were far older than the other guerrillas who were between 20 and 30 years old, and before they enlisted they had lived by rustling and banditry.[2]

This strange alliance forged between political activists and fugitives was far from uncommon in the early period of the resistance; however, scholars have either downplayed the presence of these 'scoundrels', or presented them as patriotic Robin Hoods who were transformed gradually into model guerrillas following enlistment in ELAS. For instance, Mark Mazower notes that 'sometimes the ... andarte and the brigand overlapped', but underlines that 'the insurgency in the mountains had moved beyond the understanding and values of the traditional brigand entrepreneur'. Mazower is equally critical of those who presented the guerrillas as 'fodder' for the Party, arguing instead that the 'backbone' of the guerrilla movement was formed by 'the young men from the mountains' whose decision to 'take up arms was an assertion of everything that was admirable in the Greek spirit – a fierce patriotism, a refusal to calculate where matters of honour were concerned, a stoic acceptance of enormous hardship and a determination to act together against overwhelming odds'.[3]

While such men were not uncommon in the guerrilla ranks, patriotism alone was seldom enough to convince the peasants to leave their families behind and embark upon an adventure with an uncertain future. Despite his 'exhortations' and constant reminders of the 'holiness of our struggle', noted an ELAS cadre from central Greece who tried to raise a band in mid-1942, 'I kept facing the same difficulties ... everyone tried to find an excuse to avoid volunteering for the band. The one is afraid of reprisals against his family; the other predicts that we will end up becoming bandits ourselves, and yet another asks for a reprieve until harvest time.'[4] So, why did men join? Guerrilla leaders like Xinos were not free agents – their actions and decisions were shaped by the constraints of the environment in which they operated, their ideological beliefs and by the resources available to them. The first guerrilla groups operated in a suffocating environment; Xinos's band was hemmed in by Greek gendarmes, Italian Carabinieri and Vlach legionaries. Their foremost concern was, therefore, to recruit men who would be politically trustworthy, and such men could only come from the ranks of the Communist Party and fellow travellers. However, this was not the only constraint faced by recruiters. Guerrillas led a spartan existence; they slept rough, lacked food and clothes and were in constant danger. Understandably these conditions made service in the guerrilla bands unappealing for all but the most desperate. However, even when recruits were willing to overlook these trials and come forward, the resistance bands often had to turn them away since they lacked provisions, materiel and guns.

The bulk of recruits came from three sources during this period: the first group were political cadres, most of whom had an urban background;

the second was the extended families and fellow villagers of band leaders; and the third was the numerous outlaw bands that operated in the Greek mountains. These men joined for diverse reasons: family ties motivated some, others had a problem with the law or looked for adventure, and a large number simply lacked any other choice. Recruitment during this period was highly personalised, and recruits were as a rule accepted only after they had been approved and vetted by the band leaders. The gradual creation of free territories in the mountains of central and northern Greece, and the arrival of the British Military Mission, changed the patterns of recruitment and allowed the resistance organisations to recruit in ever-growing numbers. British financial help played a particularly important role in this respect, as it allowed the resistance to offer generous benefits to prospective recruits and their families. Material benefits made enlistment a much more attractive option, especially for poor young peasants for whom participation in a band offered a worthwhile alternative to backbreaking labour in the fields and with the flocks, as well as boosting their personal status.

However, this trend came to an abrupt end after the outbreak of clashes between ELAS and EDES during October 1943. These clashes decimated the guerrilla ranks, which were further thinned by desertions as many new recruits found the realities of guerrilla warfare very different from what they had hoped. Both ELAS and EDES were at least in theory all-volunteer forces; accordingly, guerrilla leaders preferred to attract highly motivated, ideological recruits. However, the dire need for recruits led the resistance to resort increasingly to coercion. Guerrilla bands initially targeted regular army officers, village presidents and community leaders, as they believed that the participation of such men would encourage more to enlist. However, they gradually broadened their scope and began harassing ordinary peasants and threatening those who refused to enlist. Such tactics enabled the resistance to replenish its ranks as the increasing political sectarianisation and fear of repercussions led large numbers of peasants, many of whom had opposed the resistance beforehand, to enlist. However, such men tended to be politically and militarily unreliable and many of them would defect at the first opportunity in search for safety, revenge or simply a better pay-out.

Bandits, cadres and peasants: recruitment in the first resistance bands

In October 1942 Giannis Katsantonis, a schoolteacher from the small village of Mirofilon in Thessaly, was despatched by EAM to set up a resistance band in the uplands of Agrapha in Thessaly. Katsantonis was a popular and energetic man; however, he found recruiting particularly hard: 'we had many difficulties with recruiting guerrillas, our first five guerrillas were dispatched by EAM from the town of Larissa'.[5] Such difficulties were not confined to this area. The economic crisis that had devastated the cities had largely spared the countryside, but had made the peasantry averse to any ventures that might jeopardise their precarious safety; furthermore, rural areas lacked, with a few exceptions, both a tradition of political activism and the cadres necessary to raise these bands. An ELAS report on the area of Arta underscored the difficulty of recruiting from the peasant population that was no doubt common to most rural areas: 'our area was completely devoid of any revolutionary political traditions and the party organisations were in an embryonic state since our province was agricultural ... these factors created an asphyxiating situation ... we had to fight very hard in order to be able to recruit guerrillas in this small province of 60,000 in this situation'.[6] During this period, guerrilla bands relied on a small cadre of political activists, many of whom were of urban extraction, and professionals in violence: gendarmes, rural guards, regular army officers and criminals.

In the summer of 1942 political activists predominated in the first band fielded by ELAS in the Parnassus area. This group was intended initially to be 25-strong. However, as noted by Giorgos Houliaras, the *kapetanios* of this band, they were unable to achieve this number: 'by late June 1942, out of 25 guerrillas promised by the local [KKE] organisations in the 14th May meeting, only three were willing to follow plus three more bandits'.[7] Unable to muster a sufficient number of men, the local Party committee finally 'agreed to make participation in the group a Party obligation to several members of the Parnassida committee and the west Locrida subcommittee and form the basic nucleus of the group with them'.[8] Seven out of nine members were activists and fellow travellers, and while all had a peasant background, most came from the upper strata of peasant society, were well educated and worked in cities. Loukas Kathoulis was a lawyer, Giorgos Kouroubis an agronomist, Giannis Alexandrou had studied law, Giorgos Houliaras was an employee of the Electricity Company in the city of Lamia and Dimitris Dimitriou was a regular army officer.[9] These men were later joined by a motley assortment of brigands, outlaws and rustlers, the most famous of whom was Dimos Karalivanos and his followers from the village of Segditsa, Theoharis Polihronis, Giorgos Fisekis, Kostas Sarantis, G. Kasioutas and Loukas Tzitziras.[10]

Initially, few of the leaders were keen to recruit brigands. Gakis Spirou, an ELAS *kapetanios* from Epirus, warned his comrades that 'after the liberation these men will be the first that we'll have to shoot'. Spirou was justly wary – brigands were tough, brave and experienced guerrilla fighters. However, they lacked discipline and were often unwilling to abandon their old ways.[11] The Agouridis–Tzivaras gang that plagued the uplands of Fokida during 1941–42 continued operating its numerous rackets, which included kidnapping and rustling, long after they joined ELAS.[12] Several members of the Boudouris–Gratsounas gang who joined EDES and ELAS in Epirus were no different. They requisitioned provisions, rustled, fought turf battles with other local gangs and even robbed Red Cross vehicles.[13] No different were the bands of Spiros Tsouknidas, an infamous highwayman who led a detachment of ELAS in the Fanari area of Epirus, and Nasis Giohalas, an escaped convict who operated in the adjoining Parga and Margariti areas. Between them these men were responsible for numerous acts of violence including the robbery and murder of four local peddlers.[14]

However, the dearth of recruits left the ELAS cadres with no choice but to enlist such men. The first band fielded by ELAS in the district of Arta comprised a mixture of students, such as Haralabos Gekas and Nikos Tsakas, who was also a KKE member; political activists like Mitsos Lakkas, an agronomist by trade; professionals of violence such as Fanis Tsakas, a gendarme; and outlaws like Vissaris Pournaras and Vasilis Bourganis, both of whom were fugitives from justice.[15] Brigands were the mainstay of the band of Vasilis Tselios, which appeared in Xiromeron in late 1942. The first two recruits to this group were Vlahomitros and his partner Kitsos Korozis, a notorious brigand who came originally from the village of Trovato in Agrafa, and plied his trade in the lowland area of Fiteies.[16] Korozis was noted both for his bravery and his religious fervour. He once tried to steal a relic, allegedly a fragment of the Holy Cross, which was owned by the monastery of Trovato in the hope that it would render him immune to bullets.[17] He was later joined by his relatives Thomas and Spiros Korozis. Later, Tselios also enlisted the bandit Sotiris Pitsinelis and his gang.[18] Some of the first ELAS recruits in western Thessaly were, according to a pro-EAM source, 'young men with no steady jobs who were attracted to the life of the vagabond', many of whom 'believed that by being guerrillas they will manage to live better'[19] and who requisitioned food and valuables 'without thinking if this was plunder or robbery'.[20] Such men also predominated in the first ELAS bands that appeared in the environs of the city of Ioannina. A local schoolteacher noted that:

> when the guerrillas appeared ... the first people who took up arms and joined them were the tough highlanders, many of whom had escaped from prison during the first days of the occupation and more generally the vagabond element, since the bourgeoisie and the *nikokiraioi* [affluent peasants] were loath to expose themselves at this early stage.[21]

The motives of bandits and outlaws are not always clear. Some popular historians highlight a certain affinity between bandit culture and that of the outlaw in ELAS.[22] However, this is highly doubtful. Bandits were individualists who admired personal strength and bravery, saw wage labourers and peasants as lesser men, and idealised the free life of the shepherds and the *keradji* muleteers from whose ranks most of them came.[23] These values were sharply opposed to the egalitarian and modernist ethos of the left. Some EAM apologists suggested that a number of these outlaws were moved by the dignity and bravery of the communists they encountered in prison during the Metaxas dictatorship.[24] However, this seems highly improbable; these men were attracted to ELAS for more practical and mundane reasons.

Banditry had a brief resurgence between the winter of 1941 and the summer of 1942; however, its halcyon days were over by late 1942. Out of the 45 gangs numbering more than 300 men that operated in central Greece during the autumn of 1941, only five remained six months later.[25] A few outlaws opted to declare allegiance to the Italian authorities and operated briefly under their auspices as anti-guerrilla fighters; however, this was not an inviting prospect, especially after the Italian authorities reneged on their promise and shot some of those who had surrendered.[26] By mid-1942 the remaining bandits who were already hard pressed by the Greek and Italian authorities faced a novel and unexpected competitor: the guerrillas. The guerrilla bands were often poorly armed; however, they were well organised and had a broad support base that enabled them to strong-arm the scattered bandits, whose star was on the wane. ELAS and EDES dispersed several bands and gave their members a simple choice – enlist or be shot. As the walls closed in, more and more brigands joined the resistance in the hope that this new guise would guarantee their safety and allow them to continue their old trade.[27]

Initially, such men were rarer in EDES. Zervas needed recruits as much as his ELAS rivals; however, his dependence on local elites and, more importantly, his political ambitions for the post-war period led him to abstain from incorporating this element in his bands. Thus, when Koutsokostas, a notorious brigand from Valtos, presented himself to Zervas and offered his services, he was 'politely turned away, because he [Zervas] did not want to start building his organisation by enlisting bandits'.[28] EDES guerrillas were frequently portrayed as mercenaries, probably because EDES offered a small monetary compensation to its recruits; however, very few men were initially attracted by this reward. Iosif Papadakis noted in the autumn of 1942 that 'we toured the villages in order to raise their morale and encourage them to rise up, however, they were rather unwilling'.[29] The lack of enthusiasm among the peasantry was also underlined by Giorgos Agoros, the commander of the 3/40 EDES regiment, who noted in his diary: 'very few are willing to fight and most of them are young men from the city of Arta. The majority of the peasants in Megalohari, Mesopirgos, Skoulikaria are only interested in gaining as much as they can from our leader's patriotic effort.'[30]

Agoros's assertion was largely correct; the first EDES recruits were not impoverished peasants, but rather educated and ambitious men, many of whom came from the upper strata of the peasantry and had lived in the cities before the war. The first EDES recruit in the area of Arta was Apostolis Papakostas from the village of Skoulikaria. Papakostas came from a poor but historic family. Through sheer determination and hard work, he became a successful leather hides merchant. Papakostas was unusual among his peers for his love of reading; he was particularly fond of Victor Hugo, and aspired to intellectual status. After the war, he wrote several articles and a fascinating autobiography.[31] Other recruits included Giorgos Papas, a 22-year-old man from the village of Mesopirgos. Papas left his village at the age of 15 to continue his studies at the gymnasium of Agrinion, where he also worked as a waiter to support his family. In 1941 he returned to his village following an absence of seven years. Papas also aspired to intellectual status; after the war he continued his studies at a private grammar school and became a successful journalist and leader in the veteran community.[32]

In the nearby village of Piges, the first recruits included the village priest, Spiros Zafeiris, and the Voulgaris brothers, Elias, an undergraduate, and Giorgos, a gendarme.[33] Meanwhile, in the adjoining village of Megalohari, two of the first recruits were Nikiforos Kossevakis, an agronomist, and Giorgios Kossevakis, a gendarmerie officer. Further south in the village of Sintekno, EDES was joined by Dimos Arvanitis, a retired gendarmerie officer, and his 16-year-old son and gymnasium student, Giorgos. Other recruits came from the more traditional segments of society, such as Spiros Kolonikis or Karabinas, a charcoal burner. Kolonikis was illiterate but was admired by his fellow villagers both for his personal bravery, which he exhibited by serving as a guerrilla in the 1914 northern Epirus struggle, and his abilities as a hunter and a practical doctor. 'His sagacity was admitted by all and his opinion and cures were highly sought after', noted an EDES officer who served alongside Kolonikis; 'he was a practical doctor, a dentist, a veterinary and a midwife and a very honest man if we consider the times that he lived in'.[34]

The factors that led these men to enlist are quite complex; some considered it their duty as veteran fighters and community leaders, for example Father Zafeiris and Kolonikis. Others were attracted by the prospect of adventure or believed that by enlisting in the resistance they would perform their patriotic duty, a view no doubt shaped by their education which abounded in patriotic and militaristic imagery. Politics played a less important role in their decision; however, it is certain that most of these men were anti-communist. Radovizi was a staunchly conservative area; Papas, who lived for several years in the 'red' city of Agrinion, had no affinity with the left and the same can be presumed for the other recruits.[35]

However, the number of available recruits was limited and eventually EDES, like ELAS, was forced to turn to an existing pool of men – the brigands and outlaws who roamed the mountains of Epirus. Alekos Papadopoulos, the legendary commander of the Xerovouni battalion, formed his first group from a mixture of rustlers, veteran guerrillas of the Balkan wars and former bandits from the villages of Sklivani and Anogi, some of whom had been members and affiliates of the renowned Rentzos gang that terrorised north-western Greece during the 1920s.[36] No less notorious was the Padazis gang led by Zois Padazis, a shepherd from the village of Labanitsa in Epirus. Comprising between 10 and 15 men, all of whom belonged to the same extended family, this gang began its career by robbing a flour mill and wounding its owner. Padazis and his entourage had demonstrated little inclination towards outlaw life before the war; however, they quickly acquired a notorious reputation, as a local EDES guerrilla noted: 'before the war they were nothing but during the war everything was possible'.[37] Hunted by the Greek gendarmerie and the Italian army with whom they clashed repeatedly, they gradually attained the status of local heroes, especially among the shepherds in areas of the Skala and Douskara regions, who provided them with shelter and food. Padazis finally joined EDES in March 1943, and formed a band comprised exclusively of his extended family and fellow villagers.[38]

Such bands were far from unique. Peasants were often unwilling to risk their lives and those of their families during these uncertain times; however, kinship ties could often override or at least ameliorate these concerns. Furthermore, most guerrillas felt safer and more comfortable when they were led by local leaders and fought alongside men whom they knew and trusted from their civilian days. The importance of these ties is reflected both in the composition and the recruitment methods of the early bands. The first ELAS band fielded in western Crete during June 1943 was comprised exclusively of peasants from the hamlet of Meskla, the home village of Nikos Tsamantakis, an important local cadre:

> Mihalis, Hristos and Stratos Boloudakis, Batonas Giorgos and Nikos Tsamantakis had a private discussion and decided that each of our families should provide two guerrillas. At mid-day Vasilis and Stavros Papoutsakis, Antonis Louloudakis and Apostolos and Drakos Drakakis arrived in our house in Agrelia … we had already arranged which of our own people would take part in the group and agreed about its composition. We told them to be at Meskla in our cottage tomorrow evening at 6 with their gun and their knapsack.[39]

This pattern of recruitment was no less common outside Crete. The first ELAS group in the area of Grevena, named Astrapi [lightning], consisted of nine men, five of whom hailed from the village of Kidonies with the remainder coming from two adjoining villages. It is indicative that these men not only shared a common place of origin and family ties but also belonged to a similar occupational and linguistic subculture. They were all stonemasons, a semi-nomadic social group who shared a cryptic language known as Koudaritika that was spoken in parts of Epirus and western Macedonia.[40] Similarly, the first ELAS group to appear in the highland area of Evremanthos in Achaea comprised seven men all recruited from the village of Brakoumadi.[41] The nucleus of the 24th ELAS regiment in Thesprotia was formed in similar way. This unit was led by Spiros Kokkoris, a schoolteacher from Paramithia; however, its real leader was Tsilis Mastoras, an infamous outlaw whose numerous exploits earned him nationwide notoriety during the 1920s when he arrested the commanding officer of the local gendarmerie and proceeded to declare his province an independent statelet. Mastoras brought to the band his brother-in-law and fellow outlaw, Nikos Kiamos, his two sons, Giannis and Kostas, and his son-in-law, Vasilis Giotopoulos. The band was later joined by Thodoris Katselis, a cellmate of Kiamos, his son Mihalis and his wife Thalia. Other members included Kirka Gekas, a gun smuggler and former associate of Mastoras, who was followed into ELAS by his brother, Nikolas, and his cousins, Thanasi, Spiros and Hristos. Gekas later convinced four members of the Zaharias family, also from the village of Tsaggari, to enlist.[42]

Family and regional ties played an even more important role in the formation of EDES bands. The majority of the EDES groups during the early period were raised by local men, known as *oplarhigos* – band leaders who occupied a position of prominence in their societies either because of their education and affluence or their capacity for violence. Some studies presented the EDES *oplarhigos* as romantic peasant outlaws;[43] however, many were educated men and some were quite affluent. Fotis Kitsos, who commanded a large band and later a platoon in the EDES 10th division, was an agronomist by trade and before the war had served as leader of the EON chapter in Paramithia.[44] Kostantinos Mavroskotis and Aristeidis Strouggaris, who also commanded bands in the area of Paramithia, were lawyers,[45] as were H. Tsoggas and D. Zikos[46] in the area of Lakka Souli and A. Kostantinides in the area of Lakmos, a brave, charming but unstable man whose allegiance was contested between ELAS and EDES, since he 'commanded great respect in the villages of Mikri and Megali Gotista which were located in a strategic area'. Kostantinides joined ELAS in June 1943, defected to EDES a few weeks later and, after another brief spell in ELAS, returned finally to EDES in the autumn of 1943.[47]

Other band leaders were schoolteachers, like Apostolis Goulas who raised a band in Tetrakomon,[48] N. Dokopoulos who raised a band in Dovla[49] and K. Kourtis who raised a band in Popovo; or civil servants like Nikos Giannoulis in Kapsala.[50] A large number were also peasants. Some were shepherds like the Mitrokostas brothers from Krapsi,[51] who owned thousands of sheep, or Vasilis Baloumis from the village of Spatharati,[52] while others were farmers like Thomas Nakis from the village of Senitsa.[53] Finally, a number of *oplarhigos* were professionals of violence, such as Giorgos Ioannou, a rural guard from the village of Grava in Thesprotia, Thanasis Bakas, also a rural guard from the village of Senitsa, and Nikos Tzanis, a former policeman and Bakas's fellow villager, who was described by one of his men as 'somewhat of a gangster', a reputation he acquired following his mysterious dismissal from the police ranks in Athens.[54]

Giannoulis's diary offers invaluable insights into the formation and culture of these bands and the complex web of alliances used to mobilise and recruit their compatriots. Like most *oplarhigos*, Giannoulis was approached by a representative of EDES, in his case Major G. Agoros, who asked him to join EDES and promised him financial backing. Agoros was not successful, since Giannoulis was a hard-line royalist who had little sympathy for EDES's politics or its leader, Napoleon Zervas. However, the repeated entreaties of fellow royalist and local power-broker Dr N. Tsirogiannis from Voulgareli, who had already joined EDES, and the creation of an EAM committee in his village by men Giannoulis considered beneath him socially, finally convinced him to act. Giannoulis recruited the men who comprised his band from among his extended family, which numbered over 100 men and women in the villages of Tetrakomo and Kapsala. He also supplied the weapons and ammunition. The second-in-command was his brother, Napoleon, who also enlisted his father-in-law, Ioannis Kapsalis, along with several men from the family.[55]

Giannoulis proceeded to raise another band in the nearby community of Tetrakomo. His first contacts were P. Spais, the local Liberal Party boss, and retired teacher Apostolis Goulas, a royalist like Giannoulis and president of the village council before the war. Once the three men had agreed to set aside their political differences and unite to face the new threat of EAM, they decided to proceed by 'creating a committee of the more respectable men from each village clan to raise the whole village in revolt'. Moreover, it was decided that even though Giannoulis would lead the whole venture, he would remain in the shadows initially. They were afraid that placing an outsider at the head of the Tetrakomo band would be seen as an affront by the locals who might decide to shun him and back local-led ELAS instead. Giannoulis's band chose Sunday 10 January 1943 to make their first appearance. Escorted by his men, Giannoulis posted a notice outside the building that hosted the local EAM committee, which declared its dissolution for being 'in opposition to the village's popular will'. The notice further declared: 'I undertake myself the suppression of banditry and theft in my area and all those who trespass this notice will be shot in the spot.' The same notice was posted in the village's coffee shop. Afterwards, Giannoulis and his men moved to the church where he proclaimed the beginning of the uprising in his village. Following the conclusion of his speech, Giannoulis and his men took an oath to fight against the 'German and Italian occupiers and every enemy of the fatherland, the religion and the family'.[56]

Nonetheless, the success of an *oplarhigos* was determined ultimately neither by education nor by wealth, but rather by his capacity for inflicting physical violence. Dionisis Nikolaou, one of the two *opharhigos* of the Radovizi village in Epirus, unlike his colleague Vasilis Labros (a witty, hardworking peasant who also raised a band in the village with the help of his five brothers), was 'not much loved'. However, his fiery temperament ('he was a savage man' recalled a man who served under his command),[57] quickly got him noticed as someone to be reckoned with during this turbulent period and earned him a significant following. Like Nikolaou, Fotis Kitsos lacked both the means and the prestige required for the position of *opharhigos*. Kitsos became an orphan at an early age and was adopted by a family of modest means. The most obvious candidate for leadership of the local band was a member of the much more numerous Karras clan who had already provided a band leader during the 1912–13 war. However, despite their glorious past, the Karras' reputation diminished after the murder of their headman and the inability of his children 'to take revenge'. After that 'people did not really take them into account'. Kitsos's personal bravery, forceful character and distinguished record of service in the 1940 war convinced his compatriots to follow his lead.[58]

Despite the efforts of such men, the guerrilla bands remained little more than local militias who found recruitment outside the leader's circle very difficult. Peasant unwillingness was not the sole problem faced by the resistance organisations. Even when recruits could be found, the bands had little to equip them with, since both ELAS and EDES lacked guns, ammunition, boots and uniforms. Indeed, in many areas, only recruits who brought along their own equipment were accepted, while as late as January 1943 several bands contained men who were equipped with shotguns or were completely unarmed. The provisioning situation was equally bad; bobota, a heavy corn bread, was the staple of the guerrilla diet, sometimes supplemented by herbs and dandelions. Bill Jordan, a New Zealander attached to EDES as a liaison officer, was impressed by the hardiness and poverty of the early bands: 'the food they carried in their rough bags, sufficient for a few days, would have made one good breakfast for an Australian or New Zealander'.[59]

Recruitment was further hindered by the lack of free territories. Up to early 1943 recruitment was conducted in a highly clandestine manner, even in the isolated highlands of central Pindus. Houliaras noted that there was a strict rule of not allowing recruits to join on the spot. Peasants who wanted to enlist did not follow the guerrillas when they left the village, but 'they came to us the next day when we have moved into another village. The reason for that was that the new guerrillas wanted to keep their enlistment in ELAS a secret in order to protect their families from the occupiers and the Greeks who had received arms and collaborated with them.'[60] The fear of infiltrators also made the guerrilla leaders increasingly careful about whom they enlisted. From autumn 1942 onwards, several men volunteered for the Xinos band; however, only a handful were recruited. 'We examined who they are, where they came from, if they had been tested etc. Several of them were not accepted.'[61] ELAS groups in Peloponnesus also subjected recruits to a careful screening and at least in the early period avoided recruiting from among the peasantry, whom they saw as politically suspect: 'the new recruits at least in the early period had to be trusted persons and the only place these could be found was from among EAM's urban cadre where the level of "consciousness" as many of the EAM organisers said was much more advanced'.[62] Such precautions helped ELAS and EDES to retain their cohesiveness and deter desertion and betrayal. However, as the guerrilla groups expanded and needed more and more manpower, this personalised model of recruitment would become obsolete, and new motivations would arise.

Guns and welfare: the politics of recruitment from the creation of the Joint Guerrilla HQ to the civil war

On the morning of 10 February 1943 a reinforced Italian detachment burned and looted the village of Oxineia in Thessaly. A few hours later, the unsuspecting Italians were ambushed and killed by a group of ELAS guerrillas and armed villagers. A few weeks later, another Italian battalion was annihilated in Fardikabos in western Macedonia. These successes were the culmination of a low-key but effective guerrilla campaign that, by June 1943, had driven the Italian army to abandon the mountainous hinterland, thereby allowing the resistance groups to form a free zone 'entirely independent of the influence of or contact with occupying Powers or the Quisling administration in Athens'.[63] This zone stretched from the Gulf of Corinth to the Greek–Yugoslav border. Territorial expansion allowed the resistance organisations to draw from a much larger pool of recruits and suspend the personalised system of recruitment that had previously afforded undue influence to local commanders.

By mid-1943 recruitment offices had been set up in the local ELAS and EDES headquarters where recruits were interviewed and examined by officers and medical professionals. The guerrilla organisations also imposed age limits; only men between 18 and 46 were allowed to enlist. Recruiters were encouraged to select men who were politically conscious, had no prior criminal convictions (the recruitment of bandits in the resistance's ranks had tarnished its reputation among the peasantry) and possessed some military experience, preferably as veterans of the recent war. However, the final arbiters were the local commanders, who were allowed to select men who were untrained or below the age limit if they deemed that they 'could withstand the rigours of military life'.[64]

These changes also allowed ELAS and EDES to conduct a much more aggressive recruitment campaign. Recruitment brigades, comprising a mixture of EPON youths, ELAS guerrillas and EAM political activists, roamed the countryside. The guerrillas and the activists would take turns to speak to the assembled villagers, proclaiming the justice of their cause and lionising the achievements of ELAS. The speeches were followed by patriotic plays performed by the various travelling troupes attached to ELAS. Frequently, authors were commissioned to write special plays that would be performed at such events. Poems and songs were also performed by guerrilla choirs, following which the guerrillas would make a last call for volunteers. Written propaganda played an equally important role. EAM had absolute control over the flow and distribution of information in the countryside and used its propaganda machine to promote guerrilla achievements. Stories were recounted of underage guerrillas who defied their parents' wishes to make the ultimate sacrifice for the fatherland, alongside obituaries of fallen partisans and narratives of battles that pitted lone guerrillas against scores of German soldiers.[65]

However, the expansion of the guerrilla organisations was not uniform across Greece. In Crete and eastern Macedonia, ELAS remained in an embryonic state. In eastern Macedonia, ELAS numbered less than 100 men in December 1943, the majority of whom were strangers to the area and came from the city of Kavala and the island of Thasos. Despite the repeated efforts of the ELAS leaders, they were unable to attract a significant number of local recruits, and the local 26th regiment only reached battalion strength (700 men) in July 1944. The distrust of the local peasantry, many of whom were Turkophone Pontic Greeks, a notoriously conservative and xenophobic community, was to a great extent responsible for ELAS's failure to attract recruits; however, it was not the only reason. The lack of free territories, the presence of a large number of Bulgarian troops and above all the lack of funds stalled ELAS's development. The first representative of the SOE reached the area in late 1943. However, he soon became convinced that ELAS was not worth the money or the effort and instead chose to back the local nationalist bands of Tsaus Anton. Isolated and poorly armed, the ELAS guerrillas lacked the necessary strength to muscle their nationalist rivals as they did in the rest of Greece and were a much less attractive option for young local peasants who thought of becoming guerrillas.⁶⁶ The emaciated appearance of the local ELAS men convinced peasants like Panagiotis Aberiadis, a shepherd seeking a band in which to enlist, that 'I would not be able to withstand these tribulations'. Rather, the locals opted to join the Tsaus Anton groups, which were lavishly funded and armed by the British.⁶⁷

The lack of free areas had an equally detrimental effect on the recruitment efforts of the Cretan section of ELAS. A British officer who worked in the region noted in mid-1943 that 'the essential difference between Crete and the mainland is the absence of safe areas. There is thus no secure base ... no opportunity for maintaining satisfactory army dumps, and no fixed spots from which W/T [wireless telegraphy] sets can work.'⁶⁸ The situation led the local BMM to oppose the build-up of guerrilla forces, especially after an abortive local uprising in the Viannos area that cost the lives of hundreds of peasants,⁶⁹ instead encouraging the creation of clandestine groups whose main task was to collect intelligence and engage in political propaganda. Eventually, some armed groups emerged who were tasked with protecting the wireless telegraphy stations and the British officers who coordinated subversive activities on the island.⁷⁰ However, lack of funds, arms and provisions (the few guerrillas who lingered in the highland areas suffered extreme hardship and sometimes went for days with nothing but bread and water) stalled recruitment both among ELAS and its rivals, whose combined forces were estimated at a total of 800 men a few weeks before the liberation.⁷¹

Despite the profound problems faced by ELAS in some areas, the strength of the guerrilla bands continued to increase to the point that the guerrilla organisations were forced to turn away recruits by September 1943. ELAS, which numbered 1,600 guerrillas in January, had reached 15,000 by August 1943. EDES forces developed accordingly from 300–350 men in January 1943 to more than 4,000 guerrillas six months later.⁷² How can we explain this surge? There are several factors. The first was the stunning success of Operation Animals, which convinced large parts of the peasantry that liberation was imminent and led hundreds of peasants to enlist in the hope of gaining some last-minute laurels.⁷³ The militarisation of the guerrilla bands played an equally important role: in June 1943 the ELAS GHQ decreed that the scattered bands and commands be designated as battalions, regiments, and divisions; medical services, logistic corps and staff offices were also created. A month later ELAS, EDES and EKKA agreed to form a Joint Guerrilla Headquarters under the aegis of the SOE and the Middle East allied command.⁷⁴ As Christopher Woodhouse noted, this move 'had an appeal to the vanity of the guerrillas. To be a soldier in an army was much more satisfying than to be an outlawed bandit.' This innovation attracted the more respectable rural element to the resistance as well as an overwhelming number of officers, more than 1,000 in EDES alone, who, as Woodhouse noted sarcastically, 'were more easily attracted out of the coffee shops when they heard that they were to command Divisions and army corps, than when they were only to lead guerrilla groups and bands'.[75]

Ideology also played an important role in attracting men to the guerrilla ranks. For many rural youths like Giorgis Dafermos, a worker from a small Cretan village, enlistment in ELAS was not only a patriotic duty, but also a struggle for social change and the restructuring of society along socialist and egalitarian lines. Before the war Dafermos worked as a farmhand and ironmonger's apprentice, a life he found 'tyrannical'. In 1943 he first joined EAM and then KKE on the recommendation of a fellow villager. In his memoir, he underlines that he had little knowledge of politics but was attracted to EAM's declaration that 'we would fight to stop the exploitation of one man by another'. Dafermos had little understanding of Marxism and admitted that 'the people were completely ignorant about Marxism'. However, he added,

> Marxism was evident in … everyday life. By that I meant that you saw injustice, you saw that the monasteries had great properties … you saw the inequality in the peasant world, people were really hungry, people being paid 20 drachmas for a day's work … so it was a necessity of life, it was the injustice that you saw.[76]

However, while ideology provided an important impetus there was no direct link between support for EAM and participation in the resistance bands, and often communities where EAM had enjoyed widespread and unrivalled support from the very beginning produced very few recruits. The village of Protopapas, a 1,000-strong community where over 90 per cent of adults were enlisted in EAM, contributed only nine guerrillas.[77] This was far from rare. ELAS was unable to recruit a single guerrilla from the mountain town of Pogoniani, a community 'where the political organisation [EAM] was very active'.[78] ELAS faced similar problems in Crete; none of the 834 male members of EAM in the province of Apokoronas had enlisted either to the regular or the reserve ELAS by September 1944.[79] The same situation prevailed in Thessaly, where out of 40,000 adult male members in the province of Karditsa, only 1,000 enlisted,[80] and in western Macedonia where only 950 of 18,859 EAM members had joined ELAS by late 1943.[81] Indeed, EAM often had great difficulty mobilising even some of its high-ranking and supposedly more committed members. An EPON cadre from east-central Greece dismissed the local EPON functionaries as 'cowards', noting that 'on many occasions our cadres have exhibited a petty-mindedness that is far from helpful in the effort to stimulate a revolutionary spirit'.[82] This was not an isolated incident. A cadre from lowland Thessaly noted that 'several of our cadres had refused to join ELAS',[83] a problem that ELAS also faced in western Macedonia where in early 1944 'a great many failed to show up in the latest call up for the reserve ELAS and many of them were Party members. This is a very serious issue to which we had paid no heed until now.'[84]

To what can we attribute this lack of enthusiasm? Like most villages in the plain of Ioannina and Kalamas, Protopapas was spared from the famine that wreaked havoc in the cities, while many peasants made small fortunes selling wheat and corn on the black market. Furthermore, the area was largely free from Axis interference until the end of the occupation and did not suffer any violence or reprisals, with a few exceptions. The same factors account for the paucity of recruits in the prefecture of Karditsa. The catastrophic harvest of 1941 was followed by two excellent yields. The abundant harvest and the scarcity of working hands also led to a rapid increase in agricultural wages. Farmhands, most of whom came from the poor highland regions, could easily gain between 30 and 40 oke of corn for a day's work, enough to provide for their families and have a surplus to peddle in the local black market. Finally, with the exception of the villages near Karditsa, the Axis presence in the area was quite sparse, both in the highland areas and the villages situated in the foothills of the Agrapha mountains.[85]

The insistence on ideology has blinded scholars to the fact that individuals might have their own separate reasons for enlisting or refusing to enlist in a guerrilla group. Moreover, it has led them to ignore the importance of material benefits on participation. Food, living conditions and material rewards were often much more relevant to prospective enlistees, who took a more pragmatic approach to enlistment than scholars have believed. This can be observed in the response given by a young peasant from an Ileian village to an ELAS *kapetanios* who asked him to join his band: 'they [Ethnikos Stratos, a local royalist organisation] are willing to give me money, are you going to pay me as well?'[86] Such men were not exceptional. In the uplands of Epirus and Thessaly, 'most people saw enlistment during this period from an economic rather than an ideological perspective'.[87] Personal testimonies point towards the ubiquity and importance of such motives, even among the seeming vanguard of EPON. Vasilis Papananos, a law student from the city of Agrinion and a KKE member who enlisted 'to fight and to die for a better world ... and abolish social classes', expected his fellow fighters to be equally determined. However, he soon discovered that they had far less idealistic motivations. A few weeks after enlisting, Papananos noted in his diary: '70%–80% of those who became guerrillas did so either because they were hungry ... or because they committed a crime'.[88] He reiterated this opinion following an encounter with the first recruits of his regiment's exemplary EPON platoon. After the first roll call, Papananos noted:

> A group of 6–7 derelict men appeared ... when they fell in line the spectacle was even more disheartening, they were dressed in tatters, their shoes were filled with holes, many of them had their jackets slung on their soldiers or wore the one sleeve, how can you cooperate with these people? I am really desperate ... unfortunately the first EPON groups are comprised of the most rotten and useless elements of our society, burglars, homosexuals, bootblacks and other dregs ... who only joined us so as to get a plate of food.[89]

This is not surprising. The difficulty of recruiting from the more 'respectable' element led band leaders to seek recruits from those 'whose criminal records were larger than a blanket', in addition to men who had no ideological impetus 'but came for the food and nothing else'[90] – unemployed youths, tenant farmers, hired hands and the lumpenproletariat, from whose ranks most of Papananos's comrades came. Before the war, such men had found an outlet in temporary migration to the cities and the more productive lowland regions, while a significant number sought their fortunes overseas. The occupation and the ensuing economic crisis precluded such options, leading many to join the resistance in order to survive. According to a British liaison officer, in many of the poverty-stricken villages of northern Pindus, 'many Andartes originally joined for food and not to fight'.[91] Vangelis Haliatsos, an 18-year-old peasant from the mountain village of Radovizi in Epirus, joined ELAS in the summer of 1943 after losing his job as a farmhand in the town of Paramithia. 'I had no work, I was hungry, so when ELAS came by our parts me and ten other lads from our village joined them.'[92]

A similar case was that of Vasilis Kourelis, the younger son of a large farming family, who left his native village of Mavrilo in central Greece at the age of 13 for Athens, where he undertook various menial jobs. However, in the winter of 1942 he found himself unemployed and homeless and 'almost died from hunger'. Kourelis decided to return to his village; 'however, things were no better there', and his family made it clear that they were unable to support him. In desperation he decided to join a local ELAS band, hoping that 'once we throw out the occupiers we, the guerrillas, will eat with golden spoons'.[93] These guerrillas were also joined by vagrants and unemployed labourers from nearby cities, for example 'Atsigaros', an underage boy whose parents had perished during the famine in Athens. After his parents' death 'Atsigaros' relocated to the lowlands of Boeotia, sometimes working and often begging, until he learned that ELAS guerrillas had appeared in the mountains and went to join them.[94]

Material benefits came to play an even more important role after the formation of the Joint HQ. Even though ELAS and EDES had no problem in attracting itinerant youths to their ranks, they faced significant difficulties attracting recruits from more conventional backgrounds – farmers, artisans and professionals. According to an EAM report from western Macedonia, such men were loath to enlist since they were afraid that their departure would condemn their families to penury. The report advised that the only way to reverse this was to provide 'immediate financial help to these families and assist them with their agricultural toil and accommodation'.[95] However, neither ELAS nor EDES was initially in a position to provide any significant help. The creation of the Joint HQ changed this situation. The HQ prohibited the paying of money to individual guerrillas; however, it allowed two significant exceptions. Guerrilla families who were deemed to be destitute received a weekly quantity of flour as well as soap, oil, butter and other food and a monthly allowance. Furthermore, families who were not considered destitute but whose primary breadwinner had enlisted were entitled to a monthly allowance to the equivalent of his previous monthly income.[96]

These measures encouraged hundreds of men to enlist in the hope of securing better living conditions for their families, since the provisions and salary provided by the guerrilla organisations were often significantly better than what they had earned as civilians. Lack of work had led brothers Kostas and Spiros Malamos to leave their native town of Tsamantas and seek work in the Vourkos region of Albania to support their widowed mother and young brother, who was studying for his high-school diploma in Ioannina. Living conditions were hard; the two youths often slept in the open and were paid in kind. When they learned that ELAS representatives had appeared in their village with the promise of 'free food, a uniform, boots and half a sovereign per month', they negotiated 30 miles of rough mountainous terrain back to Greece in order to enlist. 'Their maternal uncle, he was married, had already enlisted and so their mother told them you should enlist as well, you'll eat, you'll get clothes and you'll use the half sovereign to help your brother.'[97] Mihalis Bolosis, a farmer from the village of Koristiani in Souli, enlisted for similar reasons. Several of Bolosis's family members had enlisted in ELAS and EDES; however, he was hesitant. He was newly married and he had no other source of income, apart from a few fields. However, he was finally convinced after a local EDES recruiter assured him that he would be able to help himself and his family by enlisting: 'I had no one to help me, my father had died, my mother remarried … and he told me, you should enlist to put clothes on your back, to eat and drink, to get paid. OK, I shall do so. I became a guerrilla in the Zervas organisation.'[98]

However, the wide availability of funds and the complete freedom given to local commanders in their distribution led to gross misuse, especially in areas where ELAS and EDES vied for control. The region of Thesprotia presents a characteristic example. ELAS was unable to recruit more than 50 men by the spring of 1943 because of 'the lack of financial means'.[99] However, between July and September 1944 numbers increased to over 900 as ELAS and EDES began a frantic struggle to attract more men to their ranks, often making wildly inflated promises. Local EAM cadres gave new recruits two sovereigns upon enlisting and promised continuation of payment for at least two more months, as well as a gun and a uniform and leave to return to their villages during the harvest and lambing seasons.[100] This situation shocked many of the original ELAS guerrillas who complained that the promises and preferential treatment shown to prospective recruits, especially those who had formerly served in EDES, gave the impression that 'there are two categories of guerrillas in ELAS ranks; the favourites and all the rest'.[101] However, the necessity of material motivation was admitted: 'the living standards … in the area are extremely low, and the locals are willing to sell themselves for a few breadcrumbs … neither we nor our rivals [EDES] can claim that they prevail in this as the side that is willing to give the most to the locals will be the one to finally prevail in this area'.[102]

EDES did not shy away from using equally underhand tactics; 'emboldened by constant supply drops they developed a frantic activity and by distributing money, clothes and guns … they managed to lead astray many peasants', noted an EAM cadre, who further argued that 'EDES turned the national struggle to a patriotism marketplace, the EDES command which differed little from a bazaar, corrupted, blackmailed, and bribed … it is enough to underline that in order to break our influence in the village of Popovo, EDES spent within 18 days over 32,000,000 drachmas'. An extra sum was promised to men who would defect from ELAS to EDES.[103] This situation was not confined to Epirus but was common to all areas where ELAS coexisted with the other resistance organisations, and it persisted well into the autumn of 1943, despite the repeated instruction of the BMM that it was 'not allowed or possible to offer or promise money … in order to move Andartes to their org'[104] and the strict prohibition against guerrillas remaining 'in or near their place of residence'.[105]

Food and money were not the only incentives used to attract new recruits. The guerrillas' families enjoyed a number of privileges and services that were not accessible to ordinary peasants. Guerrillas' relatives received preferential treatment in the allocation of Red Cross and Allied provisions, and EAM committees often forced 'reactionaries' to allocate part of their produce to guerrilla families and hire them on preferential terms. Moreover, EAM constructed a social welfare network for the families of guerrillas, providing food, medical care and medicine, and free working hands during harvest time.[106] In Laconia, for instance, the families of ELAS guerrillas received a quantity of olive oil, figs and other foodstuff on a monthly basis; they had privileged access to guerrilla health care facilities and received free medicine, while the organisation forced local rightists and EPON youths to work for them for free during harvest time.[107] EDES employed similar recruitment tactics; it provided a sum of money for each family dependant and provisions to all guerrilla families. Guerrillas in both organisations were given the option to serve on a part-time basis, and to return when needed in their homes to help with agricultural work. In some areas, guerrillas served from March until autumn, when most military operations took place, before returning home for the harvest period and lambing season.[108]

The income from looting and extortion offered an additional motive for recruitment. Such activities were not condoned and those who were caught in the act could even receive the death penalty; however, very many were willing to take the risk. Isolated guerrillas and groups of men extracted money and provisions from peasants whom they threatened to denounce as reactionaries, and later sold these goods on the black market or distributed them among their families. Such incidents were particularly common in the richer agricultural areas of central Greece where, according to an ELAS *kapetanios*, poor peasants 'had enlisted in the organisation for one reason only: profit'.[109] The frequency of these incidents rose steeply from the summer of 1943 when thousands of impoverished men enlisted in the organisations; a guerrilla newspaper in Thessaly noted that

> the rapid expansion of ELAS had landed in the ranks ... a number of men who are completely foreign to the character and the goals of ELAS ... they use the guns that were given them to protect the honour, the property and the freedom of the people ... to satisfy their own personal interest.[110]

Less obvious but no less important was the prestige brought by participation in an armed group and the carrying of weapons, particularly for young men like 19-year-old ELAS guerrilla Vasilis Giouris, who recalled: 'we loved guns, we loved showing that we were manly, a gun had a great emotional value ... we strutted around armed and we felt that we were strong and powerful'.[111] Giouris was far from exceptional. Twenty-year-old Vasilis Dokopoulos, who joined an EDES band in his native district of Douskara in Epirus, was similarly enticed by the sense of power and prestige brought by the carrying of arms: 'a gun changes you ... you feel powerful, I cannot describe it differently'.[112] Prestige was important. However, it was not the only advantage of being a member of an armed group. Rural Greece was an extremely volatile and violent environment and while bearing weapons was not always a guarantor of safety, it provided an undoubted advantage to the guerrillas over the civilian population and gave men a sense of security, as ELAS guerrilla Thanasis Mitsopoulos noted: 'learning how to use a gun ... made me stronger, it gave me self-confidence and a sense of assurance'.[113]

However, bearing arms was not merely a psychological boost, but also gave young men power and authority that was often disproportionate to their age and social status, as Giouris soon discovered.[114] However frail or youthful, the guerrillas came to believe that they constituted a class apart, superior to the civilians who were regarded as weak and unmanly; in the words of an ELAS *kapetanios* from Epirus, they were 'worms and vermin ... who lack manly courage'.[115] Such feelings were bolstered by the guerrillas' casual encounters with the civilian population. In areas where guerrillas became dominant, peasants grew accustomed to obeying any person who bore weapons,[116] and many veteran guerrillas still recall the ease with which they 'got into a home and seized what they liked'.[117] Indeed, for many young peasants, the greatest attraction of enlisting was neither ideology nor monetary rewards, but rather the material benefits and the prestige brought by the bearing of arms. As one EPON cadre from Epirus commented, there was no ideology, that we'll seize weapons and wreak revenge on the state, wreak revenge on the reaction ... actually, most peasants could seldom explain why they joined one faction and another one joined a different faction ... some enlisted for the benefits they could reap ... and others grabbed a gun to impress their girlfriend or to show the girl they liked that they were somebody.[118]

Between a rock and a hard place: the aftermath of the civil war and the politics of coercion

The halcyon days of the resistance were not long-lasting. The civil war between ELAS and EDES in the winter of 1943–44 and the failure of both organisations to distinguish themselves during the German anti-guerrilla operations that occurred during the same period led to growing disenchantment among the civilian population and the guerrillas. A British officer in western Macedonia noted in early 1944 that 'many villagers particularly bitter against EAM-ELAS and even well-schooled party members reported to be losing ardour'.[119] This rendered recruitment increasingly difficult. Many peasants were unwilling to enlist in an organisation whose cause they resented and considered responsible for their suffering, while others preferred to make the perilous trip to the Axis-occupied lowlands rather than join ELAS. A recruitment rally attended by 2,500 men in the province of Kozani yielded only seven recruits, while attendees shouted down the speaker, yelling that 'they had already been waiting two years for freedom in vain and had sacrificed all their belongings for the guerrillas'.[120] The situation was no better in the ELAS heartland of Evrytania. Despite the pivotal role of the region in the development of the resistance movement, ELAS encountered serious difficulties recruiting from this area. According to a contemporary report, the area 'contributes next to nothing in guerrilla recruits'. The author attributed the 'decline in militancy' to the ineffectiveness of propaganda ('we have not popularised our feats') and the oppressive behaviour of the guerrillas who took food and pack animals and commandeered houses with complete disregard of the peasants' needs. This situation had turned the peasantry against the guerrillas, and such feelings were further exacerbated by the failure of the guerrillas to measure up to their expectations during the latest German drive.[121]

Many guerrillas who enlisted in the autumn of 1943 in anticipation of the liberation had either been discharged or were reassigned to reserve ELAS units by February 1944. However, this policy, which had the purpose of 'eliminating non-Party hats', caused severe problems.[122] Even men who were deemed ideologically trustworthy and performed well in combat applied for discharge, much to the shock of ELAS commanders. The available data from western Macedonia show the extent of the problem:

> On 18 December 9 Div issued an order that any Andartes wishing to leave ELAS on compassionate grounds could return home. From the 3rd company of the 2nd battalion, 53 regiment, stationed at Morphe, 54 andartes out of a total of 135 left the company. From the 2nd company of a total 90 all wanted to leave but only 13 were allowed.[123]

The situation was similar in the 7th ELAS battalion, where after the command decided to 'allow those who wished to to transfer to their village's reserve ELAS', over 50 per cent of the guerrillas asked for a transfer. The battalion's *kapetanios* tried to dissuade the guerrillas to no avail; fearful that the regiment would disintegrate completely, 'we were forced to release another order: only those who have serious health or family issues are allowed to quit and only after their village committee verifies it'.[124]

This was not the only problem, since desertions and casualties had also thinned the ranks considerably. EDES was reduced to a few hundred men by December 1943, while several ELAS units had been rendered non-operational. The 24th and 3/40 ELAS regiments in Epirus had been completely wiped out by German and EDES strikes;[125] the 15th ELAS regiment was relocated to Albania where it was replenished with local recruits; other units like the 1/38 and 53 regiments and the Death Battalion had suffered massive casualties in the fierce battles that took place in the area of Tetrakomo during January 1944.[126] The situation was hardly better in other areas: the 30th regiment of ELAS in Macedonia lost over 30 per cent of its force between December 1943 and January 1944.[127]

After hostilities ended in February 1944, ELAS and EDES made frantic efforts to replenish their ranks using every possible means, including threats and the promise of material rewards. However, it seems that such motivations had begun to pale, since despite its grandiose promises, EDES was in reality unable to provide the benefits it advertised. Until the autumn of 1943 EDES acquired its provisions from the lowlands of Thessaly, an area that was dominated by EAM. The clashes that erupted between ELAS and EDES led the former to stop the flow of provisions and caused a dramatic increase in the price of food. The situation deteriorated further after the catastrophic German reprisals of 1943–44 and the loss of significant territory to ELAS, which rendered the salary of a sovereign per month promised by EDES virtually useless as there was 'nothing to buy, people would not sell you anything';[128] the peasants would only exchange food for parachute silk or guns.[129] Most EDES guerrillas survived for days on little else than wheat rusk and beans and were reduced to stealing vegetables from the peasants' gardens, while others had to sell guns and equipment. In some cases guerrillas chose to opt for ELAS, as the living conditions of the ELAS guerrillas were much better than those of their EDES colleagues.[130]

This situation forced EDES to intensify its propaganda efforts. Napoleon Zervas and his top commanders made repeated tours of their region's largest communities where they delivered fiery anti-communist speeches and warned the peasants about the perils of an ELAS takeover. EDES troops organised feasts and parades in the larger communities in the hope that the guerrillas' bearing and appearance would prompt young men to enlist.[131] However, these were not the only methods adopted to attract new guerrillas. According to one source, EDES tried to entice recruits by 'spreading rumours that the Germans would arrest all men aged between 16–45 years of age'.[132] EDES also tried to address the dearth of recruits by 'importing' recruits from the cities. The recruitment of urban cadres was first suggested by EDES's Athenian section and was quickly accepted by Zervas, who wrote in response, 'we are in need of non-commissioned officers, and brave, conscientious and disciplined guerrillas … be quite careful as far as undergraduates are concerned, because these youths are quite influenced by the local atmosphere and it is very difficult for them to adapt here'.[133]

Some EDES bands also made raids into ELAS territory in order to recruit former guerrillas or entice those who disliked EAM's rule to enlist. Officers were sent clandestinely to ELAS territory for recruitment purposes. Colonel Kostantinos Bouros was despatched to the area of Mesolongi in mid-1944, where he managed to recruit 13 men, most of them shepherds and farmhands from the area of Tzoumerka who worked in the area in exchange for food. The Bouros group operated in a highly secretive manner, making no public appearances and dressing in peasant clothes. Surrounded by ELAS outposts, these men followed an intricate and perilous route to reach EDES ranks. Prospective recruits were sent first to Agrinion where they were provided with counterfeit documents and then proceeded to the town of Amphilohia. From here, they were smuggled to the plain of Arta across the Amvrakikos lagoon before continuing on foot to the Xerovouni mountains.[134] However, the numbers of these men remained relatively small, since despite the pressures that they faced, not all were willing to undertake such a perilous journey.

These difficulties led ELAS and EDES to adopt increasingly radical measures. In theory, recruitment remained voluntary; however, resistance cadres were under constant pressure to produce more recruits, especially in areas contested between ELAS and its rivals. Both organisations placed particular stress on enlisting individuals of higher social status, such as schoolteachers, affluent peasants, regular army and gendarmerie officers and civil servants. They hoped such figures would encourage those who were wavering to enlist. Coercion took many forms. In EDES areas, EAM sympathisers were excluded from lists of Allied help recipients, and were often forced to contribute a significant part of their produce to the EDES struggle, while their families were harassed constantly. ELAS pursued similar strategies of coercion – fines for imaginary trespasses, anonymous threatening letters and beatings were the norm, while persecution was extended to the relatives of 'reactionaries'. P. Papadopoulos, a royalist officer from the village of Aeto in Trifilia, had been courted by EAM for most of 1943. After the local EPON members began to harass him and threaten his family, Papadopoulos took the decision to enlist and served for several months as commander of the ELAS 9th regiment. 'I admit', noted Papadopoulos in a post-war report, 'that I was not in the least willing to undertake a new adventure, but there was nothing I could do about it, I couldn't go to Athens … or to Patras because they might try to kill me, so I was forced to stay'. This was far from an isolated incident, especially in Peloponnesus where many officers found themselves enlisted to ELAS under similar circumstances.[135]

Compulsory enlistment was also introduced by ELAS in some areas between early 1943 and late 1944, including in the districts of Achaea and Corinthia in northern Peloponnesus and the prefectures of Imathia and Pieria in central Macedonia.[136] Unsurprisingly, conscripts tended to be under-motivated and performed badly in combat. In early 1944 hundreds of these men in central Macedonia defected to the local collaborationist militias or deserted, according to a report: 'the fact that many of them had been press-ganged into service was one of the foremost reasons for the cowardice they exhibited and underlined that in the future the reserves should be raised on a strictly voluntary basis after careful selection and indoctrination of prospective cadres'.[137] However, it is doubtful whether the warning given by the author of this report was heeded.

As the occupation drew to a close, ELAS and EDES intensified their pressure on the peasantry. Many of those targeted by ELAS took flight and headed to the Axis-occupied cities; ironically, these were the safest places for many peasants as the occupation drew to a close. However, this option was only available to the better off or those who had relatives who could support them. For those who remained in their native communities, neutrality was seldom possible, since those who failed to take a side were in constant danger from both and trusted by no one; this is demonstrated by the story of the Tsolis family, a pastoral clan from the Epirote village of Lippa. The Tsolis were one of the few families who had not contributed any recruits to either organisation. The local EDES authority took exception to this and in early 1943 'our father was called to the village and the *kapetanios* asked him to enrol at least one of his sons in the organisation. Our father did not agreed because he didn't want his sons to become guerrillas, and neither of my brothers wanted to have any part in this.' Tsolis's refusal heralded a sudden change for the worse; 'the nightmare began, since we were unwilling to enlist either in the one party or the other, we became pariahs'. The change began with the theft of animals ('they stole our best rams and billy goats') and continued with fines for trespassing, damage of property and a myriad other persecutions. The situation deteriorated when a fellow villager lodged a complaint with the local national committee that a member of the Tsolis family had made a disparaging comment about the EDES guerrillas.[138]

This denunciation was not motivated by political differences, but according to the Tsolis family was made out of spite: 'jealousy is the predominant feeling in the villages, especially if one peasant is a little better-off than the others ... thus the accusation reached the guerrillas' ears'. The outcome was that Takis Tsolis, the head of the family, was arrested by the guerrillas, who took turns in beating him with their rifle butts, breaking two of his ribs in the process. The Tsolis family was able to escape the worst when they pleaded their case with an *oplarhigos* from an adjoining district who put an end to the harassment. This was not an isolated incident; by mid-1944 life had become impossible for any EAM supporter or neutral in the area of Lakkas Souli and many of those who refused to enlist ended up in the prison camp of Giorganoi or worse.[139]

Such cases seem to have become the norm in areas contested either between rival guerrilla organisations or between the resistance and the various collaborationist militias, such as Epirus, parts of western Macedonia and Peloponnesus. Guerrilla leaders would often enter villages and order local men to enlist under threat of violence. In the village of Gotista in Epirus an EDES band 'used violence to recruit men ... only

20 men out of a total of 70 recruits are EDES supporters'. The same tactic was employed in the adjoining village of Matsouki. On 16 July 1944 an EDES band entered the village, encircled it with outposts and handed the authorities a list of '25 men whom they order to enlist within two days'.[140] Such tactics were not unknown to ELAS either, particularly in the areas of Tzoumerka and Radovizi where EDES had a large following. Giorgos Georgiou and his brother from the highland village of Piges in Arta were arrested in the autumn of 1944 after repeated refusals to enlist in the ELAS bands.

> They asked us 'Why didn't you join the guerrillas?' They asked my brother a dozen times to enlist and he always said, 'I can't, I have personal obligations ... I have to take care of my mother, my sister, my farm', they escorted us to Miliana, a village that was very near to ours ... they asked us again 'Why didn't you join the guerrillas?' We answered once more that we had many obligations, they started beating us, with belts, with whips, and they were shouting 'You have guns, you are hiding guns', and somebody put a gun in my mouth.[141]

ELAS employed similar methods in the areas of Kozani and Kastoria in Macedonia where, 'in order to make up the numbers of Andartes, youths in their teens were conscripted from the villages, indoctrinated and employed in firing squads'.[142] In the adjoining areas of Prespes, 150 men were conscripted from two villages in August 1944, and when 'several men ... refused to become Andartes [they] were badly beaten up by ELAS'.[143] Such tactics were equally common in Peloponnesus where a refusal to enlist in ELAS could often have lethal consequences, as the case of the Velelis family shows. The Velelis belonged to the small Jewish community of Patras. On 23 September they fled their home town for the village of Mihalaiika, high in the Panahaikon mountains, which they then left first for the village of Kalousi and then for Demestixa, where several members of the family were employed by the BMM. However, this was not the end of their adventure. Pepe and Victor Velelis were constantly harassed by ELAS for serving with the British instead of enlisting with them. In January 1944 the two men disappeared. After several months their family learned that they had been arrested and placed in an ELAS prison camp near Kalavrita. The two men were executed in the spring of 1944, just hours before a German unit reached the camp.[144]

Outright coercion was not always necessary; often men who came from right-wing families would volunteer, fearful of the consequences

Patriots and scoundrels

for their families and themselves if they remained neutral. The Nikolaou family stood out for their fierce royalism in the otherwise left-wing village of Kounina. When ELAS appeared in the area things took a turn for the worse: 'I talked with my brother Giorgis and we were afraid that they might even kill us, we heard that the guerrillas killed Dimoulas from Vodova, and they had already killed Karpouzogiorgis here'. The Nikolaou family finally decided that their best chance was the enlistment of a family member in the guerrillas:

> my brother was a lively lad ... it was better for us to join the guerrillas because this was the line followed by the village then. You couldn't do less, especially if your father was a 'Halivdokranos' [a member of a pre-war right-wing organisation] and you ran the risk of being branded a traitor at any time.[145]

After his brother joined the guerrillas the situation improved considerably. The case of the Nikolaou family was far from unique, since 'during that time even those who were right wing pretended that they supported the left'.[146]

Uncertainty, lack of ideology and the widespread use of violence by guerrilla groups also led to an increasing number of defections. Historians have paid little heed to defections; however, in many of the contested areas guerrillas and militiaman were willing to follow anyone who could provide them with food, loot and a gun, and they rotated constantly from one side to the other in search for safety for themselves and their families, revenge against their rivals or better terms of employment. Defections were particularly common in the ethnically mixed areas of northern Greece. Many Slavic peasant families in western Macedonia would send a son to ELAS, another to a collaborationist militia and a third to the Yugoslav partisans over the border. The Kalimanis family of Kalohori had members rotating between the militia and ELAS. Pashalis Kalimanis was the leader of the Kalohori militia; his relatives, Padelis and Dimitris Kalimanis, after serving under him, shifted their allegiance to ELAS; while his brother, Dimitris, also defected to ELAS, becoming a regional organiser. Spiros, Anastasios and Antonios Lazaridis of Lefki also defected from these militias to ELAS. The two brothers of Apostolos Makris, the *komitadji* leader of Mesopotamia in Kastoria (the *komitadji* were pro-Bulgarian militiamen), were recruited by EAM as was the brother of another *komitadji* leader, Evangelos Apoultsis of Mesopotamia.[147] Defections were also not uncommon from ELAS to collaborationist formations. A number of guerrillas in the prefectures of

Florina and Kastoria, who began their careers as ELAS guerrillas, defected and joined collaborationist formations in Yugoslav Macedonia.[148]

Such phenomena were equally common in Epirus and are encapsulated by the career of Ismail Haki, one of the most prominent Cham Albanian military leaders.[149] In 1942 Haki formed a band that 'remained neutral in the mountains of south Albania'. Despite being on friendly terms with both ELAS and the Albanian partisans, he 'never fought an action against the Germans' and never officially joined either. In December 1943 Haki and his band moved into Greece and fought alongside ELAS during the civil war against the right-wing EDES. A few weeks later, following an impressive volte-face, the band 'was found collaborating with the Germans and raiding Greek villages north of Filiates with German support'. The case of Haki, which was far from unique, underlines the complexity of a situation 'where groups of people in the same small village were apparently in one case fighting and in the other assisting the Germans without betraying each other but whose code of honour did not extend outside their own circle'.[150]

Anti-communist authors regarded this as proof of ELAS's lack of patriotism.[151] However, the ubiquity of such attitudes shows that ideologies including communism and nationalism had made little headway in the peasant communities, whose loyalties were still tied to family, faith and locality. These communities ultimately joined one faction or the other for a variety of reasons, including fear, profit or a sense of loyalty to a local figure of authority. However, the family and the village remained their foremost points of allegiance. Opportunism and side-changing were not planned by devious EAM propagandists who aimed at subverting the country's unity, but rather were deliberate tactics of communities to protect their well-being and safety.

Defections were no less common among the Greek population. Guerrillas would casually float between organisations depending on who offered the most, who was the stronger and who could benefit their family the most. The case of Kostas Rentzos, a shepherd from the Zagori region, 'who placed the fate of his flocks above all other considerations', exemplifies the mentality and tactics of many peasants. Rentzos's sons had enlisted in EDES; when ELAS appeared in their region in the autumn of 1943, fearful of the repercussion to his family, he presented himself at the local ELAS headquarters to report that his sons had been forcibly recruited and declared that they would be willing to change their allegiance if asked by ELAS. Such tactics were followed by many peasants whose sole concern was the survival of their family and their fortune in these troubled times. Moreover, such attitudes were shaped by the attitudes of local social elites.[152] Like many others, Rentzos's sons were recruited to EDES following the intervention of Georgios Tsoumanis, a regular army officer who came from one of the richest Sarakatsani families in the area. Tsoumanis flirted initially with EAM but finally sided with EDES in the summer of 1943. However, after ELAS attacked EDES he became convinced that his kinsmen and community risked ruin if they remained aligned to EDES. Tsoumanis convinced his relatives to defect and bribed an ELAS commander with the money he had received from EDES for the provision and recruitment of guerrillas to arrange safe passage to the plains of Akarnania.[153]

This was not an isolated case. After EDES dispersed an ELAS band in the area of Lakmos in October 1943, a dozen ELAS guerrillas volunteered on the spot;[154] the converse happened after ELAS prevailed in Epirus. Many men made a habit of changing their allegiances. SOE officer G. Heppell, who was attached to EDES, remarked on a similar case: 'Andartes brought me a man who had deserted to ELAS and been recaptured and asked what to do with him. Sent him to the local commander. Saw him weeks later back in the ranks.'[155] Such attitudes were even more common in the area of Arta where, between October 1943 and January 1944, ELAS and EDES fought a bloody civil war. An ELAS report on the 3/40 regiment noted that out of the 300 men who served in a battalion, only 29 were EAM members: 'the rest are either neutral or former EDES members'.[156] The situation was similar in EDES. Zervas noted in his diary during the same period: 'recently, we have enlisted very many men who were formerly EAM members, this is the case particularly with the 3/40 regiment'.[157] The numbers of EAM members and former ELAS guerrillas who defected to EDES in Epirus were such that the EDES leadership was worried that this was an organised effort to subvert EDES by 'making propaganda and collecting information'. They encouraged officers and band leaders who enlisted such men to be extra vigilant.[158]

Defections were equally common in the rest of Greece. Side-changing was so prevalent in the hinterland of Euboea where ELAS battled the collaborationist security battalions that the families of guerrillas and militiamen were frequently unaware of the current position of their kinsmen, and sometimes EAM village committees fined or confiscated the property of militiamen families unaware that they had defected to ELAS.[159] Defections from collaborationist formations to ELAS were less common in Macedonia, since militiamen were 'concerned that if they surrender to ELAS they will be shot or put in prison as well as that the Germans or the other reactionaries will take countermeasures against their families'.[160] Side-changing was more ubiquitous on the island of Lefkada; after ELAS shot Giorgos Papadatos, a local strongman and EDES leader in the village of Katouna, several EDES supporters enlisted in the reserve ELAS and took part in operations against their former comrades.[161] Defections between ELAS and the nationalist EOK were equally ubiquitous on the island of Crete. According to a local cadre, over one-third of the reserve ELAS guerrillas in the province of Apokoronas were formerly supporters of various right-wing organisations.[162]

The reasons for defection are quite complex; an EAM report from Zagori in Epirus underlined the importance of personal animosities and 'promises of monetary reward [and] promises of promotion'; thus 'sergeant Kentros', who was previously enlisted in ELAS, 'rose through the ranks, becoming a lieutenant within the space of a single week', while Thomas Bairaktaris 'who had no military experience whatsoever became a second lieutenant'.[163] Such cases also abounded on the other side; for instance, Spiros Papaggelis, a lawyer and EDES band leader from the village of Papigo, defected to ELAS after being passed over for promotion. Other men switched sides after a scuffle with a fellow guerrilla or officer.[164] Giorgos Dimitriou enlisted in EDES in March 1943 along with his brother Anastasis. Their decision was dictated by their financial situation. Both men worked as farmhands in the area of Fanari and were paid in kind; the appearance of EDES offered a chance to escape poverty: 'we didn't know anything about ELAS or EDES, they gave us a half a sovereign and they told us that we must fight … I didn't know anything about organisations, about political parties, my only motivation was to get the sovereign.' However, their living conditions did not improve; they survived on meagre rations, while their pay was diverted by their officer. The situation deteriorated after the outbreak of civil war and many members of Dimitriou's band refused to engage in operations against ELAS:

> We haven't been paid for three months and while we sat I went to the major and told him Mr major, Sir, we have nothing to eat, you haven't paid us for the past three months … he pointed his gun at me! He said if you want money you've got to follow me to Tzoumerka … I said you should have told us that there is no money because there are other organisations as well, he pointed his gun at me, then a lad from Karteri, Petros Sotiriou, they were four brothers from the village of Karteri, well as soon as he pointed his gun at me he turned his rifle at him and told him, well you better put the gun back to the holster … anyway he was forced to do it, and I said to myself, leave now, because you will not be able to get away from him again.[165]

The following day Dimitriou and his brother crossed over to ELAS, where they served until February 1945.[166]

However, defection was not always voluntary. In October 1943 82 EDES guerrillas were arrested by ELAS in the area of Farsala. For several days these men were paraded in villages throughout the region, where they were exposed to ridicule and taunts. ELAS forced the unit's padre to hold a banner with the inscription 'the rabble of Sourlas'.[167] Eventually, they were led to ELAS regional headquarters where 'it was underlined that they had a duty to fight in ELAS ranks'; broken, exhausted and afraid for their lives, most of these men kowtowed and enlisted in ELAS.[168] Lieutenant Miltiades Stergiopoulos and Captain Emmanuel Vazaios found themselves in ELAS hands after their band, which operated in the Farmaka mountains of Corinthia, was attacked and dispersed by an ELAS unit in September 1943. The two men decided to enlist in ELAS along with 32 other men from their band. Stergiopoulos commented years later: 'Why did I accept? Well, where could we have gone? There was no way we could back to our village, it was impossible to go to Zervas … and even if they let us go we were afraid that they would bushwhack us on our way home.'[169]

The scarcity of volunteers led ELAS to recruit from Axis deserters and collaborators. The majority of Axis recruits were former Soviet soldiers. The 9th division of ELAS had more than 750 Soviet soldiers, who fought in a separate detachment called Svoboda-Freedom.[170] The 30th regiment of ELAS included an 'international company' consisting of six different nationalities: Russians, Italians, Moroccans, Austrians, Poles and Czechs.[171] These men were seldom motivated by ideology. Many were exasperated by the brutality of the German officers and the drudgery of anti-guerrilla operations, while others were motivated by an instinct for survival, fear or a simple understanding that, by joining the guerrillas, they could continue living off the peasantry. Such was the case for 'Rosso', a middle-aged Italian soldier, who deserted in mid-1942 and formed a band with some of his fellow soldiers, 'roaming the mountains, armed to the teeth'. Rosso acted under the auspices of ELAS; nevertheless, he hardly ever took part in battles. His main targets were isolated Italian NCOs and officers, whom he abducted and tortured in order to extract money.[172]

Few of these men were the exemplary figures of post-war historiography. Soviet partisans in particularly were undisciplined, haughty and violent; drunkenness was a constant problem and fights between Russian, Ukrainian and Armenian partisans were constant. Non-Russian

A history of the Greek resistance

partisans also heavily criticised the Soviet regime. A Ukrainian partisan in Peloponnesus 'besmirched the name of the leader of the Soviet people and foremost proletarian of the world, comrade Stalin, using words of such vulgarity that we do not dare include them in this report'.[173] Some even denounced ELAS to the peasants and warned them of the dangers of communism. Violence was common against civilians as well. The career of Ali, a Caucasian Muslim, provides a characteristic case. Ali deserted from a German unit and joined ELAS in 1943; a violent man, he terrorised the villagers of southern Euboea, stealing, confiscating produce and raping. He career came to an abrupt end when his comrades, exasperated by his actions, shot him.[174]

The need for manpower led the resistance organisations to pardon and recruit collaborators in large numbers. The enlistment of such men reached its pinnacle after the fall of Italy. The demise of the Italian army deprived the collaborators of their most valuable backers, and led them to enlist in the resistance in hope of being reprieved. During the winter of 1943, ELAS in Thessaly absorbed several former members of the Vlach Legion, a collaborationist militia created and backed by the Italians that had terrorised this area for the previous two years. ELAS shot many of the instigators under pressure from the local peasantry. However, as ELAS was fighting against EDES in the adjoining area of Epirus during this period, the urgent need for manpower enabled these men to enlist in ELAS and reinvent themselves as resistance fighters.[175] This situation escalated as the occupation drew to a close and ELAS and its opponents started to prepare for a violent final stand-off. In eastern Macedonia, both ELAS and its rivals 'tried to swell their ranks' in anticipation of the liberation

> using propaganda, promises and above all by magnifying the danger that their rivals' victory represented. All the dregs of society, collaborationists, traitors, even common criminals ... found a chance and joined the guerrilla ranks ... those who were in command of the guerrilla bands were not in a position to screen them out since they were in dire need for recruits.[176]

Between September and October 1944, ELAS recruited hundreds of such men in central Macedonia: former *komitadji*, gendarmes who had collaborated with the German occupation authorities and Italian soldiers. A contemporary report noted that 'the morale of the reaction is deteriorating rapidly, we have positive information that many are thinking of defecting to ELAS ... we must be vigilant and intensify our efforts in order to convince them'.[177] However, this policy was greeted by objections from many EAM and KKE cadres:

Patriots and scoundrels

You write that some of the *komitadji* in Edessa were disarmed by the Germans and others defected to ELAS ... inducting to ELAS people who in one way or another collaborated with the occupiers and made orgies in Edessa is a misrepresentation of our policies, this tactic will have a disastrous effect for the liberation struggle. With this strategy you not only erase every boundary between the fighting people and the national traitors ... but you also provoke the hatred of the Greek element against both the Slavophones and ELAS ... you write the same thing about the Paotzides [members of a local nationalist militia], however, the policy that has been declared both by the allies and the Papandreou government is clear, they should either surrender with their arms ... or be annihilated.[178]

In the highlands of Vitsi in Florina, the predicament was even more complex. The area was garrisoned by the Vitsi Battalion, a semi-independent unit comprised of Slavic-speakers from the Florina and Korestia areas and led by Elias Demakis, a baker from the mountain village of Ano Melas in Korestia, who styled himself as the future leader of the area's Slavic minority. Demakis had started a frantic recruitment drive, taking in every adventurer, bandit and former collaborator willing to take up arms in this ragged area. By the autumn of 1944 the unit counted among its more than 1,000 members former *komitadji* from Greece and Yugoslavia, members of the Bulgarian fascist party, deserters from the Yugoslav partisans and common criminals who saw a chance to refashion themselves as resisters at the eleventh hour. Demakis's unit lacked 'even the most elementary discipline';[179] they survived by robbery and plunder, their foremost targets being the Grekomans and the Greek-speakers of the area. The lack of discipline was such that the local KKE committee asked Demakis 'to stop all recruitment and make a thorough search of the guerrillas' background both from the battalion and the political organisations'.[180] Demakis refused. According to some, he was preparing a coup whose purpose was to incorporate the Slavic-speaking areas of Macedonia into the newly socialist Yugoslavia; however, it is more likely that Demakis was trying to muscle EAM in order to improve his personal standing in the local hierarchy. Fearful that Demakis might be preparing a coup, the ELAS HQ finally acquiesced to the repeated protests of ELAS cadres and party members that the lack of discipline had rendered this unit an embarrassment and threatened the unity of the organisation in Macedonia. Consequently, an attack was ordered on the Demakis band in October.

The situation was similar in Epirus, where ELAS began an extensive programme of recruitment among the local Muslim Albanian minority.

According to one source, the local ELAS had recruited between 400 and 700 men by December 1944.[181] Some of these men had served previously with ELAS or the Albanian left-wing resistance; however, a large number had been involved in anti-guerrilla operations against both ELAS and EDES partisans in the spring of 1944. The pace of recruitment accelerated during and after the battles between ELAS and EDES in December 1944.[182] However, the unruly attitudes of many of these neophytes, who had no qualms about robbing civilians of any political persuasion, and the violence they exhibited against civilians who backed EDES caused uproar. This was even the case among EAM members, who threatened to quit or take action against them, and forced ELAS to relocate this unit to the town of Tsamantas, a highland community located a few miles from the Albanian border.[183]

The People's Armies were never a purely voluntary force, nor were all the men who enlisted inspired by political ideology; fear, want, a desire for adventure and a propensity for violence had played an important role in attracting recruits to guerrilla bands since the early days of the resistance. However, these men were not the majority and a number eventually came to espouse their group's goals and ideology. The onset of the civil war changed this and led both groups to rely increasingly on coercion. Ideological volunteers became more and more scarce and defections rose sharply as groups and individuals rotated from one group to the other in search of safety and material benefits. The number of these recruits increased further on the eve of liberation when hundreds of men rushed to enlist in order to gain absolution for their previous misdeeds and prove that they had left their past behind. Some areas had so many recruits that ELAS was unable to provide them with food, clothes or guns, and the strength of a few units increased within the space of three months by over 50 per cent.[184] Yet these developments completely changed the character of ELAS and EDES. As the occupation drew to a close, the People's Armies were transformed from a volunteer force to a mass of disgruntled, press-ganged recruits who had no stomach for fighting and were kept in line through fear. A British officer noted in mid-1944 that

> the war-weariness of the civil population is very marked and the dissolution of ELAS is as heartily desired ... inside ELAS the same forces are active; I consider that more than 60% of ELAS rank and file are eager to leave ELAS, if they can do so with any chance of safety.[185]

Notes

1. ASKI/AKKE/Box 429/File-26/4/13.
2. Arseniou, *I Thessalia*, pp. 107–9, 129.
3. Mazower, *Inside Hitler's Greece*, p. 321.
4. Giorgos Houliaras (Pericles), *O Dromos einai asotos* [The long and winding road] (Athens: Oionos, 2006), pp. 94–5.
5. Katsantonis, *Polemontas tous kataktites*, p. 18.
6. DIS/ADN/File 2/Ekthesi pros ton kathodigitiko pirina tou kommatis tis VII merarxias/20/12/44
7. Houliaras, *O Dromos*, p. 94.
8. Houliaras, *O Dromos*, p. 95.
9. Giannis Privovolos, *Monimoi axiomatikoi ston ELAS oikeiothelos i ex anagis* [Regular officers in ELAS, volunteers or coerced] (Athens: Alfeios, 2009), p. 348.
10. Foivos Grigoriadis, *To Antartiko ELAS/EDES/EKKA-5/42* [The Andartiko ELAS/EDES/EKKA-5/42] (Athens: n.p., 1964), vol. 1, p. 54.
11. Lazanis, *Anamniseis apo to metopo tou 1940*, p. 78.
12. Grigoriadis, *To Antartiko*, pp. 240–2.
13. G. Papanikolaou, 'O orkos tis Paraskevis', *Ethiki Antistasi* 15 (1978), pp. 66–8.
14. P. Giourgas, *Martiries kai viomata* [Testimonies and experiences] (Athens, 1998), pp. 178–81.
15. Fanis Tsakas, *Martiries gia tin antistasi kai ton diogmo* [Testimonies about the resistance and the persecutions] (Athens: self-published, 1982), pp. 37–9.
16. Ziagos, *Ethniki antistasi*, vol. 2, p. 156.
17. http://www.agrafiotis.gr/content/view/142/121 (accessed 20 October 2015).
18. Ziagos, *Ethnike antistasi*, vol. 2, pp. 158–9.
19. 'To hroniko tis Moutsiaras' [The chronicle of Moutsiara], *Istoriko Arheio Ethnikis Antistasis* 9 (1959), p. 29.
20. Arseniou, *I Thessalia*, p. 98.
21. Lazanis, *Anamniseis apo to metopo tou 1940*, p. 78.
22. Dionysis Haritopoulos, *Ares o arhigos ton atakton* [Ares, leader of the irregulars] (Athens: Topos, 2009)
23. For a comprehensive study of brigandage in Greece, see Ioannis Koliopoulos, *I listeia stin Ellada, 19os aionas* [Banditry in Greece, nineteenth century] (Thessaloniki: Epikentro, 2005)
24. Ziagos, *Ethniki antistasti*, vol. 1, p. 158. General Ioannis Metaxas was the leader of a military dictatorship known as the Fourth of August regime that governed Greece between 1936 and 1941. His reign saw the re-establishment of the monarchy and the restructuring of the state along traditionalist, authoritarian and corporatist lines. Some historians have described the

Fourth of August regime as fascist. Metaxas did introduce symbols and practices that bore a close resemblance to those of the Mussolini regime, but the similarities were only skin deep: 'despite his openly expounded authoritarian views, the truth is he [Metaxas] never indulged in public commendation of the fascist states abroad, neither before or after the establishment of his dictatorship, or did he ever admit that he was in any way trying to create a similar system'; Constantine Sarantis, 'The ideology and character of the Metaxas regime', in Robin Higham and Thanos Veremis (eds), *The Metaxas Dictatorship: Aspects of Greece, 1936-1940* (Athens: Hellenic Foundation for Defense and Foreign Policy and Speros Basil Vryonis Center for the Study of Hellenism, 1993), p. 149. For a general survey of the Metaxas regime, see P.J. Vatikiotis, *Popular Autocracy in Greece, 1936-1941: A Political Biography of General Ioannis Metaxas* (London: Routledge, 1998).

25 Kostantinos Antoniou, *Istoria Horofilakes* [History of the gendarmerie] (Athens: n.p., 1967), vol. 3, pp. 1641-5.
26 Dimitriou, *Antartis*, vol. 3, p. 298.
27 Lazanis, *Anamniseis apo to metopo tou 1940*, p. 78.
28 Papadakis, *To Imerologio*, p. 25.
29 Papadakis, *To Imerologio*, p. 36.
30 DIS/AGA/Agoros, Diary, p. 10.
31 Apostolos Papakostas, memoir, unpublished, Skoufas Library Arta, pp. 5-6, 16-17.
32 Papas, *Anamesa stous protagonistes*, p. 35.
33 Giorgos Georgiou, personal interview, Arta, 2009.
34 Kostas Ioannou, 'Iroikes morfes tou agona: O Spiros Karabinas' [Heroic figures of the struggle: Spiros Karabinas], *Istoriko Arheio Ethnikis Antistasi* 2 (1958), p. 16.
35 Papas, *Anamesa stous protagonistes*, p. 34.
36 Lazanis, *Anamniseis apo to metopo tou 1940*, p. 78.
37 Evangelos Haliatsos, personal interview, Igoumenitsa, 2008.
38 Vasilis Dokopoulos, personal inteview, Igoumenitsa, 2007.
39 EDIA/Arheio Nikolaou Tsamantaki/I Antistase sta Meskla, p. 4.
40 Hristos Vittos, *Ta Grevena stin katohe kai sto adartiko: Istorike Meleti Dekaetias 1940-1950* [Grevena during the occupation and the civil war: a historical study of the 1940-1950 decade] (n.p., 2000), p. 196.
41 Panagiotis Stouras, 'The Greek resistance in the area of Kalavryta and Aigialia between 1941 and 1944', PhD thesis, University of Johanesburg, 2012, pp. 64-9.
42 Kostantinos Tsipis, personal interview; Giorgos Dimitriou, personal interview; Vasilis Pavlidis, *Oi Alvanotsamides tis periohes Paramithias* [The Albanian Chams of the Paramithia region] (Athens, 2008), p. 46.
43 See Vangelis Tzoukas, *Oi oplarhigoi tou EDES stin Ipeiro 1942-1944* [The band leaders of Edes in Epirus] (Athens: Estia, 2013).

44 Vangelis Nakos, personal interview, Gardiki, 2008. EON (Ethiniki Organosi Neon) was a paramilitary youth organisation created by the regime of General Ioannis Metaxas, and fashioned after the fascist Italian *ballila*.
45 Thomas Karakitsos, personal interview, Paramithia, 2008.
46 Harilaos Tsogas, *Aima kai dakria* [Blood and tears] (Ioannina: self-published, n.d.), p. 19.
47 GAKI/AMM/15, p. 3.
48 Aristofanes Tsakas, *Trilogia* [Trilogy] (Athens: self-published, 1988), p. 55.
49 Vasilis Dokopoulos, personal interview.
50 GAKKI/Small Collections/Box 116/K.D. Giannoulis, diary, p. 1
51 Dimitris Papas, *To progefiroma tou Lakmona* [The bridgehead of Lakmonas] (Athens: self-published, 2000), p. 25.
52 ELIA/APME/Gerasimos Priftis.
53 Giorgos Dimitriou, personal interview.
54 Giannis Naskas, personal interview, Eleftheri, 2008.
55 Giannoulis, diary, p. 6.
56 Giannoulis, diary, p. 7.
57 Evangelos Haliasos, personal interview.
58 Engangelos Nakos, personal interview.
59 William Jordan, *Conquest without Victory* (London: Hodder & Stoughton, 1969), p. 51.
60 Houliaras, *O Dromos*, p. 157.
61 ASKI/AKKE/Box 429/File-26/4/13.
62 Moutoulas, 'To EAM stin Ileia', pp. 116–17.
63 Richard Clogg, *Greece 1940–1949: Occupation, Resistance, Civil War* (New York and London: Palgrave, 2002), p. 118.
64 DIS/File/922/B/Odigies Prosorinou Kanonismou Stratologias.
65 ELIA Press Archive/Antartika Neiata/1/January 1944.
66 Tasos Hatzianastasiou, *Antartes kai Kapetanioi I ethniki antistasi kata tis Voulgarikes katohes tis anatolikes Makedonias kai tis Thrakes* [Guerrillas and *kapetanioi*, the national resistance against the Bulgarian occupation of eastern Macedonia and Thrace] (Thessaloniki: Kiriakidis, 2003), pp. 31–3.
67 Panagiotis Aberiadis, *Mia prosfigiki oikogeneia sta oreina tis Kavalas 1922–1952* [A refugee family in the highland of Kavala 1922–1952] (Kavala: ILAK, 2005), p. 193.
68 Cambridge University Archives/012 MS.Add.8683/McKitterick/Personal Report 30 May 1944 to Major O'Toole, p. 2.
69 Antonis Sanoudakis, *Kapetan Manolis Mpantouvas, O arhigos tis ethnikis antistasis Kritis: Ta polemika tou apomnimonefmata* [Kapetan Manolis Mpantouvas, leader of the Cretan national resistance: war memoirs] (Athens: Knossos, 1979), pp. 318–22.
70 Liddell Hart Centre for Military Archives (henceforth LHCMA)/The

Personal Papers of Count Julian Dobrski/37 in 36-44/Report on Crete and the islands of the Aegean, p. 1.
71 ASKI/AKKE/Box 418/File-24/2/71B/p. 6
72 Baerentzen (ed.), *British Reports on Greece*, p. 78.
73 This operation, which involved extensive sabotage and ambushes against Axis columns, took place across mainland Greece between June and July 1943. The aim of the operation was to divert attention from the imminent Sicily landings, and lead the Axis command to believe that a landing was about to happen in Greece.
74 EKKA (Ethniki kai Koinoniki Apeleftherosi – National and Social Liberation) was a republican resistance organisation.
75 LHCMA/The Personal Papers of Christopher Woodhouse/5/1/1/ in 2/7-9, 3, 4 & 5/1/1/History of the Allied Military Mission in Greece, p. 96.
76 Antones Sanoudakes, Athanasios Psaroulakis and Giorgis Dafermos, *Ta limeria tou ELAS* [The hideouts of ELAS] (Athens: Knossos, 1993), p. 45.
77 Evangelos Vekris, *Protopapas, istoria kai paradosi* [Protopapas, history and tradition] (Ioannina: self-published, 2008), pp. 178–81.
78 Kostoulas, *Katohikes istories*, p. 71.
79 ASKI/Arheio Markou Ntoukaki [the Archive of Markos Ntoukakis] (henceforth AMN)/File 12/Miniaia Organotiki Ekthesi III tmimatos EAM eparxias Apokoronou 1-31 Oktomvrio 1944.
80 ELIA/AEPK/Organotiki Katastasi tou Mina Iouliou 1944/Eparhiake Epitropi Mouzakiou.
81 ASKI/AKKE/ Box 415/File-23/8/1α.4.12.43
82 ASKI Digital Archives/http://62.103.28.111/neolaia/rec.asp?id=53400 (accessed 4 January 2015).
83 ASKI Digital Archives/http://62.103.28.111/neolaia/rec.asp?id=51631& nofoto=0 (accessed 20 January 2015).
84 ASKI Digital Archives/http://62.103.28.111/neolaia/rec.asp?id=51631& nofoto=0 (accessed 4 January 2015).
85 ELIA/AEPK/Ethniko Apeleftherotiko Metopo (EAM) Eparhiaki Epitropi Palama/27/6/44.
86 Moutoulas, 'To EAM stin Ileia', p. 80.
87 Stefanos Filos, *Agnanta Artas* [The village of Agnanta in Arta] (Athens: self-published, 1989), p. 119.
88 Vasilis Papananos, *To Anti-iroiko imerologio tou antartoeponiti Vasili Papananou* [The anti-heroic diary of the antarto-eponite Vasilis Papananos] (Athens: Oddyseas, 2006), p. 71.
89 Papananos, *To Anti-iroiko imerologio*, p. 86.
90 Papadakis, *To Imerologio*, p. 31.
91 LHCMA/The Personal Papers of Captain Albert Henry Lingen/2/8/ Appreciation of situation in area one/p. 1. *Andartes* is the Greek word for guerrillas, and was frequently used in British army documents.

92 Evangelos Haliasos, personal interview.
93 Stelios Katsogiannos, *I Agnosti alitheia gia ton ELAS* [The secret truth about ELAS] (Athens: self-published, 1994), p. 38.
94 Gianni Manousaka, *Hroniko apo tin antistasi* [Chronicle of the resistance] (Athens: n.p., 1976), p. 176.
95 ASKI/AKKE/Box 412/ File-25/5/194.
96 DIS/File 914/ST/11/Apofasi Iparithmon 14/25-8-1943.
97 Pinelopi Vezdrevani, personal interview.
98 Mihalis Bolosis, personal interview.
99 DIS/AGA/File D/ Ekthesi gegonoton 24 Sintagma pezikou ELAS pros VII Merarhia, p. 5.
100 Kosmas Antonopoulos, *Ethnike Antistase 1941–1945* [National resistance] (Athens: self-published, 1964), p. 1644.
101 DIS/AGA/File D/Ekthesi gegonoton 24 Sintagma pezikou, p. 4.
102 ASKI Digital Archives/http://62.103.28.111/neolaia/rec.asp?id=51445&nofoto=0 (accessed 10 January 2015).
103 DIS/AGA/File D/Ekthesi gegonoton 24 Sintagma pezikou, p. 5.
104 LHCMA/The Papers of Brigadier Edmund Charles Wolf Myers/Myers 1/4 in 1/4-6/National Band of Rebels/JGHQ, Instruction No. 7, 18 August 1943.
105 LHCMA/Myers/Myers 1/4 in 1/4-6/Instruction No. 15 National Bands of Rebels/JGHQ.
106 ASKI/AKKE/Box 412/ File-25/5/194.
107 DIS/File 922/Z/4/Ekthesi gia to Peloponnisiako sinedrio tou EAM, pp. 1–4.
108 DIS/AGA/File D/1-109/Deltion Plirofoion apo 20 Martiou me 3 Apriliou 1944.
109 Dimitrios Vlahos Grivas, *To Hroniko enos agonisti, mnimes kai gegonota apo ton B Pagosmio Polemo stin Attiko-Beotea* [The chronicle of a fighter, memories and events from the Second World War in Attiko-Beotea] (Acharnes, 1996), pp. 48–9.
110 ELIA Press Archive/Flabouro/6/January 1944.
111 ELIA/OTA/Vasilis Giouris interview.
112 Vasilis Dokopoulos, personal interview.
113 Thanasis Mitsopoulos, *To Trianta Sintagma tou ELAS* [The 30th regiment of ELAS] (Athens: self-published, 1987), p. 49.
114 ELIA/OTA/Vasilis Giouris interview.
115 Labros Tatsopoulos, *Nihtologio, 1940–1949* (Ioannina: self-published, 1998), p. 107.
116 Papagiannis, *Kravges tis mnimes*, p. 491.
117 Giorgos Dimitriou, personal interview.
118 Vasilis Sarvas, personal interview, Filiates, 2009.
119 LHCMA/The Papers of Major Ronald R Prentice and Captain Arthur H

Wickstead/ Prentice/Wickstead 19/1 in Prentice/Wickstead 5/ Drive into Pindus, p. 8.
120 Polixhronis Enepekides, *I Elliniki antistasi 1941-1944* [The Greek resistance 1941-1944] (Athens: Estia, 1964), p. 125.
121 ASKI Digital Archives/http://62.103.28.111/neolaia/rec.asp?id=53359&no foto=0 (accessed 1 February 2015).
122 Nicholas Hammond, *Allied Military Mission in West Macedonia* (Thessalonica: IMXA, 1993), p. 29.
123 Hammond, *Allied Military Mission*, p. 30.
124 Douatzis, *Imerologio*, pp. 368-9.
125 DIS/ADN/File 2/Ekthesi pros ton kathodigitiko pirina; Giorgos Dimitriou/ Personal interview.
126 Tsakas, *Trilogia*, pp. 90-100.
127 TNA/HS5/701/Report on Kaimaxala by Major TC Johnson, p. 26.
128 Giorgos Dimitriou, personal interview.
129 Giorgos Romanos, *Mia Athinaiki vengera tou 1944, imerologio apo tin Eleftheri Oreini Ellada* [An Athenian banquet in 1944, diary from free mountain Greece] (Athens: Potamos, 2008), pp. 144-5.
130 IWM/The Private Papers of Major M Ward/13345/Report on visit to Greece – 21 Oct to 25 Dec 1943 by Capt. M. Ward, p. 5.
131 DIS/ADN/File 2/4/Polemiki Ekthesi gia tin Drasi ton EOEA, p. 5.
132 DIS/ADN/File 2/4Minaio Deltio Pliroforion epi EDES minos Maiou.
133 GAK/KI/AMM/Small Collections/Box 197/Pros ton Adelfon Konstantino Giannaraki.
134 DIS/AGA/File 4/1-109/Enorki Exetasi Martiros Eis Halkiopoulos tin 5 Maiou, p. 1.
135 Antonopoulos, *Ethnike*, p. 1246.
136 ELIA/Arheio 12 Sidagmatos ELAS [the Archive of the 12th ELAS regiment] (henceforth AER)/File 15/14/2/1944.
137 ASKI/AKKE/Box 413/File-23/6/7 p. 3.
138 Kosta Vlahou, *I antistasi stin Lakka Souli 1943-1944* [The resistance in Lakka Souli 1943-1944], unpublished, Zosimaia Library Ioannina, p. 15.
139 Vlahou, *I antistasi*, p. 17.
140 http://arxeiomnimon.gak.gr/browse/resource.html?tab=tab02&id=206316 &start=20 (accessed 5 January 2015).
141 Giorgos Georgiou, personal interview.
142 Hammond, *Allied Military Mission*, p. 30.
143 Hammond, *Allied Military Mission*, p. 161.
144 Maria Filosofou, 'Katohe kai Antistasi stin Achaea' [Occupation and resist ance in Achaea], PhD thesis, University of Peloponnesus, Patra, 2009, pp. 241-2.
145 Priovolos, *Mia alisida mnimes*, p. 250
146 Priovolos, *Mia alisida mnimes*, p. 250.

147 Athanasios Hrisohou, *I katohe en Makedonia, I drasi tis Voulgarikes Propagandas 1941–1944* [The occupation in Macedonia, the activities of the Bulgarian propaganda] (Thessaloniki: Etairia Makedonikon Spoudon, 1950), vol. 2, pp. 206–8, 334–5.
148 ASKI/AKKE/Box 415/File-23/8/53.
149 The Chams were an Albanian Muslim group of approximately 20,000 who lived in the area of Thesprotia in Epirus. During the occupation a large number of Chams collaborated first with the Italian and then the German militaries. For a detailed account of the Cham issue, see Eleftheria Manta, *Oi Mousoulmanoi Tsamides tis Ipeirou* [The Muslim Chams of Epirus] (Thessaloniki: IMXA, 2004).
150 TNA/WO/204/9348, p. 5.
151 Dimitris Zafeiropoulos, *To KKE kai I Makedonia* [KKE and Macedonia] (Thessaloniki: self-published, 1948); Hariton Labrou, *Tsamides kai Tsamouria* [The Chams and Tsamouria] (Athens: self-published, 1949).
152 DIS/Ligerakis Archive/File 1/Ekthesi lohagou Ligeraki peri ton gegonoton pou proigithikan tis genikis epitheseos tou ELAS kata tou EDES/p. 6.
153 Diamantis, *Mnimes*, p. 81.
154 Papas, *To progefiroma*, p. 105.
155 TNA/HS5/696/Lieut. GAW Heppell/Report on Operations in Epirus/21/12/44, p. 4.
156 ASKI Digital Archives/ http://62.103.28.111/neolaia/rec.asp?id=54561&nofoto=0 (accessed 3 January 2015).
157 Zervas, diary, p. 315.
158 DIS/Arheio Kostantinou Mavroskoti [Konstantinos Mavroskotis Archive] (henceforth KMA)/File 1/319-467/March April 44/Arhigeio Ipirou diatagi peri metron pros apofigin dieisdiseos eamiton stis grammes EDES/8-3-44.
159 ELIA/Arheio Gianni Douatzi [Giannis Douatzis Archive] (henceforth GDA)/File. 2.2/7o sidagma diatages (1943–1944)/Ethnikos Stratos ELAS/Y taxiarxia pros to anexartito tagma/9.9/44.
160 ASKI/AKKE/Box 495/File-30/3/175.
161 Logothetis, *To hreos*, pp. 79–80.
162 ASKI/AMN/File 12/Katastasi Apostelomenon eis II tagma efedrikou ELAS Ebrosnerou/24/9/1944
163 DIS/AMM/908A/Ekthesi tis EPON Ioanninon tou ethnikou apeleftherotikou metopou gia tin katastasi stin perifereia tis to etos 1943, pp. 1–2.
164 Diamantis, *Mnimes*, p. 78.
165 Giorgos Dimitriou, personal interview.
166 Giorgos Dimitriou, personal interview.
167 Giorgos Sourlas was a local EDES band leader who recruited these men.
168 Nitsa Koliou, *Agnostes ptihes katohis kai adistasi 1941–1944* [Unknown aspects of the occupation and the resistance] (Volos: self-published, 1985), vol. 1, p. 1005.

169 Giannis Priovolos, *Monimoi axiomatikoi ston ELAS, oikeiothelos i ex anagis* [Regular officers in ELAS, volunteers or coerced?] (Athens, 2009), p. 158.
170 Kostas Avgitidis, *Oi Sovietikoi mahites stis grammes tis Eamikis ethnikis antistasis* [Soviet fighters in the national resistance] (Athens: Sinhrone Epohe, 2007), p. 75.
171 Avgitidis, *Oi Sovietikoi mahites*, p. 65.
172 Romolo Galiberti, *Tripies botes, apo tin Merarxia Pinerolo stous andartes* [Torn boots, from the Pinerolo division to the ELAS guerrillas] (Athens: Filistor, 1998), pp. 40–3.
173 DIS/File 954/G/9lg/Anafora gia filonikies Rosson me Ellines antartes, p. 3.
174 Kostas Sapounztis, *Atafoi kai lismonimenoi sta vouna tis Euboeas, 1942–1949* [Unburied and forgotten in the mountains of Euboea, 1942–1949] (Athens: self-published, 1995), p. 82.
175 Stavros Papagiannis, *Ta Paidia tis likainas, oi epigonoi tis 5hs Romaikis legeonas kata tin diarkeia tis katohis* [The children of the she-wolf, the descendants of the fifth Roman legion during the occupation] (Athens: Sokolis, 2004), p. 194.
176 Aberiadis, *Mia prosfigiki oikogeneia*, p. 258.
177 ASKI/AKKE/Box 412/File-23/5/202.
178 ASKI/AKKE/Box 410/File-23/2/70.
179 ASKI/AKKE/Box 415/File-23/8/70.27.9.44, p. 1
180 ASKI/AKKE/Box 415/File-23/8/67.22.9.44. p. 1.
181 TNA/FO/371/48094/report by Lt. Col. C.A.S. Palmer on visit to northern Greece 9–14 April 1945, p. 2.
182 TNA/WO 204/9348, pp. 2–3.
183 DIS ADN/Files b-12/Ekthesi epi tis exelixis stin Thesprotia stis 25/3/45 kata tin period tis katohes mexri tis apeleftherosis (1941–1944).
184 ASKI/AKKE/Box 418/File-24/2/41.09.4.44.
185 Hammond, *Allied Military Mission*, p. 183.

3

Not by bread alone: combat, everyday life and the formation of guerrilla identities

Nikos Hatzinikolaou was not unaccustomed to hardship. Like most tobacco farmers in his native district of Xanthi, he lived a harsh life, working long hours for little pay in trying conditions. However, neither his upbringing nor his familiarity with military life (he was a veteran of the Greco-Italian war) prepared him for what he encountered when he enlisted in ELAS, where he served for two years leading an 80-strong band. Hatzinikolaou recalled his time in the resistance as 'the harshest life possible'. According to Hatzinikolaou, the greatest tribulation was neither hunger nor want, but rather the isolation, loneliness and boredom that characterised their everyday existence, which lacked even the most elementary comforts of civilian life: 'warm food, a hearth … pleasant conversation'.[1] Guerrilla life had few graces and even less excitement; combat was infrequent and the guerrillas would spend most of their time marching and foraging for food. Conditions were even harder during operations, when guerrillas would live for days in the open, hiding in the woods during daylight and moving from wood to wood at night.[2] Forays into villages were accordingly infrequent and were often marked by tension between the peasants trying to protect their property from these unwanted guests, and the guerrillas who believed that their toils entitled them to the villagers' cash and food.[3]

Hatzinikolaou's sober depiction of everyday life and relations with civilians is quite rare, as few memoirists and even fewer historians have expressed any interest in this aspect of guerrilla life. Consequently, we still know very little about daily life in the bands, relations between guerrillas and the peasantry, or the ways in which the guerrillas experienced combat, treated prisoners and were socialised into the use of violence.

Even less is known about the intricacies of guerrilla life: provisioning, leisure, health care and the organisation of life in the guerrilla encampments. The present chapter will delve into this neglected region; it will examine the material conditions of the guerrillas' daily lives and explore how their experiences in the field shaped their self-image, social attitudes and their relations with the civilian population.

For most guerrillas, the resistance was a novel and unexpected experience. The Albanian war certainly acquainted a large number of men with the nuts and bolts of military life and gave them a foretaste of what was to follow. However, guerrilla warfare was a different kind of war altogether and required a set of skills and knowledge that very few men possessed and most had to learn from scratch. Unlike regular soldiers, the guerrillas had no home front where they could rest, no logistical corps to provide them with the necessities of everyday life, and most units operated without a medic. The guerrillas, therefore, had to learn a series of skills from treating wounds to locating edible herbs, finding shelter and evading enemy patrols; more importantly, they had to learn how to fight.

Partisan warfare was a very different affair from regular war. However, the essential component remained the same – killing. This was a task for which most men were ill-prepared, especially when it involved hand-to-hand combat, which was often the case. Hatzinikolaou's first assignment was to assassinate a well-known collaborator. However, as he approached his target's village, he began having second thoughts: 'I had never killed a man. I still had some time to choose between a gun and a knife, I have never used a knife not even for slaughtering a chicken.'[4] Such experiences were far from unique. Historians have often presented the partisans as natural fighters and pointed to the long tradition of guerrilla fighting in the mountains. However, the situation was different in the field. Moreover, while such traditions sometimes shaped the way the guerrillas viewed their task, they were hardly adequate to convince the guerrillas to break the foremost social taboo – taking the life of another human being. The resistance organisations were acutely aware of this, as well as the need to accustom men to perpetrating violence. Socialisation rituals and violent initiation rites played a very important part in this respect, as they helped facilitate the guerrillas' passage from the civilian to the military realm.

These ordeals had a profound impact on the way in which the guerrillas viewed themselves and their task as well as their relations with the civilian population. Isolation, hardship and socialisation rituals led the guerrilla groups to develop an agonistic culture that celebrated violence and hardiness as the true signs of masculinity. The guerrillas saw themselves as a class apart, men of 'iron will and stout heart'[5] who were superior to the peasants, whom they often derided as cowardly and ungrateful. Such perceptions bred distrust and hostility between the peasants and the guerrillas that was further exacerbated by the rampant corruption and constant impositions of the guerrillas, which often outran the patience and capacities of the civilian population.

From the pavement to the mountain: everyday life in the bands and the construction of guerrilla identities

Giorgos Evangelakos had not considered enlisting in a resistance band until the Italian financial police confiscated the wares he was peddling in the lowland villages near the town of Trikala:

> I decided to take revenge, I thought I won't be able to survive, I will become a *klepht* [brigand], after a while I learned that someone I knew had joined the guerrillas, I thought if he can do it why can't I? I took some bread, a shepherd's cape and a blade from home and from that moment onwards I severed my ties with law abiding society, from then on I was an outlaw.

Evangelakos's experience was not uncommon. During this period, the mountains of western Thessaly teemed with desperate men who joined the resistance in search of glory, revenge or mere survival. However, imagining oneself as an outlaw and becoming one were two very different things, especially for a man like Evangelakos who had no experience of or ties to the mountain communities.[6]

Unfortunately, Evangelakos's narrative focuses on his martial adventures and offers little information on how he was able to locate and join a band, his everyday life or the way that he experienced life as a guerrilla. Evangelakos is equally silent about the fate and reactions of his family. Could the lack of reference to his family mean that they were against his decision? It is certainly not implausible. Some parents showed unwavering support; the mother of Mihalis Dafermos actually encouraged him to join ELAS: 'my mother never told me, son don't go' noted Dafermos, who fled his village to escape being arrested for his political activities; 'she said better in the mountain than in a cell'.[7] Others were much less happy with their children's decision. Fifteen-year-old Nikos Arvanitis from Aigion, who ran away from home to join ELAS, was disowned by his family for abandoning them 'to join the communists'.[8] H. Aberiadis's mother was equally unhappy with his decision to skip service in the

Bulgarian labour battalions and enlist in a band. She lashed out, accusing him of being an ungrateful son who did not care for the repercussions that might befall his family. Aberiadis's mother was afraid that their family would be persecuted by the Bulgarian authorities because of her son, a fear no doubt shared by many resisters whose families lived in occupied areas.[9] Vasilis Papananos noted in his diary a few days after he enlisted that he 'felt rotten' for placing his family in danger, even though feelings such as 'weakness, passions, tenderness, family life, forgiveness and love must not exist, but be submerged by the IDEA [sic]'.[10]

Evangelakos noted that a friend helped him reach a guerrilla band but details about how he located it or the enlistment procedure are not clear. Nevertheless, it is probable that Evangelakos was helped by a *sindesmos*, an EAM cadre who brought him into contact with a guerrilla band and vouched for him, since few men, at least in the early period, were foolhardy enough to join a band without the help of an intermediary. An anonymous narrative written by a guerrilla of the 16th ELAS regiment gives a good idea of the difficulties involved in contacting and enlisting with a band. The author and his seven comrades set off from Veroia in the winter of 1943. After meeting their EAM contact, 'we proceeded in pairs and kept a distance between 500–700 meters between us, trying to look as inconspicuous as possible'. However, 'many of the peasants looked at us with suspicion, we each carried a sack with clothes and they probably thought that we were Jews who were trying to escape Hitler's mania'. After they had crossed the plain of Veroia, they were taken to a safe house in the village of Koumani where they remained hidden for three days. They set off again at night after they were given a gun and some bullets each. After a day's walk, they crossed the Aliakmon river and reached the monastery of Prodromos in the foothills of the Pieria mountains, where they spent the night and dined on some leftovers. It was then that they realised that their ammunition was of the wrong type and calibre for their rifles, and they were barely able to escape from a collaborationist militia. The next day they climbed higher into the mountains where they met their band, which comprised 27 men, of whom only seven were armed.[11]

It was there that the group probably took the guerrilla oath. Enlistment was not automatic but relied on the guerrilla's willingness to take an oath of allegiance and, in the case of ELAS, adopt a pseudonym. Little attention has been paid to the role of symbolism and ritual in the construction of resistance identities. Rituals such as blood brotherhood played a pivotal role in rural life and culture; they were used to resolve conflicts, cement friendships and business ventures and create fictive kinship ties among men who were engaged in marginal and dangerous occupations, such as stonemasons, tinkers and brigands. These rituals were later adopted and enriched by the various irredentist societies that were created during the late nineteenth and early twentieth centuries.[12] The guerrilla groups elaborated their own rituals which were borrowed from these traditions to forge new collective identities among the diverse men who comprised the bands and reinforce cohesion between new and old band members.

Initially, the oaths of both ELAS and EDES contained strong religious overtones; often the resisters would swear on a Bible or an icon; sometimes a gun or a blade would also be used. Ceremonies were frequently conducted in chapels and monasteries. The EDES band of Kostas Giannoulis took the oath after Sunday service. Giannoulis spoke briefly to the assembled worshippers and afterwards 'I recited the oath which was repeated by all the guerrillas who stood in front of the icon of Christ crucified'.[13] This ritual played a pivotal role in forging a new identity for the initiated, since it both heralded their passage from the civilian to the military realm and denoted that they were distinct from and superior to the peasants. They were now members of a confraternity reserved for the select, the bravest and the most daring. The importance of the oath is underlined in several testimonies. ELAS guerrilla Giorgos Katsikas noted that, after giving the oath, 'I felt as if I had reached the sun … an incredible feeling, I saw … myself in each and every one of these men … as if I was one with them'.[14] Notis Mastrogiannis, a guerrilla in the 7th ELAS battalion in Euboea, commented similarly that 'our training lasted for a few days, when this was over we took the oath, this was a very important event for us back then'.[15]

The completion of the ceremony would sometimes be marked by a lavish celebration and the bestowal of some clothing, a gun and other military paraphernalia to the new recruits, and among ELAS guerrillas by the adoption of a *nom de guerre*. This practice, which was probably borrowed from the Macedonian freedom fighters, was commonplace until early 1944 but eventually subsided as ELAS became more militarised. ELAS memoirists attributed the adoption of pseudonyms to a need for anonymity; however, the oath and the adoption of *noms de guerre* not only facilitated anonymity but, along with the adoption of a uniform and a weapon, served to create a new warrior identity. It is characteristic that many guerrillas described this ceremony as a 'baptism'.[16] Vasilis Papananos adopted the *nom de guerre* Charon, after the mythical overseer of souls who in local lore was represented as a fierce, dashing warrior who had to beat in combat the young and the brave before carrying them off to the underworld – a clear indication of what Papananos aspired to and how he wanted to be perceived by his comrades. Papananos took the oath and received some military clothing and a gun, which completed the transformation from civilian to guerrilla. 'I discarded my coat, and put on a pilot's jacket and an ammunition belt, this gave me a somewhat military look', noted Papananos: 'thus the last traces of Vasilis were finally erased, and in his position stood Charon armed and ready'.[17]

However, men like Papananos were often unprepared for what was expected of them. The first few weeks of his service were marked by a series of shocks that included uncooperative peasants, bad weather conditions, unfamiliar food and disease. Papananos was further hindered by his background. He had a strong constitution but no idea about how to survive in the mountains. In this respect, he was not unique; few of the early guerrillas knew how to slaughter and cook an animal, distinguish between edible and poisonous herbs or deal with the men who populated the mountains: nomadic pastoralists, foresters, smugglers and monastic hermits.

Shepherds were often the only presence in the isolated mountain areas where the guerrillas moved and, according to circumstances, they could be the best friend and the worst enemy of the guerrillas. These pastoralists were the real kings of the mountain; they knew every passage, fountain and cave where the guerrillas could take shelter, while their transient and violent lifestyle made them ideal recruits. In the areas of Thesprotia and Preveza in Epirus the huts of Vlach pastoralists were the only safe haven for the EDES and ELAS bands during 1942–43.[18] The Sarakatsani shepherds played an equally important role in eastern Macedonia.[19] These shepherds offered food, intelligence and occasionally manpower for the bands and in some cases paid dearly for it. However, their help was not completely disinterested, since in exchange they received protection from rustlers and unfriendly peasants, especially in the ethnically mixed areas of northern Greece. Monastics played an equally important role; like the shepherds, they lived isolated and dangerous lives, threatened by the elements and by land-hungry peasants and bandits who were attracted by their fabled wealth. Monasteries often made alliances with brigands in order to protect themselves from peasants, and sometimes monks became bandits themselves. In the chaotic period of 1941–43 monasteries sheltered fugitives, provided food to the guerrilla bands and in a few rare cases even provided recruits.

Guerrillas often had to learn their trade in a harsh way. In January

Not by bread alone

1943 ELAS managed to field four bands numbering a total of 100 men in the mountainous area between the prefectures of Kavala and Drama. Within a few weeks less than a dozen remained, the rest having deserted or been captured, poisoned or murdered. The majority of these men, who were lowland peasants, workers and intellectuals most of whom had no experience of guerrilla warfare, were easy prey for the experienced Bulgarian search parties who had their own network of informants in the highlands. These experiences led the remaining men to adopt a series of set rules in their dealing with the peasantry. 'We decided', Nikos Hatzinikolaou, the leader of the band, wrote in his memoir, that

> the shepherds should never know our real strength, therefore we always asked for much more milk than we actually wanted, also, we made them drink the milk in front of us, this way we made sure that they would not poison us. We had the same rules in our dealings with the peasants, whenever we went to a village for provisioning during the night we always asked for much more food than we actually needed.[20]

Other bands learned their trade from the real outlaws, the bandits and rustlers who populated many bands from early on. Men like Giorgos Floros, a Vlach shepherd and rustler who joined the band of Nikos Xinos in the summer of 1942, taught the guerrillas how to survive in the open, evade their pursuers and live off the land.

> Floros ... knew how to march during the night, he led and the others followed him as if they were marching during daylight ... he was able to find paths where none existed ... with him it was impossible to get lost and we always find the best hideaways. The other guerrillas learned the ropes next to him.

Brigands like Floros also brought along with them a whole network of informants and helpers from their bandit days.[21] The logistics corps of ELAS in the Souli area were the Tsipis family, a large pastoral clan whose association with local ELAS leaders Tsilis Mastoras and Nikos Kiamos dated back to the beginning of the century and their bandit days. The Tsipis' help was invaluable since they provided food, information and safe houses to the guerrillas.[22]

Hardship challenged the expectations and endurance of many guerrillas. One EDES resister noted that

> it is impossible to describe the life we lead ... we're no different to beasts, we don't care about anything, and above all you cannot conceive that once you were a human being or that you might become one again. Every

conversation revolves around our job, laughter and wit, these demarcations of humanity have become unknown to us.[23]

Some men would take their own lives or desert, and most would pine for home and the life they left behind, unable to deal with hunger, disease and exhaustion.[24] One guerrilla of middle-class origin noted that he missed nothing more than 'the smell of gasoline, dust and asphalt'.[25] Longing and nostalgia were common to all: 'the main feeling of the guerrilla during the hours when he is not occupied with something is nostalgia', noted one EDES resister; 'nostalgia for our homes, our loved ones ... nostalgia for better, quieter days'.[26] However, these feelings were stronger among urban resisters who were often shocked and depressed by the strangeness of the landscape, and the poverty of the inhabitants. Upon returning to his native Athens, one nationalist resister noted: 'I felt that I was returning to Europe'.[27]

Nevertheless, gradually most guerrillas became accustomed to this sort of life. One EDES guerrilla noted that

> day by day we managed to adapt. Thus we were brought closer to nature, the trees, the soil, one became more experienced and keen, a passage in the mountains was easier to detect ... you could hear from a long distance, and tell if a noise came from a village or a herd ... inside us city kids the most ancient human instincts were re-awakened, our movements became firmer, we rarely got lost during the night or stumbled.[28]

Facing and overcoming these challenges was experienced by many as a rite of passage which enabled them to mature both physical and mentally and attain a more authentic masculinity that had been lost among the civilians. Papananos noted on the anniversary of his enlistment,

> A year! Hardships, marches, hunger, battles ... superhuman efforts that I will always remember. Through all these tests it is true that I have become much stronger both in regard to my psychic and physical strength, and have learned to deal coolly with situations, and to be indifferent to adversity ... nothing can move me any more as it could a year ago. This romantic situation that I suffered from a year ago is cut with a knife.[29]

However, gaining acceptance from one's peers was not easy. Rituals may have served to induct new members into the band, however, young men like 18-year-old Vasilis Zahodanis, who joined ELAS in early 1943, often found themselves marginalised and scorned. Zahodanis noted that 'us young lads ... the older guerrillas ... held us in really low esteem ... they said we couldn't become warriors, that what they needed was others, hardened men'.³⁰ Guerrillas, particularly younger recruits, had to prove that they had the character to respond to the challenges posed by guerrilla life. Young guerrillas would swear profusely, take up smoking, swagger defiantly and brawl in an effort to build an image of élan and military aggressiveness. EDES resister Giannis Beratis, a veteran of the Albanian war in his mid-30s, was struck both by the youth and by the machismo of the guerrillas. The first group he encountered 'were very young, almost kids … thick beards … filled their young faces' and they had a 'rough behaviour that they [tried] to make as pronounced as possible'.³¹

The performance of these masculinities played a crucial role in being accepted as a member of the peer group. EDES guerrilla Vasilis Dokopoulos was often subjected to the taunts of his comrades, some of whom were considerably younger than him, because of his short stature and leanness. He finally became accepted and respected due to his physical strength, which he demonstrated through his ability in wrestling:

> I became respected, I got a name, after a particular incident, you know there was a wrestling contest, between my unit and another unit, they came and asked who fights, and I said I do, and went there and won it for us. I was very good at that, and people would know and respect me because of that, because you see it was important to have a name.³²

Wrestling contests were an important part of peasant culture that transferred to the guerrilla bands. Contests between the men of the 30th ELAS regiment and other units operating in the Paikon area occurred frequently and were eagerly anticipated.³³ Wrestling was equally popular among the ELAS bands that operated in the Olympus area and organised contests.³⁴ It was not only a pastime but also a way to prove one's masculinity in front of one's peers. The guerrilla world was highly agonistic and reputation played a foremost role; however, reputation 'could only be made and maintained on the basis of physical force and courage'.³⁵ Guerrillas had to prove their courage and demonstrate their ability to withstand hardship and pain and retain their calmness in the face of danger. Stergios Valioulis, a schoolteacher, was the most educated man in his band; however, his urbanity did not render him any more respected by his peers. On the contrary, men like Valioulis had to prove even more than their peasant comrades their toughness and agility. Appearing indifferent to hunger and pain were very important in this respect. Valioulis admitted that 'it is a damn lie to say that one gets used to being hungry', but underlined that repeated complaints could result in loss of face: 'it was shameful to put too much stock in the rumblings of your stomach

... you keep that a secret, you pretend that you do not care in order to maintain your decency and prove that you've got guts, that you are brave'.[36]

Becoming accepted by his comrades was the proudest achievement of Dimitris Bouzoukas, a 16-year-old boy from a small village in Boeotia, especially since it coincided with his actual coming of age. During this time Bouzoukas had his first shave and later began to grow a beard, being envious of his older comrades, and smoked his first cigarette. Cultural activities were equally important to Bouzoukas, who described the ELAS bands as 'my best and greatest school'. It was during these years that youths like him first watched a play, read literature or attended poetry recitals. Bouzoukas remembered several decades later how a recital of some of the works of the left-wing poet Varnalis moved him to tears.[37]

Participation in the resistance also marked the first time that Bouzoukas and thousands of men like him had travelled outside the environs of their village. These journeys were often dangerous and exhausting, but they exposed the guerrillas to new sights, landscapes and customs. Mountaineers such as Ioannis Papazisis, a peasant from the uplands of Grevena, saw the sea for the first time: 'I didn't know what the sea looked like, I saw the sea for the first time in 45 in Plataria'.[38] Meanwhile, lowland peasants, who were traditionally hostile to the mountaineers, came into contact for the first time with the world of the mountains. They were impressed by the rugged beauty as well as the austerity and poverty of the inhabitants. Dimitris Dimitriou and his men, most of whom came from the lowlands of eastern Greece, were awestruck by the beauty of the mountains. Some of the vistas were so beautiful that 'we forgot our tiredness and all our sorrows and we walked as if we were enchanted ... captivated and awestruck trying to absorb this majesty'.[39] It was these experiences, according to an ELAS guerrilla from Epirus, that 'made us conscious of our humanity, we learned so many things within just two months, they made us human ... they taught us a new ethos'.[40]

The mountains not only offered new experiences but also freedom from constraint and social norms. Young men like Bouzoukas and Dokopoulos were not allowed to frequent the village café, drink or smoke in front of their elders or pursue an occupation independent of that of their families. The resistance gave these men a chance to escape familial supervision and pursue lifestyles that were out of bounds for them at home. The first band in Dokopoulos's village was raised by his father. However, he chose to enlist in a different band:

I did not join my father. I was a lively lad, but I couldn't even smoke in front of my father. I was ashamed to smoke ... back then we neither played cards nor did we smoke in front of our fathers, nor could we jest, in front of them, only serious talk ... others stole; me, I didn't dare to steal an ounce of grain because my father would beat me.[41]

This situation changed as soon as Dokopoulos enlisted. He took up smoking and along with some other men began raiding local flocks to prove 'they had guts'.[42] Theft was condemned by the resistance organisations both because it caused peasant hostility but also because it was at odds with their ethos and mission, which was to protect but also to provide spiritual and political leadership to the civilians. The guerrilla was envisioned by the ELAS authorities as 'a fighter, a leader, a missionary'. Education was very important in this respect since the guerrillas were envisioned as 'the guides of the peasantry' who 'enlightened them about our national struggle ... and opened their eyes to bright and wide horizons'. Bravery might be important; however, without moral and personal integrity, little could distinguish the guerrilla from his adversaries. 'Since the guerrilla is a missionary he must be first of all honest and moral'; drinking, gambling, fighting, swearing and illicit sex were therefore condemned as unbefitting to the national role and ethos of the guerrilla. Such attitudes were extended to the treatment of enemies; prisoners should be treated 'with chivalry, the guerrilla would tenderly bind his wound, give him a drink from his canteen and share with him his sparse meal ... at the same time he should convince him about the justness of his struggle, about the holiness and the justness of their mission'.[43]

However, not all guerrillas conformed to this image and most took to the role of outlaw with gusto. Indeed, what would have been condemned in young men's civilian lives as inappropriate or shameful behaviour was embraced as a staple of guerrilla masculinity and used to establish a reputation. Their struggles also gradually gave rise to a shared consciousness of belonging to an elect group of men who stood above the rest of society. The guerrillas saw themselves as a class apart, hardy, selfless and courageous, superior to the docile and effeminate peasantry and the cowardly bourgeois. An EDES guerrilla-poet wrote: 'I have no love for the offerings of peace ... I don't long for the bourgeois quiet life/ but for struggle, war and fire ... I don't want death to find me tired ... old and sick like a nightlight that withers away ... I want death to find me standing tall and fighting in the bloom of my youth/ strong and full of passion.'[44] The man who wrote this poem, Dimitris Soutzos, was not a typical guerrilla; he came from an old and rich aristocratic family whose roots dated back to the sixteenth century. However, the feelings and themes he expressed – the vigour of the guerrilla, his manliness and superiority over the civilians – were shared by many of his comrades in both organisations and recurred in guerrilla songs and publications.

Soutzos was a heavy drinker and a daring fighter who was admired by his comrades of all social classes; he was also a violent man. On one occasion he stole the clothes of some Italian prisoners and beat them badly after they complained to his superior officer. Soutzos was far from unique in this respect. Theft under the guise of requisitioning was common, as was drinking, the use of recreational drugs[45] and shooting in the air, a practice that often led to the death or injury of guerrillas and civilians alike[46] as 'village-type rebels … let off fusillades of shots every time they get drunk'.[47] Such habits were not the work of a few marginal elements within the guerrilla movement but were widespread, and while condemned by the guerrilla authorities, they were accepted by most men who saw them as a prerogative of their status as well as a means of emphasising both their separateness from civilian society and their dominance over civilians.

Giannis Douatzis, the *kapetanios* of the 7th ELAS battalion in Euboea, was forced to court-martial several of his men after ordering them repeatedly to desist from discharging their guns in the air because they had 'terrorised' the villages with their attitude.[48] However, these measures did little to curtail such behaviour. Drunken guerrillas from Douatzis's unit casually threatened civilians, trashed shops and had open sexual relations with prostitutes and women who had been tried for collaboration and treason. Such attitudes shocked the conservative Arvanite villagers of Euboea. Douatzis admitted that his men 'had made a mess'[49] and despite severely lacking recruits he was forced to court-martial and expel several ELAS men whose behaviour had been particularly shocking to local communities.[50]

The guerrillas' self-perception as a class apart led them to believe that, as members of the 'liberation armies', they should be provided for and even feted by the peasantry. Failure to comply with their wishes resulted in violence. ELAS guerrillas in western Macedonia taunted the peasants by exclaiming that 'all those who didn't take up arms are not men and they better put on skirts' and they thrashed peasants who dared to 'criticise the army'.[51] In the central Greek village of Karia, several ELAS guerrillas publicly flogged a middle-aged peasant for refusing to let his daughter tend to an injured ELAS *kapetanios*. His refusal 'was viewed as an affront by the guerrillas', who arrested him. After holding him under

Not by bread alone

guard for several hours, they led him to the village piazza where he was stripped naked and beaten unconscious by the guerrillas, who took it in turns to thrash him with belts and whips.[52] The attitudes of guerrillas differed little in other areas. EAM cadres from the village of Liggari, a small community nestled in the foothills of the Pangaion mountain in central Macedonia, protested that ELAS guerrillas who visited their village 'had a feast while the villagers were dispatched to guard duty' by the group's drunken commissar, who terrorised the peasants by shooting in the air with his rifle. The peasants also complained that they were constantly harassed to offer more and better quality food, till the guerrillas' fields and chop wood for them, while village women were forced to visit the guerrillas' encampments to serve as cooks and cleaners. They even accused the guerrillas of using their position to settle personal rivalries and murder their enemies.[53]

On a similar occasion a group of inebriated EDES guerrillas in the Lakka Souli area savagely beat a peasant in the village of Ardosi while shouting 'you are busy with your fields and don't care that we fight for the fatherland'. Afterwards they arrested and held hostage several peasants in the same community; 'they forced the villagers to enter the church and put guards on the doors, then they made them chant the funeral service and were threatening to shoot them, when the chanting stopped they beat up several peasants and asked for wheat, meat and raki in order to let them go'.[54] This violence had no anti-clerical bent; the guerrillas, like the peasants, came from a highly religious society and in all probability were practising Christians. The goal of such transgressive practices was to underline the guerrillas' outlaw identity and underscore their dominance over the 'tame' citizenry. The use of profane and blasphemous language among the guerrillas, which often led the peasants to protest to the guerrilla authorities, had an analogous purpose – to underline the guerrillas' dominance over and disregard for the mores of civilian society.[55]

Bread and bullets

However, while guerrillas often scorned the peasantry, they were ultimately dependent on them for food, provisions and shelter. Guerrillas might have tried to appear nonchalant while they marched on empty stomachs, but food was an important concern both for individual men and bands. Lack of food decimated bands and created tensions among band members; disputes and fights over food were common in many bands and hampered recruitment. Often guerrillas would neglect their duties and concentrate all their energy on procuring food, raiding barns, fields and houses. Arranging a steady supply of food was pivotal but also led guerrillas to clash with those whom they were assigned to protect. Procurement was, as a rule, voluntary; however, the threat and fear of violence was often present and few peasants would attempt to refuse the guerrillas' demands for food. Kostas Kipouros, a member of the Olympus band, recalled:

> The band moved only during the night. Provisioning was also done during the night when we requisitioned sheep from the shepherds. The shepherds took us for bandits, after all that's how we acted to take what we wanted. I remember once when we went to the village of Skamnos in Elassona to take a sheep. Two of us went to the shepherd and asked for a sheep. The rest of us were hiding at a distance of 30–40 metres and were moving the rifle bolts to intimidate him ... the shepherd asked us, 'lads if my boss asks me who took the sheep what am I supposed to say?', comrade Papas told him to say that 'some hungry men with guns came by and took it'.[56]

This was far from an isolated incident. Most bands relied on tactics that differed little from those adopted by bandits and organised crime. Some of the first ELAS bands in Epirus and central Greece sent notes to local merchants and landowners asking for money and provisions. Those who did not heed the call – like Nikos Papageorgiou, a rich merchant from Sperheiada,[57] or N. Bousis,[58] a businessman who owned a fishery and a salt-mine on the outskirts of Arta – were abducted and were only released after their families paid large ransoms. Others, like Dimitris Stergiou, a rich farmer from Almyros who refused the guerrillas' demands for provisions, were brutally murdered.[59] The situation was similar in the rich plain of Ileia in Peloponnesus, where ELAS operated an elaborate protection racket whereby local notables, merchants and landowners provided the local bands with a set amount of provisions and material in exchange for protection. Those who refused were threatened or had their properties vandalised by the guerrillas:

> In the village of Rodia a number of peasants provided ELAS with provisions, however, most of them did so under duress. In the village of Kavasila, Giannis Giannikopoulos, a local merchant, was threatened that unless he provisioned ELAS he would be executed. In Sabanaga, the notable Hristos Anagnastopoulos provided food and provisions to the guerrillas who in return protected his property.[60]

Guerrillas also derived a large part of their revenues from 'taxing' peddlers, smugglers and black marketeers for the privilege of doing business in their territory.[61]

Not by bread alone

Sometimes the line between procurement and banditry became completely blurred as whole bands, like the one led by 'Olympus' in Pineia, robbed and plundered for their personal gain. Olympus, whose real name was Aggeletos Spentzeris, was a transient Roma from the Peloponnesian town of Vartholomio. In late 1942 Spentzeris joined and later deserted from ELAS, along with a man known as Odysseus, under unknown circumstances. In the spring of 1943 he returned along with his comrade to his native town where the local EAM committee granted him permission to raise a band. Spentzeris was a gifted commander; however, his violent temperament and avarice eventually prevailed. Spentzeris's band requisitioned wheat from local farmers, part of which they sold on the black market. They robbed a monastery, robbed and executed some peddlers whom they accused of collaborating with the enemy, and in one case even received money from a peasant woman to kill her antagonist. Spentzeris's career came to an abrupt end when he was executed by ELAS in unknown circumstances. According to one author he refused to join the newly formed 12th ELAS regiment and his men were scattered among various ELAS units.[62]

Bands like those of Spentzeris became increasingly rare as the resistance groups became more organised and expanded their activities to the richer lowland areas. EAM had created two distinct services by the summer of 1942: the 'Fanela tou Antarti' [The guerrilla's vest] created during August 1942 in Athens whose main task was to provide the guerrillas with boots and clothes; and the 'Epitropi Prostasias Antarton' [Committee for the protection of the guerrillas], created in the countryside during the same period. In the spring of 1943 both organisations were merged into ETA [Epimeliteia tou Antarti – the guerrilla logistics corps].[63] Contributions during this period were largely voluntary and came from organisation members both in the cities and the countryside. However, the most importance source of income and provisions was the British Military Mission. Between June and October 1943 ELAS received over 36,000 gold sovereigns to procure food and supplies, and a total of 136,000 gold sovereigns was supplied over the entire occupation. This assistance was interrupted during the winter of 1943–44, since ELAS was considered to be responsible for the outbreak of hostilities against EDES, and resumed, albeit on a smaller scale, from March 1944.[64]

The civil war and the anti-guerrilla operations of 1943 placed ELAS under considerable strain, especially after the BMM stopped supplying them with money and provisions. This crisis led ELAS to introduce taxation both on agricultural production and commerce. Tax was paid both in kind and cash, and ranged between 5 per cent and 10 per cent on agricultural produce. Mill owners were taxed at a flat 10 per cent, while commercial transactions were taxed between 15 and 20 per cent. Producers and merchants who failed to pay the allocated tax had their whole crop and wares confiscated and were liable to be court-martialled as saboteurs.[65] However, taxation alone could not cover all the needs of ELAS. It was estimated that in mainland Greece ELAS guerrillas consumed over 18 tons of meat and 130 tons of bread weekly and needed over 160 tons of fodder for their animals.[66]

In addition to the food shortages, many resistance groups lacked clothes, weaponry and medical supplies. In certain areas, only those who could afford their own weapons and provisions were allowed to enlist and it was not unusual for guerrillas to kill isolated soldiers 'because they were shoeless and dressed in rags and were tempted by their leather coats, the boots and the steyr automatics'.[67] The guerrillas wore a wide array of uniforms. In Epirus 'no one wore a full military uniform. One wore ... military breeches and on top a homespun garment, another one wore an army greatcoat and his civilian trousers ... you could occasionally see old men wearing shorts and a shepherd's coat.'[68] Guerrilla dress was even more disparate in central Greece, where

> bits of British uniform alternated with items of captured Italian dress; khaki side caps, German fatigue caps and Greek *fesia* [fezzes] jostled for pride of place; jackboots trod the cobbles in the company of pompommed *tsaroukhia* [sandals]; battledress trousers vied with Italian breeches and indigenous *foustanelles* [kilts]. The variety of clothing was as nothing compared with the medley of armaments ... it seemed that every museum piece in the Balkans had been pressed into service.[69]

Often it was impossible to differentiate between ELAS and EDES guerrillas, and during the clashes between the two groups some fell victim to friendly fire, since they all shared the same semi-military uniform.

However, 'this policy of laissez-faire' was not merely an outcome of want and 'the inconveniences of life in the mountains', but also 'a badge of resistance in much the same way that the revolutionaries of Fidel Castro made a special display of their hirsute chins. In the Greek case, there was [also] an underlying desire to emulate the traditional manly appearance of the *klephts*.'[70] Many guerrillas were induced initially to go to war through stories of heroism narrated by relatives or found in literature and film. It was to be expected that some men would seek to emulate the appearance and deeds of these idealised heroes. Nevertheless, these efforts should not be dismissed as plain imitation. Rather, they had a particular gender dynamic: by re-enacting these romanticised forms of masculinity, men strove to forge a link with an idealised past. Thus, they were symbolically appropriating the masculine qualities deemed fitting for a guerrilla. Additionally, the men's flamboyance was used to highlight their irregular identities. Guerrillas did not view themselves as simple soldiers, but as rebels who defied authority and stood in a long line of irregular fighters who had challenged organised society and its norms.[71] The adoption of these styles and items provided men with a sense of distinctiveness, as well as continuity with the past at a personal level; kilts, fezzes and damascene knives were recast from museum pieces into operational items. Tied in with the everyday life of the guerrilla, they became potent proof of the individual's connection with a semi-mythologised heroic past.

Weaponry was equally varied. The guerrillas of the 54th ELAS regiment sported Italian carbines, British and Greek rifles, and some even had nineteenth-century Turkish muskets. This situation persisted well into 1944, despite the considerable amount of supplies despatched by the SOE.[72] The situation improved radically after the Italian capitulation of 1944 which enabled ELAS to re-equip units with modern equipment, while the resumption of British assistance further helped deprived units. The lack of weapons was not the only problem; during the same period, many guerrillas had to make do with looted or homespun clothes. A British officer in Epirus noted that 'Their living conditions were bad owing to extremely wet and cold weather and their lack of greatcoats, groundsheets or gas caps.'[73]

The lack of clothing caused serious health problems. During the winter of 1943, 45 out of 196 men in the ELAS 30th regiment suffered from frostbite, and five died.[74] Bronchitis, colds and malaria were also acute problems, as were lice which were responsible for periodic outbreaks of typhus. The guerrillas tried to address this by boiling their clothes in hot water at least twice a month, but such measures were ineffective. A medical report on the 54th ELAS regiment stated that

> The health situation among the guerrillas is far from satisfactory ... the lack of items of clothing and underwear and more generally the living conditions of the guerrillas ... undermine their health ... We had 15 cases of typhus ... Furthermore because of the almost complete lack of footwear we had 10 men with frostbite.[75]

The situation was equally bad among the 28th regiment of ELAS. Many men in these two units were dressed until the spring of 1944 'in civilian

A history of the Greek resistance

clothes and goatskin slippers and were poorly fed'; as a result over one-third of the guerrillas suffered from malaria and rheumatic fever.[76] The 10th and 15th regiments of EDES faced equally serious problems with clothes and provisioning. A junior officer reported in June 1944 that 'the men lack boots and wear old and tattered uniforms', while many were equipped with antique weapons, some dating back to the Balkan wars.[77]

The health situation was aggravated by the lack of doctors and medical provisions. The guerrillas' greatest fear was getting injured; wounded men were sometimes left behind and were often tortured for information. Even when a medical station was nearby, things were difficult: 'when an andarte … became a casualty he received no medical treatment apart from the application of a dressing by his companions until he could get back … most wounded had to walk … wounds were treated considerably longer after they had been received than they are on more "civilized" battlefields'.[78] The guerrillas often had to rely on folk remedies administered by villagers. In Epirus, 40 doctors were responsible for tending to 9,000 guerrillas and more than 100,000 civilians.[79]

The dire conditions were a shock to many volunteers who expected guerrilla warfare to consist of constant movement and adventure. However, action was rare; some guerrilla groups would engage in no more than four or five actions in a year, while a few were restricted to carrying out garrison duties. An SOE officer stationed in central Greece described the situation as follows: 'Outstanding individuals and their comparatively small forces always carried the whole brunt of the fighting. While the remaining garrisoned the villages and fortified the gospel.'[80] The most common and fierce enemies of the guerrillas were not the Axis troops but rather the cold, hunger, disease and monotony of everyday life, interspersed with bouts of activity that were so violent that guerrillas were left dumbfounded. Papananos noted in his diary, 'it is very difficult to define the psychological state that I am in … the idle waiting in this boring village for so many days on end has really exhausted me'.[81] Two months later, Papananos's mood had hardly changed: '25/8/43 the same monotony of the mountains, 26/08/43 the only thing that soothes me is that I will soon be out of here, I hope in no more than 10–15 days, 27/8/43 nothing interesting, 30/8/43–nothing, 31/08/43–nothing … 06/09/43 I am going mad with this monotony.'[82]

EDES guerrilla Faidon Maidonis was similarly exasperated by the lack of action: 'we came here, filled with rage to fight the … enemy, and they have been keeping us here … to trudge like tramps in the narrow streets of Derviziana … every single morning is the same thing, hunger, lots

Not by bread alone

of theory and idleness'.[83] Maidonis's complaints were certainly justified since his unit, the 24th regiment of EDES, saw very little action between May and July 1944. However, other formations were much more active; for instance, the 30th regiment of ELAS in Macedonia fought more than forty actions between May and October. Nonetheless, such bouts of activity were rare even for this crack unit and were usually followed by several weeks of inactivity. A British liaison officer jestingly noted that 'I believe that the first question that should be put to any volunteers for such [guerrilla] work is: "How long can you sit doing nothing?"'[84]

Living conditions deteriorated sharply during punitive operations by the Axis forces. The guerrillas were harried continuously by enemy troops; they marched relentlessly, with little or no food and water, and were forced to stay hidden in the remoter highland areas, where they were exposed to the fury of the elements. They were ravaged by lack of water, and sleep was rendered almost impossible by fear, stress and cold. Sometimes exhausted partisans would fall asleep while walking, and wake with terrible frostbite.[85] Even in safe conditions, sleep was difficult; lacking blankets and firewood, men would cover themselves with their greatcoats and tree branches, embracing their comrades to keep warm.[86] Such difficult situations could be exacerbated by harsh weather conditions. An ELAS officer in Peloponnesus noted in his diary:

> 16/4/1944: the enemy is pursuing us so quickly and with such intensity that we have no time for rest but continually move from mountainside to mountainside … I was so exhausted that I thought that … this is the end for me … 17/4/1944 … from the afternoon onwards we keep on marching against all the elements of nature, cold, rain and forests so vast that I have never imagined or seen before. We are walking corpses … 18/4/1944: all my men are in a shocking state.[87]

However, such violent bouts of activity were rare and guerrillas spent most of their time engaged in the more basic activities of guard duty, setting up camp, cleaning weapons and marching. Most guerrillas lived a peripatetic existence, constantly on the move so as to reach enemy targets, procure food and avoid Axis troops. Papananos noted, in early 1944: 'I calculated this year's toils … I must have walked more than 1,500 kilometres which is more or less equal in length to the whole German–Soviet front and have resided in more than 75 villages.'[88] However, there was a pattern in marches, as there was in combat. Guerrillas followed the habits of pastoral shepherds; between April and October they lived in the high pastures and moved towards the plain in winter. Life was more difficult in the winter because of the cold and the lack of food, but it was also much quieter because of the lack of operations.[89]

Life in the guerrilla encampments differed greatly from that in the regular military since the partisan armies were often accompanied by scores of non-combatants: black market peddlers, prostitutes, entertainers and the guerrillas' spouses, siblings, children and mistresses. The 15th regiment of EDES was accompanied by scores of civilians including the guerrillas' families and girlfriends who followed them to the mountains 'for safety reasons'.[90] The presence of these civilians created serious problems. Non-combatants placed a serious strain on the guerrillas' food and provisions, especially during the winter months. Combat performance was equally affected, since during operations guerrillas would often abandon their positions in order to help their families escape their pursuers and salvage their belongings. Such problems were equally common to ELAS units. The commanding officer of the 12th regiment was forced to forbid 'the stay of the family or relatives of the fellow comrades … near the unit encampments', as well as the hiring of women of dubious origin by many units 'as seamstress or nurses'. Such women were sometimes the girlfriends of guerrillas; more often, they were prostitutes brought to the mountains from the towns of Aigion or Patra. The regimental authorities asked that all such women 'be immediately fired … these services will from hereafter performed by the political organisations'.[91]

Prostitution was not uncommon in the 'free areas', and even though the guerrilla organisations did not condone it, they were unable to forbid or regulate it. Even some of the high-ranking members patronised brothels. Most of the women who engaged in this trade belonged to socially marginal groups such as Roma; others were unmarried mothers, widows or former girlfriends of Axis soldiers. It is also probable that some women were forcibly brought by guerrillas who prostituted them. Sex was not only exchanged for money; often food, a pair of trousers or parachute silk was enough for those who sought pleasure in the several houses of ill repute located in the larger villages and market towns.[92]

However, buying sex was not the only perk available in villages. A stay, however brief, allowed guerrillas to visit a coffee shop or a tavern, buy some sweets or cigarettes and, if the village was sufficiently friendly, be billeted in peasants' homes and spend a night in an actual bed. A stay in a village also gave the chance for some much-needed recreation. Sometimes the guerrilla officers would organise a dancing contest between the men; shadow theatre was equally popular, while occasionally a local EPON troupe would stage a play for the benefit of the guerrillas.

Not by bread alone

However, no activity was so simple or as loved as storytelling. Many guerrillas came from a predominantly oral culture, in which sharing and narrating stories provided a way to induct the young into the dominant culture, as well as offering an avenue for escapism. Guerrillas had a penchant for the macabre and the fantastic; tales about ghosts, spirits and demons who roamed the mountains were particularly popular, especially when narrated by charismatic storytellers such as Father Pantelis, an Orthodox priest who served in the 26th ELAS. Several decades after the war his platoon commander recalled that

> no one could rival Father Pantelis, he could narrate from sunrise to sunset without tiring his audience. Goblins, and flying beasts ... lords and beautiful damsels, slaves locked in a harem, thieves and treasures and witches ... and poor devils who always managed to brave all difficulties and emerge as winners ... these were the heroes in his stories that he so brilliantly narrated.[93]

The presence of a guerrilla detachment would often put a great strain on the peasants' daily life and provisions. Guerrilla bands might have travelled light in the early period of the occupation; however, as the pace of operations escalated and their numbers increased, they came to resemble more and more a regular army. During operations guerrilla units were accompanied by a host of non-combatants: cooks, gunsmiths, muleteers, medics, blacksmiths and a number of civilians who followed the guerrilla columns in the hope of laying their hands on some loot. This multitude needed food, shelter, provisions and fodder for their pack animals, all of which had to be extracted from the peasants. Unsurprisingly, peasants tried to avoid these unwanted guests as much as they could, since the guerrillas often made excessive demands for food, and their hygiene was questionable at best; partisans would often infest peasant homes with lice. Most had a laissez-faire attitude with regard to the peasantry's supplies, clothes and firewood. Guerrillas would often destroy fences for firewood, and requisition pack-animals' fodder and other supplies.[94]

Upon learning that a column was approaching, peasants would hide their pack animals and provisions and try to find excuses to keep the guerrillas out of their homes. Guerrillas were often shocked by the 'ungrateful' attitudes of the civilians and the lack of sympathy for their plight. Papananos noted that peasants often refused to sell them their produce, or help ill and injured guerrillas: 'we tried to buy some cherries from the peasants, and even though we offered them money, these beasts would not sell to us. We should have done as the Italians did, and taken what we wanted by force.'⁹⁵ This was not the only time that Papananos and his comrades were denied assistance. On another occasion, despite the cold, peasants declined to take the guerrillas into their homes, 'and told us to go away and sleep in the open ... as if we were stray dogs'.⁹⁶ Papananos noted angrily that 'these scumbags forget that they live free and enjoy their goods thanks to us'.⁹⁷

Papananos's opinions were shared by many other guerrillas who often described the peasants as unpatriotic or indifferent towards their cause, and argued that civilian efforts compared unfavourably with their own sacrifices. This might have been true in the early days of the resistance; however, by the time Papananos wrote those lines the situation had changed radically. A British officer who travelled in Thessaly and the EAM-held parts of Epirus in the winter of 1943–44 was struck both by the desolate look of the upland villages and the huge disparity in the lifestyles of the guerrillas and the peasantry:

> where the village stocks have not been seriously depleted by the Germans in their various drives, they are depleted by the andartes ... The ELAS requisition wheat, beans and livestock on a percentage basis, without any attempt at recompense. I have not yet seen an ELAS outpost where the andartes were not eating wheat bread and having a meat meal at least once every three days.⁹⁸

This situation made the peasants more and more intolerant of the guerrillas' interloping and boastfulness and increased tensions between the civilians, who desperately tried to cling to the last vestiges of their belongings, and the guerrillas, who saw anything short of complete cooperation as tangible proof of the peasants' unworthiness.

The tip of the iceberg

Combat might have been less frequent than expected; however, it was after all both the purpose and the ultimate test for the guerrilla. Surprisingly, guerrilla testimonies are very sparse with regard to accounts of fighting. To what can we attribute this reticence? Combat was certainly traumatic, since it not only involved crossing the foremost social taboo — killing — but also resulted in the loss of loved ones and comrades. Furthermore, in the period that followed the civil war the left tried to dissociate itself from the image of the bloodthirsty *simmoritis* [bandit] and instead stressed the sacrifices and tribulations of the guerrilla, rendering him a martyr and a victim instead of a killer. Yet guerrillas killed, and many found killing and combat not just a duty but an enjoyable, almost transcendent, experience.

The attitudes of men during combat have been scrutinised by a host of scholars, beginning with S.L.A. Marshall's pivotal study of American servicemen in the Second World War. According to Marshall, the foremost problem faced by the American army during this period was the soldier's reluctance to take active part in combat. Marshall estimated than no more than 15–20 per cent fired their weapons, even in the thick of battle. Marshall and subsequent studies attributed this to a fundamental resistance to transgressing the foremost social taboo – killing a fellow human being.[99] Dave Grossman argued that

> there is ample indication of the existence of the resistance to killing and that it appears to have existed at least since the black-powder era. The lack of enthusiasm for killing the enemy causes many soldiers to posture, submit, or flee, rather than fight; it represents a powerful psychological force on the battlefield; and it is a force that is discernible throughout the history of man.[100]

More recent studies have contested this view, pointing instead towards instances of 'joyful killing'. Such studies highlight the importance of training and cultural narratives in the facilitation of killing.[101]

Training could not prepare men for the realities of the battlefield; nevertheless, it was a necessary precondition for 'control and motivation on the battlefield', thereby helping men withstand the 'shock … of battle' and turning the scattered groups 'into cohesive units'.[102] Training in the guerrilla bands was elementary if not entirely non-existent. Many guerrillas and EAM cadres saw training as completely useless for a guerrilla army like ELAS, and believed that political education and ideological belief could help guerrillas overcome any obstacles. Moreover, guerrillas in both organisations disliked training because they believed it was at odds both with the free life of the mountains and the fiercely independent personas of the bandit-heroes, whom they regarded as their cultural ancestors. Such attitudes were shared by many guerrilla officers, particularly of the irregular kind, who were equally obdurate in their dismissal of training and military procedures in general. An SOE officer attached to the 85th ELAS regiment in Epirus noted of its leaders that 'neither … had the slightest idea of any military matters, nor did they display any interest in such matters'.[103]

Lack of training was also a result of the constant movement of groups and the lack of instructors. In theory, ELAS bands were ruled by a triumvirate of a *politikos* or commissar, who was responsible for propaganda and ideological education; a *kapetanios*, who was responsible for recruitment and provisioning; and a *stratiotikos* – an officer of junior rank responsible for all military matters. However, until early 1944 such men were notable by their absence, especially from ELAS. Many units had no military training until well into 1944, since guerrillas and their leaders believed that 'the military lessons that were common once in bourgeois armies ... were probably useless'.[104]

However, guerrilla organisations were not unaware of the need to socialise guerrillas to engage in violence. ELAS and, to a lesser extent, EDES published hundreds of articles in which they luridly described the atrocities perpetrated by the Germans and the reaction and encouraged the guerrillas to kill and show no mercy. Guerrilla groups tried to accustom the men to committing violence in more direct ways. A few days after his enlistment in ELAS Papananos was summoned by some of his comrades to witness an interrogation, in this case a euphemism for the torturing of a suspect. Papananos was encouraged to partake in order to 'get bloody'; at first he hesitated but after some time he joined in, later noting in his diary how much he had enjoyed his 'baptism of fire'.[105] Recent studies on armed groups have underlined the importance of violent initiation rituals in the building-up of morale and group loyalty. Armed groups prompted novice fighters to take part in the killing or molestation of their political opponents in order to inure them to committing violent acts, thereby facilitating their integration into a new moral landscape.[106]

ELAS and, to a lesser extent, EDES used similar tactics. Young guerrillas were used frequently in execution squads and encouraged to kill prisoners with knives and bayonets in order to 'bloody' themselves.[107] A young guerrilla who joined the 51st ELAS regiment in Boeotia was regaled with stories about the killing of collaborators from his comrades who gave him advice about the best way to use a knife: 'you first stab him in the throat, then you cross his chest and you finally give him one in the gut'.[108] Such talk was often mere bravado and was used to scare and haze new recruits; however, it is certain that sometimes such practices were used to initiate new men into the bands, especially those who came from 'high-risk' backgrounds such as gendarmes, civil servants and petty thieves. Such men were forced to perpetrate violent acts and sometimes murder prisoners in order to be adopted as fully fledged members of the group.[109] Such rites were associated closely with ideals of masculinity. The guerrillas partook in a hyper-masculine culture which saw the ability to perform and withstand violence as the most important attribute of masculinity. An ELAS *kapetanios*, who ordered his men to watch the torture and execution of two collaborationists, berated those who expressed concerns over this, scolding them that 'a guerrilla should not hesitate, he must not be afraid of anything; a guerrilla mustn't be a coward and flinch in the sight of blood like a little girl'.[110]

The usefulness of these methods must be assessed with care. The man who witnessed the previous incident quit ELAS in disgust, while despite its usefulness propaganda could not prepare the guerrillas for being shot at or seeing their comrades lying dead and wounded next to them. However, it is certain that there were many men in the guerrilla bands who felt no inhibitions about taking their fellow men's lives. Unlike conscript armies that recruited from all segments of society, the guerrilla forces contained a disproportionate number of men who came from the margins: brigands, rustlers, professionals of violence, men who were attracted not by ideology but by the opportunity to exercise violence. There were men among the guerrillas, according to Romanos, who 'would as easily kill a man so as to see if he would die screaming or crying … people who would simply kill somebody just for the thrill of it'.[111] Similarly, Maidonis noted the presence among his fellow guerrillas of men who enjoyed 'narrating with an undertone of sadism the killings they committed, as if they were professional hired killers'.[112]

Such behaviour might have shocked these urban middle-class men, but violence was not viewed as deviant or reprehensible among peasants. Indeed, in these societies, violence, manliness and honour were fundamentally linked: 'honour is … primarily contingent on physical strength and bearing'.[113] The ability to exercise violence effectively was highly esteemed as a sign of manhood, according to the anthropologist John Campbell, who argued in a study of social mores in a Greek highland community that

> strength and prowess … matter more than ethical goodness. Indeed a man is only good when he is … able and strong. Although aimless violence is dishonourable there is no missing the pleasure it gives when a man is forced to kill; nor the prestige which it brings him. For there is no more conclusive way of showing that you are stronger than by taking away the other man's life.[114]

However, many guerrillas soon found out that there was a significant disparity between these idealised depictions of violence and the reality of combat. Despite its brief duration, irregular fighting was terrifying and intense. Stelios Giatroudakis, a guerrilla in the 40th ELAS regiment, noted that

> as soon as firing started I got really scared ... and I said to myself. You fool! How did you end up here! And really I would not believe anyone who said that he took part in combat and was not scared a bit ... this is a blatant lie. This was my true combat baptism.[115]

Axis troops were well equipped with heavy machine guns and mortars, whose effect on young, inexperienced guerrillas was considerable. EDES officer Giorgios Patsis described an action in which his platoon attacked a German outpost in the village of Louros in north-western Greece:

> Some of the German soldiers were hurling insults at us in perfect Greek, flares were lighting the sky and their searchlights were blinding us ... they were less than 150 metres away, anyone who dared to move was cut to pieces, one of my men shouted 'they are going to cut us into pieces tonight' ... maybe the others believed that as well, but they tried to keep it to themselves.[116]

EDES officer Nikiforos Kossevakis also related how during an ambush, 'the Italians were pouring on us with machine guns and mortars ... we fell back and returned fire sporadically. The men became panicky because of the mortars. It was very difficult to keep them in order.'[117]

Heavy guns had a detrimental effect on guerrilla morale. Partisan bands could withstand superior forces and exhibit extraordinary spirit; however, most men were unable to withstand a barrage for more than a few minutes since they lacked the appropriate training. Guerrillas who faced artillery fire would quickly break ranks and flee, despite the pleas of their officers. An EDES guerrilla commented:

> after the barrage started everyone fled ... I turned my head to look and I was the only one left along with another guerrilla who had fought in Albania. We knew the war with machine guns, with rifles ... but we still hadn't taken the baptism with the artillery ... everyone else had fled, they thought we had been killed.[118]

Guerrillas would sing, swear and exchange insults in an effort to intimidate opponents and contain their fear. 'The bandits', noted the officer of a pro-German militia in a post-operation report,

> were pouring in on us ... they interrupted their fire from time to time, they called to our troops to surrender and arrest their officers, promising them that they bear no responsibility and that they will not be hurt, when they

saw that this led nowhere they started swearing against them and their officers, our units responded by firing and singing patriotic songs.[119]

Many guerrillas derived courage from alcohol, others would vomit or defecate, while a few felt nauseated during battle. ELAS guerrilla Giannis Voultepsis stated that 'I felt as if my soul was leaving my body'.[120] Among inexperienced units the loss of a single comrade was sufficient for a whole unit to lose its nerve. An EDES officer described the situation as follows: 'The men of my battalion had never taken part in a battle with Germans before, nor did they have the experience of the war in Albania, and now standing opposite a German battalion ... suffering a casualty or having one of our men injured sufficed ... to destroy their morale'.[121] Some officers used force to make their men stay in their positions. Antonis Lainakis, an ELAS officer, contained his panicked men by waving his sub-machine gun and threatening to shoot any man who tried to turn tail and run.[122] ELAS officers Giannis Kontakis and Dimitris Papas also had to threaten their men: 'The morale of the men became affected. Dimitris Papas and I tried to encourage them ... at the same time we made it clear that nobody was allowed to flee, and threatened that anyone who tried to do so would be shot on the spot by Papas.'[123]

Most guerrilla actions, particularly in the early period, were small-scale ambushes involving 30–40 men from each side. Guerrillas were usually armed with rifles and more rarely with machine guns, at least until late 1943, and it was only during early 1944 that the guerrillas attacked fortified positions or villages in numbers. They preferred to bring the battle to the enemy using hit-and-run tactics. Their success rested on their 'ability to ... move lightly and with little food ... to hide and strike again without thinking of fixed terms of defence', and sometimes this enabled them to achieve 'remarkable success at practically no cost to themselves',[124] since they were 'favoured by their knowledge of the ground, by their mobility ... [and] ... by the local support of the villagers'.[125] Some of the more impressive successes of the resistance, such as the battles of Oxineia, Fardikabos and Stavros, were won precisely because of the guerrillas' knowledge of terrain and peasant support.

However, mastering the art of guerrilla warfare was not easy. The guerrillas' disdain for military procedure and ignorance of guerrilla tactics during those early days led them to commit grave mistakes. Guerrilla bands would often wander into ambushes or camp next to Axis search parties; many units failed to post guards or send scouts to scan the area. Furthermore, very few men had any military experience. A report of the

3/40 ELAS regiment estimated that less than 30 per cent of the guerrillas who had enlisted in this unit up to December 1943 had served in the last war; the situation was similar and sometimes worse in other units.[126]

This lack of experience led to frequent debacles. A large ELAS party stationed in the village of Theologos in Euboea was put to flight by a small Italian detachment which chased the guerrillas out of the village where they were stationed and seized their supplies and equipment; 'thirty demoralised Italians ambushed us and we were not only unable to do what we should have done but we were unable to protect our equipment. After all this damage that was due to our military incompetence we sooth ourselves for having killed one Italian.'[127] This was a broader problem; the inexperience of many guerrilla leaders, their unwillingness to suffer casualties and the lack of training and 'poor knowledge' of weapons and tactics often led guerrillas to open fire too early and from too great a distance, thus blowing their cover during ambushes. Furthermore, the lack of coordination between the different bands seriously curtailed their capabilities.[128]

Operation Animals underlined both the abilities and the inadequacies of the guerrilla bands. Guerrilla bands scored impressive successes, the most important being the battle of Makrinoros. However, time and again inadequate training, lukewarm commanders and bad fire discipline led to mishaps. Edmund Myers, the head of the Allied Military Mission in Greece, noted a few weeks after the completion of the operation that

> I rely upon my British and American officers for being the spirit behind all future operations, not for the reasons that the Andartes have no spirit, but that their training is such that they are not reliable soldiers, particularly in a tight corner; when things are going right, their morale is right up in the clouds, but immediately things start going wrong it is extremely difficult to raise their morale.[129]

However, increased exposure endowed the guerrillas with a more professional and workmanlike attitude towards combat, which they viewed as a job that had to be carried out effectively and dispassionately. Little by little, men learned how to take cover, give first aid, and handle and maintain their equipment, and many men developed a fetishistic fascination with their weapons, naming them after their girlfriends or relatives. They also learned to approach enemy wounded with caution, as German soldiers often feigned injury so as to get away or take a final shot at the guerrillas.[130] Many were also increasingly attracted by combat. The feeling of pursuit, of being shot at and the sound of enemy guns all had an exhilarating effect on some guerrillas. Combat, according to one EDES resister, elevated and sharpened the senses and even facilitated a sense of rejuvenation that made a welcome contrast to the abject drudgery of non-combat duty:

> In a little while we hear machine guns, mortars, guns. This is the baptism of fire … They … attack during the whole day. After a while, one gets accustomed to the noise, and indeed shortly afterwards the whole affair becomes really enjoyable. It is a real game with fate and one's mood is really uplifted. Who will be the lucky one, who will die, who will live? I am in a terrific mood, I joke, I flirt, I eat, and I work … The next day the whole affair starts over. It is a game and it is really enjoyable.[131]

Others found an almost mystical fascination in combat. Faidon Maidonis was a dedicated patriot and a conscious anti-fascist. He noted in his diary: 'these chosen Hitlerite boys, they deserve a thousand times to go through knife, iron and fire'.[132] However, for Maidonis, death and killing also held a fascination unrelated to political ends. After attending the funeral of a fellow fighter, he wrote: 'It is so beautiful, so manly for someone to die so young, without having lived, without having as much enjoyed. There is so much beautiful sorrow in the loss of one so young.'[133] For Maidonis, combat held something unique that set it apart from the mundane pace of everyday life. It was a chance for men to 'overcome fate' and 'conquer death, conquer our destiny, conquer life'.[134] However, combat had other more mundane, but no less conspicuous, pleasures. One of its more appealing aspects was its nature, which facilitated personalised killing. Maidonis remarked that 'when you fire a cannon or a mortar you don't know if you have really made a kill. You cannot really taste the blood, the spirit, of the man you killed.'[135] Guerrilla warfare gave men the chance to enjoy all the sensations of close-quarters combat. Maidonis noted a few hours after an ambush:

> I was feeling that I was so drunk that I was not a part of this world any more. I was drunk with the sound of automatics, with the smell of gunpowder, with the flames that burst from the machine gun's barrel … The machine gun is the most exhilarating weapon. You enjoy using it, you feel that you are actually fighting; you hear the sound of Mars' iron armour thundering next to you.[136]

Some men developed an aesthetic fascination with the sights and sounds of combat. Explosions, the sound of machine-gun or artillery fire and the colours from a burning building created an almost surrealistic landscape that had an undeniable attraction: 'the strange juxtaposition of

A history of the Greek resistance

gruesome horror with natural beauty and alien landscapes contributed to a sensuous fascination with war'.[137] ELAS guerrilla Vasilis Papagiannis described an act of train sabotage in lyrical terms:

> A series of explosions spread from one carriage to another. It was a fascinating yet sad spectacle, something that we could never have imagined, or even seen in a film ... carriages exploding sky-high ... the colours from the explosive bullets ... burning pieces of iron falling from the sky ... Just like those red ribbons that girls use to tie their hair.[138]

Giannis Voultepsis described the sight of an exploding German ammunition depot as 'a grand spectacle'.[139] ELAS guerrilla Elias Kainourgios remarked that, during a railway sabotage, 'the whole area was alit, as if day had suddenly arrived amidst the darkness of the night. The sounds were deafening, and the carriage looked like a beast that was on fire. This was like watching one of those extravagant stage-shows actually unfolding in front of your very eyes.'[140] ELAS guerrilla Thanasis Nikas noted how gunfire and SOS flares during an ambush 'turned the whole affair ... into a spectacle that seemed as if it had been designed by some artist'.[141]

Although descriptions of pleasure and exhilaration are not uncommon, expressions of remorse are rare. Men often described participation in the resistance as a hardening process, which matured and strengthened them both physically and mentally. As Reid Mitchell noted in his study of masculinity during the American Civil War, hardening can be accompanied by a 'growing lack of reaction to suffering and death'.[142] Rodis Roufos argued pointedly in his autobiographical novel *To Hroniko mias stavroforias* [The chronicle of a crusade] that many men became very cynical following a stint in the resistance: '[a] feeling of callousness slowly but steadily eroded us'.[143] Guerrillas would become indifferent to the death around them, as one EDES guerrilla noted: 'during that time you pitied the bullet [you spent] and not the man you killed'.[144] Maidonis wrote in his diary:

> During the afternoon the German artillery pounded Mouzaka. Fortunately none of our boys was there; it's some other [unit] from a different area. I mean they're still ours, but less proximate ... We might mind them getting killed, but certainly it won't be as bad as having some of our boys killed. [So] here is what becomes of man. He becomes like a beast, he doesn't care about many things and he doesn't care about the fate of the many.[145]

These attitudes were reflected in a disregard for human life and rising levels of violence in which the foremost victims were civilians and prisoners. The killing of prisoners was very common. Often they would be murdered by men who wanted to avenge the death of a comrade or relative. EDES *oplarhigos* Spiros Karabinas, on learning of his brother's death, burst into the area where they were being kept and executed 11 Italian prisoners.[146] Sometimes enraged peasants who saw their houses and properties go up in flames would attack and lynch prisoners. Some of the more widespread killing of prisoners took place during the battle of Amphilohia, when ELAS decided to raid a building where a German detachment was stationed. Unbeknown to the guerrillas, another detachment had arrived in the town during the same day, and the Germans had scattered among several civilian homes. Subsequently, the raid descended into a series of gun fights, during which the guerrillas tried to dislodge the Germans from a number of separate residences. After a day of fighting and numerous casualties, the guerrillas managed to break into one of the main fortified houses they had been besieging. No prisoners were taken. Despite their pleas, the Germans were machine-gunned and finished off with knives. In the same action, an ELAS officer ordered the killing of several Greek gendarmes who had sided with the Germans and shot at wounded guerrillas and medics, despite their pledge of neutrality.[147]

However, it must be noted that the killing of prisoners was not just a spontaneous action, but was the official ELAS policy until the summer of 1944. An ELAS order dating from the summer of 1943 noted that guerrillas tended to treat the non-German auxiliaries better than regular soldiers. The order condemned such attitudes and stated

> the fate of every guerrilla that might fall into the hands of the Germans is well known to all of us – death by torture. Being more humane than them we'll repay them only with death. From receipt of the present order you will shoot on the spot every prisoner that you take after you've extracted any information that he might have.[148]

The number of killings would escalate further when operations took place against fellow Greeks or collaborationist militiamen. In the clashes between EDES and the Albanian Chams in Preveza and Thesprotia, neither side gave quarter; the wounded were finished off and prisoners were killed by both sides.[149] In the clashes between ELAS and EDES during the winter of 1943–44, ELAS proved particularly averse to taking prisoners. At least 14 EDES prisoners of war were executed by their ELAS captors in Lavdani. Two men were shot immediately after they surrendered, while a further 12 were transferred to the school of Lavdani where they were beaten to death with rifle butts by a group of ELAS guerrillas. Such attitudes were far from uncommon in the area, where local *kapetanios* like Fotis Kontopanos, aka Kapetan Annivas, were famous for their policy of taking no prisoners. During the same period Annivas's band ambushed and captured an EDES supply column and executed all 17 guerrilla-muleteers, whose bodies were thrown into the Kalamas river. On another occasion he personally executed six EDES prisoners in the village of Aetopetra.[150]

Such atrocities were by no means unique; EDES guerrillas executed 16 ELAS prisoners after the battle of Preveza in the autumn of 1944. According to one guerrilla present,

> the [ELAS] lads ... raised a white flag, and as an EDES lieutenant walked towards them, Sideris Kirlas drew his gun and he killed the lieutenant ... after this was done the guerrillas broke in, they tied them all up and made them dig their own graves in Pantokratoras and there they killed them ... this was not pre-planned, it was done for revenge, that's how things had turned out.[151]

Killing was even more widespread during clashes between collaborationist formations and left-wing guerrillas on the island of Euboea. After the village of Vathia fell to ELAS an orgy of killing ensued:

> last night the village was taken by storm ... when ELAS succeeded in breaking through the perimeter wire, many of the defenders scattered and took refuge in houses, which parties of ELAS then set on fire ... the andarte took no prisoners: wounded left behind ... were finished off, and more than one civilian from a burning house was killed at the same time as the soldier to whom he had given shelter.[152]

Prisoners were also casually mistreated. One SOE officer in Epirus noted that in the local EDES and ELAS prison camps, Italian soldiers 'were being beaten and robbed daily by their antarte guards, and were not getting their food'.[153] EDES prisoners in Zagori were made to carry their ELAS captors on their backs for miles.[154] Torture was equally prevalent. Gerasimos Maltezos, the leader of the 3/40 ELAS regiment, and several of his men who were arrested by EDES were 'robbed of any item they possessed, watches, money, pens, glasses even their uniforms ... afterwards Maltezos and his men were beaten mercilessly'. After this, the prisoners, still naked, 'were tied to the saddle horns of their captors and were dragged to all the area's villages where the assembled peasants jeered and spat at them'.[155] EDES officer Theodoros Harvalakis was subjected to similar treatment by his captors; after he was beaten and robbed he was stripped naked and had his beard and hair shaved off and was then paraded around the villages.[156] Such practices were common in Peloponnesus where even the corpses of nationalist militiaman were desecrated by ELAS men.[157] Axis prisoners did not fare any better; Dimitris Dimitriou noted that a group of his guerrillas saddled an Italian prisoner, hung a cow-bell round his neck and rode him like a donkey.[158] Prisoners were also robbed of money, rings, watches and clothes and molested by the guerrillas if they resisted. An ELAS military priest noted that

> I stumbled upon a group of … guerrillas who had seized a group of Italians and were stripping them of their possessions. Each of them stole whatever took his fancy; one would grab a watch, another one a coat … and so on … I pleaded with them, but who would listen. I was alone after all, and these savages would have no second thoughts about putting a bullet in my head.[159]

Some men even collected trophies such as ears, noses or heads, which were often exhibited publicly. When the ELAS guerrillas in Hanthi executed a local collaborator, Barba-Stavro, they proceeded to cut off his head and place it on a pike at the entrance to his village. Mutilation, both facial and genital, was common.[160] One such atrocity took place after an ambush by ELAS against a group of German soldiers near the village of Kleisoura on 5 April 1944. After neutralising the Germans' resistance and finishing off the wounded, the guerrillas proceeded to mutilate the bodies, cutting off the genitalia of all seven men and then placing them in their mouths.[161] A similar case occurred when a band of nationalists ambushed an ELAS band in eastern Macedonia: 'They killed them all … then they cut off the officers' heads and hung them from the branches of nearby trees. Then they cut off their genitals, and placed them in their mouths.'[162] In the district of Thesprotia in Epirus, EDES guerrillas mutilated the bodies of Italian soldiers and Albanian militiamen, stripping the corpses naked, mutilating them and cutting off their genitals.[163] Similar incidents had been recorded in a number of areas from the uplands of central Macedonia[164] to southern Peloponnesus where ELAS guerrillas and collaborationist militiamen engaged in trophy taking and the mutilation of their enemies' corpses.[165]

The identity of the men who committed these atrocities is not always clear. We do not know whether they were novices or hardened veterans, or if these actions were prompted by the loss of a friend or relative or simply by the enjoyment of violence. However, the callousness and ubiquity of these actions clearly underlines a shift in attitudes among the guerrillas. Irregular warfare was an unexpected and, in some ways, a shocking experience for the men. They soon discovered that life in the field differed significantly both from their previous experiences in the Albanian war and from the idealised narratives of guerrilla warfare that proliferated during the pre-war period. The guerrillas learned their trade in a harsh way, and many suffered personal loss as a result. Their endurance was challenged by the nature of the war, the tribulations that they underwent and the often primitive conditions in which guerrilla warfare was waged. Simultaneously, these experiences bred a rough, homosocial culture that celebrated violence and demeaned civilians as unmanly and undeserving.

It would be unwise to describe the experiences of guerrillas as a long descent into brutalisation. Participation in the resistance also broadened their horizons by affording the opportunity to escape a narrow, hierarchical environment, encounter new vistas, and gain exposure to new ideas and political and cultural activities that often had a great impact on them. Nonetheless, there was a darker aspect to this experience. The hardship they endured, and the nature of guerrilla combat, had a hardening effect on many, as exemplified in the guerrillas' treatment of prisoners and civilians. Such tendencies became increasingly prominent as the occupation and war dragged on, creating an unbridgeable rift between the guerrillas and the people in whose name they fought.

Notes

1 Hatzinikolaou, *Taragmena hronia*, p. 38.
2 IWM/Report by Major KF Scott MC, RE Officer No1 area, Cairo December 1944, p. 8.
3 Hatzinikolaou, *Taragmena hronia*, p. 39.
4 Hatzinikolaou, *Taragmena hronia*, p. 55
5 Hatzinikolaou, *Taragmena hronia*, p. 39.
6 ELIA/APME/Evangelakos Giorgos.
7 Antones Sanoudakes, Athanasios Psaroulakis and Giorgis Dafermos, *Ta limeria tou ELAS* [The hideouts of ELAS] (Athens: Knossos, 1993), pp. 54–5.
8 ELIA/AER/File 22/katathesis Vasileiou Arvanite/23/08/44.
9 Panagiotis Aberiadis, *Mia prosfigiki oikogeneia sta oreina tis Kavalas 1922– 1952* [A refugee family in the highland of Kavala 1922–1952] (Kavala: ILAK, 2005), p. 199
10 Papananos, *To Anti-iroiko imerologio*, p. 77.
11 IAM/Box 140/ ELAS/X Merarhia/16 sintagma pezikou/sinoptiki istoria sintagmatos, pp. 1–3.
12 Keith Brown, *Loyal unto Death: Trust and Terror in Revolutionary*

Macedonia (Bloomington, IN: Indian University Press, 2013), pp. 70–5.
13 GAKKI/Small Collections/Box 116/K.D. Giannoulis, diary, p. 9.
14 Georgios Katsikas, *Agones kai thisies* [Struggles and sacrifices] (Athens: self-published, 1990), p. 27.
15 ELIA/GDA/Martiries Agoniston/Fakelos 13/Ipofakelos 2/Martiria Noti Mastrogianni.
16 ELIA/APME/Zahos Kostas.
17 Papananos, *To Anti-iroiko imerologio*, p. 74.
18 Giorgos Dimitriou, personal interview.
19 Hatzinikolaou, *Taragmena hronia*, p. 49.
20 Hatzinikolaou, *Taragmena hronia*, p. 50.
21 Arseniou, *I Thessalia*, pp. 120–1.
22 Kostantinos Tsipis, personal interview.
23 Romanos, *Mia Athinaiki vengera*, p. 49.
24 Dimitriou, *Antartis*, vol. 3, p. 265.
25 Rodis Roufos, *To hroniko mias Stavroforias* [The chronicle of a crusade] (Athens: Okeanida, 2004), p. 279.
26 Romanos, *Mia Athinaiki vengera*, p. 76.
27 Alexandros Zaousis, *Anamniseis enos anti-iroa* [Recollections of an anti-hero] (Athens: Estia, 1980), p. 212.
28 Sotiris Tsabiras, *As min vrexei pote* [Let rain never fall] (Athens: Elliniki Evroekdotiki, 2005), p. 64.
29 Papananos, *To Anti-iroiko imerologio*, p. 141.
30 Papagiannis, *Kravges tis mnimes*, p. 283.
31 Giannis Beratis, *Odoiporiko tou 43* [A chronicle of 43] (Athens: Ermis, 2000), p. 29.
32 Vasilis Dokopoulos, personal interview
33 Thanasis Mitsopoulos, *To Trianta Sintagma tou ELAS* [The 30th regiment of ELAS] (Athens: self-published, 1987), p. 254.
34 Arseniou, *I Thessalia*, p. 164.
35 Anton Blok, 'Rams and billy-goats: a key to the Mediterranean code of honour', *Man* 16 (1981), p. 433.
36 Stergios Valioulis, *Politis B katigorias* [A second-rate citizen] (Thessaloniki: Ellinikes Ekdoseis, 1985), p. 324.
37 Dimitris Bouzoukas, 'Anamniseis apo ton ELAS' [Recollections from ELAS], *Ethniki Adistasi* 34 (1983), p. 38.
38 ELIA/OTA/Ioannis Papazisis.
39 Dimitriou, *Antartis*, vol. 3, pp. 62, 77.
40 Skopouli, *Sta aposkia tis istorias*, p. 149.
41 Vasilis Dokopoulos, personal interview.
42 Vasilis Dokopoulos, personal interview.
43 ASKI/AKKE/ Box 493/File-30/1/58/1943.

44 Dimitris Soutzos, 'O Pothos tou Antarti' [The guerrilla's longing], *Istoriko Arheio Ethnikis Antistasis* 12 (1959), p. 17.
45 Tsabiras, *As min vrexei pote*, p. 150.
46 ELIA press archive/Miniaio Deltio/01/02/1943.
47 Baerentzen (ed.), *British Reports on Greece*, p. 82.
48 Douatzis, *Imerologio*, p. 278.
49 Douatzis, *Imerologio*, p. 279.
50 Douatzis, *Imerologio*, p. 363.
51 ELIA/OTA/Sotoris and Agni Matsika interview.
52 Thanasis Trigas, *To Arhigeio Lokridas tou II/42 Tagma tou ELAS stin Karia* [The headquarters of the ELAS II/42 battalion in Karia] (Karia: self-published, 2007), pp. 33–4.
53 ASKI/AKKE/Box 412/File-23/5/202.
54 Kosta Vlahou, *I antistasi stin Lakka Souli 1943-1944* [The resistance in Lakka Souli 1943-1944], unpublished, Zosimaia Library Ioannina, p. 21.
55 DIS/KMA/File 468-572/15 sidagma/21/5/44/diatagi tis 8is merarhias peri siberiforas antarton/(08/05/44).
56 ASKI/AKKE/Box 429/File-26/4/13.
57 Kosta Karagiorgou, *I Roumeli stis floges, Elliniki ethniki antistasi 1941-1944* [Roumeli in flames, the Greek national resistance 1941–1944] (Athens: self-published, 1979), pp. 72–3.
58 Gerasimos Maltezos, *EAM-ELAS, anamniseis kai zitimata stratigikis kai taktikis* [EAM-ELAS, memories and questions of tactics and strategy] (Volos: self-published, 1987), p. 149.
59 Ioannis Ladas, *Anamniseis apo tin ethniki antistasi kai tin katastoli tis kommounistikis antarsias* [Memories from the national resistance and the subduing of the communist rebellion] (Athens: Hilektron, 2006) p. 333.
60 Moutoulas, 'To EAM stin Ileia', p. 181.
61 Maltezos, *EAM-ELAS*, p. 150.
62 G. Bouratzis,'To antartiko kinima Ileia Peloponnisou 1943–1944' [The guerrilla movement in Ileia Peloponnesus], *Istoriko Arheio Ethnikis Antistasis* 13 (1959), p. 71.
63 Andrea Moraitis, 'I epimeliteia tou antarti' [The guerrilla logistics corps], *Istoriko Arheio Ethnikis Antistasis* 3 (1958), pp. 14–15.
64 ASKI/AKKE/Box 493/File-30/1/70.
65 ASKI/AKKE/Box 493/File-30/1/74.
66 Andrea Moraitis, 'I epimeliteia tou antarti' [The guerrilla logistics corps], *Istoriko Arheio Ethnikis Antistasis* 4 (1958), pp. 54–61.
67 Nikos Paikos, 'Megales ekatharistikes epixiriseis tou exthrou tin anoixi tou 1944' [Major anti-guerrilla operations in the spring of 1944], *Ethniki Antistasi* 42 (1984), p. 105.
68 Romanos, *Mia Athinaiki vengera*, p. 68.

69 Michael Ward, *Greek Assignments: SOE 1943–1948 UNSCOB* (Athens: Lycabettus Press, 1992), p. 74.
70 Ward, *Greek Assignments*, pp. 72–3.
71 Faidon Maidonis, 'To Imerologio tou Fiadona Maidoni (24.6–10.9.1944)' [The diary of Faidon Maidonis], *Mnimon* 9 (1984), p. 100.
72 DIS/File 922/ST/1b/24-2-1944/54 Sintagma pezikou, p. 3.
73 TNA/HS5/697/General Report of Capt I.D. Ross, p. 3.
74 TNA/HS5/701/Report on Kaimaxala by Major T.C. Johnson, p. 26.
75 DIS/File 922/ST/1b/24-2-1944/54 Sintagma pezikou, pp. 3–4.
76 LHCMA/The Papers of Major Patrick Hutchinson Evans/2/1/7 in 2/1/Post-operation Report, p. 16.
77 DIS/KMA/File 468-572/8 merarhia/ekthesis epitheoriseon/16/5/44.
78 TNA/HS5/695/Capt. J.H. Childs/Report on my stay in Greece – May 1943–April 1944, p. 9.
79 TNA/HS5/697/Capt. J.A. Peters RAMC/Activities in Greece from Oct 14th to Dec 17th, p. 9.
80 LHCMA/Woodhouse/5/1/1/ in 2/7-9, 3,4 & 5/1/1/History, p. 73.
81 Papananos, *To Anti-iroiko imerologio*, p. 72.
82 Papananos, *To Anti-iroiko imerologio*, pp. 108–10.
83 Maidonis, 'To Imerologio', p. 85.
84 LHCMA/Woodhouse/2/7-9, 3, 4 & 5/1/1/History, p. 23.
85 TNA/ HS5/701/Report on Kaimaxala by Major T.C. Johnson, p. 25.
86 TNA/HS5/694/History of ELAS OCTU, p. 15; Mitsopoulos, *Anamniseis agoniston*, pp. 19, 105; Hatzinikolaou, *Taragmena hronia*, p. 38.
87 Giorgos Konstas, 'I Zoi mou sto antartiko' [My life with the guerrillas], *Ethniki Antistasi* 15 (1978), pp. 29–31.
88 Papananos, *To Anti-iroiko imerologio*, p. 141.
89 IWM/Micklethwait Guy/Interview.
90 DIS/KMA/File/1/702-844/8 merarhia/10/08/44/Diatagi GA peri oikogeneion antarton/2/8/44.
91 ELIA/AER/File IE/I Taxiarhia/12o sintagma/arith.pro 694/16/3/44/EAM and KKE.
92 LHCMA/Dobrski/34/29-35, Letter to Adv Force 133 (HQ) Att HQ LF and MC(O) CMF; LHCMA/Dobrski/ 34/29-35/Letter from J. Mulgan Lt Col. Cond. Adv. Force 133 to Welfare officer HQ Force 133 MEF dated 18th of February, 1945; IWM/10514/The Papers of J.E. Lawson, The Second World War memoirs of Captain J.E. Lawson, p. 160.
93 Valioulis, *Politis*, p. 348.
94 GAK Digital Archives/ http://arxeiomnimon.gak.gr/browse/resource.html?tab=tab02&id=206315 (accessed 5 January 2015); Ioannes Bougas, *Matomenes mnimes 1940–1945* [Bloodstained memories 1940–1945] (Athens: Pelasgos, 2009), pp. 204–5, 232.
95 Papananos, *To Anti-iroiko imerologio*, p. 86.

96 Papananos, *To Anti-iroiko imerologio*, p. 103.
97 Papananos, *To Anti-iroiko imerologio*, p. 80.
98 IWM/Ward/13345/Report on visit to Greece, p. 5.
99 David Grossman, *On Killing* (New York: Little, Brown, 1996), p. 3.
100 Grossman, *On Killing*, p. 28.
101 Bourke, *An Intimate History of Killing*, ch. 1.
102 Stephen Fritz, *Frontsoldaten – The German Soldier in World War II* (Lexington, KY: University of Kentucky Press, 1997), p. 1.
103 TNA/HS 5/697/Cpl. S. Morgan/General Report/p. 1.
104 ASKI Digital Archives/http://62.103.28.111/neolaia/rec.asp?id=53865 (accessed 5 January 2015).
105 Papananos, *To anti-iroiko*, p. 69.
106 Peter Singer, *Children at War* (Berkeley: University of California Press, 2006), pp. 70–6.
107 Denys Hamson, *We Fell among Greeks* (London: Jonathan Cape, 1946), pp. 124–5 n. 3; GAK/AET/Apostoli A/File 3/Ekthesis tis en ti elefthera oreini Ellada kratousis katastaseos mehri telos Noemvriou os kai ep auti kriseis ipilarhou S.D/11, p. 5.
108 GAKKI/AET/Apostoli A/File 2/9
109 Priovolos, *Mia alisida mnimes*, p. 59.
110 Beratis, *Odoiporiko tou 43*, pp. 51–3.
111 Romanos, *Mia Athinaiki vengera*, p. 66.
112 Maidonis, 'To Imerologio', p. 92.
113 Blok, 'Rams and billy-goats', p. 432.
114 John K. Campbell, *Honour, Family and Patronage: A Study of Institutions and Moral Values in a Greek Mountain Community* (Oxford: Oxford University Press, 1974), p. 318.
115 ELIA/APME/Stelios Giatroudakis.
116 Vasilis Patsis, *Sta ori ta Thesprotika* [In the Thesprotika mountains] (Athens: self-published, 2009), pp. 71–2.
117 Kossevakis, *I Triti alitheia*, p. 163.
118 Vasilis Dokopoulos, personal interview.
119 ELIA/GDA /File 6.1/Giorgou Tsirini tagmatarhou tagmaton asfaleias Eubeoeas/Ekthesi Drasis kata tou ELAS Eubeoas, p. 19.
120 Giannis Voultepsis, *Sinagonistis Akelas* [Fellow comrade Akelas] (Athens: Alkion, 1997), p. 121
121 Patsis, *Sta ori ta Thesprotika*, pp. 28–9.
122 Antonis Lainakis, *Anamniseis apo tin ethniki antistasi* [Recollections from the national resistance] (Chania: self-published, 1984), p. 119.
123 Giannis Kodakis, 'Mahi Marathiti Fortetsas' [The Battle of Marathitis Fortetsa], *Ethniki Antistasi* 71 (1991), p. 35.
124 LHCMA/Lingen Papers/1 in 1/Appreciation of situation, p. 1.
125 Barentzen (ed.), *British Reports on Greece*, p. 17.

126 DIS/AND/File 2/Ekthesi pros ton kathodigitiko pirina tou kommatos tis 8hs merarhias/20/12/43.
127 Douatzis, *Imerologio*, p. 319.
128 TNA/HS 5/696/Sgt Hotchkiss, M/General Report Epirus/9 Jan 1945, p. 1.
129 LHCMA/Myers Papers/1/3/23 in Myers 1/3/Greece and the Greeks of Today, pp. 13–14.
130 ELIA/GDA /File 13.2/Daktilografimenes martiries agoniston
131 Romanos, *Mia Athinaiki vengera*, p. 180.
132 Maidonis, 'To Imerologio', p. 77.
133 Maidonis, 'To Imerologio', p. 67.
134 Maidonis, 'To Imerologio', p. 67.
135 Maidonis, 'To Imerologio', p. 148.
136 Maidonis, 'To Imerologio', pp. 142, 144.
137 Fritz, *Frontsoldaten*, p. 123.
138 Papagiannis, *Kravges tis mnimes*, p. 286.
139 Voultepsis, *Sinagonistis*, p. 189.
140 Elias Kainourgios, 'To Sabotaz sto stathmo Dadiou kai tin Palavitsa' [The sabotage at the station of Dadi and Palavitsa], *Ethniki Antistasi* 71 (1991), p. 77.
141 Thanasis Nikas, 'I mahi ston Ahladokabo Argolidas' [The battle of Ahladokabos Argolidas], *Ethniki Antistasi* 71 (1991), p. 50.
142 Reid Mitchell, *The Vacant Chair: The Northern Soldier Leaves Home* (New York and Oxford: Oxford University Press, 1993), p. 10.
143 Roufos, *To hroniko*, p. 447.
144 Ioannis Naskas, personal interview.
145 Maidonis, 'To Imerologio', p. 87.
146 Stylianos Houtas, *I ethniki antistasi ton Ellinon* [The Greek national resistance] (Athens: self-published, 1961), p. 74.
147 Themis Moshatos, *I mahi tis Amphilohias* [The battle of Amphilohia] (Athens: self-published, 1986), p. 64
148 ASKI/AKKE/Box 493/File-30/1/81.
149 ELIA/APME/Gerasimos Priftis interview; Thomas Karakitsos, personal interview, Paramithia, 2008.
150 Kostoulas, *Katohikes istories*, pp. 201–5.
151 Giorgos Dimitriou, personal interview.
152 TNA/HS5/694/Report by R.P. Griffin on work with mission Chatham 25/9/44–18/1/44, pp. 9–10.
153 TNA/HS 5/697Lt A.C. McCloy, R.A/22/1/45, p. 5.
154 Nikolaidis, *Ta hronia*, p. 50.
155 Apostolos Papakostas, memoir, unpublished, Skoufas Library Arta, p. 384.
156 Tsabiras, *As min vrexei pote*, p. 61.
157 Anna Stamatopoulou, *Feneos 1944, I gi tis odinis* [Feneos 1944, the land of suffering] (Athens: Pelasgos, 2010), p. 33.

158 Dimitriou, *Antartis*, vol. 2, p. 135.
159 Germanos Dimakos, *Sto vouno me to stavro konta ston Are* [In the mountain with the cross fighting next to Ares] (Trikala: Protipes Thessalikes Ekdoseis, 2004), p. 211.
160 Htzinikolaou, *Targamena hronia*, p. 57.
161 Stratos Dordanas, 'Antipoina ton Germanikon arhon katohis sti Makedonia 1941–1944' [Reprisals by the German occupation authorities in Macedonia], PhD thesis, University of Thessaloniki, 2002, pp. 560–1.
162 Hatzinikolaou, *Taragmena hronia*, p. 63.
163 ELIA/APME/Gerasimos Priftis interview.
164 Dordanas, 'Antipoina ton Germanikon arhon', p. 465.
165 Bougas, *Matomenes mnimes*, pp. 363, 407.

4

Cause, comrades and faith: morale in the guerrilla armies

Takis Kapralos had served for less than a month in EDES when he wrote to his family to inform them that he was doing well and adapting quickly. His first impressions of the guerrillas were good; he found them amicable and noted that 'morale was excellent', even though 'the majority of men have no consciousness … by that I mean they do not really know why they fight, you do understand that we have an enormous task ahead of us and currently we try to address the ideological shortcomings of the struggle with the help of articles and talks'.[1] Kapralos was not the first person to observe this paradox. ELAS commissar Dimitris Kremmos commented in early 1943: 'I have noticed that there are very many guerrillas who do not even know why they took up arms',[2] an assertion that was repeated a year later in a report to the GHQ of the ELAS 8th division, which noted 'the men's morale is excellent … however their level of [political] education is very low … we have almost no political cadres'.[3]

Guerrillas have been described during both the occupation and the post-war period as political soldiers who were inspired to fight and risk death as a result of their allegiance to a specific ideology; however, the quoted statements suggest that some men demonstrated little understanding of or interest in politics and hint that motivation may have come from other sources. Ideology was, of course, far from irrelevant. Guerrilla groups made persistent efforts to impart their beliefs, and it seems that some guerrillas, especially poor rural youths, developed an almost messianic faith in the cause of their organisations. However, indoctrination was seldom an easy task; many units lacked the necessary material and cadres for this task while guerrillas were often reluctant or indifferent towards such efforts. Even the most fervent believers were not immune to the rigours of war, and while political beliefs might have played an important part in shaping the men's perception of their task, ideology alone could not help them deal with the exertions of campaigning or the loss of comrades.

So, for what did men fight? Guerrilla testimonies point to a series of factors: primary group loyalty, fear of punishment, ideas of honour and religion among others. Guerrilla groups were often composed of men who had known each other in civilian life and sometimes even shared kinship ties. These connections helped to endow the guerrilla groups with an often surprising degree of cohesiveness that was further bolstered by shared experiences of hardship and loss. Primary group ties were also carefully cultivated by the guerrilla organisations, which were keenly aware of their importance. However, such ties were a double-edged sword as group loyalties often undermined the guerrillas' loyalty to the organisation and encouraged indiscipline and corruption. Such problems were exacerbated as the resistance groups expanded, leading the People's Armies to adopt increasingly stringent measures. This was especially true following the catastrophic winter of 1943–44, during which EDES was almost destroyed and ELAS suffered badly in a series of bloody engagements both with the opposing guerrilla group and with the German army.

Guerrilla groups responded with a radical reform of their structures and disciplinary approach; they reintroduced military-style discipline, made increased use of the death penalty and restored a series of privileges to the officers, in the hope of limiting the autonomy of the guerrilla bands. These reforms managed to curb indiscipline but ultimately undermined the combat performance of the People's Armies as they weakened the nucleus of the guerrilla fighting machine – the primary group. The outbreak of the civil war had an equally detrimental effect on morale. It led many guerrillas to believe that the resistance had strayed from its intended goal of national liberation and political reform and reverted to a naked power struggle. So, why did the guerrillas persist? Fear was a powerful motivator, as were group ties that might have weakened but were far from diminished. Moreover, at the same time that the pace and nature of war changed, guerrillas found new ways to cope with this situation; many turned to religion and developed elaborate ritualistic practices and beliefs that helped them cope with the situation and reassert a degree of control over a frightening and chaotic world.

Faith will inspire sacrifice: the scope and limits of political ideology

In mid-1943 the ELAS GHQ commissioned a small booklet titled *O Antartis tou EAM–ELAS* [The EAM/ELAS guerrilla]. The booklet's purpose was to serve as a how-to guide for aspiring guerrilla commanders. It contained sections on various issues: tactics, relations with civilians, command and finally morale, which took up the largest part of the publication. The pamphlet noted that ELAS started with a disadvantage since it lacked the means to wage warfare against a better equipped and highly trained rival. However, this imbalance mattered little since, according to the author, the key to victory was neither numerical superiority nor materiel but ideological fervour and determination. As long as the guerrillas possessed these two, they could overcome any obstacle:

> the human factor had never ceased to play a foremost role in warfare … this is even truer in guerrilla warfare … the men who choose to become guerrillas must have several traits: experience, courage, manliness, perception, willpower and above all they must know what are they fighting for … the guerrilla must be bristling with enthusiasm, quiver with faith for the holiness of our struggle, the human material of guerrilla warfare must be fanatical.[4]

This fanaticism would be inspired by consistent and careful political indoctrination. 'Political education is necessary' to inspire 'faith that will lead to self-sacrifice … each and every fighter must understand the reasons for which he fights'.[5]

Ideology would not only strengthen morale but would eventually render obsolete the methods used by the army to inculcate discipline and build morale. Many EAM cadres viewed the pre-war army as an instrument of oppression whose reactionary nature forced it to rely on fear and coercion to induce the demoralised soldier to fight; 'the nature of the old army led it to rely on blind discipline', noted a leading EAM cadre, who continued: 'the military hierarchy was a machine that oppressed and degraded any sense of human decency'. The soldiers were only looking forward 'to leaving the hell that the army was'. In contrast to the pre-war army, ELAS was envisioned as 'an instrument of the people', an egalitarian force where relations between the ranks would be based on camaraderie rather than deference and soldiers would fight out of conviction or 'conscious discipline'.[6] EAM and ELAS cadres believed that ideology would not only render training and conventional discipline useless, but would inculcate a spirit of sacrifice and fanaticism that would allow ELAS to overcome any obstacle. As a guerrilla-journalist noted, 'those who follow conscious discipline will say ... do what you wish with me, take my whole being and devote it to the cause of the people, I am ready to sacrifice my life whenever our struggle demands it'.[7] EDES did not prioritise political indoctrination until mid-1943. This negligence was due to the absence of educated cadres and the regular army background of its founder. However, the increased influx of educated officers and middle-class cadres from mid-1943, alongside the increased antagonism between ELAS and EDES, convinced the latter's leadership of the need for 'counter-propaganda' and led to the reversal of this situation.[8]

However, the ELAS leadership was aware of the limits of this military Stakhanovism. Furthermore, while cadres, like the author of the pamphlet, believed that the peasants' heroism and willpower would allow ELAS to overcome all obstacles, they were also keenly aware of the shortcomings of the recruits and the dire need for education. One ELAS officer noted that 'there are very few intellectuals among us ... our human material is pure but their level of education is deplorable'.[9] The resistance took several approaches to education. Guerrillas were prompted to publish weekly or monthly newspapers and create mobile libraries comprising rudimentary Marxist texts and other 'progressive' material. In central Greece, the reading material constituted mostly Soviet tracts, such as the works of Ilya Ehrenburg; *The Fall of Paris* was a particular favourite, along with a book on the Life of Soviet Women, which was published in 1942 in the Soviet Union and 'comprised ten short stories that exalted the actions of the Soviet woman and also discussed the atrocities perpetrated by the Germans in the countryside'. Furthermore, the more educated guerrillas were encouraged to write short stories for publication in clandestine newspapers.[10]

The press was the foremost instrument for the dissemination of propaganda and education. Several ELAS units began to publish newspapers from early 1943 onwards, and by the autumn of 1943 there was hardly a regiment that did not publish a newspaper. Moreover, the Party press of KKE and the various publications of EAM were widely circulated. EDES units also began to publish newspapers of which there were at least ten by early 1944. However, with a few exceptions, the guerrilla press scorned political analysis and focused instead on four issues: news of the war in Europe; short stories and chronicles about the guerrillas' everyday lives; reprints of the decisions of the GHQ of the guerrilla organisations and their political branches; and eulogies. The purpose of this material was not so much to educate the guerrillas ideologically, but rather to help them identify with the organisation and their comrades on an emotional level; 'the press', noted an ELAS circular, 'must be a mirror where each band and each member of EPON will recognise himself and learn how his brothers fight and die'.[11]

Short stories and chronicles conveyed an idealised image of the peasantry and their relationship with the guerrillas. In these narratives, peasants appeared selfless and enthusiastic; they hosted the guerrillas eagerly, shared their meagre food with them and some even declared in a frenzy of enthusiasm that they offered all their belongings to the struggle. According to one such chronicle, a rich farmer in the village of Kosmati in Grevena pledged all his belonging 'to the struggle' after his first encounters with a local ELAS band, an act that convinced the rest of his fellow villagers to follow his example and promise 'everything for the struggle'.[12] Another article in a publication of the ELAS 9th division saw a village headman address the ELAS men as 'heroic guerrillas, guardians of the people's interest' and thank them for pulling the peasantry out of the 'darkness of ignorance the old society had kept us in'.[13] Such representations made the guerrillas feel appreciated and respected and helped convince those who had encountered mostly hostile peasants that their efforts were appreciated and the peasantry supported them.

Furthermore, there was an abundance of combat narratives and tales of atrocities. An article entitled 'Primitive Huns with modern weapons' recalled a raid during which the German soldiers 'entered the church and used the baptismal font to wash their clothes, used the icons as firewood to cook [and] one of the Hitlerites shot at Christ's icon shouting Christ is a communist and it is these people who decided to civilize Europe these cannibal scum'. Such representations might have shocked EDES followers like Kapralos, who believed ELAS to be a radically anti-religious movement; however, the very notion that communism was little different to Christianity, as expressed in the above article, highlights the attention paid by ELAS to the religious feeling of the guerrillas. Religious imagery and themes abounded in ELAS and EDES propaganda. The same article used apocalyptic tones to call on the guerrillas to 'avenge those who have been martyred for freedom, the beast is thirsty and as the days of his power run out he craves more blood. Endless numbers of patriots are sacrificed every day. The martyrs cry for revenge.'[14] The rhetoric and imagery of martyrdom were adopted by both sides and some ecclesiastics such as the Bishop of Kozani, a prominent EAM supporter, urged the EAM/ELAS authorities to commission and circulate a martyrology of ELAS supporters.[15] The purpose of such representations was not just to rally the faithful – rural Greeks were highly religious and both resistance organisations sought to present themselves as defenders of the faith, enrolling large numbers of clerics to their ranks – but also to associate death in combat with Christian martyrdom and to equate the enemy soldiers with the antichrist so as to endow service in the resistance with a higher meaning and purpose.

Images of martyrdom pervaded guerrilla narratives. The association between death in combat and Christian martyrdom was particularly common in short stories, poems and chronicles, where fallen comrades were described as 'bloody offerings to freedom and the people's rule'.[16] Such narratives helped attach a positive meaning to loss, since death not only offered redemption to the guerrilla-martyr, but also served a higher purpose – the salvation of the nation and the regeneration of Greece. A guerrilla poet wrote that death in combat 'nourished the roots of the new just world and gave meaning and worth to our lives'.[17] Simultaneously, such representations endowed new guerrillas with a sense of purpose by tasking them with avenging the deaths of their comrades. Fallen guerrillas attained the properties of Christian saints; they were the protectors of their living comrades and guardians of the cause and the fatherland that was 'sanctified' by their sacrifice.[18] These representations served to polarise the differences between 'us' and 'them', by reframing the resistance war as an apocalyptic struggle between good and evil. The Italian, and later the German, troops were portrayed as an almost demonic force, 'the insatiable beast',[19] according to an EDES guerrilla poet. In an article titled 'Two worlds, fighters and traitors', a guerrilla journalist argued that the resistance war was not a simple political conflict; rather, it was a struggle to the death between the 'rot, the profane, the more foul segment of … society, the world of dishonour and betrayal … [and] the world of honour and sacrifice that is headed by the guerrillas of ELAS'. In this Manichean struggle, the article continued, there could be 'neither neutrality nor compromise … death to the German hordes, death to the traitors'.[20]

Often the guerrilla organisations held commemoration ceremonies to honour fallen comrades and civilians who died during combat or were shot in reprisals for guerrilla actions. Such ceremonies were frequently followed by athletic exhibitions and amateur plays performed by the guerrillas. These often elicited powerful emotional responses from the participants. One ceremony held in the village of Tohova in western Macedonia where 13 locals were shot, including a leading Communist Party cadre, concluded in the village's cemetery where the leader of the

ELAS detachment 'gave a brief speech while standing by the grave of three brothers who were shot by the Germans ... their father, who stood next to us, asked us with tears in his eyes to avenge his sons, their mother also cried while she repeated the same words'.[21]

These rituals and representations played an important role in fostering group and organisation loyalties, since they not only provided a link between new and old group members, but also provided new cadres with a conduct guide and role models. However, they were not the only activities aimed at the guerrillas. ELAS groups organised lectures and courses, which were delivered by commissars and Party functionaries. The 30th regiment organised a

> rigorous programme of lectures and courses, which were delivered in their headquarters ... attendance was compulsory, only the seriously ill and those assigned guard and combat duties were exempted. We taught a variety of political and military courses; our main goal was to enlighten our men with regard to political and ideological matters, and thus properly prepare them for war.[22]

The 1/38 regiment had an equally active programme: 'in the preceding period we have delivered various courses: on the programme of ELAS-EPON, on the latest events, with regard to the war, with regard to fascism'. Some indicative lecture topics were 'Fascism and the youth', 'National popular struggle and internal struggle', 'The People's Army', 'Why is the Red Army victorious', 'The people's rule', and 'The [18]21 struggle and the contemporary struggle'.[23] A significant amount of time was devoted to reading and analysing the press. Every group was divided into two subgroups led by the more educated guerrillas. After the reading was completed the commissar answered the guerrillas' questions. Tongue-tied guerrillas were given separate assignments and were allocated a specific issue to present to their fellow fighters. Such activities were equally important to EDES. Political education classes were held four times a week for half an hour, under the supervision of the platoon commanders. The weekly programme for the 3/40 regiment included 'a history of the creation of national bands of EDES', 'the contribution of the national bands towards the assurance of the people's rule',' the freedom of the individual and the improvement of the working people's position', 'Italian aspirations and the reactions towards the completion of our national ideal (north Epirus, the Dodecanese issues, the Heptanisa)', 'the 1923 incident at Corfu', 'the Macedonian question', 'Bulgarian brutalities in Macedonia and Thrace', 'German policies towards Greece' and

A history of the Greek resistance

'the contribution of British policy during the previous struggles of liberation and the current one'.[24]

Lectures and reading groups were not the only methods used by the resistance to disseminate its ideology. Songs and plays were equally important and often more popular. Singing was a significant part of guerrilla life; based on Soviet melodies and pre-war Greek tunes, the songs were usually scripted by the more literate guerrillas. Upon enlisting, a guerrilla learned the songs from his comrades and commissar. There were various types of song. Some would refer to a particular battle; one popular song described the guerrillas' actions and celebrated the killing of the 'German dogs'.[25] Many songs referred to the post-war period, professing an almost apocalyptic faith that a new world would emerge after the war, thus justifying the guerrillas' sacrifices. The song *Anemoi Thieles* [Winds and storms] declared:

> Winds and storms rage against us/ the sons of darkness are pursuing us/ we are engaged in the final battle/ and an unknown fate awaits us/ the workers are starving, they are dying in front of us/ how long, brothers, will we have to accept this/ young heroes, don't be frightened by the gallows and the punishments/ we will hold high the banner/ always with pride, we'll always go forth/ sometimes faltering but always prevailing/ we redeem the enslaved nations and peoples.[26]

The guerrillas were the deliverers who intended to establish a utopia, 'a new world, a world of dreams', in which 'the whole world would live like brothers'.[27] EDES songs also declared their faith in 'a greater Greece' that would expand beyond the national frontiers and 'bring to the people a new life, a life that is just and happy'.[28] These songs had multiple functions. By presenting an idealised image of the future world for which the guerrillas fought, they provided a sense of mission and a rationale that justified their sacrifices; thus, they made more bearable and meaningful the loss of life and extreme hardships endured by the men. At the same time, the repetitive recitation of slogans and catchphrases acquainted the men with the spirit and aims of the resistance groups, educating them about their goals at a basic but effective level. As John Lynn notes in his study of the French Revolutionary armies, 'as a medium of political education in the army, songs enjoyed special advantages ... catch phrases and slogans became indelibly printed on men's minds, not just on torn paper', and served to propagate 'patriotic idealism within the army'.[29] Finally, the narratives of battle sacrifice, and the continuous celebration and appraisal of the guerrilla's prowess which placed him a cut above the rest of the population, served to create a shared consciousness, a sense of belonging to a micro-society of men with their own myths, standards of conduct and virtues. This helped the new recruits acclimatise to the guerrilla way of life.

Nonetheless, the shape of the future world proclaimed in countless guerrilla songs was often unclear in the narratives of both ELAS and EDES. ELAS was particularly careful to distance itself from the practices of the Yugoslav and Albanian partisan movements, which proclaimed openly their purpose of building a socialist state after the war. Left-wing imagery was used widely and the Soviet Union was habitually praised in ELAS songs and publications; however, ELAS stopped short of using terms such as 'socialism' and 'communism' to describe the regime it aimed to establish, preferring instead to use the term *laokratia*, people's rule. Mark Mazower argued that *laokratia* was used to denote a type of populist 'radical democracy' and claimed that

> ELAS stood not for Bolshevik rule but for the emancipation of the *chorio* [the village] from domination by the 'political world' of the capital ... they linked this to a language of independence that described the country's traditional elite as the lackeys of an international plutocracy and demanded Greece's liberation from the shackles of 'British capital'.[30]

Nonetheless, the meaning of *laokratia* varied widely in ELAS publications and it is clear that, for many cadres, it meant little more than a socialist-type regime that would cultivate a spirit 'opposed to individualism'. An EAM publication assured its readers that it 'would not rely on the exploitation of the many for the benefit of the few but the joyful toil of everyone for the collective happiness'.[31] Neither this nor similar publications explained how EAM was going to build this utopia or elaborated on its economic programme or the political institutions of the new society.

EDES publications were often much more blunt. This disparity between the EAM and EDES programmes was present from early on; it is characteristic that EDES did not shy away from declaring in its 1941 manifesto it would use force to keep the royalist faction at bay and build a democratic and socialist regime. These proclamations were viewed with disdain by many, even among EDES ranks, who believed that Zervas and his entourage wanted to establish a left-wing dictatorship, and they were denounced violently by EAM/ELAS publications, which accused EDES and its supporters of being 'faux' socialists who were using this rhetoric to lead astray the peasant and worker masses from their natural home in EAM/ELAS.[32] The EDES programme had two founding principles: the

A history of the Greek resistance

first was the creation of a 'Greater Greece' that would incorporate parts of Bulgaria and Albania in its national territory. This aggressive irredentism was combined with a fierce critique of the Metaxas regime, capitalism and the establishment politicians and a distinctly left-wing rhetoric. In contrast to EAM, which shied away from the word 'socialism' in its publications, *Ethniki Floga*, the official publication of EDES, declared that the ultimate aim of the organisation was the creation of a 'greater, democratic and socialist Greece' that would become the 'wellspring of freedom, justice and civilisation'.[33]

Anti-capitalist references abounded in EDES publications. One guerrilla journalist reminded his readers that 'capitalism lies in wait', and continued:

> they know that their rotten edifice is about to crumble and they fight to retain it ... capitalism is the number one enemy of the people ... if the great capital is controlled by a conscientious government then it is possible to fulfil all the needs of the people and make them understand that they will not find happiness in Marx's theories and the dictatorship of the proletariat.[34]

As with EAM, the propaganda of EDES had a distinctly populist bent. Both organisations idealised 'the people', a social category incorporating the peasants, the workers and the lower middle class, as the nation's foundation and proclaimed their contribution to the resistance. This rhetoric was often combined with attacks on the 'bourgeoisie' and the 'upper classes', whom they critiqued for their cowardice and their unwillingness to support the struggle.[35]

Such criticisms also abounded in ELAS publications, which condemned the 'bourgeoisie', the residents of Kolonaki (an upper middle-class district in Athens) and those who lingered 'in the salons and the cafés'[36] for their nonchalance and unwillingness to contribute to their struggle, but this criticism took a distinctly violent form in EDES propaganda. An EDES journalist wrote characteristically: 'we call the bourgeoisie to wake up ... and face reality ... they bear a heavy burden because they left the cause of the nation to a handful of people and the masses of the impoverished peasantry'. He continued:

> let them open their eyes and see what is going on in today's war, the British, the American and the German aristocracies fight in the front lines. But here even the middle class are absent from the struggle, their leaders turned them into eunuchs with their bickering ... [they] ... shut themselves inside their homes waiting to be redeemed by the heavens.[37]

Cause, comrades and faith

The EDES brand of socialism lacked the collectivist aspect of EAM's *laokratia* and had a distinctly liberal and corporatist bent. EDES publications dismissed class struggle and underscored the need for cooperation between the 'bourgeoisie' and the 'people'. Despite its stringent criticism, EDES did not dispute the importance of, or need for, a social elite; moreover, it criticised the Greek upper classes for failing to fulfil their role. However, it also stressed the need for social mobility and maintained that the future elite must be composed of resisters from all classes. EDES agitators were also careful to dissociate their programme both from Marxist ideas and from the Soviet Union, which they dismissed as an oppressive regime. This underscored their commitment to the Western camp and, particularly, Britain and the United States, which they described as 'brother' nations and common allies in the fight against eastern absolutism.[38]

As the occupation progressed, however, the guerrilla propaganda placed less stress on social critique and enemy atrocities, and focused increasingly on denouncing the internal enemy. EDES publications abounded with stories of ELAS guerrillas desecrating churches and robbing peasants of the fruits of their labour,[39] and warned parents of the corrupting potential of EPON for their children, often describing in lurid detail sexual acts between guerrillas and the female members of EPON. EDES commanders also warned their men repeatedly about the dangers of an ELAS victory. The latter was little more than a front for the KKE, 'whose main aim was to lead the children of the people astray and turn them into communists'. ELAS's leaders were denounced as 'thieves' and 'scoundrels' by their rivals, who described them as no better than bandits whose sole aim was to live at the expense of the peasantry.[40]

Conversely, ELAS propaganda narratives focused disproportionately on denouncing EDES and its leaders as mercenaries whose intention was to restore the status quo with the help of the British. EDES was often described by ELAS cadres as an 'anti-national and treasonous organisation', far worse than the Germans.[41] This accusation was emphasised in a host of circulars and orders that reminded the guerrillas that 'the Germans are not the only enemy but every reactionary and every rival of ELAS'.[42] As with their EDES counterparts, ELAS propagandists accused their rivals of lacking national sentiment; one ELAS circular referred to them as 'Greek-speaking Huns'.[43] Another ELAS bulletin accused the EDES officers of plotting a massacre of EAM supporters: 'Zorbalas and Kostantopoulos … said that out of nine million Greeks only one third, the true Greeks, must survive and the rest must perish'. The same officers were reported to have said that 'Metaxas should have killed them instead of putting them into prison', and that 'we don't care if the British bring the king back, even if they decided to set up Rastafari as a king we would kneel down in front of him, what else can we do'.[44] Such denunciations were accompanied by graphic tales of torture and rape allegedly committed by EDES troops.[45]

How effective was this propaganda? If the various ELAS circulars and reports are to be believed, ideology was the single most important determinant of guerrilla morale. A post-operation report of the 1/38 ELAS regiment underlined the importance of ideology and attributed the guerrillas' endurance to their belief in the resistance's cause:

> The non-stop marches and the deprivation had a detrimental effect on the lads ... yet they marched in the snow, shoeless and scantily dressed without ever complaining ... *katsamaki* was our only food and even that was meagre and always in short supply ... no other army would be able to endure these hardships, and still retain such a high level of morale. No other group of young men would be able to endure these tribulations but the Eponite who was conscious of the reasons [why] ... he fought.[46]

Such documents must be read carefully since the functionaries who compiled them were often unsuited for this task and were more interested in 'filling in the blanks on notional lists, [and] reporting that morale was "healthy"', rather than in 'what was really going on in their men's heads'.[47] Nevertheless, it is certain that the violent millenarian rhetoric that abounded in ELAS publications was appealing, especially to young men from poor and marginal rural backgrounds who believed fervently that they 'were taking part in the birth of a new age'.[48] These men saw the resistance as an apocalyptic struggle that would result in the resolution of all social tensions and establish a reign of justice once and for all. Such views were undoubtedly influenced by the religious beliefs of the partisans themselves and the apocalyptic imagery prevalent in ELAS propaganda, as evidenced by the following song written by an anonymous ELAS guerrilla in Crete. The song, entitled 'The Russians', proclaimed 'Dear Mother of God summon here those who love equality/ as soon as the Russians will come there will be justice ... the Russians will come and will right all wrongs/ if the Russians come there will be no rich no poor ... by next year there will be no poor'.[49]

Such beliefs were often combined with an almost irrational hatred, especially among rural guerrillas, of everything pertaining to the world of the cities, the state and the educated classes. When Ioannis Triantafillidis,

Cause, comrades and faith

a doctor and nomarch of Drama who was arrested as a reactionary, asked one of his ELAS captors to release him from his handcuffs 'since I was in great pain and I was an elderly man and a doctor and there was hardly a chance that I'd try to escape, he told me angrily that it is exactly you, the old and the educated, that deserve to be killed'.[50] Some of the more fanatical guerrillas made sure to adopt their outward appearance to their beliefs; they sported red scarves or shirts and some even carved a five-pointed star or a hammer and sickle into their weapons.[51]

Such fanaticism was not unknown on the other side; many EDES guerrillas tended to believe even the wildest accusations and were afraid that an EAM victory would destroy traditional peasant mores and plunge rural society into anarchy and debauchery. An EDES guerrilla was asked by an elderly peasant 'why do EAM and EDES fight? EAM will give us land, bread, money.' He responded angrily that if EAM won

> he won't be the master of his house any more, his daughter will be ass-fucked, they will shut down the Church ... and confiscate his farm, that he will end up working for others ... and much more ... in the end he told me – those accursed, those faggots ... we should kill every one of them.[52]

Political tensions often led to violent episodes, especially in areas such as Tzoumerka where guerrillas from the two organisations coexisted during 1943. In one case, an EDES guerrilla stabbed an ELAS partisan to death[53] while several men were injured in a melee that started after a group of EDES guerrillas entered a café in the town of Voulgareli and shouted to the assembled ELAS guerrillas and supporters 'you are all faggots from the oldest to the youngest and we're going to fuck your sisters' cunts'.[54]

Such feelings were not limited to peasant guerrillas but were shared by educated officers; for example, Lieutenant Ioannis Katsadimas, a middle-class officer from the town of Arta, believed that ELAS was 'the greatest danger that threatened to turn Greece into a wasteland'. Unlike his peasant colleagues, Katsadimas was sufficiently informed to know that ELAS did not present any dangers to morality; however, like many conservative officers, he was afraid that an EAM victory would result in the destruction of the existing institutions and plunge the country into an adventure for which it was ill prepared. 'They have no need for tradition', noted Katsadimas, 'they want to cut all ties, they want to destroy [everything] and then rebuild'.[55] Katsadimas's beliefs merit further scrutiny since they can shed light on the mentalities and perceptions of the junior leaders who constituted EDES's backbone.

Katsadimas was not a bigoted devotee of the old regime. He believed that the military should not be involved in political activities since they 'belong to the fatherland and not to parties'. It is quite plausible that his attachment to EDES derived more from his admiration for Zervas than his belief in EDES's political agenda; as he wrote in a letter, 'Zervas is an IDEA, he is the personification of the national struggle, he has reached immortality'.[56] Katsadimas had no sympathy for the old political parties and believed that EAM 'benefited from the bickering between the bourgeois parties who tried to settle their differences upon the ruins of Greece',[57] while his diary bristles with derogatory expressions towards the 'idiotic bourgeoisie'. In spite of these misgivings, Katsadimas remained a resolute conservative who noted in early 1944 that the outcome of the war had been settled and a new struggle between 'capitalism and communism' was brewing, which would lead to a 'new synthesis that will set the foundations for a new historical period' under the supervision of the 'Anglo-Saxon ruling class'.[58] However, Katsadimas was a pessimist as far as Greece was concerned; he had little faith in the capabilities of 'the people' or the resistance's promises of social equality.[59] In mid-1944 he noted, 'the only thing that we have achieved in Greece for the past one hundred year was to destroy what the others had built for the only reasons that it was built by them and not by us and thus to start all over again. Of course since we lack continuity we find ourselves perpetually starting over.' He believed that the 'Greek people is in dire need of EDUCATION', preferably according to 'the Anglo-Saxon model', which would enable the 'next generation to create something new'.[60]

It is difficult to discern how widespread such views were among EDES's ranks. Katsadimas noted in his diary that his opinions 'reflect the opinions of hundreds of Greek officers who fought ... for our homeland, our families and our faith'.[61] Other testimonies and archival evidence also show that such apolitical moderates constituted a strong presence in both organisations. A confidential SOE report highlighted that 'sympathies are mixed' in both organisations and suggested that 'although the [ELAS] leaders are probably communist the bulk of the rank and file are moderate democrats of the French Republican type'.[62] The same report noted that many EDES sympathisers had turned towards the right in the aftermath of the 1943–44 civil war; however, it also stressed that 'the rank and file though possibly sympathetic towards the monarchy are essentially democratic'.[63] A British officer who travelled to Epirus and Thessaly between December and March 1943 noted similarly in his post-operation report that travelling through ELAS territory I formed the impression that the average rank and file are not vitally interested in the political outcome, and are certainly not aware of EAM aims. They are drawn from peasant stock, where the chief preoccupation is the morrow's food, and have joined ELAS as being either the local, or in their opinion the best resistance organisation. Most of them are not fighting for political reasons.[64]

Indeed, it seems that extremists who were 'only interested in the post-war question'[65] were a minority in both organisations, with the majority being either moderates or completely apolitical. This lack of ideological commitment was not only due to peasant ignorance as the previous report suggested. The fact is that the comprehension and internalisation of ideology also depended on the presence of suitable cadres, which neither the minuscule Communist Party nor EDES could produce at a satisfactory rate. Most of the early ELAS bands were supported by a Communist Party member who acted as a *politikos*-commissar. However, as the resistance groups expanded, the pool of experienced political cadres dried up, while there was less and less time for educational activities and many groups functioned without a *politikos* for months on end.[66]

Equally often the *politikos* were unsuited to their role; some were middle-aged working-class activists, who had a very different mentality from that of the rural guerrillas, and many completely lacked education. Often their only qualification was their blind faith in the KKE, and they could do little more than misquote Marxist slogans.[67] However, even when capable cadres were present, guerrillas displayed little aptitude or interest and were often scornful towards the men who tried to indoctrinate them. Panananos soon became frustrated by the indifference of the guerrillas to the educational activities he coordinated. He complained constantly in his diary of the indifference of his fellow guerrillas, who preferred drinking and playing cards to hearing his lengthy diatribes on socialism and the future of Greece: 'I can't bear these people any longer. Even if I teach those men ten different things every day, they are not going to understand anything … hoodlums will always be hoodlums and scum will always be scum, no matter what.'[68]

Papananos's students were far from exceptional; often guerrillas were at a loss about their organisation's goals and aims and had difficulty explaining their programme and cause, even in the most elementary terms. A report of the ELAS 50th regiment noted that that 'political and ideological emancipation of the guerrilla, their sense of selflessness, heroism and self-criticism and conscious discipline … are not of the first order … we must admit that we have profoundly overlooked the political and ideological education of our guerrillas'.[69] These problems were not only present in units that operated in mountainous isolated areas such as the 50th regiment but were also profound in regions such as Euboea, located next to the ELAS heartland of central Greece and less than 80 miles from Athens. A report of the local ELAS 7th battalion noted in mid-1944 that 'both the party members and the non-affiliate guerrillas ... are completely devoid of discipline and comradely spirit ... our cadres are terribly backwards both in regard to theoretical and political education'.[70] EDES units fared little better, and despite the repeated pleas of the GHQ many officers and most band leaders shown a complete indifference towards ideological indoctrination. A report dispatched to all units in 22 February 1944 noted that

> I have realized to my great sorrow that many of our colleagues are completely uninterested about the enlightenment of our guerrillas and their education about the sacred purpose of our national struggle. There are many guerrillas who had not listened even once to their officer explaining to them both their obligations as fighters and the great benefits that will result for them and their families from the fruition of our struggle ... all our officers should undertake with apostolic zeal the task of the enlightenment of our fighters ... we must not ignore that our national struggle still has to face many difficulties and trials and that the strengthening of our national spirit is of the outmost importance in facing them successfully.[71]

Even men who exhibited great ideological commitment were seldom immune to the exertions of combat and the grim living conditions in Free Greece. A few days after he enlisted in EDES, philology student Faidon Maidonis noted in his diary his determination 'to fight and to die for the death of Bolshevism, for the new world that is just rising over the mountain'.[72] However, the apathy of his fellow fighters and the dire repercussions of guerrilla operations on the everyday lives of the peasants radically altered radically Maidonis's views. Two months after he enlisted he noted that 'one day it will be proved that the guerrilla organisations, the liberation armies, all this shit ... brought only destruction with their actions'.[73] Furthermore, ideology could not prepare the men for combat. Several decades later, veterans recounted with trepidation the sight of dead and maimed comrades and rivals, and recalled feelings of stress, fear and guilt.

We fight for our brothers: primary group ties, honour and officership

Notwithstanding their misgivings, most men kept on fighting. Maidonis proved to be a resolute and determined fighter, losing his life in combat four months after he enlisted. What kept men like him fighting? Maidonis's diary is full of reference to his comrades, their lives, background and habits. Even though he was an outsider – most men in his group were farmers and shepherds from the Lakka Souli region – he quickly formed his own group of comrades. Maidonis was often ambivalent towards his fellow fighters. He noted repeatedly that he found it difficult to communicate since none of them shared his interests or background; however, common experiences of combat, hardship and loss eventually led Maidonis to identify with his comrades. Later entries in his diary abound with familial metaphors and denote his admiration for the bravery, pride and 'natural chivalry' of his guerrilla 'brothers', and the pride he felt when his bravery was recognised and praised by his colleagues.[74]

Honour, camaraderie and affection towards one's comrades played a particularly significant role in guerrilla morale. An SOE operative noted in his memoir of the Yugoslav resistance that

> a large element of partisan morale rested on the fact of companionship, of sharing evils, of enjoying interest in the same affairs no matter how obscure; the pressure of war had brought us so close together that we drew strength and encouragement from each other ... the individual had sunk his identity into the group, and from that moment onwards he could feel himself neither desperate nor alone.[75]

Peer-group loyalties were not shaped simply by circumstances, but were carefully cultivated by the resistance organisations. Central to guerrilla life in both organisations was the *omada*, a group of 10–20 people, most of whom had joined at the same time and many of whom came from the same area. In ELAS, each *omada* was ruled by a triumvirate of *stratiotikos* – usually an NCO or a junior officer responsible for the planning and implementation of operations; the *kapetanios* – a civilian and often a Party member who raised the band, recruited the guerrillas and was responsible for provisioning and logistics; and the *politikos* or commissar. The latter was often represented as the *éminence grise* of ELAS bands. The *politikos* was not a simple propagandist; he was the second in command in military affairs, he was responsible for espionage and counter-intelligence, he was the liaison between the political organisation and ELAS, the book-keeper of the unit and even the teacher for those guerrillas who were illiterate. He was responsible for giving a 'political direction to all activities of the band'.[76]

These three positions were considered equal in terms of authority and all decisions were taken during a mandatory weekly meeting, while all differences between them were arbitrated at regimental level.[77] However, true power lay in the hands of the *politikos*.[78] The *politikos*, like the *kapetanios*, were Party men and were often chosen for their fealty rather than their abilities. Few of the *stratiotikos* were Party members initially; however, the difficulty of attracting regular soldiers to their ranks and the constant bickering between them and their fellow commanders led the ELAS GHQ to create its own cadet school, and by end of the occupation over 60 per cent of the ELAS officer corps were graduates of this school. The majority of these officers were peasants, clerks, labourers and shop assistants; most had no previous military experience and were less than 25 years old, while fewer than 3 per cent were educated, middle-class professionals.[79]

The guerrilla slept, ate and fought alongside the same group of men for the duration of his service in the resistance. The shared local and often familial ties between the men (most groups were recruited on a regional basis) further strengthened the group's cohesiveness. All group decisions and actions were debated and decided during the *olomeleia*, the monthly and sometimes weekly meeting between the guerrillas and the leaders. During the *olomeleia*, men took turns to present issues for debate and engaged in lengthy self-criticism sessions. The *olomeleia* and the self-criticism sessions were seen as the 'main feature of ELAS internal democracy'.[80]

However, their aim and purpose were much more intricate. The public presentation of ideas and the self-criticism sessions enabled political officers to spot and deal with unreliable political attitudes within the group and control Bonapartist tendencies. The *olomeleia* enabled younger members to benefit from the experience of veteran guerrillas; additionally it permitted men to express their frustration and discontent and thus reduce tensions and deal with internal strife and animosities between group members before they exploded. Issues discussed by the *olomeleia* included combat performance and morale, relations between the guerrillas and relations with civilian communities. The agenda was set by the political officer; however, individual guerrillas were permitted to propose issues for discussion. Participation was compulsory and all guerrillas had a right to talk and vote on issues presented. Moreover, the *olomeleia* could decide on the punishment of unit members and even officers who had demonstrated cowardice or committed a crime against civilians. However, the *olomeleia* had no authority to execute such decisions whose final approval and implementation rested with the regimental authorities, nor did it have the ability to reject regimental decisions or policies, and a regimental representative was present as a rule.[81] In some areas, such as Crete, the *olomeleia* also had the power both to elect and dismiss officers and *kapetanios*.[82] The *olomeleia* was not institutionalised in EDES; however, as EDES resister Giorgos Romanos noted in his diary, the guerrilla 'won't obey as a soldier … in order to carry out an order he would have to scrutinise it'. All issues concerning the unit, including regimental decisions and policies, were subjected to rigorous criticism and debate.[83]

These activities endowed the guerrillas with a powerful sense of belonging and enhanced unit cohesion, since all men were rendered responsible for the fate and actions of the primary group. Group ties were further strengthened by the feelings of isolation borne out of everyday experience. Guerrilla warfare had no home front to which the men could return to rest; leave was rare and some men did not see their families for years. 'Nostalgia overwhelmed us', noted one EDES guerrilla, 'those [we] had left behind seemed more distant and unreachable than a friend who lives today in Australia or Bolivia'.[84] The resistance organisations also tried to restrict emotional and social ties as much as possible. Fraternisation with civilian women was strictly prohibited and occasionally punishable by death. Marriages and engagements were also forbidden since 'they encumber the feelings of sacrifice and bravery that are imperative for our struggle, which as servants of the Greek people we are obliged to carry out without letting anything stand in our way'.[85] This situation rendered the primary group the only place where the guerrillas could find support, express their concerns and receive affection.

Correct behaviour was encouraged with the help of moral punishments based on shared codes of honour and masculinity. Temporary disarmament was the most serious reprimand; according to ELAS *kapetanios* Vaggelis Saltamanis, 'there was no graver insult to a guerrilla than disarming him'.[86] This was followed by exclusion from the *olomeleia* and temporary isolation. Repeated and serious offenders ran the risk of much more brutal punishments; for instance, one EDES band leader publicly flogged two deserters and after he was finished he paraded the men in front of all units, who jeered, swore and spat at them. Such reprimands had both a symbolic and an immediate effect.[87] While the

A history of the Greek resistance

guerrillas' participation in combat separated them from the civilians and reinforced the link between their masculine identities and the exercise of violence, disarmament relegated them to the status of the unmanly civilian. Thus, they were cut off from the masculine brotherhood of the *omada* and deprived of their only source of moral and material support. Furthermore, the strongly regional character of most bands meant that news of inappropriate behaviour reached their home areas. This further served to make guerrillas conform to their group expectations since any mishaps would not only destroy their reputation but also that of their families.

These experiences endowed the guerrilla groups with a large degree of cohesiveness. Giorgos Romanos, an EDES member and a lawyer in civilian life, noted in his diary that the guerrillas 'have a solidarity that is hard [for an outsider] to comprehend'.[88] Group solidarity and honour culture also bolstered combat performance, since guerrillas were aware that cowardice would expose them to the taunts of their peers and might lead to loss of status. Group ties also increased rapport and confidence among the guerrillas since they knew that if they were injured they would not be left behind in the field and would be taken care of by their friends. The lengths to which guerrillas went to protect wounded comrades is both touching and extraordinary; in one engagement between ELAS and EDES near Bisdouni in Ioannina, four ELAS guerrillas lost their lives while trying to help a wounded comrade.[89]

Guerrillas developed fierce attachments to their comrades and often employed familial metaphors to described life and relations within the primary group. An intelligence report of the ELAS 3rd division noted that 'there is a great degree of solidarity among them … they will share a piece of bread or an apple … as if they were brothers'. Similar terms were employed to describe the relations between the guerrillas and their leaders.[90] Guerrillas often described themselves as *paidia* (children or boys), and officers were described accordingly as fathers, like Mihalis Papazisis, the 40-year-old commander of the ELAS Parnassida battalion,[91] uncles or elder brothers. Ilias Loutsaris, a 50-year-old ELAS officer, and Illias Katsios, a 45-year-old EDES officer, were known among their men as the uncles. Napoleon Zervas, the EDES leader, was affectionately known among his men as *o papous* (the grandfather), as was Major Thodoris Zizopoulos, the commanding officer of the ELAS 30th regiment.[92]

Such representations reflected the age and status stratification within the guerrilla groups. The majority of the guerrillas were young men, some barely adults, who occupied an analogous position within their households to the one they held in the resistance, and who were accustomed to viewing themselves as under the authority of their father or older siblings. At the same time, they provided a model for relations between the ranks and the creation of hierarchical structures that would be acceptable to the guerrillas. This model was not democratic, since it clearly showed a discrepancy in status between men and officers. Indeed the very fact that the guerrillas were represented as children signified their need for authoritative leadership. However, it was sharply different from the model found in the regular army, since it signified that men and officers did not belong to different 'tribes' but were part of the same family. In order to be effective, an officer, like a good father, had to share his men's hardships and impose discipline through persuasion and personal example, as an EDES cadre noted:

> The cohesion and functioning of the guerrilla group is solely dependent on its military leader. He must not command as a regular soldier; excessive kindness is not advisable, while too much strictness will also bring no results. Bravery, defiance of danger, living as rough as any guerrilla, shedding all distinctions ... in dress, in food, in accommodation; a genuine concern for the needs of the guerrilla ... supporting the guerrilla when he is in trouble with his superiors, turning a blind eye to looting; these are the factors that can make a guerrilla leader stand up.[93]

Officers who exhibited such traits were revered by their men, for instance Lefteris, an ELAS *kapetanios* in central Greece: 'to the ordinary Andartes he was almost a god, not only on account of his obvious power of leadership, but also because, unlike many others in the higher positions, he would spend much of his time in chatting and joking with them'.[94] A similar case was that of Nikos Roussopoulos, a junior leader in the ELAS 28th regiment, who 'did not impose his authority as a regular officer', but 'when it was needed he would act as a commander, and when things were different he would become both a friend and a teacher'.[95] Day-to-day interaction and leading by example was equally important, an ELAS guerrilla noted: 'It was the actions of the *kapetanios* that set the example. We would share the same food, and smoke the same cigarette. There wouldn't be any distinctions whatsoever.' In one case, an officer gave away his new boots to a guerrilla who 'was staggering, because his sandals were torn, and his heels were covered with wounds ... It was this example and many others that made us love them so much, and made us so disciplined and so devoted to each other.'[96] Bravery played an equally important role. Nikos Koustas, an officer in the 2/39 ELAS regiment, noted that 'defiance of danger' became almost 'pathological and morbid'. Guerrilla leaders had to constantly expose themselves to danger in order to convince their subordinates of their masculinity; moderation and carefulness were accordingly seen as 'a sign of cowardice, I was a commander and therefore I was obliged to outdo the others'.[97]

The egalitarianism of the guerrilla forces was shocking to many officers. An EDES officer noted in a confidential report to the Greek government in exile that 'The EDES GHQ had prohibited officers from receiving any kind of compensation and forced them to eat along with the guerrillas.' He found this situation 'very demeaning' since 'we had to join a throng of guerrillas and borrow their spoons and plates which afterwards we had to wash in order to be able to eat, it must be underlined that this treatment, befitting to POWs was endured even by high ranking officers'. The attitudes of the guerrillas and their lack of deference were equally shocking to this officer, who noted that 'there was no discipline of any kind and the rank and position of the officers was not taken seriously by anyone'. Ultimately, the hardship of guerrilla life and disappointment with the guerrillas, whom he described as 'a motley rabble', prompted this officer to leave EDES in early 1944.[98] The situation was no different in ELAS; 'our men ... asked for equality in everything', noted an ELAS *kapetanios*:

> they demanded that their commanding officer should queue in order to eat from the communal pot ... when we gave an officer a new pair of breeches they protested, arguing that there was a guerrilla who was in more need. Many argued that we had no need of professional officers, and that all new officers should rise from the guerrilla ranks.[99]

However, these bonds not only worked for the primary group, but often led to complications that threatened to subvert discipline and combatworthiness. Catherine Merridale noted that 'tightly-knit groups of comrades are as capable of fomenting a mutiny or conspiring to desert as they are of fighting heroically together and the guerrillas were no exception to that'.[100] Individual guerrillas had no qualms about stealing from their organisation to provide for their comrades, while officers often abused their authority to provide their men with perks such extra rations, boots and clothes with complete disregard for the needs of other units. Furthermore, the *olomeleia* was used frequently by the guerrillas to overthrow regimental decisions and safeguard their autonomy from outside influences. Many units refused to submit their resolutions for approval to their regimental headquarters, and instead used the authority of the *olomeleia* to subvert regimental and divisional policies. Decisions pertaining to unit policies, including rationing, the procurement of armaments and the punishment of dissenters, were taken by the *olomeleia* and were executed on the spot. It was not unusual for suspects to be questioned, tried and executed within the space of a few hours. Guerrillas also used the *olomeleia* to scrutinise operational policies and decide whether their units would take part in operations. It was not uncommon for the guerrillas to desist from fighting if they deemed that a prospective action might put the unit into unnecessary danger, and sometimes units would call an *olomeleia* in the midst of fighting, abandoning their positions to debate the course of the battle and decide whether or not the unit should stay in the field.[101]

This situation undermined the military capabilities of ELAS to the point that many units had turned into 'disorganised bands'. A circular sent to all units by the ELAS headquarters in late 1943 blasted the men's abuse of the *olomeleia* which undermined ELAS's military efforts 'during this critical moment for our struggle', and accused those who disobeyed orders as cowards whose sole concern was 'to save their own skin by abandoning [their] fellow fighters to the enemy's lethal fire'. The document further added that 'we took up arms to fight the occupiers and we must understand that there is an 80% chance to die and a 20% chance to survive' and concluded by warning the guerrillas that 'refusal to carry out orders is a court-martial offence and will be punished severely'.[102] Such problems had an equally important impact in EDES where, to the amazement of officers, guerrillas often left in the midst of combat or refused to take part in operations unless they first scrutinised their impact and purpose and agreed to a detailed plan. Officers who refused to subject their decisions to this scrutiny often found it impossible to reach an accord with their men. Consequently, sometimes only 30 or 40 men out of a total of 200 would follow their leaders into combat, 'most of whom would ask for some rewards in exchange for this'.[103]

The ardent regionalism of many guerrillas and their leaders also created a series of problems. Most mid-level guerrilla leaders were local men whose authority depended on the acquiescence of their men and the local population who provided support, manpower and material in a tacit agreement that they would be sheltered from the worst effects of the war. Similarly guerrillas were enlisted on the understanding that their foremost task was to defend their homes and families. As a result, local commanders often refused to fight outside their district and vetoed any operations that might cause harm to their areas, fearful that this would turn the local population and their men against them. A report to the

EDES GHQ in June 1943 warned that 'the guerrillas insist on staying in their home areas ... and it is likely that we will face problems if we have to move them'.[104] This problem was no less common in ELAS. A commissar from the area of Konitsa in Epirus noted that the localism of these men created difficulties:

> they all want to join units that are stationed close to their villages in order to be able to stay close and help their families. However, we cannot create a separate army for each region. This is a serious problem that must be urgently dealt with by our higher military and political authorities. Very many guerrillas have recently deserted their units claiming that they needed to help their families, however, it is difficult to consider these men as deserters ... often we don't really know how to deal with them.[105]

While these attitudes did not create any problems in the early period when most guerrilla bands differed little from localised militias, the situation changed from mid-1943 onwards, as both ELAS and EDES bands were called repeatedly to fight outside their districts.

Such problems peaked in the winter of 1943–44 when thousands of men from both sides were ordered to leave their home districts and fight against their Greek and foreign rivals in the area of central Pindus. However, a few days after the operations began, the first cracks appeared, with many units refusing to fight and demanding to return to their home district. The 85th regiment of ELAS was one of the first units to abandon the struggle in early January 1944, despite the efforts of other guerrilla commanders to deter them; 'we told them that this was a serious breach of discipline ... we asked them to think what would happen to ELAS if every single unit decided to return to its area'.[106] The unit moved back to its home area after less than two weeks of fighting. Such problems were quite widespread, as an ELAS officer who took part in the fighting noted in his memoir: 'localism was very intense in many units and seriously affected their combativeness and discipline'.[107] The situation was more serious in EDES, with guerrillas refusing to fight and openly defying the orders of their officers. The EDES leadership tried to contain the situation by promising improved living conditions, appealing to the men's sense of honour and promising a swift victory. These efforts brought no results and desertions accelerated during mid-January, when sometimes entire units abandoned the fighting and returned to their areas. Napoleon Zervas wrote in his diary that he feared EDES would completely disintegrate if the fighting continued, noting that 'dealing with those people is a martyrdom; they have no faith in the cause'.[108]

Cause, comrades and faith

These problems were not limited to this region. During the same period, a large number of guerrillas from the 1/38 (Thessaly) regiment of ELAS refused to follow their unit in operations outside their area.[109] ELAS faced similar difficulties in central Macedonia as many of the guerrillas in the 16th regiment refused to fight outside their territory and had to be reminded that 'our duty is to fight wherever we are called'.[110] The situation was even more serious in Peloponnesus where the ELAS 12th battalion lost one-third of its men during the anti-guerrilla operations of early 1944, since hundreds of men deserted their units and returned home to protect their families and deal with the loss of property and animals.[111]

Desertions were not due solely to regionalism. Guerrillas would not think twice about abandoning their unit if they thought they were being slighted by their commanding officers. Furthermore, individuals and sometimes entire units would often desert in the midst of operations upon learning that plunder was available nearby.[112] This behaviour was often encouraged by the antagonism between local band leaders, who looked to augment their unit's size and were willing to enlist anyone, regardless of their past or transgressions. Thus, men who had abandoned one unit could easily join a different one with the certainty that their new leader would protect them from any possible repercussions for their previous actions. The EDES GHQ strictly prohibited the enrolment of such men, warning band leaders that 'under no circumstances should they enlist guerrillas who used to serve in other bands', albeit to no effect.[113]

The arcane system of command in both organisations gave rise to complications and rivalries between officers, band leaders, commissars and *kapetanios*, who vied for control of their bands. The dislike of the ELAS *kapetanios* for the officers and their sense of pride in having created and raised their bands from scratch led them to disdain their presence. Many officers in their turn viewed the *kapetanios* as amateurs and resented their interference with military affairs. This antagonism had a detrimental effect on the performance of ELAS and despite the efforts of the ELAS HQ it persisted well into 1944.[114] Rivalries between regular officers and band leaders were equally commonplace in EDES since many leaders saw the officers as upstarts and refused to cooperate with them. It was not unusual for band leaders to threaten defection if an officer was posted to their unit or the organisation refused to acquiesce to their demands.[115] Such threats were seldom carried out and the few who went as far as deserting were quick to return to the fold, for example Zois Padazis, an EDES band leader who defected and proclaimed his band an independent organisation after he was refused a promotion to captain and corresponding pay.[116] However rare, such actions underscored both the potentially disruptive effects of primary group ties and the undue power wielded by many band leaders. They often held the officers and the organisation to ransom with their threats and created an explosive atmosphere that threatened the cohesion of their organisations.

The civil war and the crisis of morale

The persistence and depth of these problems led both ELAS and EDES to revise their policies dramatically. From late 1943 onwards the organisations reintroduced some privileges to the officers in the hope that this would raise their prestige among both the guerrillas and the citizenry. They also simplified the system of command: the position of *politikos* was abolished and unit leadership was shared between the *kapetanios* and a regular officer; meanwhile, in EDES, all band leaders were flanked by a mandatory military adviser. The *politikos* were replaced in ELAS by the EDA [Epitropi Diafotisis Adartou], the committee for the enlightenment of the guerrilla, whose tasks included propaganda and surveillance of political attitudes. The command of the guerrilla groups also became much more centralised: during September 1943 the ELAS GHQ decreed that the scattered bands and commands be designated battalions, regiments and divisions; medical services, logistics corps and staff offices were also created. EDES followed the same path from February 1944 onwards.[117]

ELAS also made significant efforts to politicise its army by introducing separate EPON squads to each unit. EPON, EAM's youth organisation, was, according to one acerbic observer, more akin to the fascist *ballila* than the Komsomol.[118] These groups were first created in August 1943; however, they did not reach any significant numbers until the first half of 1944. The formation of the 'exemplary' EPON squads was a clear move towards the further politicisation of ELAS. Despite their many merits, the regular army officers and the gendarmes who had military command of most guerrilla groups, and the apolitical peasants who composed them, continued to foster distrust. The creation of the exemplary platoons and their eventual expansion would help replace these men with politically trustworthy cadres who were more suited to the role of propagandist and less hesitant to fight the 'internal enemy'. The 1943 order that decreed the creation of EPON underlined its role as the ideological vanguard of ELAS: 'it is necessary to combine military training with the appropriate political instruction and education on the goals of EAM, EPON and the spirit of the popular army so ... as to render them a breeding ground for cadres'. The same order also made explicit that the role of EPON was not only limited to the military tasks of the liberation struggle, but also 'the enlightenment ... and organisation of the youth and the people in the organisations of the EAM-ELAS-EPON and the obliteration of every fascist venture of our nation's internal enemy'.[119]

This move was accompanied by the creation of a sophisticated surveillance apparatus. Many ELAS cadres had come to attribute the problems that plagued their organisation to the work of subversives and enemy spies in the guerrilla ranks. ELAS responded by placing undercover intelligence officers in many units. The role of these men, who were, as a rule, trusted party cadres, was to provide reports on dissenting attitudes among the rank and file and the officers. The surveillance apparatus was further reinforced by the creation of Party nuclei in each unit, from platoon level upwards. Party members comprised the 'hard core' in individual *omades*; each unit had a three-man 'Party office' whose members were tasked with reporting and policing dissension and helping to keep non-affiliated members in line with EAM and Party policies.[120]

ELAS also adopted increasingly stringent measures to deal with desertion, indiscipline and cowardice. Capital punishment was used increasingly to punish desertion and cowardice, a punishment that, until then, had been reserved largely for infractions such as rape or treason. In January 1944 the ELAS 12th regiment executed seven men for desertion and cowardice in the face of the enemy[121] while the ELAS 30th regiment condemned seven men to death for similar reasons.[122] A further four men who served in the 36th and 3/40 regiments were condemned to death for cowardice and negligence of duty.[123] The 1/38 regiment of ELAS took equally stringent measures during this period; between January and February 1944, four guerrillas were executed for desertion, cowardice in the face of the enemy and theft. A further three were sentenced to life in prison for the same reasons and ten more were given penalties ranging from one to ten years in prison for desertion and cowardice.[124] The use of the death penalty subsided gradually; however, cowardice and abandonment of position remained punishable offences. Nineteen men who served in the ELAS 9th division were tried for such offences between April and June 1944; four were sentenced to life in prison while the remainder were given prison sentences ranging from six months to ten years.[125] EDES, on the other hand, largely abstained from adopting such severe punishments, and while it made some efforts to intensify propaganda and surveillance in the ranks, it stopped short of adopting ELAS's methods.

These reforms curbed some of the worst excesses; they stemmed the tide of desertions and were able to rein in the rampant regionalism and indiscipline. However, they were not entirely adequate and in some cases they backfired. Despite their unruliness, the independent bands' mobility and knowledge of the terrain and the local situation enabled them to conduct a low-key yet effective guerrilla campaign against the Axis troops. The transformation into a regular army reversed this situation, since it deprived junior leaders of the necessary freedom of movement, limited their field of action and led to the concentration of large numbers of troops in set locations where they were vulnerable to Axis incursions. As a British liaison officer noted,

> ELAS henceforth believed that they were in fact an army which operated on army lines with army tactics. This apart from the introduction of lengths of red tape ... also encouraged the establishment of fixed lines of defence, orthodox methods of attack and so on. All this should have been quite foreign to a proper guerrilla army, which must operate on irregular unorthodox lines; it was increasingly to hinder, rather than help operations.[126]

EDES was not free from such problems, as most 'believe in lines of battle and mountain ridge to ridge formations' and devoted their time to 'long, useless typewritten orders talking of regts [sic] and other non-existent units'.[127]

ELAS and EDES were repeatedly warned by the Allied liaison officers that this change would prove 'unsuitable for guerrilla warfare' as it 'destroys essentials of guerrilla ability to strike, when surrounded to hide and strike again without thinking of fixed terms of defence'.[128] However, these warnings were not heeded by the guerrilla authorities. The effect of these changes became apparent during a series of anti-guerrilla operations that took place between November 1943 and February 1944. The ease with which the Wehrmacht troops penetrated guerrilla defences shocked the ELAS GHQ. Some reports noted that several units 'abandoned their positions without even returning fire even from a distance with the attacking columns'.[129] The extent of demoralisation was underscored by the abandonment of the dead and wounded to the hands of the German troops – 'in many cases we neglected our sacred duty to recover the dead and those who were badly wounded' – and the desertion of scores of officers, particularly among ELAS, who 'in many cases ... abandoned their units in the midst of fighting and sought refuge in the more peaceful and less dangerous sections of the front'.[130]

The repeated setbacks during the winter of 1943–44 prompted the ELAS GHQ to reconsider its tactics. In a circular addressed to all units, ELAS commander-in-chief Stephanos Sarafis noted that

> the tactics used by our units during the latest mopping-up operations were not completely appropriate … our divisions created static defence fronts hoping that they would be able to repulse the Germans … however this tactic is not correct. Our army lacks both the organisation, the manpower and the firepower to engage in a static defence struggle against the Germans.

Sarafis suggested the adoption of a more elastic defence 'that will rely on counterattacks against the flanks of the advancing Germans'. In order to achieve this, Sarafis suggested the creation of small raiding parties that would go deep into enemy territory to collect information and stage ambushes, 'a return to guerrilla warfare'. Such raiding parties according to Sarafis would slow down mopping-up operations and create havoc in the German lines, causing great casualties.[131] The ELAS GHQ took ever more strident disciplinary actions and gave repeated instructions to 'take measures so as to deal with indifference and eliminate unwillingness and cowardice'.[132]

However, the performance of ELAS did not improve. During the operations of June 1944 in western Macedonia 'guerrillas on nearly all occasions fought little and badly … it was a walk over for the Germans', who managed within a few days to destroy two ELAS divisions.[133] A series of ELAS operations against the towns of Vonitsa and Nafpaktos in central Greece a month later were no more successful. In Vonitsa, the 300-strong ELAS 24th regiment that was tasked with taking out the German garrison stationed in the town beat a hasty retreat after a brief firefight with the Germans, without suffering or incurring any casualties. The attack on Nafpaktos turned into a panicked rout, with a handful of militiamen putting to a flight the ELAS 36th regiment. Having lost their guides a few minutes after entering the town, the guerrillas were seized by panic when the few militiamen who defended the town started shooting at them; 'anarchy prevailed … our men fired towards all directions and it is a miracle that we did not have casualties from friendly fire'. The situation deteriorated completely as soon as the carts that were despatched to carry the loot and evacuate the wounded appeared: 'the unit dissolved entirely … everyone broke into shops as if looting was the foremost reasons for this operation ... many guerrillas deserted in the midst of the operation and left Nafpaktos to save their loot'.[134]

The faltering capacity of ELAS was affirmed again during the Noah's Ark operation during September–October 1944.[135] Despite the repeated calls of the ELAS GHQ to 'multiply the strikes against the occupier' and 'strike them everywhere without mercy', many units in central Greece and Thessaly displayed little appetite for action, thereby allowing the retreating German troops to traverse their territories unharmed.[136] German troops were able to best the guerrillas even a few weeks before their departure; in October 1944 a battalion of the 54th regiment of ELAS in the Pelion area scattered 'without firing a single shot', leaving the civilians to bear the brunt of reprisals. The unit commander underlined in his post-operation report that 'morale was not good ... there were many cases of desertion and cowardice'. He also noted that the lukewarm performance of ELAS exasperated even trusted EAM and KKE members who 'called the guerrillas scum' and prompted the peasantry to stop supporting them.[137]

This was not the whole picture, however; some units continued to perform remarkably. For instance the 16th and 30th ELAS regiments 'fought very hard during the anti-guerrilla operations that took place during the summer of 1944 even though they lacked arms and ammunition and were very much outnumbered by a good and highly trained force'.[138] The picture was similar in EDES where a number of superb units such as the 3/40 regiment and the Xerovouni battalion commanded by Alekos Papadopoulos, a contractor in civilian life and 'a tremendous disciplinarian ... with a savage love of war',[139] operated next to mediocre units such as the notoriously incompetent 9th division, commanded by Lieutenant Colonel Constantinides, a 'rather old and decrepit officer [with] an enormous staff – at one time this contained 300 officers – who are generally so tied up in masses of paper that they are unable to give the simplest information'.[140] Such independent units, which according to an estimate comprised 25–30 per cent of EDES forces, were 'the backbone of the movement, they had done practically all the hard fighting ... and are always keen for action against the Germans'[141] while many guerrillas who served in them 'have requested to fight outside Greece after the war here is ended'.[142]

What set these units apart was the quality of leadership and training and their strongly regional character. The majority of Papadopoulos's guerrillas were recruited from a small cluster of villages on the Xerovouni mountain of Epirus and were led by local notables: schoolteachers, reserve officers and veteran guerrilla leaders of the 1912–13 Balkan wars.

Unlike many of his colleagues, Papadopoulos was a stickler for discipline and training. He introduced British Army drill in his unit and did not shy away from imposing severe penalties for looting and cowardice. Such measures were naturally resented by some of the guerrillas; however, his personal bravery (he was repeatedly wounded in combat), strong roots in the community, spartan lifestyle and uprightness earned him the respect and loyalty of his men.[143] However, units like those of Papadopoulos had become exceedingly rare. The militarisation of the People's Armies was accompanied by a massive recruitment campaign which reached its height during the autumn of 1943 and landed ELAS and EDES with scores of men who were untrained, undisciplined and under-motivated. This rapid increase had a detrimental effect on unit morale as it diluted the regional character of the units and dismantled the closely knit primary groups.[144] Some voices in ELAS suggested a radical decrease of strength and a downsizing of the units; however, this was not possible. Indeed the outbreak of the civil war led the guerrilla organisations to further step up their recruitment efforts, often recruiting former convicts and boys as young as 15 who were eager to surrender or run away at the first chance they got.[145]

Group ties were further undermined by the growing autarchy of guerrilla commanders who, in their effort to justify the continuous debacles, unleashed a witch-hunt for subversives who 'lurked everywhere' and sabotaged ELAS's work.[146] Many unit commanders abolished the *olomeleia* altogether, since they saw it as a tool for dissent, and made increased used of corporal punishment to punish even the slightest infractions. In some units these measures terrorised the guerrillas to the point that they were even afraid to talk in the presence of their officers.[147] A no less important role was played by the growing disparity in living standards between the rank and file and officers who often used their unit's resources to fund their lavish lifestyle.[148] Corruption had reached such proportions that, in June 1944, the ELAS GHQ decided 'to review the proceedings of ELAS … from the beginning of the revolution until now … we already know, and it will be further proved that widespread fraud has taken place'.[149]

The rampant corruption, the continuous decline in combat performance and the growing autarchy were symptoms of a broader crisis of morale that was triggered by the outbreak of the civil war in the winter of 1943–44. The clashes between ELAS and EDES caught by surprise guerrillas and senior cadres alike, many of whom were at a loss to understand why 'we started killing each other'. A few days after the outbreak of hostilities a senior EDES member noted in his diary:

> We have no clear information ... the GHQ sends us regularly some badly written circulars and orders hoping to galvanise the people against EAM, however, the people do not really believe that they are in danger from EAM and read these circulars with a notable apathy and calmness ... I haven't been able to understand why we declared war myself even though I am constantly in contact with the GHQ ... they claim that EAM has proclaimed the dictatorship of the proletariat, however, I highly doubt if one in a hundred EAM members really know what this means.[150]

The feelings of surprise and despondency expressed in this passage were even more widespread among rank-and-file guerrillas who voted with their feet, deserting their units *en masse*. One EDES guerrilla commented that 'I pretended that I was sick, I wanted to leave because I saw that we are going to start killing each other'.[151] Such feelings abounded on the other side as well, with an ELAS guerrilla from Epirus recounting in his memoir

> the whole excitement of being a guerrilla, a liberator was gone, enthusiasm was gone, songs were gone and were succeeded by despondency and gloom, the guerrillas marched with their heads down and most were tortured by a single question – why did we really join up ... in the morning our platoon was less than half since many have deserted.[152]

The end of the civil war did not signal the end of hostilities, and cadres on both sides struggled to justify the continuing need for vigilance, violence and counter-accusations against fellow Greeks and the lack of action against the occupation troops. An ELAS report noted that 'we must be ready to face practically and ideologically this situation, our troops have come to believe that nothing separates us from EDES any more and that we can boldly shake hands with our enemies ... thus revolutionary vigilance is diminished among the mass of our troops'.[153]

EDES authorities found galvanising their troops equally difficult. The press and leaders might have thundered about the dangers of communism and 'pan-slavism', rejecting any reconciliation with EAM; however, the mood was much more subdued among the rank and file.[154] A confidential report sent to all unit commanders in the aftermath of the Plaka agreement which put a brief end to the clashes between the two organisations underlined both the fall of morale among the guerrillas, many of whom failed to understand why EAM and EDES had been fighting in the previous months, and the need to boost anti-EAM feelings: 'you should bolster the morale of your men and explain to them that when the time comes we might need to take action again in order to avert the humiliating prospect of kowtowing to EAM'.[155] Such feelings were also underlined in a British report which noted that many 'simply despair and lament that at the end of it all there will be no Greeks left alive ... [and] agree that the only hope of solution is in the Anglo-American Allies and never cease asking: Are they sending an army to save us? And how soon?'[156]

Fatalism had become predominant among the ranks. An EDES partisan confided to his comrades that he was afraid the war would go on forever with both sides locked in a perpetual stalemate; he stated that 'God had abandoned us, he has moved further on high.'[157] Even the more ideologically motivated cadres like Papananos had become restless and disappointed; he noted repeatedly in his diary how he longed 'to leave behind this whole charade'.[158] Exhaustion was equally widespread in civilian ranks; a British officer in Macedonia noted in mid-1944 that 'the war-weariness of the civil population is very marked and the dissolution of ELAS is as heartily desired ... inside ELAS the same forces are active'.[159] As morale slowly deteriorated, guerrillas and officers abandoned all pretensions and used their position to obtain profits by appropriating material and funds and victimising the peasantry, who became increasingly exasperated by their haughtiness and violence. In mid-1944 Zervas noted in his diary that faltering performance and increasing tensions with the peasantry had reached boiling point in the EDES heartland of Lakka Souli where he feared a general insurrection against the guerrillas.[160]

Mistrust, fear and disappointment led many men to seek new ways to deal with the rigours of combat and everyday life. Some men turned to drink while others increasingly sought refuge in religion and the supernatural. Often, men who had exhibited little feeling for or interest in such matters found themselves increasingly drawn to such beliefs. After a few months in the field, ELAS officer Giannis Lainakis developed a fascination with the supernatural and began visiting mediums in the villages where his unit was stationed, seeking counsel on military and personal matters despite his initial prejudice towards 'these devilish things which I had never belief beforehand'.[161] Of course religion did not appear as a factor only after the onset of the civil war; it played a vital role in the lives of many guerrillas from the very beginning. Comrades might have offered affection, and agitators were able to provide a host of reasons for which one should fight; however, neither could help men address their more fundamental anxieties: the fear of death or injury, and worries over the fate of their loved ones. The available testimonies suggest that such beliefs became increasingly important as the war dragged on, enveloping the men in a situation for which they were not prepared. These beliefs offered respite, helped them to deal with the psychological effects of combat and enabled them to attach meaning to and explain a situation that appeared to be increasingly chaotic and meaningless.

Historians have often ignored the religious beliefs of the guerrillas, seeing them as being at odds with the ideological façade of the resistance. However, as Kenneth Slepyan noted in his study of Soviet partisans, 'partisans cannot be separated from the society from which they emerged'.[162] The guerrillas came from a particularly religious society in which Orthodox Christianity coexisted with a set of quasi-religious and superstitious beliefs. Demons and apparitions were commonly reported, while the casting of the evil eye could have a devastating effect on a man's fate. However, men and women were not without protection in this bewildering universe, since they could use a variety of 'prophylactic means ... some of them are magic substances with apotropaic power, others are symbolic objects, words or rituals, through which the Grace of God confronts and defeats the power of evil'.[163] Peasants would seek the help of sorcerers and fortune-tellers, who explained dreams and foretold the future. The guerrillas adopted this complex web of quasi-religious beliefs, developing their own systems. Orthodox religious practices coexisted alongside superstitions and taboos about sexuality, dreams and the body, which were applied to combat and everyday life, and whose function was to act as a shield against death and evil.

Faidon Maidonis had no direct experience of the civil war clashes. He joined EDES in spring 1944 and did not see any combat until midsummer. A fervent believer in the EDES cause, he expected his comrades to share his dedication; however, after some weeks he not only noticed an almost complete absence of ideological belief, but also began to note a series of beliefs and attitudes by which he was both repelled and fascinated. Maidonis soon came to realise that individuals and sometimes units had developed an intricate series of rituals, beliefs and practices that they used to predict fate and avert bad luck. Maidonis refused to espouse such beliefs despite the prompts of his comrades, but admitted that even men who had joined with him had begun to give credence to them, noting in disgust that 'they eventually became pawns to superstitions and omens, some sought solace in their belief in God, and others became blind fatalists'.[164]

Maidonis disparaged his fellow guerrillas for being feeble and squeamish. However, such men were far from the exception. ELAS officer

Cause, comrades and faith

Dimitris Dimitriou noted how, in the headquarters of his battalion, a guerrilla had created a lucrative trade by posing as a psychic and claiming that he could foretell the future by 'reading the cards'. According to Dimitriou, 'the men were flocking' to have their future told by this man, and they 'said that the psychic was a genuine one and that all his predictions were undoubtedly correct'. Encouraged by his NCOs, Dimitriou, who was worried about the fate of his family, not having seen them for several months, eventually visited the man himself. However, after a while and under pressure from his *kapetanios*, he ordered the man out and forbade similar displays among his men.[165] Such a medium established an equally lucrative career for a period in the ELAS 30th regiment.[166] When a fortune-teller was not close at hand, the guerrillas would appoint the role to one of their own. In Maidonis's platoon, this role was given to a guerrilla officer on the eve of operations.

> In Mouzaka ... the officers had a game of cards, afterwards they read the cards ... to see if the Germans were going to attack us ... the cards showed that the Germans were actually going to attack ... and they believed in it ... they believed in cards, in omens, like the old women back in 1800.[167]

Guerrillas developed a remarkably complex web of rituals and habits to predict the future, some borrowed from their civilian lives, others invented in the moment; 'if the omens are bad ... every discussion stops ... they all withdraw into themselves, drinking and smoking'.[168] Dreams and astronomical or weather phenomena, such as eclipses or thunderstorms, were regarded as omens for future events, and often affected the decisions and psychology of the men. One SOE officer noted how an eclipse threw a guerrilla band into disarray during an operation: 'Just before our start a blood-red, almost full moon came up and there was a very good eclipse, which caused a good deal of consternation and uneasiness among quite a few of the Andartes. Many wanted to stop over another day or quit altogether.'[169] Some men believed that the dreams one had on the eve of battle could foretell whether a man would survive or be killed. This was also in accordance with rural beliefs, which, according to the anthropologist C. Seremetakis, held that 'the advent of death engages a sequence of events and practices, beginning with warning dreams, visual and acoustic apparitions that announce impending death'.[170] EDES officer Vasilis Patsis recounted such a dream:

> I saw in my dream that I was in a certain encampment ... I understood that the soldiers in that encampment were my men ... Close by a wolf

was roaming ... The wolf attacked and managed to capture one of them. He dragged him away and disappeared into the forest and I was unable, despite the soldier's screams of agony to enter the forest ... Then I saw the mother of one of my guerrillas, Bakolas, crying and ripping out her hair and shouting ... She was the mother of the soldier whom the wolf had carried into the forest ... I woke up in agony ... because in my village they believe that if one sees a wolf in one's sleep ... it is a sign of impending death.[171]

ELAS officer Nikos Hatzinikolaou noted a similar incident:

A guerrilla called Mihalis Gouralis came to wake me up in order to tell me about a dream he had seen ... Mihalis insisted that the next day he would be killed and he wanted to tell me to look after his family ... I tried to convince him that dreams have no resemblance to reality ... but Mihalis would not believe this, but he was also one hundred per cent sure that dreams foretell the good or bad luck of men.[172]

ELAS officer Giannis Dimitroglou was also considered a savant by his men, who would often seek his advice about their dreams, especially on the eve of battle.[173]

However, even if fate was all powerful, the men had ways of stemming its advance through a complex web of rituals and taboos. One of the stronger taboos concerned the avoidance of sexual intercourse. The men believed that abstaining from sex would help them avoid death in combat. Furthermore, they believed that committing rape would certainly lead to one's demise in battle: 'There is a moral law, and also a human law, that everyone fears and all are subjected to. This law is tested in life ... If you dishonour ... a woman ... a deadly bullet will take you, the Grim Reaper will hunt you down and he will no doubt catch you.'[174] Left-wing resister Giorgos Kotzioulas noted that female sexuality had negative connotations for many of the guerrillas. Kotzioulas quickly exchanged the first gun he was issued, upon learning that the previous owner had been killed over a sexual affair: 'I considered it a bad sign fastening the bandoliers of a man killed over an affair with a woman'.[175]

These perceptions were consistent with the traditional understanding of female sexuality as 'something which is unseemly or out of alignment ... [and] that in some way ... pollutes'.[176] Male potency, honour and strength were all connected with sexual purity, which translated into the restriction of sexual intercourse to purposes of procreation only, and into strict control of the sexual activity of men and particularly women, who were seen as weak and prone to lust. Therefore, sexual intercourse was viewed as an activity that threatened the men's honour, since lust would weaken their will and self-control, thereby rendering them easy prey to the comments of other men and the workings of fate and supernatural powers. This was felt to be especially the case during wartime, when men needed to master all their strength and seek divine assistance to survive the tribulations of war. An EDES veteran noted that

> We were preparing for large scale operations, it was the summer of 1944, we were all fearful of our lives, but were also excited, a man in our company, from Lakka I think, while on leave had raped a woman, we believed that having intercourse while being an antarte was bad luck, women were for the fighter bad luck in general, but committing such an infamy with a woman was like signing your own death warrant, we implored him not to join us in the battle, to ask for leave, even to desert, he did not do it though, in the very next day during a skirmish a bullet struck him in the forehead and in an instant he was dead.[177]

Guerrillas were also careful to avoid people with physical deformities. Such conditions were ascribed to bad luck or even an evil disposition that could have repercussions for others if they did not keep away. ELAS guerrilla Stathis Geronikolas commented that he and the other guerrillas in his detachment became panicked when they spotted a baby that had six fingers: 'Nature had wreaked its revenge on this tender soul … but I, and perhaps many others as well, couldn't stop thinking all night, or close my eyes, because I was certain that something bad was going to happen to me the following day.'[178]

Taboos in relation to killing were equally important for the guerrillas; men tried to keep away from comrades who had committed a crime, or who had engaged in torturing prisoners. Such actions were seen as an 'evil and unnatural deed where supernatural sanctions rightly operated',[179] and it was thought that the spirits of the men and women who had suffered under their hands were pursuing them during combat. Sotiris Tsabiras was advised by a fellow guerrilla to avoid such a man in his unit. He was told 'Go away or you are lost. It is him that the shells are after. The murderer.'[180] Other men believed that such supernatural sanctions applied even if one killed an opponent in battle, and that a particular procedure had to be followed in order to avoid being 'seized by blood'; in other words, haunted and driven mad by an apparition of the victim. Maidonis was told by a fellow guerrilla that 'if you kill an enemy during battle, then you must smell the gunpowder from your gun, otherwise the blood of the dead man will seize you … and you get dizzy, you feel remorse … fear gets hold of you. The gunpowder … makes you drunk, it gives you strength.'[181] Others believed that tasting your victim's blood could avert this situation and enhance potency and bravery in combat. In some cases, prisoners had their throats slit by guerrillas who sought to improve their potency.[182]

Such beliefs coexisted with Orthodox Christian religious practices and customs. Many men wore amulets, attended services and beseeched the saints for favours by offering alms to the church. A group of ELAS guerrillas in Peloponnesus, while en route to join their detachment, stopped at a monastery to receive the abbot's blessing and take communion, and received a piece of holy bread as a talisman.[183] Many men would also wear crosses and icons under their vests, since it was believed that such items had protective powers both during and following combat, by shielding a man from death and illness.[184] It was believed that men who were particularly successful in combat or in avoiding enemy ambushes possessed extremely powerful talismans, usually a piece of the Holy Cross. Cretan nationalist leader Nikos Boutzalis was famed among friends and foes for being in possession of a piece of the Holy Cross that rendered him immune to bullets.[185] Equally famous among his comrades in the ELAS 9th regiment was guerrilla Giannis Kotsakis, who believed that 'bullets had no effect on him'. Some attributed this to Kotsakis wearing a fragment of the Holy Cross, while others attributed his immunity to a visit from female spirits during his youth.[186]

Some men would offer gifts to particular saints, most frequently to Saint George, Saint Demetrius or Saint Theodore, all of whom were seen traditionally as protectors of military men. Lainakis visited a church before embarking on some crucial operations with his unit and beseeched Saint George to help him survive: 'When we set off ... I prayed ... and called for the help of my protector and patron saint, Saint George, and I made a promise to do something in the church of my village which I indeed carried out during the liberation.'[187] Many guerrillas in Tsabiras's EDES unit also attended church often. During one break from operations, he noted, several men visited a country church and used the small quantity of oil they had left to light the church's chandelier, 'as a gift to the Virgin Mary'.[188] The guerrillas also attended church during religious holidays, and open-air services were particularly common in some ELAS units. ELAS guerrillas in Macedonia would attend services and often join in the singing of hymns and psalms.[189] When a priest was present in a guerrilla unit, the men would often ask for a service to be held or to receive the sacrament. Even men like Faidon Maidonis, who scorned the religiosity and superstition of his comrades, did not fail to attend a service or visit a church when he had the opportunity, noting 'we need God from time to time. Our hearts need something to grasp when we have no other consolation.'[190]

Maidonis's gradual transformation from an ardent ideologue to a sceptic and then to a man of religion exemplifies the peril inherent in attributing combat resilience to a single core factor. The conduct of war is essentially a deeply dynamic process. Men who enlisted for glory or political beliefs would often become disillusioned with guerrilla life and seek respite in faith, drink and group ties, while those who joined for material benefits sometimes became true believers. Ideology played a pivotal role in morale and unit cohesion during the early period. However, as the resistance bands expanded and the nature of war changed, the causes that led men to fight and endure hardship transformed accordingly. So, was ideology completely irrelevant? The answer must be no. Guerrillas needed to identify at least at an abstract level with their group's ideology in order to continue fighting; however, it is obvious that this was far from being the main factor and as the resistance dragged on it became less important and new factors begin to emerge, coercion, fear and religion being the most important.

However, while the significance of ideology diminished at the ground level, it continued to exercise a pivotal role on the ways in which the guerrilla groups tried to deal with and overcome the problems that emerged. ELAS and EDES faced similar problems: regionalism, insubordination, desertion. However, they sought and implemented different solutions to these challenges. ELAS used violence extensively and formed an elaborate surveillance apparatus to police political attitudes and stem dissent among the ranks. EDES also tried to reinstate discipline along regular army lines; however, it took a much more measured approach. It abstained from using the death penalty and while it placed increased stress on the guerrillas' political education, it stopped short of spying on the men or targeting dissenting political voices. In both cases, these choices were ultimately dictated by ideology. ELAS was formed and led by men who were reared in a Stalinist political environment, where fear of infiltrators and spies was almost pathological and where violence was not just seen as a necessary means to an end but celebrated as the hallmark of the true revolutionary. However, neither ELAS nor EDES managed to address the problem of morale and while sternness prevented the collapse of ELAS, it also bred corruption and disenchantment among the rank and file.

A history of the Greek resistance

Notes

1 Lelou Artemis and Popi Kostadinidou, *Treis Ierolohites* [Three men of the Holy battalion] (Athens: self-published, 1998), p. 24.
2 Dimitris Kremmos, *Hroniko, 1941–1944* [Chronicle, 1941–1944] (Athens: Politis, 2001), p. 109.
3 DIS/AND/File 2/Ekthesi pros ton kathodigitiko pirina tou kommatos tis VII merarxias/20/12/44.
4 ASKI/AKKE/Box 493/File-30/1/58.
5 ASKI/AKKE/Box 493/File-30/1/58.
6 ASKI Digital Archive/http://62.103.28.111/neolaia/rec.asp?id=61201&no foto=0 (accessed 5 January 2015).
7 ELIA Press Archive/Iho tou Vermiou/Issue 1/20/12/1943.
8 GES/DIS/Arheio Ioanni Katsadima [the Archive of Ioannis Katsadimas] (henceforth AIK) /Diary, p. 13.
9 ASKI Digital Archive/http://62.103.28.111/neolaia/rec.asp?id=56040&no foto=0 (accessed 5 January 2015).
10 Vasilis Rotas, *O agonas sta Ellinika vouna* [The struggle in the Greek mountains] (Athens: self-published, 1982), pp. 122, 123.
11 ASKI Digital Archive/http://62.103.28.111/neolaia/rec.asp?id=52579&no foto=0 (accessed 5 January 2015).
12 ELIA Press Archive/Eleftheri Makedonia/Issue/20/01/1944.
13 ELIA Press Archive/Eleftheri Makedonia/Issue/20/01/1944.
14 ELIA Press Archive/Laikos Stratos/Issue 1/19/10/1943.
15 ELIA Press/Eleftheri Makedonia/Issue 7/15/04.
16 ELIA Press Archive/Smolikas 29/01/1945.
17 ELIA Press Archive/Smolikas.17/11/1944.
18 *Megali Ellada, Periodos 1943–1945* [Greater Greece 1943–1945] (Athens: self-published, 1998), p. 89.
19 ELIA Press Archive/Dervanakia/15/01/1944.
20 ELIA Press Archive/Dervanakia/15/01/1944.
21 ASKI Digital Archive/http://62.103.28.111/neolaia/rec.asp?id=55411 (accessed 5 January 2015).
22 Thanasis Mitsopoulos, *To Trianta Sintagma tou ELAS* [The 30th regiment of ELAS] (Athens: self-published, 1987), pp. 101–2.
23 ASKI Digital Archive/http://62.103.28.111/neolaia/rec.asp?id=53792&no foto=0 (accessed 5 January 2015).
24 DIS/AGA/File IB/Geniko Arhigeio/1943/Kanonismos kai Antikeimena Ekpaideuseos.
25 Dimitris Votsikas, *Palevodas gia tin Lefteria* [Fighting for freedom] (Athens: self-published, 2001), p. 47.
26 Dimitrios Kremos, *Epilekta Tragoudia tou EAM-ELAS (1941–1944)* [Select songs of EAM-ELAS] (Athens: self-published, 2001), pp. 51, 43.

27 Kremos, *Epilekta*, pp. 18, 25.
28 Riki Van Boeschoten, *From Armatolik to People's Rule: Investigation into the Collective Memory of Rural Greece, 1750–1949* (Amsterdam: A.M. Hakkert, 1991), pp. 331, 374.
29 John A. Lynn, *Bayonets of the Republic* (Urbana and Chicago: University of Illinois Press, 1984), pp. 142, 143.
30 Mazower, *Inside Hitler's Greece*, p. 315.
31 ELIA Press Archive/Ginaikeia Drasi/25/07/1943
32 ELIA Press Archive/O Fanos tis Ipirou/1944.
33 ELIA Press Archive/Ethnike Floga/Issue 21/23/07/1944.
34 ELIA Press Archive/To Glikoharama/Issue 10/13/09/1944.
35 ELIA Press Archive/To Glikoharama/Issue 10/13/09/1944.
36 ELIA Press Archive/Ginaikeia Drasi/25/07/1943.
37 *Megali Ellada*, p. 16.
38 ELIA Press Archive/Ethniki Floga/30/07/1944; Epanastatis/Issue 47/07/08/1944.
39 *Megali Ellada*, p. 16.
40 GES/DIS/AGA/File E/EAM Ipirou perifereias Artas kai Prevezas 1943–1944.
41 ASKI/AKKE/493/File-30/1/55.
42 ASKI/AKKE/Box 493/File-30/1/55.
43 ASKI/AKKE/Box 496/File-30/4/140.
44 DIS/AGA/File 4/1-109/Ektakto deltio pliroforion, p. 3.
45 DIS/AGA/File 4/1-109/Ektakto deltio pliroforion, p. 3.
46 ASKI Digital Archive/ http://62.103.28.111/neolaia/rec.asp?id=54206&no foto=0 (accessed 2 January 2015).
47 Merridale, 'Culture, ideology and combat', p. 313.
48 C.M. Woodhouse, *Something Ventured* (London: Harper Collins, 1982), p. 68.
49 Gazis Kostas, *Antartika Tragoudia* [Guerrilla songs] (Athens: n.p, n.d.), p. 106.
50 ELIA/Arheio Athanasiou Triantafillide [the Athanasios Triantifillidis Archive]/File 2/p. 1.
51 GAKKI/AET/A/File/2/9, p. 5.
52 Maidonis, 'To Imerologio', p. 72.
53 DIS/AGA/File E/EAM Ipirou perifereias Artas kai Prevezas 1943–1944.
54 DIS/AGA/File E/EAM Ipirou perifereias Artas kai Prevezas 1943–1944/Epistoli/Anthipolohagos Haralabos Haraklias/19/08/1943.
55 GES/DIS/AIK/Diary, p. 6.
56 DIS/AIK/Epistoli/4/9/43/File E/159-172
57 GES/DIS/AIK/Diary, p. 11.
58 GES/DIS/AIK/Diary, pp. 11–13.
59 GES/DIS/AIK/Diary, p. 14.

60 GES/DIS/AIK/Diary, p. 14.
61 GES/DIS/AIK/Diary, p. 16.
62 LHCMA/Dobrski Papers/21/3 in 21/1-12/Maintenance of order in Greece, HQ Force 133, MEF.
63 LHCMA/Dobrski Papers/21/3 in 21/1-12/Maintenance of order in Greece, HQ Force 133, MEF.
64 IWM/Ward/Report on a visit, p. 4.
65 Baerentzen (ed.), *British Reports from Greece*, pp. 72–3.
66 ASKI/AKKE/Box 413/File-23/6/34.
67 G.E. Papageorgiou, *Pareleipomena tis ethnikes antistasis, anamniseis apo tin drasi tou 50ou sintagmatos tou ELAS* [Neglected aspects of the national resistance, memories from the actions of the 50th ELAS regiment] (Athens: Sinhrone Epoxe, 1981), pp. 200–1.
68 Papananos, *To Anti-iroiko imerologio*, p. 101.
69 ASKI/AKKE/ Box 413/File/23/6/7.
70 ELIA/GDA/File 16/Kommatiki Epitropi tou 4 tagmatos 7ou sidagmatos apofasis tis KO tou sidagmatos.
71 DIS/KMA/File 1/201-318/EOE/Arhigeio Ipirou/diatagi peri diafotiseos/16/2/44-22/2/44.
72 Maidonis, 'To Imerologio', p. 71.
73 Maidonis, 'To Imerologio' p. 111.
74 Maidonis, 'To Imerologio', pp. 108, 123.
75 Basil Davidson, *Partisan Picture* (Bedford: Bedford Books, 1946), p. 163.
76 ASKI/AKKE/Box 493/File-30/1/45.
77 ASKI/AKKE Archive/ Box 493/File- 30/1/45.
78 TNA/HS 5/Cpl. S. Morgan/General Report, pp. 1–2.
79 TNA/HS5/694/History of ELAS OCTU, p. 20.
80 ASKI/AKKE/Box 493/File-30/1/45.
81 ASKI/AKKE/Box 493/File-30/1/45.
82 Antonis Sanoudakis, *Oi teleftaioi Kourites* [The last Kourites] (Athens: Knossos, 2006), p. 111.
83 Romanos, *Mia Athinaiki vengera*, p. 65.
84 Tsabiras, *As min vrexei pote*, p. 67.
85 GES/DIS/File.954/E/104/Koinopoiesi genikis diatagis tou genikou stratigeiou peri gamon kai arravonon.
86 Tasos Karadis, *Oi Anamniseis tou Agonisti Vaggeli Saltameni* [The recollections of the fighter Vaggelis Saltamanis] (Athens: Lihnos, 2005), p. 289.
87 Romanos, *Mia Athinaiki vengera*, p. 153.
88 Romanos, *Mia Athinaiki vengera*, p. 65.
89 ASKI Digital Archive/http://62.103.28.111/neolaia/rec.asp?id=55254 (accessed 4 January 2015).
90 ASKI Digital Archive/http://62.103.28.111/neolaia/rec.asp?id=54339 (accessed 4 January 2015).

91 Foivos Grigoriadis, *To Antartiko ELAS/EDES/EKKA-5/42* [The Andartiko ELAS/EDES/EKKA-5/42] (Athens: n.p., 1964), vol. 1, p. 93
92 Maidonis, 'To Imerologio', p. 61.
93 Romanos, *Mia Athinaiki vengera*, p. 65.
94 John Ponder, *Patriots and Scoundrels: Behind Enemy Lines in Occupied Greece 1943–1944* (Melbourne: Hyland House Publishing, 1997), pp. 24–5.
95 Giannis Lalos, 'Apo tin Drasi tis Ipodigmatikis Dimoirias tis EPON tou 28ou Sigmatos tou ELAS' [From the activities of the exemplary EPON squad of the 28th regiment of ELAS], *Ethniki Adistasi* 78 (1993), p. 43.
96 Apostolis Delidiamadis, 'Apo Kariotisa Pelas ston ELAS' [From the village of Kariotisa in Pela to ELAS], *Ethniki Antistasi* 99 (1998), p. 24.
97 ELIA/APME/Nikos Koustas.
98 GAKKI/AET/Apostoli A/File 3/Ekthesis tis en ti elefthera oreini Ellada kratousis katastaseos, p. 2.
99 Fanis Tsakas, *Martiries gia tin antistasi kai ton diogmo* [Testimonies about the resistance and the persecutions] (Athens: self-published, 1982), p. 83.
100 Catherine Merridale, 'Introduction', *Journal of Contemporary History* 41 (2006), p. 205.
101 Tsanaklidis, *To 13o sintagma*, p. 67.
102 GAK Digital Archive/http://arxeiomnimon.gak.gr/browse/resourse.html?tab02&id=206315 (accessed 18 March 2014).
103 GAKKI/AET/Apostoli A/File 3/Ekthesis tis en ti elefthera oreini Ellada kra tousis katastaseos, p. 2.
104 DIS/KMA/File 1-101/Diatagi Peri Antartikon Omadon/29/06/43
105 Kremmos, *Hroniko*, p. 250.
106 Katsantonis, *Polemontas tous kataktites*, p. 232.
107 Katsantonis, *Polemontas tous kataktites*, p. 233.
108 Napoleon Zervas, diary, unpublished, Skoufas Library Arta, pp. 305, 314.
109 ELIA Press Archive/Iho tou Vermiou/20/12/1943.
110 ELIA Press Archive/Pindos/23/04/1943.
111 ELIA/AER/Dikastikin Epitropi 1ou tagmatos/File 22/30.4.44
112 DIS/File 1/A/Arheio Ligeraki/Ekthesi Lohagou Ligeraki peri ton gegonoton pou proigithikan tis genikis epitheseos tou ELAS kata EDES, pp. 16–17.
113 DIS/KMA/File/1/702-844/8h merarhia/koinopoiesis/16/8/44/diatagi genikou arhigeiou peri tis afthairetis metakinisis antarton.
114 ASKI/AKKE Archive/Box 493/File-30/1/44/29.4.44.
115 GAKKI/Small Collections/Box 116/K.D. Giannoulis, diary, p. 17.
116 GES/DIS/KMA/File 468-572/15on sidagma/19/05/44 diatagi 8hs merxarxias peri sillipseos antarton/17/05/44.
117 Sarafis, *ELAS: Greek Resistance Army*, pp. 155–7, 167–8.
118 Ponder, *Patriots and Scoundrels*, p. 36.

A history of the Greek resistance

119 GAK Digital Archive/http://arxeiomnimon.gak.gr/browse/resource.html?tab=tab02&id=206314 (accessed 5 February 2015).
120 Nitsa Koliou, *Agnostes ptihes katohis kai adistasi 1941–1944* [Unknown aspects of the occupation and the resistance] (Volos: self-published, 1985), vol. 1, p. 506.
121 ELIA/AER/I taxiaraxia/II tagma/12 sidagma/arith.prot. 210, pros ton 5on, 6on kai IIon loho polivolon/13/2/44; ELIA/AER/ELAS/1/2/44/arith. prot.1496.
122 IAM/Box 141/30 sintagma minaia ekthesis pepragmenon Dekemvriou.
123 Aristofanes Tsakas, *Trilogia* [Trilogy] (Athens: self-published, 1988), pp. 95–6; Giannakos-Giannis Mastrogiannis, *Hroniko to laiko kinima sto nomo Artas, 1931–1945* [Chronicle, the popular movement in the prefecture of Arta, 1931–1945] (Athens: Petra, 2004), p. 59; Rigas Georgios Skoutelas, *Ta Theodoriana Artas* [Theodoriana village in Arta] (Athens: self-published, 2006), p. 233.
124 ASKI/AKKE/Box 495/File-30/3/113.04.44; ASKI/AKKE/Box 495/File-30/3/133; ASKI AKKE/ Box 495/File-30/3/175/31.7.44; ELIA Press Archive/Antartika Neiata 4/March 1944.
125 ASKI/AKKE/ Box 493/File-30/1/80.
126 LHCMA Prentice/Wickstead Papers/2/5/1 Post-operation Reports, p. 3.
127 TNA/HS 5/695 The Andarte Movement in Epirus Jun 43–Feb 44, Major P. Bathagate, p. 3.
128 LHCMA/The Papers of Major Patrick Hutchinson Evans/Post-operation Report/2/1/7 1945, p. 1.
129 ASKI/AKKE/Box 493/File-30/1/52.
130 DIS/File 954/E/31/XVI merarhia ELAS pros tis monades tis koinopoiesis diatagis/24/11/1943; DIS/AGA/File Z/I Merarhia ELAS pros monades, koinopoiesis paratiriseon gia tin taktiki tou Germanikou stratou, pp. 1–3.
131 ASKI/AKKE/Box 493/File-30/1/52.
132 ASKI/AKKE/Box 495/File-30/3/52.12.10.44.
133 LHCMA/Evans Papers/Post-operation Report/2/1/7 1945, p. 3.
134 DIS/AGA/File ST/2/36 Tagma ELAS pros lohous, paratiriseis gia tin mahi tis Nafpaktou/9/07/1944.
135 The Noah's Ark operation was undertaken by ELAS and EDES with the help of several Anglo-American special forces units. The purpose of this operation was to harass the German troops as they gradually withdrew from Greece and cause the greatest number of casualties possible.
136 ASKI/AKKE/Box 494/File-30/2/103.12.10.44.
137 DIS/File-954/G/54 sintagma pezikou, ekthesi gia tis epiheiriseis tis 5/10/44 stin Portaria/9-10-1944, pp. 2–3.
138 IWM/Report by Major K.F. Scott MC, RE Officer No. 1 area, Cairo December 1944, p. 8.
139 Baerentzen (ed.), *British Reports from Greece*, p. 147.

Cause, comrades and faith

140 TNA/HS5/695/Lt. Col. Barnes NZE/Report on Zervas Andarte Movement/ Epireus HQ/Aug 14, 1944, p. 4.
141 Baerentzen (ed.), *British Reports from Greece*, p. 147.
142 TNA/HS5/695/Lt. Col. Barnes NZE/Report on Zervas Andarte Movement/ Epireus HQ/Aug 14, 1944, p. 4.
143 Spiridon Ioannou, *Katohe sto horio* [The occupation in our village] (unpublished, personal collection), pp. 3–4; NA/HS 5/695/Report by Lt. A.T. Curtis/21 Dec 44.
144 DIS/File 954/XVI merarhia ELAS pros tis monades tis, koinopoiesi diatagis tou genikou arhigeiou/24/11/1943.
145 DIS/File 954/XVI merarhia ELAS pros tis monades tis, koinopoiesi diatagis tou genikou arhigeiou/24/11/1943.
146 ELIA Press Archive/Laikos Agonistis/19/08/1944.
147 ASKI/AKKE/Box 410/File-23/2/27/15/6/44.
148 ASKI/AKKE/Box 410/File-23/2/22.
149 ASKI/AKKE/Box 410/File-23/2/21.9.6.44.
150 Romanos, *Mia Athinaiki vengera*, p. 64.
151 Skopouli, *Sta aposkia tis istorias*, p. 128.
152 Evangelos Vekris, *Protopapas, istoria kai paradosi* [Protopapas, history and tradition] (Ioannina: self-published, 2008), p. 299.
153 DIS/AGA/File/a.1 diatagi.
154 Baerentzen (ed.), *British Reports from Greece*, p. 124.
155 DIS/KMA/Arhigeio Ipirou/File 1/201-318/Diatagi peri diapragmatefseon EAM-EDES /20/02/44.
156 Baerentzen (ed.), *British Reports from Greece*, p. 150
157 Maidoni, 'To Imerologio', p. 67
158 Papananos, *To Anti-iroiko imerologio*, p. 142.
159 Nicholas Hammond, *Allied Military Mission in West Macedonia* (Thessalonica: IMXA, 1993), p. 183.
160 Zervas, diary, p. 352.
161 Lainakis, *Anamniseis*, p. 75.
162 Kenneth Slepyan, *Stalin's Guerrillas: Soviet Partisans in World War II* (Lawrence, KS: Kansas University Press, 2006), p. 5.
163 Campbell, *Honour, Family and Patronage*, p. 344.
164 Maidonis, 'To Imerologio', p. 77.
165 Dimitriou, *Antartis*, vol. 3, pp. 30, 31.
166 Lainakis, *Anamniseis*, p. 75.
167 Maidonis, 'To Imerologio', p. 100.
168 Romanos, *Mia Athinaiki vengera*, p. 81.
169 TNA/HS5/701/Report on Kaimaxila Area by Major T.C. Johnson, p. 12.
170 C.N. Seremetakis, 'The ethics of antiphony: the social construction of pain, gender, and power in the southern Peloponnese', *Ethos – Journal of the Society for Psychological Anthropology* 18 (1990), p. 486.

171 Patsis, *Sta ori ta Thesprotika*, pp. 53–4.
172 Hatzinikolaou, *Taragmena hronia*, p. 103.
173 Giannis Dimitroglou, 'Anamniseis apo tin Drasi tou 36 Sidagmatos ELAS' [Memories from the activities of the 36th ELAS regiment], *Ethniki Antistasi* 71 (1991), p. 68.
174 Maidonis, 'To Imerologio', p. 103
175 Giorgos Kotzioulas, *Otan imoun me ton Ari* [The days I was with Ares] (Athens, 1965), p. 127.
176 Campbell, *Honour, Family and Patronage*, pp. 276–7.
177 Giorgos Papas, personal interview, Igoumenitsa, 2007.
178 Stathis Geronikolas, 'Pareleipomena agoniston' [Overlooked experiences of fighters], *Ethiki Antistasi* 61 (1989), p. 59.
179 Campbell, *Honour, Family and Patronage*, p. 197.
180 Tsabiras, *As min vrexei pote*, p. 219.
181 Maidonis, 'To Imerologio', p. 133.
182 Antones Sanoudakes, Athanasios Psaroulakis and Giorgis Dafermos, *Ta limeria tou ELAS* [The hideouts of ELAS] (Athens: Knossos, 1993), p. 88.
183 Kossevakis, *I triti alitheia*, p. 321.
184 Lainakis, *Anamniseis*, p. 123.
185 Sanoudakis, *Oi teleftaioi Kourites*, p. 131.
186 Giannis Shinas, *I Ethniki antistasi stin Messinia* [National resistance in Messenia] (Athens: self-published, 1984), pp. 108–9.
187 Lainakis, *Anamniseis*, p. 123.
188 Tsabiras, *As min vrexei pote*, p. 82.
189 Koliou, *Agnostes ptihes*, vol. 1, p. 263.
190 Maidonis, 'To Imerologio', p. 101.

5

A society at war: guerrilla governance and everyday life in Free Greece

Few of the Italian soldiers who set off from the town of Arta on 16 January 1943 could have foreseen that their venture would end with their unit's annihilation a week later by the guerrillas of Spiros Karabinas, an illiterate charcoal burner and EDES band leader. Desperate to return to Arta, they tried to negotiate a truce with the help of the local teacher. Fearful for his own life, the teacher tried to persuade Karabinas that his demands were excessive and might result in the resumption of hostilities; however, 'he refused to change his tone' and told the teacher to 'make sure that you say what I told you just now, I am the government here'.[1] Karabinas was never a humble man, but his success and popularity among his guerrillas led him to develop a proprietorial attitude towards his district and the civilians who resided in it. Karabinas refused to cooperate with the regular army officers who were despatched by the EDES GHQ as military advisers, intervened in the affairs of the civilian committee that was appointed by the EDES authorities to replace the old village council and run day-to-day affairs, and used his position to settle grudges, in one case by murdering the son of an old rival.[2]

The case of Karabinas exemplifies the perils and complexities of guerrilla governance in Free Greece. Band leaders on both sides often believed that their sacrifices entitled them to the unquestioned fealty of the populace, an opinion that was seldom shared by the peasants or their political superiors. Such complications should not, however, simply be attributed to the guerrillas' vaingloriousness. Neither the men on the ground nor those who recruited them had any experience of such ventures. Guerrilla warfare had a long history in the mountains of Greece, but the predecessors of ELAS and EDES were seldom interested in the organisation of the civilian realm and were content with the shape of things as long as the peasants were willing to provide them with life's necessities: food, shelter and money. However, both ELAS and EDES were aware of the need to engage in state-building. EAM's manifesto clearly indicated that its purpose was to build a parallel state that would be run by its own cadres and committees and took active steps towards implementing this by forming nuclei of cadres in rural Greece. These measures were deemed necessary since EAM's leadership was fearful that the concentration of administrative authority in the hands of military leaders would give rise to Bonapartist tendencies within ELAS, and it believed that separation of powers would curb the autonomy of military commanders and make them more compliant to their requests. However, this was not the only advantage of state-building. An important study of rebel governance noted that the formation of state-like structures helped to establish 'a physical haven for the security of its leaders and continued development of the movement … demonstrated the weakness and ineffectiveness of the government to control and protect its own territory and population' and provided 'at least an aura of legitimacy' to the insurgent group.[3]

This chapter will describe and analyse how the People's Armies ruled the territories under their control. The formation and institutions of Free Greece have drawn the attention of historians from early on. Most studies have focused on the social and political origins of these institutions, discussing the extent to which the resistance institutions were influenced by the rural traditions of self-administration and the role of the Communist Party, among other issues.[4] These studies offered important insights into the formation and development of resistance institutions. However, they omitted a series of very important issues such as the background and motivations of the men and women who ran the institutions, their reception by the peasantry and their impact on the everyday life of rural communities.

Before the resistance organisations ventured to create their state, several issues had to be addressed such as the role and limits of the guerrilla armies and the institutions required to oversee day-to-day affairs. The answer to these problems was not self-evident, and the solutions adopted by the guerrillas often differed considerably from one area to another. Free Greece has been variously presented as a totalitarian state and a haven of democracy; however, the truth is that rebel governance might had a single aim, but it had many facets. Differences in political culture played an important role in this respect, while the character and background of the cadres who created and ran Free Greece were no less important. Only a small number of the men and women who ran these institutions were seasoned politicians, and fewer still had been involved in activist politics before the resistance's appearance. So, why did they join? Some were true believers; however, ambition played an important role, and nepotism was no less important. Many guerrilla leaders simply dismissed the existing village councils and appointed their relatives, and fear was often more important than political commitment. The arbitrariness of recruitment and the often haphazard manner in which these institutions were formed resulted in a chaotic situation in which cadres, civilians and guerrillas vied over the running of day-to-day affairs, with the latter coming out on top more often than not.

The resistance organisations tried to bring some order to this chaos during the summer of 1943 when, in cooperation with the British, they imposed a common administrative code for the entire liberated area. The civil war that broke out between ELAS and EDES and the devastating raids launched by the Wehrmacht during the winter of 1943–44 put an end to this experiment and changed radically the face of Free Greece. The inability of the resistance to defend its territory and the emergence of a host of collaborationist formations raised by the political rivals of EAM/ELAS led to a profound crisis of legitimacy. EAM/ELAS responded with a crackdown against dissidents and intensified its state-building efforts. Violence helped to stem the tide of defections and restore order in Free Greece, but ultimately it failed to check the expansion of the collaborationist formations.

Despite these problems, the guerrilla organisations enjoyed a noteworthy degree of support among significant swathes of the population. Ideology played an important role in this. However, not everyone was a true believer; many were attracted by the benefits that accompanied membership of the resistance and it was not uncommon for rank-and-file members, and even senior cadres, to change their allegiance when a more suitable patron appeared. Several scholars have argued that the resistance changed the clientelistic and family-centric model of rural politics and introduced ideological mass politics for the first time in the countryside. However, the persistence of such attitudes and the widespread corruption among EAM officials suggests that clientelism not only survived but was actually reinforced during the occupation. The advent of the resistance created a new class of notables; some of them were poor peasants who rose through the ranks but most were members of established families and veteran political brokers who aligned themselves with the resistance in the hope of retaining and furthering their power or obtaining revenge against their rivals.

Building the people's state

The guerrilla state did not materialise until mid-1943. Of course, a measure of self-rule existed in some isolated enclaves, such as the villages of Fournas and Kleitsos in the highlands of Evrytania; nonetheless, most EAM and EDES civilian committees functioned in a highly clandestine manner and were limited to the dissemination of propaganda and the recruitment of cadres. The appearance of the guerrilla bands and the gradual liberation of occupied territory enabled these men and women to come into the open. Elias Regas, the senior EAM cadre in the village of Lidizda, a small village in the Mourgana area of Epirus, announced the existence of EAM to his fellow villagers only after the first guerrilla band appeared in the area in January 1943.[5] Standing next to Spiros Skevis, the local ELAS *kapetanios*, Reggas apologised for keeping the organisation secret for the past year and a half, but insisted that 'secrecy was deemed necessary to protect the organisation from treason ... today finally free and without fear we call everyone, all patriots, to join this organisation'. Reggas's prompt was met with enthusiasm, although the first EAM institutions were not created until three months later.[6]

This delay was due largely to the lack of cadres. Reggas had recruited 12 men from a village of 500 inhabitants, half of whom went on to join ELAS, and while the peasants often responded enthusiastically, finding and convincing the appropriate people to join the various committees was seldom easy. The situation was particularly difficult in regions like Tzoumerka, a mountainous area spread over three districts and encompassing more than 50 villages numbering approximately 25,000 inhabitants, where EAM had no more than 150 cadres. In such regions, the institutions had to be created from above and often the source of cadres were the guerrillas' extended families.[7] Nepotism was no less prevalent in areas where cadres abounded, since ELAS *kapetanios* and senior cadres tended to fill most positions with people from their personal and familial network. In Lidizda, most senior positions were taken by Reggas's family members; the various EAM committees in the neighbouring village of Lia were occupied by the Skevis clan, who ran their community and broader area as their private fief; while the situation differed little in the highland communities of Tetrakomo and Mesounta in the Arta prefecture, where the Tsakas and Tsoumanis clans lorded over their fellow villagers.[8]

So, who were the men and women who ruled Free Greece? The available evidence is controversial to say the least. Several dispatches to the exiled government described senior EAM cadres as unscrupulous tyrants who were either imported from the nearby cities or came from the lower strata of rural society.[9] Such people were certainly not uncommon in the resistance ranks; however, they were not the majority and it seems that many cadres were affluent and influential men and women who had occupied positions of authority in pre-war society. Reggas ran the only shop in his native village and his family, as he admitted, was one of the more affluent in the area. His brother, Spiros, was one of a handful of youth in the whole Mourgana area who had experienced higher education, studying law at the prestigious Athens University.[10] Apostolis Tsoumanis, the EAM *ipefthinos* in the village of Mesounta, was one of the wealthiest men in the region; he owned hundreds of sheep and had been president of his community for several years before the war.[11] EAM cadres in the nearby villages of Athamanio and Agnada were professionals, law undergraduates, doctors and merchants.[12]

EAM cadres were drawn from similar social strata in other areas; the Papadimitiou clan who ruled the village of Rahoula in the uplands of Karditsa was one of the most affluent families of the region, and before the war had acted as *kommatarhes*, party bosses for the Liberal Party.[13] Dimitris Raptis, the *ipefthinos* of the village of Stagiades, also in Thessaly, was an affluent merchant. Raptis was active in local politics before the war, as he noted in his memoir: 'I was involved with merchants, lawyers, teachers, I followed political discussions, I read the papers, I took part in some events.' Nonetheless, he had little sympathy for the left and during the Metaxas years he was even appointed to a senior position in the local EON. Raptis was elected by acclamation after an ELAS band headed by Nikos Kafantaris, a firebrand *kapetanios* and lawyer in civilian life, visited his village and announced that it was their responsibility to help in the 'dual struggle against the foreign occupiers and the native enemies'. Kafantaris told the assembled villages that ELAS would be 'pitiless and we'll strike them wherever we find them … but in order to achieve all this we need to become organised and your village needs to be organised, you must elect an *ipefthinos* … the whole village shouted Dimitris Raptis'. Raptis tried to get out of this position; however, he was convinced to accept after Kafantaris warned him that not accepting would be viewed as treason. Raptis was well liked by his compatriots and proved to be an affable and moderate leader who remained popular throughout the occupation.[14]

This situation persisted well into the following year. An EAM report from Thessaly in April 1944 underlined the profound lack of peasant cadres in most administrative positions ('we haven't paid any attention to the need for creating peasant cadres') and noted that most local committees and the prefectural committee were dominated by educated, affluent men: 'it is indicative that only three out of twelve cadres in the prefectural committee are peasants, the rest are teachers, lawyers and doctors'.[15] As was to be expected, the persistence of the old guard in EAM's state was not always viewed positively.[16] The peasants of Rahoula complained to an EAM representative that despite the proclamations of change, the village remained a Papadimitriou fief.[17] The presence of such individuals in senior positions was also greeted with anger by many EAM members in the Macedonian prefecture of Edessa, who complained that despite EAM's denunciation of the Metaxas regime and proclamations of social change, local committees were often dominated by men and women associated with the dictatorship.[18]

Why did these people join the resistance? Kinship ties were certainly important; however, they were not the sole reason. Fear of being branded a reactionary was an important motivation, particularly for those like Raptis who had strong associations with the previous regime. Others saw their participation as a chance to perpetuate their dominance and defend their position from local rivals. Tsoumanis had been at loggerheads with most of his fellow villagers, who resented his dominance of the village's social and economic life. After the first EAM band appeared in the area, he rushed to offer his services in the hope that their support would enable him to strengthen his position *vis-à-vis* his local rivals. EAM's support rendered the Tsoumanis family the undisputed leaders of the area between 1942 and 1945.[19] Others believed that their support would enable them to expunge a less than agreeable past and even take revenge against their enemies. The village *ipefthinos* of Koutsoufliani, Nikos Ziogos, and his brother-in-law and second in command, Nikos Mouhekas, had started their careers as informants for the Italian army according to one source. Their motivation was not political, however, and it seems that the people who were denounced by the two men were their personal enemies. After the first ELAS bands appeared both men volunteered their services, hoping that this would pre empt their rivals' designs on revenge:

> when the guerrillas appeared they asked to be placed in senior positions. Ziogos had stashed away several guns which he rushed to give to the guer-

rillas and this made them think that he was a patriot. Kostas Lipas and Athanasios Misiakas did the same, they were also relatives of Ziogos. The guerrillas didn't ask anyone else. They took over all the posts; this way, Ziogos and Mouhekas found the chance to exterminate all their rivals.[20]

No different was Thanasis Giannopoulos, the EAM *ipefthinos* of the Ileian village of Klidonia, who, according to many of his fellow villagers, was driven to enlist by the prospect of power and wealth. Giannopoulos was neither affluent nor influential; however, he possessed several characteristics that rendered him an ideal candidate for this position. He was determined, an able speaker and, unlike most of his fellow villagers, he knew how to read and write. These attributes were enough to convince the local ELAS band leader that Giannopoulos and his son, who became his right-hand man during the occupation, were the most suitable men to run the village.[21] The EAM organisation of the nearby village of Koukouvitsa was also run as a family fief. The *ipefthinos* was Giorgis Mihalopoulos, who was probably selected because, like Giannopoulos, he was one of the few local peasants who was literate; however, Mihalopoulos must have been less sure of his success since he quickly surrounded himself with relatives, beginning with his brothers Kostas and Nikos, who became the *ipefthinos* for the local reserve ELAS, thus concentrating all power in the hands of the Mihalopoulos clan.[22]

Finally, a smaller number of men like Nikos Lenis, a 26-year-old labourer from the uplands of Tzoumerka, were appointed to positions because of their ideological beliefs. Lenis was the middle child in a family of nine whose father, a teacher, had died when he was very young. After graduating from high school in 1933 aged 16, he migrated to Athens where he worked as an apothecary. Lenis spent most of his free time in a labour club near his workplace where drinks and coffee could be purchased at knockdown prices. By reading the papers and engaging in conversations with other men, he soon became attracted to left-wing ideas. His mentor was Giannis Katsigiannis, a barber and fellow villager, and the two soon became friends and roommates. Katsigiannis introduced Lenis to left-wing literature, lending him Friedrich Engels's *The Origins of Family, the State and Property*, and he recruited him into the Communist Party. From 1935 to 1938 Lenis served in the army; later on, unable to find work, he returned to his village where he set up a Communist Party cell and, in 1943, he became the EAM *ipefthinos*.[23] Thanasis Giannoukos, the *ipefthinos* of the mountain town of Dimitsana in central Peloponnesus, had a similar background to Lenis. He came from a middling peasant family and finished the local high school, where he probably became acquainted with left-wing ideas, and then made a moderate living as a peddler. In 1936 Giannoukos was arrested and spent the next five years in various prisons. His resilience during those difficult years (Giannoukos declined to provide any information on his fellow comrades or sign a declaration of repentance) earned him the respect and admiration of his comrades and during the occupation netted him the enviable position of the *ipefthinos* in the province of Dimitsana.[24]

Men like Giannoukos developed a particularly unsavoury reputation during the occupation. Years of abject poverty and suffering at the hands of the state had rendered them particularly intransigent in their implementation of EAM's agenda and many eventually became 'satraps', who 'demanded the best food, bed and drink ... to compensate for everything they had missed'.[25] Often, such men viewed all those who had not been in exile as politically suspect and treated those who had signed a *dilosi* as 'worse than slaves'.[26] The rule of such men was often characterised by extreme violence, as real and imagined dissenters were targeted with a ferocity that shocked even seasoned EAM members.

EDES cadres tended to come from the upper strata of rural society: doctors, merchants, rich farmers, priest and teachers. Many of these men were seasoned politicians who had led their communities for years and were deeply trusted by their compatriots.[27] Unlike ELAS, EDES preferred to keep the village authorities intact unless they had been tainted by collaboration or criminal acts. However, their motivation was not uniform; some were driven by ambition, while others participated in these structures in order to outmanoeuvre their political adversaries. Nonetheless, the majority accepted these positions because they believed participation was both a patriotic duty and the best way to 'keep the village safe' and shelter their compatriots from the worst aspects of irregular warfare: arbitrariness, violence, looting and theft.[28] Of course, not everybody chose to take the high road; however, the intense regionalism and the paternalistic attitudes of these men, who believed that their foremost task was keeping their community structure intact, helped to prevent violence and ameliorate differences between the inhabitants.

As both EAM and EDES cadres came to realise, state-building was a slow and expensive process. The first step for both organisations was to re-establish the rule of law or at least their own version of it. Initially, justice was left to the various roving ELAS and EDES bands who took measures against criminals and moral deviants and administered their own brand of rough justice. However, this type of justice was both

A society at war

inefficient and often unpopular. The establishment and expansion of free areas facilitated the creation of a more sophisticated apparatus. EAM and EDES developed their own system of justice whose main tools were the people's courts, or revolutionary courts as they were known in EDES areas, which were composed, at least in theory, of the more educated peasants. The role of the police was played by the ELAS and EDES reserves until 1944, when they were replaced by the militia of the Ethnike Politifilake. The people's courts had a strictly local jurisdiction and were not allowed to try political cases, which were handed to ELAS and EDES court martials.

However, EAM/ELAS did not target only common criminals, but also those perceived as moral deviants, a broad category that included women and men who had extramarital relations with Italian and German soldiers, gamblers, homosexuals, wife-beaters and alcoholics. EAM's moralisation campaign is sometimes seen as gimmick whose purpose was to placate the fears of the conservative peasantry. However, this was neither the sole nor indeed the most important reason behind it. As with other left-wing movements, EAM regarded such attitudes as a deterrent to its goal of building the new man and woman who were going to populate the future people's state.[29] According to one cadre, the gravest 'weakness' of the youth in EAM's Roumeli heartland was 'immoral behaviour … wine, gambling, sexual relations',[30] an assertion that was repeated a year later by another cadre who derided the youth's idleness and 'tendency to seek sexual pleasure', which led them to forego their political duties and devote their free time to the pursuit of 'games of cards, wine, gossip'.[31]

Even though many cadres, including the two men who wrote the above reports, believed that education would suffice to stamp out these vices,[32] EAM took a much firmer line and adopted strict measures for those who displayed such attitudes. Gambling was outlawed in all ELAS-controlled areas and sometimes guerrilla squads were brought into villages to shut down cafés; in many cases, decks of cards were ceremonially burned along with the game tables.[33] Sexual 'deviants' were also punished severely; on one occasion, a young homosexual from the town of Karpenisi was abducted and murdered by ELAS.[34] Women were treated more leniently and most were released after they had had their hair cropped and the letter P for *porni* (whore) written on their foreheads; however, some were treated much more brutally and many were even murdered.[35] Extramarital relations were also strictly prohibited to guerrillas and civilian cadres, and could lead to demotion or worse. The entire EPON committee of the village of Zarafona in Laconia, whose members had become notorious for their sexual licentiousness, were demoted and drummed out of the district.[36]

Nonetheless, civilian and guerrilla conceptions of justice often differed radically, since many of the latter came to believe that their pioneering role in the national struggle and their sacrifices entitled them to dictate their own terms to local communities. Many peasants responded positively to the persecution of traitors and the punishment of anti-social elements, but eventually they came to see the guerrillas as a threat since they were not slow to use violence to punish the slightest infraction, from a derogatory comment to a refusal of food or a criticism of their methods. Such attitudes often led the guerrilla bands to clash with the EAM civilian committees, who were often unable to stop the guerrillas from savaging their compatriots, looting their supplies and punishing real and alleged traitors with shocking barbarism. These attitudes resulted in a backlash, particularly in western Macedonia where by the spring of 1943 the guerrillas were seen as no better than the occupiers by a large number of peasants. An article in *Smolikas*, the official newspaper of the local ELAS, noted that 'our relations with the people are not good ... the people see us as tyrants, as an occupation army ... instead of the protectors of their honour and property; this is because of our unscrupulous behaviour and the violence that has been so often used'.[37]

However, the peasantry were not completely helpless and eventually they were able to find ways to shape the rules and policies that emerged during the making of Free Greece and resist the impositions of the guerrillas. Defying the resistance authorities was, of course, a risky undertaking, and it could lead to arrest or worse at any time. Therefore peasants avoided direct confrontation and instead used the 'weapons of the weak'[38] – foot-dragging, cunning, sabotage – to resist guerrilla impositions. Subversion was the foremost weapon for those faced with unsympathetic officials or people's courts: 'irony was often used against the people's courts and the judges and many times the cunning peasants were able to push them into a corner with their ingenious appeals and with other schemes'.[39] Similar methods were used to protest against the overthrowing of respected community leaders. One of the first acts of ELAS after entering a village was to ask for the replacement of local leaders and the creation of an EAM committee in their stead. Peasants were rarely able to reject such demands; however, they often managed to resist and subvert them by staffing such committees with underage children or even individuals with mental disabilities. In one case an 8-year-old girl was elected as village *ipefthinos* by her compatriots. Such tactics, whose goal was to 'demean the institutions', often forced the resistance authorities to tacitly retreat and allowed communities to protect and retain their local institutions.⁴⁰

Similar tactics were also used to resist requisitioning and taxation. Peasants would mix grain and maize with dirt and sawdust and adulterate the oil, milk and dairy products demanded by the guerrillas, or hide or injure pack animals so as to make them temporarily unavailable for commandeering.⁴¹ Sabotage and protest would often force the guerrilla authorities to change their policies; for instance, a rapid increase in hoarding and smuggling forced EAM to discontinue taxing commercial transactions between the highland and lowland areas in early 1944.⁴² Bribery was also used extensively. Peasants would pay off local officials to release relatives from captivity or to exempt them from taxation and when such tactics did not work they tried to appeal to the cadres' sense of family and regional loyalty.

EDES band leaders were often susceptible to both ploys. It was not unusual for EDES band leaders to disobey orders to collect taxes or arrest local peasants, and some even used force to stop other units who tried to arrest local men. EDES band leader Apostolis Papakostas arrested a group of EDES guerrillas from an adjoining district who were despatched by the EDES HQ to arrest the priest of his native village. He said to their leader, 'What would you do if I came to your village and tried to arrest and kill people without asking for your approval? Would you be so cowardly as to accept this, or have you imagined that you can come here and do what you wish?' The guerrillas protested that they were simply following the orders of the local district commander; however, Papakostas remained intransigent and threatened to shoot them if they returned.⁴³ Such attitudes had an adverse effect on EDES's state-building efforts, since the localism of regional leaders, many of whom paid only nominal allegiance to the organisation, undermined its efforts to impose an effective and unitary authority across its area. A British officer argued caustically that the 'EDES organisations ... have the same niceness and about the same efficiency as branches of the Mother's Union'.⁴⁴ However, they also played an important role in defusing violence and shielding the peasants from the excesses of EDES cadres:

> excesses were not unusual, though if you were arrested by EDES, there was a good chance that a friend or an acquaintance in the organisation would intervene to save you. However, I believe that things were very different with ELAS since with them if you've tried to help a kinsman or a friend you could get into serious trouble.⁴⁵

Such attitudes were less conspicuous in EAM/ELAS, though numerous EAM reports show that familial and regional ties continued to play an important role. EAM and ELAS cadres would often warn their relatives about an impeding arrest, falsify reports to allow them pay less tax or even help them to escape into the occupied areas.[46] However, such resistance should not be seen as a sign of political disaffection; as a scholar of insurgency noted, 'subjects may agree with certain political goals of the ruler but still disagree with the specifics of its rule'.[47] It was not uncommon even for senior cadres to engage in subversion and sabotage when they believed that their personal or communal rights and interests were being violated by the guerrilla organisations.[48]

The situation was ameliorated after the signing of the national agreement in July 1943. This accord, which entailed the creation of a shared guerrilla headquarters and the unification of Free Greece, brought all the major resistance organisations into a single body under British supervision and managed to introduce a semblance of order to the various self-government experiments and stem the growing peasant unrest. This agreement also resulted in a charter for self-government, which was applied across Greece with a few variations, thus creating for the first time a unified authority across the country. Local government institutions, which varied widely from one area to the next, were standardised; all villages below 4,000 inhabitants were run by democratically elected people's committees that were invested with all the authority of the pre-war village councils. The self-government structures were completed by the provision of subcommittees tasked with relief, rural safety, people's courts and the creation of a rural police force. The joint guerrilla HQ also made significant efforts to reduce tensions between guerrillas and civilians and between the guerrillas of vying organisations by creating a military police force and joint court martials whose task was to curb violence against civilians and behaviour such as drunkenness, the discharging of guns in public places and theft, which had seriously damaged the reputation of the guerrilla organisations.[49]

The joint guerrilla HQ also took a series of measures to deal with rising inflation and food scarcity. The first step was the introduction of a fixed exchange rate for the gold sovereign, which had become the main currency in Free Greece after the arrival of the BMM. Food prices and services were set at fixed rates while a form of taxation in kind, ranging from 1–10 per cent, was applied to olive oil and grain producers. Provision was also made for the restoration of the communication networks and the reorganisation of the forestry and postal services and the telegram

A society at war

and telephone companies. However, these measures were not completely effective; in many cases, taxation resulted in hoarding and an increase in black market trading since peasants preferred to sell their produce to the nearby towns for higher profits. The authorities reacted by introducing severe penalties for hoarders and black marketeers and imposing limitations to food exports.[50] However, cracks had already begun to appear in this edifice and more broadly in guerrilla unity. Rivalries between guerrillas and civilians were increasing, and despite the constant shows of unity, relations between ELAS and EDES continued to be adversarial, with each organisation guarding zealously its predominance in its area. A contemporary document underlined that both the guerrillas and the members of the civilian organisations had shown that they had not understood 'the purpose and the spirit' of the new situation.[51] Indeed, it was not long before these differences led the resistance organisations into a bitter and prolonged civil war.

The civil war and the crisis of legitimacy

Civil war had been brewing since the summer of 1943 when ELAS attacked and dispersed the small right-wing resistance organisations of Panellinia Apeleftherotiki Organosi (PAO) in Macedonia, Ellinikos Stratos (ES) in Peloponnesus and Ethniki kai Koinoniki Apeleftherosi (EKKA) in central Greece.[52] Post-war accounts have presented such actions as a justified response to unwarranted provocation and even claimed that these organisations had been actively collaborating with the enemy.[53] However, EAM's desire to monopolise the resistance had been demonstrated from early on. In early 1943 ELAS bands dispersed the small republican groups of Majors Kostopoulos and Vlahos in Thessaly, and executed several of their men who had defected from ELAS, while outright fighting between ELAS and EDES was prevented only at the last minute during January 1943.[54] The creation of the joint guerrilla headquarters, Operation Animals and the subsequent landings in Sicily convinced many senior EAM/ELAS cadres that liberation was near and that a pre-emptive strike was necessary to deter the restoration of the monarchy and the establishment of a British-sponsored dictatorship. Ares Velouhiotes, ELAS co-commander along with General Stephanos Sarafis, held that Corfu would be liberated by the British 'in the next few days' and believed that this was the first step 'in bringing back the King by force ... let us not fool ourselves, the British are far worse than the Germans'. Velouhiotes asserted that a swift response was necessary and encouraged the EAM leadership towards taking this step:

A history of the Greek resistance

we must react promptly; by that I mean that we should call an EAM–ELAS–EDES–EKKA conference and ask them to sign a public declaration that they would in no way accept the return of the king and will resist with force if necessary any such effort … if they decline to sign such a declaration EDES and EKKA must be attacked and dispersed immediately even if this means that blood will be spilt.[55]

Fighting finally erupted in Epirus on 8 October 1943 and extended to parts of western and central Greece during the following days. ELAS attacked and disarmed EDES bands in Zagori, Evrytania, Thessaly and western Greece. EDES emerged victorious in much of Arta, Preveza and Ioannina where it drove off the ELAS bands. While this fighting was ongoing, the Wehrmacht unleashed some of the deadliest counter-guerrilla operations of the occupation; Operation Panther began on 18 October and had as its main goal the opening of the Ioannina–Kalabaka motorway; it was followed by operations Tiger, Puma, Adler and Hubertus. The aim of these operations was twofold: to re-open specific strategic routes such as the Giannena–Metsovo road that were held by the guerrillas, and to destroy the material and social basis of the resistance by carrying out a scorched-earth policy. The guerrillas were unable to resist the Germans; many fled, dropping their weapons and leaving the peasants to cope as best as they could. A British liaison officer to ELAS noted in his report that

> the following morning 2 November we were turned out before daylight and bundled off with a stream of refugees … the next three days was just one headlong flight before the Germans, walking about 11 hours a day most of the time, we were a rear guard to the ELAS andartes … on this trip several people dropped out and died by the side of the track through exhaustion.[56]

The devastation that began with the Germans was completed by the guerrillas as, brutalised by days of hardship, they descended into villages, looting indiscriminately and attacking those who tried to protect their property. Fear, panic and a sense of doom had 'turned the guerrillas to bandits'.[57] As an EDES cadre noted, 'the destruction they have perpetrated is often far worse than what the German did … many houses were completely looted and many people have been left without clothes on their backs … protests, curses, threats are all that we hear every single day'.[58]

The devastation in many areas was complete. A Red Cross representative who toured the villages of western Thessaly a few days after the end of the operations noted that 'the formerly flourishing communities

A society at war

of Pindus lay in ruins, their population dishevelled and devastated has taken refuge in the mountains ... all their property has been destroyed'. In the areas of Karditsa and Trikala the homeless exceeded 23,000.[59] The situation was even worse in Epirus where more than 40 per cent of the rural population had been rendered homeless, with one in three villages destroyed; 'the harvest has been destroyed ... whole villages have been destroyed, houses, barns, stables, schools and churches and there is no material left even to build a hut in order to shelter their families in the midst of winter'. The residential loss was not the only problem; food stocks and animals were almost completely depleted ('there is no fodder and no food left') and according to a report, many were reduced to eating grass and corn stems. Moreover, poverty and destitution led to the outbreak of epidemics: 'inadequate nutrition has led to an outbreak of malarial fevers ... dysentery is an even greater enemy, the sight of men and women and children emaciated and half-naked, deadly pale, staring blankly and begging for mercy as if they were convicts is both disheartening and common'.[60] These crises also had serious social repercussions, since poverty and hardship had reduced many areas to an anarchic state:

> There is no safety neither in the forest nor in the mountains ... Epirus, AeteloAkarnania, Valtos and the highland villages are living a terrible drama ... suspicion reigns ... brother suspects brother, parents their children and children their parents, a state of terrorism, anarchy and violence dominate everyday life, abduction is common and people are living in a heart-breaking angst for what will happen tomorrow. Hunger has brutalised the people and narrowed their consciousness, banditry offers relief from hunger and looting is used to quell their needs, the one village is afraid of the other, the one organisation suspects the other, old passions are taking new shape and are brought to the surface and one brother sheds the blood of the other.[61]

Destitution and fear of reprisals led to a massive relocation of the population. More than 2,000 peasants from the Fokida uplands were forcibly relocated to the towns of Tritaia and Galaxidi where they lived in horrible conditions, destitute, homeless and hungry.[62] The situation was equally serious in parts of Evrytania:

> it is impossible to give an accurate description of the homeless and destitute villagers ... many of them have taken shelter in the forests, others have relocated to the nearby villages and towns while some have returned to their native villages, living in ruins, human ruins themselves. Hunger, malarial fever and deprivation are decimating them every day ... in the Agrapha prefecture the number of deaths have increased by 17%.

A history of the Greek resistance

The number of destitute villagers exceeded 130,000 in central Greece alone.[63] The situation was equally bad in western Macedonia, which was described by a Red Cross representative as a 'Dantean Inferno' where destitute peasants

> seek shelter in nearby communities begging to be housed in barns and stables, others take shelter in the mountains, the caves, the forest and the ravines where they try in vain to keep their families alive ... finally the more daring seek refuge in Thessalonica and other Macedonia towns where day after day they see their hopes quashed.[64]

Depopulation and destruction of property and disease were accompanied by destruction of infrastructure and a massive flight of the local intellectual and political elites; civil servants, merchants and academics abandoned their communities to seek safety in the local cities and the capital.[65]

The repercussions for the guerrilla organisations were equally serious. The anti-guerrilla operations rendered the provisioning of the guerrilla bands extremely difficult, and in many areas led to a huge defection of cadres. Membership declined by more than 30 per cent in some Macedonian communities; many cadres defected while others sought refuge in the cities.[66] The situation was even worse in Thessaly, where according to a report the whole organisational edifice of EAM 'was almost in ruins'.[67] Defection and desertion were equally common in this region; 'many of our cadres deserted' noted a local cadre, who further underlined that 'the organisations declined massively ... the reserve ELAS was almost completely dismantled'.[68]

In many areas, the situation was rendered even worse by the barbaric attitude of the guerrillas, who molested and blackmailed peasants and looted their properties with complete abandon. Such behaviour shocked the ELAS authorities and prompted them to ask for a 'swift cleansing of the ranks' of 'these elements who seriously harm the relations between the people and ELAS'.[69] Such attitudes were particularly conspicuous in parts of Epirus and western Greece where EDES was predominant before the civil war. The attitudes of ELAS differed little from those of the occupation troops in these regions. After a unit of ELAS entered the village of Theodoriana, a solidly pro-EDES community, its commander warned the assembled villagers that 'if the guerrillas come and ask you for food do as you are asked ... if someone is going to die from hunger then rest assured that you will die first; we, keep it in mind, we will die last'.[70] ELAS stood true to its promise. Within two months the local peasants had contributed over 600 sheep and four tons of maize to the guerrillas. Clothes, blankets and even shoes were requisitioned, leaving the peasants 'shoeless and naked' despite the protest of local cadres. Several peasants were tortured by the guerrillas who looked for money and weapons, while two men had their ears cut off by ELAS guerrillas for spreading false rumours. Epidemics wreaked havoc in the area and many suffered from typhoid fever and malaria because of malnutrition and the lack of clothes and shelter, the inhabitants having been thrown out of their houses by the guerrillas.[71] Hundreds of peasants abandoned their homes and took shelter in the towns of Arta and Amphilohia where they lived in extremely harsh conditions.[72]

As anticipated, tensions rose between the peasants and the guerrillas and led to a plummeting of morale, as peasants became increasingly unwilling to enlist in the guerrilla forces or provide food or help in any way, since they considered the guerrillas to be equally as responsible as the Germans for their misery. A senior EDES member noted in his diary that after the destruction perpetrated by the Germans, 'the native population is hostile to the guerrillas, we do not dare show our faces in the areas that we used to hold'.[73] The peasants in the Aspropotamos region of Thessaly who had seen their houses and barns go up in flames had also turned against the resistance by early 1944. The villagers' anger, according to a local historian, 'was not directed just against the Germans but also against the guerrilla leadership since they believed that they had been betrayed by the guerrillas who had fled instead of fighting'.[74]

The situation was no better in other parts of the country. An EAM cadre from northern Peloponnesus noted that

> after the mass executions of the inhabitants of Kalavrita and the burning of the town ... all the political organisations of EAM in the 18 villages of the prefecture have stopped functioning, morale has plummeted because of the fear and terrorism to the point that even the mere appearance of a cadre or lone guerrilla was enough to make the inhabitants flee.[75]

The mood of the peasantry was no less affected in central Greece. A senior ELAS cadre who travelled through the region in early 1944 noted that 'during my last tour I observed ... a sharp decline in morale, in combativeness and in the willingness to contribute further to the struggle. This was the situation in most villages of Fthiotida and Parnassida, the situation in Dorida is far worse.'[76] EDES was denounced even by its former supporters. The conservative village president of Menidi, who saw his community destroyed after an EDES ambush, decried the guerrillas as 'despicable human beings who were unfortunately Greeks and whose base actions serve no other purpose than the destruction of the rural population'.[77]

The peasants found themselves in an impossible situation. If they left their villages, they would be targeted by the Germans as pro-resistance; conversely, if they stayed to protect their properties and tried to mediate with the Germans, they would be arrested and manhandled by the guerrillas, who accused everyone who did not flee of being a Germanophile:

> the peasants were caught between a rock and a hard place … when the guerrillas returned to the villages after the Germans left, and usually the Germans did not stay more than a few hours, they would ask around who talked to the Germans and then proceed to beat them up, as if it was easy for any peasant to refuse to talk to the Germans if they interrogated him, or to turn his back at them.[78]

The indifference of ELAS towards the plight of the peasantry was often shocking. Peasants who tried to convince local commanders to desist from fighting or pleaded with them to exchange their prisoners for their relatives who were held hostage were not only dismissed but in some cases were threatened with violence by guerrilla commanders.[79]

Anti-guerrilla operations had an equally detrimental effect on life in the urban centres. Reprisals isolated the towns from their hinterland, leading to a massive increase in food prices and bringing hundreds of destitute refugees who further depleted the meagre resources available. Urban elites were also increasingly targeted by local Wehrmacht commanders who used them as hostages and executed them after guerrilla actions; for example, in Monodendri, 118 citizens of Sparta were shot in reprisals for ELAS actions,[80] and in the town of Paramithia in Epirus 49 local notables were executed after an EDES attack that cost the lives of six German soldiers.[81] However, it was not only the elites that suffered; ordinary citizens were also liable to be arrested and taken hostage or molested by marauding bands of soldiers who sought revenge for the loss of comrades. This situation eventually led to a violent swing to the right among townsmen and peasants alike:

> violence has changed the mood among the peasantry who initially welcomed the guerrillas … now they have come to prefer the German occupation while many have begun to speak in favour of the King even though few were enthusiastic about him before … if things turn around and the peasants feel that they are protected by the state then they will seize all these

petty tyrants who rule the villages and hang them, this is what I have heard and not just by one or two persons.⁸²

ELAS publications condemned such attitudes violently and treated such criticism with derision. One ELAS newspaper in Peloponnesus noted characteristically that

> many villages were looted and put to the torch ... and the inhabitants, lacking an elevated consciousness, sometimes panicked because they didn't understood that freedom needs sacrifices, blood and more blood ... the people must be armed with more courage and must be certain that ELAS will soon make these criminals answer for their crimes.⁸³

Another article reminded readers that 'freedom and social progress does not just fall out of the sky but is achieved by sacrifices ... do not hesitate ... nothing has any worth, neither life, nor fortune while we remain slaves and all those who claim the opposite are your enemies and agents of the enemy'.⁸⁴

However, local communities remained sceptical and in many cases local elites appealed to the guerrilla forces and asked them to suspend their activities. The EDES and ELAS headquarters in Epirus were visited repeatedly by deputations comprising notables and local ecclesiastics, including the bishops of Arta and Paramithia and the metropolitan of Ioannina, who warned the local ELAS and EDES commanders of the growing 'anti-guerrilla feeling' among the peasantry and implored the guerrilla authorities to end their operations.⁸⁵ Such entreaties were rejected by ELAS; however, EDES proved to be more amenable, for several reasons; Zervas was targeting a post-war political career and widespread destruction would not sit well with future supporters. Moreover, Zervas was genuinely concerned about the future of his group since he was squeezed between ELAS and the Germans. Finally, it must be underlined that Zervas was genuinely concerned with the plight of the local population. He was a local man of peasant origin and, according to the personal testimonies that he left, he was genuinely fond of the peasants who served under him. Zervas was reported to have said to the local metropolitan that he would 'abstain from any sabotages in the future even if the middle east HQ commands him to do so because enough blood has been shed for these actions that have brought no meaningful result'.⁸⁶ It seems that he kept his promise since, according to one source, he organised an unofficial truce with the German authorities that lasted with interruptions between February and May 1944.⁸⁷

Even though the Epirus ELAS declined to request a truce, other units proved more amenable. For instance, the local ELAS 8th regiment agreed to a temporary truce with the Wehrmacht in Laconia.[88] ELAS tried to slow the pace of operations in other areas as well. Following a spate of executions in reprisal for the killing of a German doctor in an ambush, the Macedonian ELAS ordered the guerrillas to abstain from small operations that led to needless reprisals and instead focus on 'numerically strong groups'.[89] However, not all units followed this practice and ELAS remained intransigent, especially at the lower levels. One British officer noted that 'villagers often sent up deputations to implore us not to attack the Germans in their neighbourhood ... hot headed guerrilla leaders on the lower level were not always scrupulous about this, and often caused hostages to be hanged for the destruction of a German car or the kidnapping of a German NCO'.[90]

Reprisals had another, more sinister outcome: the foundation and increase of collaborationist formations. Collaborationist militias were not a new phenomenon. However, their scope and recruitment was initially limited to ethnic minorities: Slavic Macedonians, Vlachs, Muslim Albanians. Most of these militias were poorly armed and operated in a highly disorganised manner. There were also Greek bands, for example those of Colonel Georgios Poulos, a career soldier whose militia was raised among *déclassé* elements from the urban youth in search of adventure, the impoverished and the unemployed. The expansion of ELAS and EDES in the summer of 1943 had led these groups to curb their activities, and some of them almost ceased to exist after Italy's capitulation.[91]

However, during the winter of 1943–44 collaborationist formations expanded rapidly beyond the minority communities. The violence used by EAM/ELAS against real and alleged rivals had already raised the ire of large segments of the peasantry, particularly among the followers of the scattered right-wing resistance organisations who had been systematically persecuted during the previous few months. The apparent weakness of ELAS provided an opportunity for such men, whose numbers were further swelled by peasants who accepted weapons to guard their districts for fear of German reprisals. Such militias were particularly conspicuous in Macedonia where terrified peasants asked for weapons to protect their villages from guerrilla intrusions, fearful that any guerrilla activities would lead to severe German reprisals. The situation was particularly grave for EAM in the Pieria and Kozani regions, 'where the constant raids of the Germans ... had enabled the local armed reaction to mobilise its forces to such an extent that it is

A society at war

now a threat and an obstacle to the national liberation struggle in our whole province'.[92]

The village of Koukos, a lowland, ardently conservative Pontic Greek community that had supported the nationalist PAO in the previous months, constituted the nucleus of the local militias in Pieria, which mushroomed impressively in the winter of 1943–44. By January 1944 over 340 men in twelve different villages had received arms from the Germans. This alarmed the local ELAS commanders who urged their GHQ to despatch a large number of forces for a decisive strike, since the local regiment was unable to deal with the reaction by itself.[93] However, peasants did not join simply out of fear or ideological opposition, but also because of disappointment with ELAS's performance during recent operations against the Germans. It is indicative that a significant number of those who joined the collaborationist militias were former ELAS reserve guerrillas. The arming of the villagers led to the disillusion of EAM committees and the flight of many cadres to the free areas. Hundreds of villagers were also armed in the area of Kozani and Ptolemaida between January and February 1944, where the various militias numbered approximately 4,000 men in March 1944.[94]

Between November and January 1944 a host of militias known as security battalions also sprang up in central Greece and Peloponnesus. The origin of the security battalions can be traced in the ascent to power of the Rallis government. The parent unit of the security battalions was the 'Guard of the Unknown Warrior'. Initially, this was an unarmed ceremonial unit; however, in the autumn of 1943 it was re-armed by the Rallis administration whose plan was to turn it into the nucleus of a much larger armed force. The security battalions first came into existence in Athens during September 1943 and, during the winter of 1943–44, they were exported into central and southern Greece.[95] The background of the men who composed them was quite complex. A British report divided them into the following categories: the 'very poor, who joined in order to survive; criminal types, volunteers inspired by hatred of EAM/ELAS, including those whose relatives have been killed by them, political opportunists, officers who consider the fight against "Communism" a patriotic duty and members of other organisations who were attacked by EAM/ELAS'.[96] The first battalions outside Athens were formed on the island of Euboea, which numbered by January 1944 over 400 volunteers, and in the Peloponnesian prefecture of Laconia, where they were led by Leonidas Vrettakos, the brother of a nationalist resistance leader who was murdered by ELAS. By late January 1944 security battalions had

A history of the Greek resistance

been formed in most major towns of Peloponnesus under local officers. Militias were also created in Aetoloakarnania and the towns of Agrinion and Nafpaktos in February 1944 after a unit crossed from the opposite coast. By February of 1944 large areas of the lowlands in these regions were under battalion control.[97]

The collaborationist militias comprised a complex mosaic that at its height encompassed between 25,000 and 30,000 armed men distributed over fifteen different organisations. Not surprisingly, these organisations presented considerable variations in their character, composition and mode of operations. In northern Greece collaborationist units were as a rule formed on the basis of ethnicity and were comprised of ethnic minorities: Muslim Albanians, Turkophone Pontic Greeks, Vlachs and Slavophones. Conversely, the various militias that operated in southern and central Greece were formed 'on the basis of ideology'. However, the ideological agenda of these bands and the men who raised them and led them 'was negative rather than positive, anti-Communist rather than Fascist'.[98] These groups also presented significant differences in their structure and mode of operations. Most ethnic militias had a strictly local horizon; their foremost task was keeping the guerrillas off their communities and guarding strategic routes and installations. Accordingly, only a small number of these men took part in direct actions against the guerrillas outside their home areas. Most of these units were formed and commanded by local notables such as Kostas Papadopoulos, a 60-year-old veteran band leader of the Pontic Greek guerrilla struggle in 1919–22,[99] and Abdulah Santiku, the son of a rich farmer and village headman who had been killed by EDES guerrillas, who was the undisputed leader of the Albanian Muslim bands that operated in Thesprotia and Preveza.[100] The security battalions tended to be more militarised, since they contained a large number of regular army officers. These units repeatedly took part in operations outside their home district and even copied some of EAM's practices, for instance appointing enlightenment officers/commissars.[101]

Recruitment in these units was voluntary and at least initially they had no difficulty in recruiting volunteers, since in many areas EAM/ELAS rule had generated a huge amount of ill feeling even among their supporters.[102] However, as the conflict with ELAS intensified, they resorted more and more to threats and coercion. In Euboea, the local leaders of the security battalions threatened those who failed to enlist by stating that they would 'be considered deserters, moreover it will be presumed that they belong to hostile organisations and both they and their families will be persecuted'.[103] However, while a large number of militiamen joined under duress, others were attracted by the considerable material benefits offered by these organisations. The security battalion units derived funds from a series of sources; they taxed peasants and merchants, requisitioned the properties of their political rivals and were often engaged in elaborate black market and protection schemes, which yielded significant income that they used to entice prospective recruits.[104]

The expansion of paramilitary militias further fragmented the territory of Free Greece and deprived ELAS of a crucial source of food and recruits; meanwhile, fear and resentment led to an increasing number of defections to the collaborationist camps. In the area of Kozani, 'such a complete change in the situation had already taken place that it was impossible to speak of a guerrilla movement as existing any longer in that district'; the situation was hardly better in other lowland areas of northern Greece where the various militias had managed to wrest control from ELAS.[105]

The resistance groups responded with a mixture of propaganda and coercion, which frequently shocked even its supporters. ELAS's reoccupation of the villages of Mourgana that had fallen into EDES hands during December 1943 was accompanied by a spate of beatings and executions; 'ELAS … made several arrests and many of those who had publicly opposed EAM were tortured. Some of them like Dimitris Kiratsis died while in detention.'[106] The victims were not necessarily EDES supporters; rather, they were people 'whose word counted'[107] and who had an ability to influence their compatriots. The return of EAM to western Thessaly was marked by similar actions. According to an EAM cadre, 'they started executing innocent people in order to stem popular disappointment'.[108] Most victims of violence were local elite men: schoolmasters, rich farmers and professionals who had either openly supported EDES or openly opposed ELAS and criticised its military shortcomings. The culprit behind much of the violence unleashed in the villages of western Thessaly was Egripos, aka Panagiotis Odontopoulos, a seasoned KKE cadre and former exile from Peloponnesus who was despatched by EAM to restructure the organisation in the areas of Kalabaka and Chasia. Egripos, who was remembered even by local cadres as a 'man with a criminal nature', made his intentions clear early on: 'when he spoke he told us, comrades, the struggle demands sacrifices, we will show no pity, we will strike every reactionary element'.[109]

EAM responded in a similar way to challenges against its authority in Peloponnesus. Violence in this ardently royalist area was kept to a minimum until late 1943, since the local EAM and KKE bureaus had

A history of the Greek resistance

advised cadres to take a conciliatory line towards reactionaries, decreeing that 'every person who has gone to the reaction, with the exception of traitors, must be considered as someone who is misguided and is in need of enlightenment'.[110] Accordingly, executions were to be avoided unless the accused had 'been branded as traitors by the people and their execution placates popular feeling'. In December 1943 this line was reversed and it was decreed that henceforth the 'reaction must be uprooted'.[111] This decision was no doubt influenced by the meteoric rise of armed collaborationist formations that followed the dissolution of the right-wing ES by ELAS and the widespread resentment after the repeated setbacks suffered by ELAS in the area. This was especially the case in the district of Laconia, where several hundred men had received weapons from the Germans in the towns of Sparta, Molaoi and several smaller communities. ELAS exhibited its determination to strike hard at its opponents from early on. The town of Molaoi was attacked twice by ELAS; the first attack, which took place on 2 December 1943, resulted in a stalemate. ELAS then returned with much larger forces and stormed Molaoi on 27 December; it managed to prevail after a brief fight that resulted in the death of ten militiamen and four guerrillas. Immediately after the militiamen laid down their arms, ten of them were led outside the town and summarily executed.[112] A few days' later, 39 men and women who had been arrested as reactionaries and kept in the ELAS prison camp of Zarakas were executed. Other mass executions took place during the following days at the prison camps of Haradros and Agia Sotira in the Kinouria prefecture of Arcadia.[113]

Corruption and favouritism went in tandem with violence. Achilleas Blanas, the representative of the KKE central committee and nominal ruler of Peloponnesus during the occupation, was known both for his autarchic attitude and his love of the finer things in life. Blanas was not a native of Peloponnesus; originally he was from Thessaly, but he had managed to set down roots in the region after he married the sister of a senior Messinian cadre. A vain, despotic man, he surrounded himself with courtiers, many of whom were acquaintances and friends of his wife's family, leading some cadres to complain that EAM members had been divided into 'favourites and underdogs';[114] the latter 'tried to quell their hunger with a plate of beans'[115] while the former enjoyed the good life. Nonetheless, few dared dispute Blanas's choices and policies, as most cadres 'were terrified of him'.[116] The men chosen by Blanas tended to share their patron's behaviour and inclinations and, by early 1944, they had become 'satraps of the people, of the organisations and the cadres'.[117] Vrasidas Makris, the son of a poor priest from the highland village of Lagadia, was typical of the men who Blanas chose to rule his province. In 1943 Makris was appointed first secretary of the KKE's prefectural committee of Achea and chief interrogator of the prison camp of Koumani, which was described by one EAM cadre as 'the disgrace of Peloponnesus'.[118] Makris's capacity for and inclination towards violence terrified even his fellow comrades and led to his eventual downfall; in October 1944 he was eventually expelled by the KKE as his most faithful allies deserted him, disgusted by his sadistic behaviour.[119]

Violence led thousands to abandon their villages, and provincial towns became crammed with thousands of refugees who tried to escape war, poverty and persecution. For those who remained in the 'free areas', life was often unviable. Cadres and supporters were constantly under pressure to contribute material help and personal services; however, the situation was far worse for those who had supported the wrong faction during the civil war or who had reneged on their previous allegiance. EDES supporters were constantly harassed in 'red' towns such as Tirnavos and Abelonas in the plain of Thessaly where EAM cadres posted catalogues of reactionaries in the village café and on the church wall as a warning to them and those that dared to socialise with them. Such families and individuals were progressively isolated as even their closest relatives avoided socialising with them, fearing that they would be branded themselves as reactionaries, and they endured a storm of harassment at the hands of their neighbours. EPON youths played a pivotal role in this. In Tirnavos, bands of schoolchildren shepherded by their EPON handlers would encircle the homes of reactionaries in the middle of the night, chanting slogans, banging pots and screaming that their time was nigh and the gallows were being prepared for them. Beatings and house searches were also constant.[120] Families that had declared for EDES before the civil war were often overtaxed and had their pack animals confiscated, while the local EAM committees made a point of lodging passing guerrillas in their homes and requisitioning food and provisions for the needs of the struggle, thereby forcing many into bankruptcy and pauperisation.[121]

Some people reacted defiantly to this situation and a few even chose to make dangerous trips to the EDES lines; however, not all would risk such a venture and many had to endure the humiliation of signing a recantation statement 'in which they refuted EDES as a treasonous organisation and sided with EAM',[122] in the hope that they would be finally left alone. EDES supporters who refused to recant were subjected to a torrent of threats and punishments. Shepherds and peddlers were refused permits to work nearby or to move their flocks outside their village environs, and the most persistent could find themselves in a prison camp or worse; one man who refused to sign a recantation statement in the village of Raftanaioi in Epirus was beaten to death by ELAS men while another was left disabled for life.[123] The situation was seldom better in the EDES areas, according to an EAM intelligence report: 'in the entire EDES-occupied area, EAM supporters, their families and those of the ELAS guerrillas are regularly terrorised, plundered and looted'. The aim of this pressure was to force EAM supporters to defect to their camp or at least sign recantation statements. Their EAM counterparts' local officials used a series of methods to achieve the same end: threats, the offer of material benefits and the revoking of passes.[124]

This situation was rendered even worse by the organisations' irrational fear of spies and traitors, as increasingly ELAS mishaps were attributed to subversives and infiltrators. 'There are many indications', noted an ELAS circular, 'that there are fighters … in the ranks of ELAS … who sell themselves for gold and money and betray their fatherland to the domestic and foreign enemy. We must reveal them and expel them from the ranks of ELAS and from among the Greek people.'[125] Newspapers and agitators reminded the guerrillas and the cadres of the perils of careless talk and their duty to report subversion: 'our gravest duty … is vigilance', underlined an EAM newspaper, which prompted its readers to report 'even the most insignificant words uttered by the lips of the enemies of the people and the fatherland'. and reminded them that 'sentimentalism and gullibility are two psychological attitudes that hurt vigilance'.[126] Another EAM publication warned its readers that 'the enemy lurks everywhere, he hides within our ranks and in the home front; he must be crushed without mercy'.[127]

This fixation with treason and spies created a morbid climate of fear and suspicion which fragmented social ties and led to a host of denunciations as people came to see even their closest relatives as potential spies and subversives, and court martials were constantly flooded by such cases. 'The organisations see spies even while asleep', complained an ELAS *kapetanios* in Euboea; 'they believe that everyone is a traitor and everyone is spying on them'.[128] This climate was no doubt helped by the vagueness of what constituted subversion and treason; according to a document sent to the court-martial service of the ELAS 8th division, one could be tried for treason for a range of offences from possessing undeclared firearms and transmitting information to the occupation forces to 'defaming the armed forces of the nation' and spreading 'upsetting rumours' that could incite panic and 'harm the people's struggles and the people'.[129]

Such denunciations were not motivated purely by politics. During the first few weeks of 1944, several hundred people were arrested as dangerous communists by EDES unit commanders, even though 'they were completely harmless'. The EDES GHQ eventually ordered their release and castigated the commanders who had 'made indiscriminate arrests', oblivious to the fact that most denunciations derived from 'cadres who aspire to satisfy their personal hatreds'.[130] However, this was not an isolated incident, and despite EDES efforts, denunciations and private violence did not abate. A senior member of the EDES judiciary noted a few weeks later that 'most cases are initiated by members of the regional committees for national struggle. The members of these committees use their position to settle their scores with their personal rivals.'[131] A land dispute between the Dimitriadis and Nakas families from the village of Livitsko in Epirus landed Giannis Dimitriadis and his 12-year-old son Dimitris in the Giorganou prison camp, where they remained for over four months. This was not a unique case, as Dimitriadis noted:

> if someone had an issue with somebody else before the war he would denounce him ... peasants were like that, I mean if someone damaged their property then they would try to take revenge, they didn't know much about politics in the villages then, most people were illiterate, they weren't motivated by politics, they thought you hurt my pocket so I will get back at you. Most of these accusations were lies of course and it was because of these fabrications that people were killed.[132]

Such occurrences were equally common in other areas. Raptis attributed much of the violence that erupted in his home region of Chasia to personal disputes; 'everyone found a chance to settle his personal scores',[133] using ELAS as their instrument for revenge. This argument is echoed, albeit in a much blunter form, in the testimony of an ELAS veteran from Peloponnesus who argued that most denunciations were due to personal hatreds:

> somebody might have fucked the *ipefthinos'* sister, someone might have cut the water supply from his fields and it was then that he found the chance to take revenge, he told us to take this man for an interrogation and on the side passed a paper where he wrote 'he must not return'.[134]

Dimitriadis and his son were finally released after a local commander intervened in their favour and were not disturbed again by their rivals.

However, rivalries could often take a much more violent turn, as exemplified by the feud between the Gousis and Zikos families. Both families were affluent pastoralists who came from adjoining villages in the Lakka Souli area in Epirus and herded their sheep in the uplands of the Olitsika mountain range. During the war, the Zikos clan sided with EDES while several members of the Gousis clan joined EAM and two of then enlisted in ELAS. Like most herders, the two families were engaged in reciprocal animal theft; however, the situation between the two deteriorated sharply in 1943 following an altercation between a shepherd who worked for the Gousis clan and the son of Nikolaos Zikos or KolioDimitris – the family's patriarch and EDES band leader. The conflict escalated further after the Gousis failed to make amends, and culminated in the Zikos band's all-out attack on them. KolioDimitris and his men looted and torched the homes of Kostas and Vasilis Gousis and carried hundreds of sheep to their village. Unable to retaliate, the Gousis lay low until the arrival of ELAS in the area in December 1944, at which time they used their status and local knowledge to help ELAS retrieve money and weaponry, and lobbied local commanders to punish their enemies. The Gousis campaign was finally successful when, between 24 and 30 January 1945, Nikolaos Zikos, his son Spiros and 15 more members of their extended family were summarily shot by ELAS in the courtyard of the Dalamani monastery.[135]

However, the violence unleashed by ELAS did not halt defections or the rise of collaborationist militias. A few weeks after the creation of the Sparta security battalion, two more units were raised in the towns of Githeio and Mistras. By February the security battalions had come to dominate the entire province of Laconia, with the exception of a few hamlets in the mountain fastness of Parnonas.[136] Collaborationist militias expanded even more rapidly in central Macedonia, increasing from a mere 300 in December 1943 to more than 1,200 three months later. An ELAS report noted that 'the reaction … is much more numerous than the local ELAS units and has managed to secure complete freedom of movement … our units have not been able to deal them a serious blow and there is a serious danger that the whole area would be eventually armed'.[137] Such fears were far from unfounded; by March 1943 the whole plain of Pieria and parts of the lowlands of Imathia had been brought under 'the complete control'[138] of the militiamen, depriving ELAS of its most important source of food in the region. ELAS responded to this challenge with counter-violence. On 20 March 1944 ELAS troops entered the town of Velventos and executed 20 local 'reactionaries'.[139] This action was followed by an even more devastating raid against the villages of

A society at war

Riaki and Moshopotanos. Guerrillas burned houses and executed several civilians in both communities. However, these actions did not dampen the resolve of their rivals, as a local cadre noted:

> these strikes were effective, however, they failed to deal a decisive blow to the reaction … the danger is growing day by day since each day another village is armed and our units are forced to retreat deeper into the mountains … and we might soon find ourselves in the position of abandoning Pieria … the reaction must be crushed with a swift and decisive blow.[140]

This situation progressively weakened the hold of ELAS, both in the free and the occupied areas, as many cadres either opted for neutrality or defected to the other side.[141] In the areas of Karditsa and Trikala, local EAM cadres repeatedly vetoed ELAS operations against local collaborationist militias and some even brokered agreements with militia leaders who agreed to protect them in exchange for their support in case ELAS emerged victorious. Such 'tendencies towards compromise' were particularly widespread in the region, where the frightened peasantry 'oscillated between us and neutrality'.[142] Numerous EAM village committees in the area made silent agreements with nationalist power brokers, pledging their neutrality and sometimes their support to EASAD – a local collaborationist militia whose violence had shocked even their German backers – in exchange for protection from their depredations. Thus in the village of Pazaraki the inhabitants and the local EAM committee decided to 'make up with the EASAD and when it is time to opt for EAM again'.[143]

Such attitudes were no less common in Peloponnesus, where the appearance of the security battalions in the winter of 1943–44 led to a spate of desertions among military and civilian cadres. The Sparta security battalion included a large number of former ELAS guerrillas, some of whom had been captured and chose to change their allegiance in a desperate attempt to save their lives, and others who had defected under pressure from their families.[144] The most notorious security battalion commander in the lowlands of Pineia was 'Aetos', a former ELAS guerrilla. Aetos, aka Giorgos Alexandropoulos, who came from an impoverished family from the village of Kastro, had enlisted in ELAS in the summer of 1943. A year later, enticed by the promise of social advancement, Aetos defected to the other side and led the security battalion of Vartholomio in a series of violent raids against pro-EAM communities. Aetos, who had had personally murdered five EAM cadres in the adjoining communities, established a reign of terror in the lowlands of Pineia: 'he established his command in Vartholomio … and started sending letters to the adjoining EAM organisations threatening to burn their houses if they do not hand him their stocks'.[145] Aetos's violent temperament led to his demise; he became progressively unstable, was constantly drunk and on occasion even threatened his backers with violence. They finally decided they had had enough, and Aetos was ambushed and killed; according to one version he was knifed to death by his former comrades in August 1944.[146]

Such men were by no means exceptional in the region. For instance, Thanasis Karabas, a KKE veteran and *ipefthinos* of the village of Ksirohori, worked simultaneously for EAM and the local security battalion, providing them with information, money and even guns. He eventually paid with his life for this double dealing as he was apprehended and shot by ELAS. Sotiris Prinos, an EAM cadre from the nearby village of Gianitsaiika, also defected to the security battalions. He was enraged by the fact that the regional committee had chosen to appoint as *ipefthinos* Giannis Vasilipoulos, a local schoolteacher, instead of him.[147] It was during this period that EAM cadres Kostas, Giorgos and Antreas Papadopoulos, who had ruled the village of Agrapidohori in the same area with an iron fist, and had 'committed crimes' against their fellow villagers, chose to defect to the security battalions. Fear of punishment was the foremost motive of the three men who quickly managed to restore their dominance with the help of local militiamen, and 'decided who they were going to persecute, who to kill, who to rob, who to let go'.[148]

This situation led EAM/ELAS to take even sterner measures. In April 1944 the Peloponnesus bureau of the KKE decreed that 'the measures … against the reaction had been relaxed', and decided that 'we should make carefully planned disappearances of reactionaries and traitors'.[149] More precise instructions about the measures were given to local cadres in May 1944, when they were briskly informed that 'now is the time to overcome the reaction, we must not forget that we are revolutionaries, knife blade to the reaction'.[150] This decision was followed by a violent propaganda attack against the reaction; a leaflet produced and circulated by the Megalopoli EAM called the people 'to strike at the tyrant … their polluted blood must soak our fields'.[151] Such blood-curdling rhetoric was far from uncommon. A few weeks later, a proclamation of the local ELAS announced to the peasantry that

> our heroic ELAS had started to clean our fatherland from these filthy maggots. Our regiment calls all the inhabitants of our prefecture to join us … fire and axe to those who had bent the head, wipe them out, do not spare even their youngest, hot lead to these families of snakes.[152]

A society at war

These calls for radical violence were heeded and more than 150 men and women, among them children younger than ten and a disabled octogenarian, were murdered in a series of raids and round-ups that took place in the prefecture of Arkadia between 7 May and 14 June.[153]

ELAS counter-violence was equally fierce across the country. On 2 February 1944 a large detachment of the ELAS 30th regiment attacked and burned the village of Aravissos in the foothills of Paikon, executing 22 locals.[154] A few weeks later, they raided the villages of Agios Petros and Mesia with the help of a 200-strong Yugoslav detachment. A series of equally devastating raids took place in the villages of Skidra and Platania on 17 May 1944, and in the communities of Savastiani and Karidia on 20 May, which 'wiped out the reaction'.[155] ELAS violence was followed by counter-violence as militiamen from the communities of Kria Vrisi and Skidra engaged in raids against EAM-supporting communities; 'the reactionaries from around the prefecture ... make daily raids against the surrounding villages', according to an ELAS report.[156]

The same patterns of violence and counter-violence were followed on the islands of Lefkada, Ithaca and Kephalonia. The first anti-communist militias were formed on Lefkada during Feburary 1944 by the Kalantzis clan. The Kalantzis proceeded to take up arms after the clan's patriarch, Evangelos, and his son Anastasios, who operated an olive press in the village of Nidri, were murdered by ELAS for refusing to hand over a quantity of oil to a local ELAS commander. A spate of revenge killings accelerated the creation of militias on the island, which by May 1944 numbered over 500 men.[157] As in Macedonia, civil war led to profound social disintegration. The island was fractured into several warring fiefs ruled by the various ELAS and nationalist chieftains, who nominally adhered to EDES but were in reality completely independent and used their position to take revenge against their rivals, dispense favours to their supporters and enrich themselves through plunder, looting and blackmail. After the events in Nidri, noted a local EAM cadre,

> Lefkada was divided into north and south, the north was dominated by EAM while the south was divided into several captaincies that lacked any coordination and were not subjected to any central control; the Kalantzis clan controlled the villages of Nidri, Vlihos, Haradratika, Niohori, Alatro, Katohori, Poris and Efternos, the Zabelis band controlled Marantohori, Sivros, Vasiliki, the Nikolairaioi and Karagiannaioi clans controlled Agios Elias and Vournia and the Aheimastos clan Agios Petros and its environs.[158]

Personal and political motives were inextricable in the civil war that developed in Lefkada as individuals from both sides used their position to persecute and murder their rivals. Provincial doctors seized the chance to liquidate their business rivals whom they presented as agents of the reaction, merchants got rid of unwanted business partners, farmers wreaked revenge on neighbours who had been trespassing on their land, and neighbouring communities settled their differences over water access and land rights through deadly raids. Indeed, the accounts of witnesses from both side attest to the ubiquity of 'personal rivalries' and their effect on the violence that enveloped the island during 1943–45 and cost the lives of over 300 men and women.[159]

Patronage and violence: guerrilla rule in Free Greece

Violence was accompanied by renewed efforts to rebuild shattered infrastructure and help the peasants deal with food shortages and the rapid increase in prices. It is characteristic that even in the most productive areas, such as the plain of Arta, the price of maize, a staple of the peasant diet, had increased by more than 100 per cent in two months.[160] This situation inspired unease among the guerrilla organisations, which feared that, unless they managed to reinstate a semblance of order and address the urgent provisioning problems, they would face a full-blown revolt. A senior EDES cadre noted in his diary in November 1943 that

> everyone agrees that surviving the winter will be nearly impossible, that after November there will be nothing left to eat, that the entire life of the mountains is dependent on the plains that are currently in German hands and if the peasants will not be able to winter their flocks in the plains they will perish, that the refugees will attack us … [and] butcher us for causing the destruction that befell them.[161]

The efforts made by ELAS and EDES to control the available food supplies led them to place severe restrictions on the movement of goods from the countryside to the cities. At first, only the border districts were affected since ELAS imposed strict regulations on the exchange and peddling of goods across the border in conjunction with the Albanian and later Yugoslav partisans.[162] Further restrictions were eventually imposed within the free areas while all transactions with the Axis troops and the Greek collaborationist government were strictly prohibited. In the period following the civil war, both ELAS and EDES ceased all exports to the occupied areas, although EDES allowed food imports from the

A society at war

cities and the plain into the free areas 'after special permission is granted by the regional military authorities'.[163] Exporting food was rendered a court-martial offence that could result in the death penalty. However, such transactions never stopped entirely and guerrillas would often trade arms, parachute silk and boots with the civilians in the occupied areas.[164]

EAM introduced food rationing in some of the worst-affected areas, such as central and northern Peloponnesus,[165] while in Macedonia local EAM committees in conjunction with ELAS created *laika pratiria* – 'people's stores'. These were provisioned by local producers who were obliged to hand over a part of their produce at set prices. However, this experiment did not bear fruit as local cadres used the rationing system to their advantage, bartering food and misallocating coupons, while prices in the people's stores were 'no different than those in the black market'.[166] These measures were far from popular, even among EAM backers; an ELAS functionary in Epirus noted that 'many protest, because they still cannot understand that today when our people fights for its survival and liberty some common ownership of goods is necessary, and yet many of them shout "the field is mine, therefore the wheat is mine as well"'.[167] EAM tried to curb peasant reactions through an aggressive propaganda campaign. Plays, songs and newspapers denounced the British as extortionists who blackmailed EAM in order to turn it into their instrument; a popular ELAS song encouraged the guerrillas to 'eat bean and lentils with a drop of olive oil/ eat half an oka bread even its stale/ don't ask for jam and fresh tins because we'll plunge Greece into debt again'.[168]

The situation was not helped by the rampant corruption within the resistance's ranks. Corruption was rife in ELAS: provisions, clothes and arms were casually misallocated, sold to the black market or sent to relatives and friends. Papananos noted in his diary that 'I realised to my great regret that whoever is in a position to do it, either in the administration or in the mess, is stealing, despite all our ideas and sacred goals'.[169] These practices threatened ELAS's very survival during the grim winter of 1943–44 and seriously depleted its stocks. An ELAS report noted that

> After the British Military Mission halted all financial assistance we have entered a time of almost impossible financial difficulties. It is therefore necessary to make great sacrifices in order to be able to overcome this predicament. Nonetheless, very few have adequately realised the gravity of this situation. Transactions often at extortionate prices continue uninterrupted even though we have given orders to stop all transactions. Clothes are constantly fabricated and despatched and yet many or units are bereft

of clothes, thousands of pairs of boots have been delivered and yet we constantly receive demands for more new boots.[170]

Such problems were no less prominent in EDES. Guerrillas would occasionally steal provisions from other units, money was squandered and even guns and ammunition belonging to the units were sold on the black market. Some EDES commanders, such as Major N. Kostantopoulos, the commander of the EDES cadet school (or Maria school as it became known among the guerrillas after Kostantopoulos's mistress, a former collaborator and prostitute from Arta who was saved by Kostantopoulos from the firing squad), became a byword for corruption. Kostantopoulos squandered the school's provisions and even sold the cadets' clothes on the black market in Arta.[171]

Kostantopoulos was far from exceptional. ELAS and EDES unit commanders would regularly falsify their records in order to extract more food, clothes and weapons, with complete disregard for the needs of other units or the peasantry. An ELAS report noted that

> several units have repeatedly falsified their actual reserves. We have repeatedly sent instructions in regard to this issue that have been unfortunately ignored. Many units have made desperate calls in which they described their provisional situation in the bleakest colours and managed to extract orders to requisition and even confiscate the available food stocks in their areas even though they were aware that this would burden the already sorely tried people.

Such attitudes were repeatedly castigated by the ELAS GHQ, which stressed that 'everyone must understand that the supplying of all the units must be undertaken by ETA alone', and underlined that every requisition 'must be grounded on our decisions and orders'.[172]

However, these calls were seldom heeded, either by individual guerrillas who casually ventured into villages asking for food, drink and liquor, and threatened the peasants and the local EAM cadres with violence unless they complied, or by unit commanders who looked out for their units' well-being at the expense of other units and civilians. Such attitudes were equally commonplace in EDES. Hungry guerrillas would not shy away from brutalising peasants, irrespective of their political allegiances, to lay their hands on food and drink. The presidents of the committees of national struggle – the equivalent of the EAM *ipefthinos* – were the most common focus of guerrilla violence, since they were often perceived as tight-fisted and self-serving by the young guerrillas who believed that participation in the resistance entitled them to the peasants' property:

A society at war

whenever a guerrilla passed through a village, he demanded food, clothing ... [and] requisitioned provisions ... for his detachment ... very often the presidents or even simple members of the committees of the national struggle were insulted with the utmost impunity, and some were even assaulted and beaten up by unrestrained and savage guerrillas.[173]

The inability of the resistance organisations to address the growing food crisis and the fear of a complete breakdown of morale among both peasants and guerrillas led the British and American Military Missions to intervene and create a comprehensive relief scheme in Free Greece from January 1944 onwards, 'involving payments to villagers who had suffered from German reprisals, delivery of food and clothing to distressed areas, opening of medical centres, soup kitchens etc.'[174] Provisions were flown in from Cairo and later from southern Italy; however, most food and medical material was bought wholesale from the black market. Relief money was initially handed directly to the resistance organisations, but this changed after repeated accusations of misallocation, especially in EAM territory. From February 1944 the Allied Military Mission (AMM) began operating its own system in cooperation with the Church and the local elites. The AMM set up relief committees in individual areas under the command of officers. These central committees in turn appointed other committees in particular districts or villages, to which they assigned the task of creating lists of destitute persons. These lists were cross-checked by Allied liaison officers, who also took on the task of keeping accounts and securing provisions, and often distributed the money themselves.[175]

The cost of this scheme, which involved several Allied liaison officers 'grudgingly spared from operational duty', was estimated at 37,000 gold sovereigns a month.[176] The money provided on a monthly basis differed from one area to another. In Epirus, refugees were handed between ¼ and 1/3 of a sovereign per person, while in Macedonia and central Greece destitute families were provided with a sovereign for each family member.[177] An extra sum of money was provided to the regional committees for doctors' fees, medical provisions and the setting up of soup kitchens for children.[178] This system helped considerably to maintain civilian morale. However, it also led to growing animosity between the AMM and EAM cadres who were afraid that the AMM's efforts undermined their authority and demanded that relief paid to refugees be administered through the regional organisation. EAM was not entirely wrong, since many peasants came to attribute to the Allied officers stationed in their regions 'the powers and means of changing events by exercising his own authority or by appealing to his superiors to exercise theirs'.[179] Relations between the two sides almost reached breaking point in the spring of 1944; EAM supporters denounced and in some cases attacked the regional relief committees and organised demonstrations demanding a return to the original relief agreement.[180] Despite the persistent problems, neither side chose to take their disagreement to extremes. The AMM was genuinely afraid that a humanitarian crisis would lead the rural population into the arms of the Axis, while the resistance relied on AMM's funding for most of its activities, such as running schools and hospitals, procuring medical provisions and repairing the badly damaged local infrastructure, roads, bridges etc. Eventually, a semblance of normalcy returned to large parts of Free Greece in the spring of 1944, as many schools were re-opened and the rule of law was re-established.[181]

EAM attempted to augment its support by accelerating reforms and introducing new institutions in the countryside, such as farmers' and herders' associations. It took even more active steps in enfranchising marginalised groups, such as women, the youth and minorities. EAM had displayed signs of its willingness to transform women's positions in the countryside from early on by appointing women to village committees. The creation of the EAM's provisional government, the PEEA, in the spring of 1944 accelerated these changes by giving women the right to vote and join the armed forces for the first time in Greece's history.[182] Women also came to play an increasingly pivotal role in the running of day-to-day affairs in Free Greece in a variety of ways; they worked as nurses, operated kindergartens, ran soup kitchens, helped repair roads, cultivated the guerrillas' fields and organised seamstress companies that produced thousands of ELAS uniforms.[183] The nature of women's motivation is difficult to account for. Some saw in EAM a chance to address their plight and improve their social position, while others were attracted by the prospect of adventure and the chance to escape a rigid patriarchal regime. Many were driven to support EAM out of family solidarity. In the early days of the resistance, most women were relatives of EAM cadres and were often recruited by their husbands, sons and fathers.[184] However, the actual improvements in everyday life and the belief that EAM would be able to create a new type of society that would provide women with improved living conditions and better social prospects in the future progressively rendered women the more determined and fanatical supporters of EAM, and many activists developed a fierce, messianic belief that was often uncommon among male cadres.[185]

The youth were also seen as a crucial target group by EAM, which

A society at war

created its youth section, EPON, in the summer of 1943. EPON was soon divided into a military branch that was eventually absorbed by ELAS and a civilian branch that operated under the auspices of EAM. The main task of EPON was to 'organise culture in every village' and thus prepare the new generation to become the 'builders of the new Greece'. An EAM publication noted characteristically that 'we must give youth the lights of culture and civilisation and teach them to love progress deeply'.[186] EPON's main focus was cultural activities, most of which took place in its locus, the EPON club, which was often located near or in the local school. This doubled as a debating chamber, lecture hall and theatre stage, on which EPON cadres performed 'short plays crudely but vigorously acted … [that] invariably showed the triumphant adventures of virtuous "eamites" in conflict with "antidrastic" [reactionary] forces'.[187] EPON also developed a series of social actions. EPON cadres helped to rebuild burned homes and mend roads, they cultivated the fields of guerrilla families, volunteered as nurses and teachers, cleaned public spaces and often worked as agitators and propagandists.[188]

EDES demonstrated much less concern regarding these issues and only created EDEE (Ethnike Dimokratike Enosi Ellinopaidon – the National Republican Union of Youths), EPON's equivalent, in early 1944. EDEE was designed and functioned as a paramilitary organisation. All its members wore uniform and received a salary, half a sovereign per month, which according to some was the foremost reason for its staggering success in several areas. EDEE members performed a variety of tasks: they served as combat nurses and runners, guarded installations and prison camps and helped in the transfer of material. Conversely, cultural activities were much less frequent and very little effort was put into indoctrinating them.[189]

These initiatives posed a profound challenge to and in many cases radically altered the character of the rural communities that comprised Free Greece. The participation of young men and women in politics led to a reversal of power relations within the rural communities, as the young gradually came to replace the political brokers and landowners who dominated the political life of rural communities. Many youths were appointed as village *ipefthinos* while others served as presidents of the 'people's courts'. The 'generational inversion of authority' was often accompanied by a profound inversion of social relations.[190] The appearance of EAM allowed previously marginal groups such as farmhands, hired shepherds and poor farmers to enter and sometimes play a pivotal role in the social and political life of their communities. Villages like

Spilaio, a pastoral community in the uplands of Grevena, had been ruled before the war by a small group of individuals belonging to two rich families. During the occupation the old president and village council were set aside, and new people, farmers in their early twenties 'from the poorer classes', were appointed in their stead. This led to unrest as in such areas as 'the more well off and the right wingers moved away from the organisation'.[191]

The change of guard was even more profound in the uplands of central Pindus where EAM's success was due in no small part to the support of small farmers and peasants who for the first time were given the chance to wrest control of their communities from the merchants and the *tseliggades* – the rich pastoralists who had been the de facto ruling class in these communities since the early nineteenth century. The *tseliggades*, many of whom owned thousands of sheep and employed annually as many as forty people as hired hands, enjoyed an almost feudal power in their communities; they determined the rent and allocation of pastures, fixed local elections through bribery and violence and engaged in usury.[192] Tensions between these affluent pastoralists and the peasantry were intense and sometimes violent. During the 1930s shepherds and farm labourers made several 'hunger marches' from the uplands of Thessaly to the regional capitals of Trikala and Karditsa to protest against extremely low wages and deplorable working conditions. EAM managed to break the power of these elites and relieved the plight of the poorer classes by allowing them free access to pasturage and a substantial increase in wages.[193] However, these changes were not easily passed or accepted. In some communities such as Mesohora in the uplands of Thessaly, they led to violent conflict with strong class overtones that caused the deaths of seven men between 1943 and 1947.[194]

However, to present the resistance as a social revolution would be inaccurate. It is indubitable that EAM often took the side of the oppressed; however, it was equally quick to form pacts with the powerful and defend their interests when this seemed advantageous to its cause. Thus in the village of Mesounta, located a few miles west of Mesohora, EAM/ELAS was allied with the powerful Tsoumanis clan who provided intelligence, food and cadres in exchange for protection from the local peasantry. Furthermore, while EAM's ideology and promise of a just, egalitarian society had a great appeal to many, it would be wrong to think that the bulk of EAM supporters were moved exclusively by these factors, and often the crude methods and outlandish proclamations of agitators produced the opposite result. A peasant from the uplands of Arta recalled the EAM agitators as 'mere kids' who promised highland villagers that 'we'll move you to the plain and force the lowlanders to come and live in the mountains, you'll go to live in Kolonaki [an upper-middle-class district of Athens] and we'll force the rich people to move from Kolonaki to here'.[195] An Allied liaison officer who served in central Greece noted similarly that 'most of it went over the villagers' heads ... especially the older ones, they really did not understand what was going on, and they were only interested where the next bit of food was coming from it seems to me, for themselves and for their children'.[196]

Indeed, most peasants joined for much more mundane reasons and were quick to change their allegiance when a stronger party moved in. The defeat and dissolution of EDES in the lowlands of western Thessaly in the winter of 1943–44 was followed by a massive defection of EDES supporters to EAM; 'many of those who had joined EAM in Koskinas and many other villages had no real sympathy for this organisation ... when EAM began arresting EDES supporters some of them joined EAM and others tried to make themselves invisible'.[197] The situation was comparable in many areas of Epirus where entire communities defected from EAM to EDES often more than once throughout 1944.[198] The opportunism of the peasantry both shocked and angered local cadres, particularly in areas such as Messenia where many peasants, locally known as *diplokalamades*, made a habit of changing their allegiances between EAM and its rivals, or even holding dual membership.[199]

However, such attitudes should not be seen as evidence of the backwardness of the peasantry or a lack of political consciousness. The civil war that erupted in the winter 1943–44 and the consequent creation of the various collaborationist militias resulted in a profound social and political fragmentation in the countryside. Consequently, peasants had to deal with multiple authorities that coexisted side-by-side, each demanding unconditional support. This was particularly true of artisans and shepherds, whose transient lifestyle forced them constantly to move to and from the free areas. In order to reach their winter pastures, herders from the villages of the Tzoumerka range, an area controlled by ELAS, had to cross the area of Xirovouni that was in EDES hands before reaching the plain of Xiromero, whose control was disputed between EAM and a series of nationalist militias, known locally as Verides. As noted by an EAM cadre, such people were obliged to become 'good actors' and have a 'theatrical attitude'.[200] Shepherds and artisans were required to know the hymns of both ELAS and EDES, recall the names and activities of local commanders and often hold dual membership in EAM and EDES in order to be able to travel across their region unmolested. However, this was a perilous undertaking, and those who were caught were liable to lose their property and sometimes their life.[201]

Indeed, the coveted *adeia* or *paso*, a note provided by a local EAM cadre which allowed its holder free movement to and from the free areas, was often the reason that individuals joined an organisation. Joining an organisation was a way to acquire this freedom of movement that allowed one to travel, work and visit relatives. The importance of such documents was even greater in the border regions of Epirus and western Macedonia, many of whose inhabitants held property or worked in Albania and Yugoslavia. Peasants who travelled without the necessary papers were bound to be arrested or worse by the partisans who controlled these areas and often saw all Greeks as potential spies. The popularity of EAM in the highlands of Mourgana was due in no small part to the eagerness of the local *ipefthinos* to provide the peasants with the necessary papers that allowed them to travel to Albania. This often caused protests from the Albanian administration, which castigated the local EAM *ipefthinos* for 'providing papers to reactionaries'.[202]

Freedom of movement was not the only benefit of participation. EAM members and cadres were rewarded with several privileges and services that were not available to non-members, such as preferential treatment in the distribution of Allied and Red Cross help, the licence to carry firearms and improved chances of employment. In mid-1943 EAM created several 'proletarian committees' in the lowland villages of Thessaly. The purpose of these committees was to protect the interests of landless labourers and small proprietors. However, they were actually used by EAM members to muscle local peasants into hiring their members on preferential terms.[203] A similar racket was operated by EAM committees in areas of northern Peloponnesus, where farmers and shepherds were blackmailed into providing several 'no-show' jobs for the relatives of local cadres:

> there was very little work to do in the fields during the spring, however, the organisation [EAM] sent us 4–5 people who … sat idly all day and expected to be paid, when these left they just sent us even more the next day, how long can you stand by and pay these people for doing nothing?[204]

These were not the only benefits available. EAM cadres in lowland areas like Ampelonas, a market town located in the midst of the Thessaly plain, used their position to 'tax' black marketeers and peddlers who came to town to sell or exchange produce. Two women who refused to comply were gang raped and shot by EAM cadres, while in another case, a peddler who protested was arrested, tried and executed as a reactionary.[205] EAM and EDES cadres also used their position to blackmail their fellow villagers and extort large sums of money and produce by threatening to denounce them as spies.[206]

Such activities were not officially condoned or encouraged by the two organisations; however, they were often the only way to attract peasants to the resistance's ranks, especially in areas where EAM's state organisation was virtually non-existent. Scholars have often attributed the resistance's success to its state-building efforts:

> EAM/ELAS set the pace in the creation of something that Governments of Greece had neglected; an organised state in the Greek mountains … the benefits of civilisation and culture trickled into the mountains for the first time. Schools, local government, law courts and public utilities, which the war had ended, worked again. Theatres, factories, parliamentary assemblies began for the first time.[207]

This might have been the case in EAM's heartland of Evrytania and some of the adjoining regions; however, the further one moved from EAM's heartland of central Greece, the weaker was the impact of the resistance and its activities. An EAM cadre who travelled in southern Peloponnesus during October 1943 was surprised by the lack of activity in this area where EAM had been predominant for the past year and a half. He noted that 'there wasn't a trace of the organisation … the reserve ELAS was non-existent, the EAM committees were almost entirely absent while the few that existed were barely functioning … no taxes were collected'. The situation was hardly improved two months later, since many peasants declined to pay the steep taxes imposed by EAM, while most youths showed little interest in the activities of EPON, which was 'was completely unknown'. The women's movement fared no better; however, this was possibly due to the reactions of the male cadres who, in some cases, threatened to resign or even defect if EAM persisted in establishing women's organisations.[208]

This was not a unique case. A senior cadre from the area of Fthiotida described in early 1944 the state of self-government in his region as 'deplorable'. He noted that village committees were non-existent or dysfunctional, people's courts had stopped working, schools were shut and EAM enjoyed 'no authority or prestige' in much of the region. The report continued by noting that less than 20 per cent of the youth were organised in EPON, with the women's percentage less than 15 per cent, and concluded that both EAM and EPON cadres showed in most cases a complete disregard for cultural activities, with the exception of the occasional party or football game, which were sponsored by the local EPON in a desperate attempt to woo local youths.[209]

The problems faced by EAM in Fthiotida were due, to a large extent, to the ongoing strife between ELAS and a local resistance organisation, EKKA, since clashes between the two groups had led EAM to militarise its structure and disregard the local government institutions.[210] Civil war clashes had similar repercussions in the Preveza area of Epirus where the antagonism between ELAS and EDES had also led the civilian administration to atrophy. Food scarcity and fear of reprisals had pushed many communities to militarise and gave rise to a form of war-economy, with mountain communities, which for the most part supported ELAS, engaging in regular raids against lowland villages, which as a rule were either neutral or leaned towards EDES. The reserve ELAS forces of large villages such as Krania and Ano Rahi taxed rival communities, confiscated the livestock of alleged reactionaries and requisitioned food, which was brought to the community and divided among EAM supporters. Conversely both the women's movement and EPON had a negligible presence in this area.[211]

The situation was even more complex in the adjoining area of Thesprotia where the fight against the Axis was accompanied by a bitter conflict between the Greek and Albanian communities. No organised guerrilla bands existed in the area until the summer of 1943. Most formations comprised ELAS and EDES reservists who resided in their villages and engaged in guerrilla warfare and cattle raiding against their Muslim neighbours.[212] Accordingly rivalries between ELAS and EDES were kept to a minimum; an EDES officer who travelled in the area in June 1944 noted that 'the civil war and the brutalities of EAM are as foreign to them as are the latest events in the eastern front … the entire area is characterised by conservativeness, a high degree of solidarity no doubt fed by the fear towards the Muslim element and a narrow localist spirit'.[213] ELAS and EDES band leaders in the area, who often shared kinship and local ties, showed a complete disregard for the policies of their organisations; they conducted local truces, supplied each other with guns, ammunition and money and helped each other in their military ventures. Such actions were not condoned by the EDES and EAM authorities and often came as a shock to cadres from other districts who visited this region, one of whom complained that 'EAM gangs continue to operate in our area … and are unfortunately supported by our own officers'.[214] Political cadres

A society at war

demonstrated an equally cavalier attitude. It was not uncommon for a cadre and his family to defect from one organisation to the other more than once, as was the case with the Kazakis brothers who were described by an EDES official as 'rampant opportunists who have a complete disregard of ideology and even though they supported EAM in the past are now members of the EDES committee for national struggle'.[215]

The domination of civilian life by the guerrilla bands in these areas was exceptional; however, similar tensions existed in the rest of the country, particularly in the more isolated areas like Dorida in central Greece, where according to an EAM cadre, guerrilla involvement in civilian affairs was 'a usual phenomenon, since those who hold the weapons often feel that they are strong enough to ignore the will of those who support them'.[216] The situation was similar on the island of Euboea, which was ruled as a personal fief by 'Nikiforos', a veteran communist and *politikos* of the ELAS 7th Euboea battalion who governed a large part of southern Euboea between 1943 and 1944. Nikiforos was notorious for his eccentric appearance as well as his love for the finer things in life. According to a local cadre, 'he always uses a car and he is escorted by a young girl who he presents as a fellow comrade but who is in reality his mistress'.[217] After a few weeks in ELAS, Nikiforos chose to forego his military duties and began touring the Arvanite villages of southern Euboea, where he gave impassioned speeches calling for the uprooting of reactionaries and the establishment of socialism, which spread panic among the local peasantry; 'everyone is afraid of him … the attitude of comrade Nikiforos has spread fear among the people of Euboea who have begun to look at the guerrillas with increased hostility'.[218] A similar case was that of Kapetan Kitsos, a *kapetanios* in the ELAS 26th regiment, who terrorised the Poligiros area of Halkidiki and led even his fellow comrades to protest that 'he treats the villagers abhorrently and constantly asks them for provisions, threatening to execute them unless they provide them immediately … the people are very distraught and unless we keep watch on him we'll face a very bad situation'.[219]

The situation was similar in EDES areas, since many band leaders not only persisted in administering their own brand of rough justice to civilians, but also dismantled the committees of national struggle and replaced the elected candidates with their own men. The EDES GHQ criticised such actions and instructed officers and band leaders repeatedly that 'the best way to select the members of the committees of the national struggle is to ask the peasants to hold a vote … the people must be left free to elect those who wish to represent them in the current struggle, only by allowing them to do so will we prove that we respect ... its will'.[220] However, such calls fell on deaf ears and, despite the repeated admonitions, many band leaders persisted in treating their home areas as their personal fiefs with complete disregard for the wishes of the exasperated peasantry.[221]

Nonetheless, to describe Free Greece as a military dictatorship would be wide of the mark. The guerrillas knew very well that their survival and the continuation of the struggle depended exclusively on the uninterrupted help of the civilian organisations. Nor did ELAS enjoy the same control of the civilian organisations everywhere. Indeed, in areas such as southern Peloponnesus ELAS was under the complete control of EAM, and often junior cadres and village *ipefthinos* were able to veto the orders and decisions of the local HQ and to dictate operational policies to junior military commanders, who 'in many cases failed to carry out the order of their superiors because the local *ipefthinos* disagreed and gave different orders to the military units'.[222]

By early 1944 the various ELAS bands in the areas of Messenia, Laconia and Arcadia were effectively operating as the private armies of the civilian cadres and the village *ipefthinos*. This situation gradually resulted in the fragmentation of the entire region, which was eventually transformed into a series of individual fiefs ruled despotically by local cadres who used ELAS to settle their scores with rivals and raid hostile communities, and advanced their position in the organisation through a mixture of patronage and blackmail. This situation, which enraged senior military leaders, was accepted by most junior commanders since the latter 'were unwilling to engage in true military activity'[223] and preferred to linger in their home districts where they could be feted by the peasants while staying out of harm's way. This state of affairs increased corruption and weakened the performance of ELAS; a senior cadre who visited the area in the spring of 1944 argued that there was 'a complete breakdown of discipline' in the local ELAS.[224] The same cadre underlined that ELAS's finances were 'a shambles' as local EAM functionaries and village *ipefthinos* used the organisation's resources, which were 'under their exclusive jurisdiction',[225] to build and retain their own patronage networks within the organisation and the civilian society. The extensive misappropriation of funds and materials by corrupt officials left the local ELAS denuded of funds. Most guerrillas lacked boots, lived in the open and were 'dressed in tatters and had been eating nothing but carob beans for the past four months'.[226]

The same mixture of patronage, incompetence and corruption characterised many of the rural organisations. According to some scholars, EAM's introduction of mass ideological politics undermined the traditional clientelist ties that characterised the political life of rural Greece and facilitated the creation of a new inclusive polity.[227] Nonetheless, the available evidence shows that, despite EAM's efforts, clientelism not only persisted but was further strengthened as the peasants who lived in conditions of often extreme scarcity and danger rushed to attach themselves to EAM cadres who used the pre-existing political networks in the countryside to strengthen their hold.

The village of Rahoula in the prefecture of Karditsa presents a characteristic example of the factionalism that characterised EAM's rule and the persistence of patronage. The political life of the village had been dominated before the war by two large influential families, one headed by Vasilis Papasotiriou and the other by Giorgos Papadimitriou. Papasotiriou was the secretary of the prefectural KKE bureau, while Papadimitriou occupied a senior position in the local EAM mechanism. The animosity that brewed between the two men finally exploded after Giannis Kostoulas, a friend and political client of Papasotiriou, was asked to give his position to M. Zaharis, who was supported by the Papadimitriou clan. Backed by his patron, Kostoulas declined to give in. After this, the situation deteriorated completely, forcing the prefectural EAM committee, which was afraid that violence would erupt between the two families, to send a senior cadre to mediate between them. However, this proved impossible as the two men showed no signs of backing down. They accused each other of using their connections to intimidate the people's court into dropping lawsuits brought against their friends and relatives, forging documents, embezzling, using the guerrillas to blackmail and threaten their enemies and even collaborating with the Germans. The cadre despatched to the village was unable to discern whether any of these accusations were true; however, he was certain that both men were equally bad: 'they have forgotten that they are comrades and see the organisation as an instrument which they can used to fulfil their ambitions and settle their personal rivalries'. He concluded by noting that these actions 'deprecate EAM, deal a deadly blow to local government and make a joke of people's committees ... the people who guide the local organisation have always been self-seeking and they see the organisation as their personal fief'.[228]

Such attitudes were hardly exceptional among low-ranking cadres. A senior EAM member who toured Thessaly and Evrytania in the winter of 1943–44 stated in a report to the central committee of EAM that:

We always thought that the *ipefthinos* would be those forced to endure the greatest sacrifices, deprivations and hardship, yet in the countryside they have a very different idea of their position. In fact the *ipefthinos* and their relatives are those who endure the least hardship … I don't remember a time when I used the pack animal of an *ipefthinos* or saw him on guard duty … we can certainly claim that those who occupied such positions were not the appropriate persons but rather self-seeking crooks and you can certainly appreciate how much harm this does to our cause.[229]

Corruption and maladministration was the rule in many parts of Free Greece as the EAM *ipefthinos* used their positions to extort money for favours, persecute their enemies and enrich themselves and their families by appropriating EAM funds.[230] In many cases, village *ipefthinos* dissolved the elected people's courts and replaced their members with their relatives and friends. People's judges were also far from incorruptible, as many of them used their position to enrich themselves and persecute their enemies. Corruption was rife and judges showed preferential treatment to their relatives, friends and anyone who could afford to pay them off.[231] However, this was not the only problem. Often village *ipefthinos* and the peasantry showed a remarkable lack of interest in and aptitude for the running of day-to-day affairs as well as cultural activities. Despite the constant prompts of the local EAM committees, schools had ceased working even in its heartland of Agrapha and the few that did were in 'a deplorable situation … and the attendance is far from systematic and satisfactory'. Many schoolteachers, who were also often the village *ipefthinos*, preferred to linger in the cafés or occupy themselves with political machinations rather than resume their previous post.[232]

Such attitudes cannot be solely attributed to indifference or corruption. As the occupation came to a close, many cadres came to believe that a seizure of power was imminent and 'that EAM had run its course, this view is prevalent among our cadres and is slowly adopted by the rank and file, as it is evident in the lack of concern for the various EAM organisations'.[233] The creation of EAM's provisional government, the PEEA, further bolstered this perception and led to a massive surge in recruitment to the Communist Party, as octogenarians and small children, royalist gendarmes, former collaborators, EDES supporters and sometimes whole communities joined the KKE in the hope that this would ensure them immunity from persecution and favourable treatment by the future government.[234] These perceptions further increased sectarianism within communities and hardened the attitudes of the cadres. An EAM supporter from Euboea noted that many cadres believed firmly that after the liberation EAM/ELAS would be the dominant power on the political scene and they prepared themselves to capture a position in the future government, as a result, it was not uncommon that their attitude would be slavish to those higher up, tyrannical to those beneath them and arrogant towards most others.[235]

The massive influx of neophytes, the repeated setbacks suffered by ELAS, the rampant corruption and the autarchic attitudes of many cadres ultimately had a detrimental effect on civilian morale. A senior KKE cadre from Thessaly noted that such attitudes undermined the position of EAM since they 'created the impression that nothing had changed and that the people will suffer the exact same things under a new master'.[236] The Communist Party tried to address this situation by conducting an extensive 'cleansing' of the ranks during July–August 1944.[237] However, this move did not improve public morale. A British officer who toured Thessaly and Epirus in the spring of 1944 wrote in a dispatch: 'the peasants ... are opposed to the organisation and I think would back anything which offered freedom from such interference'.[238] Defeatism and war-weariness were equally widespread in the ELAS heartland of Agrapha; 'our supporters have grown tired', noted a local cadre, 'this is because of the many years that the occupation had lasted and has created serious doubts about the final outcome'.[239]

Testimonies and reports from other regions further attest to this. A senior EAM cadre reported from Crete during the autumn of 1944 that 'the political organisations of EAM are a shambles ... and even party members have become deeply influenced by the arguments of the reaction ... defeatism has reached a point when even rank and file members attack the party ... and threaten that they will murder the political cadres'. The author noted that he was repeatedly asked by local cadres to 'desist from doing anything, as many were afraid that the "Germans will wipe us out we have already suffered enough"', and concluded by noting that 'threats ... are not uncommon and we have been warned that if we do not sit still they will kill us or betray us'.[240] The situation was even worse in Macedonia, particularly after the catastrophic setback endured by ELAS during the anti-guerrilla operations of June 1944. A British liaison officer attached to the ELAS 28th regiment noted that 'in most villages the villagers have quote and unquote the Andartes ... main reason for their disgust is failure of Andartes to give good performance and fact that they left. Cases are reported of villagers openly refusing to give Andartes food.'[241] Such views were further exacerbated by the great disparity in living conditions between the guerrillas and the civilians who saw their properties going up in flames; as a British

A history of the Greek resistance

liaison officer noted, the peasants 'were furious with the Andartes, whom they had fed throughout the winter, for abandoning them'.[242] He added that 'on the quiet locals tend to speak against EAM and ELAS quite harshly, complaining of requisitioning and shooting of non-party people ... many would welcome a British occupation until an honest plebiscite was held'.[243]

The Indian summer of Free Greece was over. As the occupation drew to a close, most peasants were certain of two things: first, that the German army was going to depart soon; and second, they could no longer bear the People's Armies. The state the guerrillas had built was neither homogeneous nor always effective, and local differences were apparent from the very beginning. However, as the occupation ended, this state no longer served its purpose, since it offered no amenities to civilians nor it could protect them from the rage of the occupation troops. Rather, it had become an unsustainable burden on the peasants, who were longing for a quick release from the dual yoke of the Germans and the men who had appeared as liberators. As an Allied liaison officer noted, 'the people have, therefore, lost their enthusiasm for the liberation movement. The national Risorgimento has degenerated into a political brawl. This view is common to moderate elements in all quarters; in the towns, in the mountains, and in ELAS itself.'[244]

Notes

1 Apostolos Papakostas, memoir, unpublished, Skoufas Library Arta, p. 104.
2 Papakostas, memoir, p. 160.
3 Robert W. McColl, 'The insurgent state: territorial bases of revolution', *Annals of the Association of American Geographers* 59 (1969), p. 614.
4 Hristos Tirovouzis, *Aftodoiikisi kai laiki dikaiosyni 1942–1945* [Self-government and popular justice] (Athens: Proskinio, 1991).
5 Reggas, autobiography, unpublished, personal archive, p. 113.
6 Reggas, autobiography, p. 114.
7 Gerasimos Maltezos, *EAM–ELAS, anamniseis kai zitimata stratigikis kai taktikis* [EAM–ELAS, memories and questions of tactics and strategy] (Volos: self-published, 1987), pp. 153–4.
8 Dimitris Papanikolaou, *Enas daskalos thimatai* [A schoolteacher remembers] (Athens, n.p., 1985), pp. 34, 73.
9 GAKKI/AET/Apostoli A/File 2/Deltio pliroforion 1/12, p. 2.
10 Reggas, autobiography, p. 113.
11 Papanikolaou, *Enas daskalos*, p. 73.
12 Kostas Stasinos, *To Athamanio ton Tzoumerkon* [The village of Athamanio in Tzoumerka] (Athens: self-published, 2000), p. 73.

13 ELIA/AEPK/Pros to Thessaliko grafeio tou KKE/03/02/1944.
14 Raptis, *Apomnimonefmata*, p. 8.
15 ELIA/AEPK/Ethniko Apeleftherotiko metopo (EAM) eparhiake epitrope palama/27/6/44.
16 Raptis, *Apomnimonefmata*, p. 8.
17 ELIA/AEPK/Pros to Thessaliko grafeio tou KKE/03/02/1944.
18 ASKI/AKKE/Box 412/File/23/5/219.
19 Papanikolaou, *Enas daskalos*, p. 73.
20 Raptis, *Apomnimonefmata*, pp. 32–3.
21 Moutoulas, 'To EAM stin Ileia', p. 92.
22 Moutoulas, 'To EAM stin Ileia', p. 92.
23 Antigone Lenis, 'Sinedefksi me ton Niko Leni' [An interview with Nikos Lenis] *Tzoumerkiotika Hronika* 7 (2006), pp. 160–3.
24 Moutoulas, *Peloponnisos*, p. 523.
25 Hatzinikolaou, *Taragmena hronia*, p. 61.
26 A *dilosi* was a statement of recantation; political prisoners who signed it were set free and could resume their normal lives without further repercussions. Hatzinikolaou, *Taragmena hronia*, p. 61.
27 Papanikolaou, *Enas daskalos*, p. 33.
28 Giannis Haliasos, personal interview, Faskomilia, 2008.
29 Sheila Fitzpatrick, *Everyday Stalinism: Ordinary Life in Extraordinary Times: Soviet Russia in the 1930s* (Oxford and New York: Oxford University Press, 1999), pp. 74–7.
30 ASKI Digital Archive/http://62.103.28.111/neolaia/rec.asp?id=53019&nofoto=0 (accessed 2 January 2015).
31 ASKI Digital Archive/http://62.103.28.111/neolaia/rec.asp?id=53104&nofoto=0 (accessed 2 January 2015).
32 ASKI Digital Archive/http://62.103.28.111/neolaia/rec.asp?id=53104&nofoto=0 (accessed 2 January 2015).
33 ELIA/APME/Kiriakos Labros; Koliou, *Agnostes Ptihes*, p. 322.
34 Giorgoulas Beikos, *I Laike exousia stin Eleftheri Ellada* [Popular rule in Free Greece] (Athens: Themelio, 2005), vol. 2, pp. 251–2.
35 Vagias, *I Arta tis katohes*, p. 148.
36 Moutoulas, *Peloponnisos*, pp. 526–7.
37 ELIA Press Archive/Smolikas/Issue 1/18/07/1943.
38 James C. Scott, *Weapons of the Weak: Everyday Forms of Peasant Resistance* (New Haven, CT: Yale University Press, 2008), pp. 350–1.
39 ELIA/GDA/File 14.1/viografikes periseuma/ipoloipa/diafora/Haris Spatharis autodoiikisi kai laike dikaiosine stin voireia Euboea, p. 7.
40 Arseniou, *I Thessalia*, p. 279.
41 DIS/KMA/File 573-701/8h merarhia/diatagi peri sillipseos melon EEA/29/07/44; ASKI/AKKE/Box 493/File-30/1/74.
42 ASKI/AKKE/Box 493/File-30/1/103.

43 Papakostas, memoir, p. 424.
44 Baerentzen (ed.), *British Reports on Greece*, p. 25.
45 I.S., Igoumenitsa, 2008; the person who provided me with this testimony wished to remain anonymous.
46 ASKI/AKKE/Box 415/File-23/8/46.8.5.44.
47 Anna M. Arojna, 'Civilian resistance to rebel governance', Households in Conflict Network Working Paper 170 (2014), p. 22.
48 DIS/KMA/File 573-701/8h merarhia/diatagi peri sillipseos melon EEA/29/07/44.
49 DIS/File 914/ST/Ethnikes omades antarton/koino geniko stratigeio apofasi up'arithmon 6/16-8-1943.
50 DIS/File 914/ST/Ethnikes omades antarton/koino geniko stratigeio apofasi up'arithmon 8/25-8-1943.
51 DIS/File 914/ST/Ethnikes omades antarton/koino geniko stratigeio apofasi up'arithmon/7/18-8-1943.
52 Spiros Gasparinatos, *I Katohi* [The occupation] (Athens: Sideris, 1998), vol. 1, pp. 366-7.
53 Thanasis Mitsopoulos, *To Trianta sintagma tou ELAS* [The 30th regiment of ELAS] (Athens: self-published, 1987), p. 42.
54 Houtas, *I ethniki antistasi*, pp. 128-9, 138-40.
55 ASKI/AKKE/Box 493/File-30/1/46.
56 TNA/HS5/697Personal Report/L/Sjt. Smith, K./H.q. Force 133/M.E.F/10 Jan 44.P.
57 Romanos, *Mia Athinaiki vengera*, p. 173.
58 Romanos, *Mia Athinaiki vengera*, p. 201.
59 ELIA/AVZ/Comite central du Dist. De Trikala/Trikala le 9/11/43/commission de gestion pour les secours en greece. D.3/Div.
60 GAK/AET/Apostoli A/Fakelos 2/Ekthesi epi tis katastaseos ton piropathon periohon Ipirou kai Aitoloakarnanias, p. 2.
61 GAKKI/AET/Apostoli A/Fakelos 2/Ekthesi epi tis katastaseos ton piropathon periohon Ipirou kai Aitoloakarnanias, p. 3.
62 ELIA/AVZ/Eggrafo 65/ellinike politeia/nomarhia fokidos/pros to ipourgeion esoteriko/diefthinsis topikis aftodoiikiseis, p. 3.
63 ELIA/AVZ/Pros ton k.proedron tis epitropis diaheiriseos ton voithmaton en Elladi/DK.ES./3/9/43, p. 1.
64 GAKKI/AET/Apostoli A/File 2/Ipiresiaki epitropi perithalpseos pathonton kai piropathon Ditikis Makedonias, p. 1.
65 GAKKI/AET/Apostoli A/File 2/Ekhesi epi tis katastaseos ton piropathon Thessalis kai perifereias Lamias
66 ASKI/AKKE/Box 412/File-23/6/10 II.1944.
67 ELIA/AEPK/Pros tin Panthessalikin epitropti tou EAM /01/05/44.
68 ELIA/AEPK/File 1/Ekthesi/Provlimata.
69 ELIA Press archive/Kokkinos Mahites/3/01/1944.

70 Rigas Georgios Skoutelas, *Ta Theodoriana Artas* [Theodoriana village in Arta] (Athens: self-published, 2006), p. 228.
71 Skoutelas, *Ta Theodoriana*, pp. 259–61.
72 Georgia Skopouli, *Aftes pou eginan ena me tin gi.* [The women who became one with the earth] (Athens: Dodoni, 2008), pp. 53–4.
73 Romanos, *Mia Athinaiki vengera*, pp. 226–7
74 Dimitris Kostantinides, *Epixeirsi Panthiras* [Operation Panther] (Trikala: self-published, 2009), p. 189.
75 ELIA/AER/Fakelo 1/1N-10 pros tin dioikisin tis I taxiarhias.
76 ASKI/AKKE/ Box 496/File-30/4/147.31.3.44, pp. 2–3.
77 ELIA/AVZ/Pros tin en Elladi sevastin dioikisn erithrou stavrou/dia tas koinotikas arhas Amphilohias, p. 2.
78 GAKKI/AET/Apostoli A/File 2/9, p. 9.
79 Stratos Dordanas, *To aima to athoon: adipina ton Germanikon arhon katohis sti Makedonia 1941–1944* [The blood of the innocent: reprisals of the occupation authorities in Macedonia] (Athens: Estia, 2007), pp. 168–9.
80 Moutoulas, *Peloponnisos*, p. 487.
81 Vasilis Pavlidis, *Oi Alvanotsamides tis periohes Paramithias* [The Albanian Chams of the Paramithia region] (Athens, 2008), pp. 102–3.
82 GAKKI/AET/Apostoli A/File 2/9, p. 6.
83 ELIA Press Archive/Dervanakia/Issue 2/15/01/1944.
84 ELIA Press Archive/Dervanaia/Issue 2/15/01/1944.
85 DIS/KMA/File 3/1-32/Anakoinosis pros ta oikogeneias ton ektelesthedon Tsamourias, tou Fanariou, tis Dragoumis kai olis tis Tsamourias pros tous Ipeirotes kai olon ton Ellinikon laon.
86 Vagias, *I Arta tis katohes*, pp. 210–11
87 Herman Franke Meyer, *Aimatovammeno Edelvais* [Bloody Edelvais] (Athens: Estia, 2009), vol. 2, p. 113.
88 ASKI/AKKE/Box 496/File-30/4/147.31.3.44, p. 3.
89 ASKI/AKKE/Box 493/File-30/1/78.
90 LHCMA/Woodhouse Papers/Woodhouse 5/1/1/in Woodhouse 2/7-9, 3,4 & 5/1/1.History of the Allied, p. 111.
91 Stratos Dordans, *Ellines enantion Ellinon* [Greeks against Greeks] (Thessaloniki: Epikentro, 2006), pp. 49–50.
92 ASKI/AKKE/Box 413/File-23/6/7.
93 ASKI/AKKE/Box 413/File-23/6/7
94 Dordanas, *To Aima*, p. 514.
95 GES/DIS/File 956/A/Aggliki ipiresia pliroforion, anaphora gia ta tagmata Asfaleias, pp. 5–6.
96 GES/DIS/File 956/A/Aggliki ipiresia pliroforion, p. 16.
97 GES/DIS/File 956/A/Aggliki ipiresia pliroforion, pp. 16–24.
98 Stathis N. Kalyvas, 'Armed collaboration in Greece, 1941–1944', *European Review of History–Revue européenne d'histoire* 15 (2008), p. 133.

A history of the Greek resistance

99 Dordanas, *Ellines*, pp. 245–6.
100 Giorgos Dimitriou, personal interview, Igoumenitsa, 2008.
101 Ioannis Karakatsanis, 'I Mani ston polemo' [Mani during the war], PhD dissertation, University of Athens, 2010, pp. 239–41.
102 GAKKI/AET/Apostoli A/File 2/9, p. 6.
103 ELIA/Douatzis Archive/File 1.2/Diefthinsis evzonikon tagmaton Eubeoas/Arith. Protokolou 6418/Prosklisis/O stratiotikos diefthintis ton tagmaton asfaleias Eubeoas/13/9/44.
104 ELIA/Douatzis Archive/File 1.2/Elliniki politeia/Nomarhia Eubeoas/Arith. Prot.5315 pros ton dimo Halkideon.
105 DIS/File 956/A/Aggliki ipiresia pliroforion, pp. 48–9.
106 Reggas, autobiography, p. 145.
107 Pinelopi Vezdrevani, personal interview, Igoumenitsa, 2008.
108 Raptis, *Apomnimonefmata*, p. 24.
109 Raptis, *Apomnimonefmata*, p. 25.
110 ASKI/AKKE/Box 418/File-24/2/90.
111 ASKI/AKKE/Box 418/File-24/2/90.
112 Moutoulas, *Pelloponnisos*, pp. 495–8.
113 Kosmas Antonopoulos, *Ethnike antistase 1941–1945* [National resistance] (Athens: self-published, 1964), pp. 1143, 1150–1.
114 ASKI/AKKE/Box 418/File-24/2/90.
115 ASKI/AKKE/Box 418/File-24/2/90.
116 ASKI/AKKE/Box 418/File-24/2/90.
117 ASKI/AKKE/Box 418/File-24/2/90.
118 ASKI/AKKE/Box 418/File-24/2/90.
119 Kosta Karali, *Istoria dramatikon gegonoton Peloponnisou* [History of the dramatic events of Peloponnesus] (Athens: self-published, 1958), pp. 231–3.
120 Papagiannis, *Kravges tis mnimis*, p. 125.
121 ELIA/OTA/Petrou Ioannis.
122 Nikolaidis, *Ta hronia*, p. 56.
123 DIS/AGA/File IA/Geniko arhigeio 1944/Ar.50-70/Epistoli/Eleftera oreini Ellas/Ethnikes Omades Ellinon Antarton/Genikon Arhigeion/IIon grafeio/pros to geniko stratigeio ELAS/6/7/44.
124 DIS/AGA/File D/1-109/ELAS Ipeirou/ VII Merarhia/arhigeio Tzoumerkon-Artas/3/40/S.E/15 SP/24 SP/85 SP/2/39 SE/VI merarhia 1943-1944/Ekthesi sinoptiki gia tis paravaseis tou EDES apo tin mera tis ipografis tis simfonias tis Plakas/apo 21/02/1944 mexri 31/03/1944/perioxi VI merarhias.
125 ASKI/AKKE/Box 495/File-30/3/120.06.05.44, p. 2.
126 ELIA Press archive/Miniatikos Antartis/Issue 6/June 1944.
127 ELIA Press archive/Laikos Agonistis/9/18/08/1944.
128 Douatzis, *Imerologio*, p. 318.
129 DIS/ADN/8 Merarhia/Diefthinsi dikastikou/Arith.Prot.5394/20/07/44.

130 DIS/KMA/File/1/201-318Diatagi Peri Sillipseos atomon me kommounistiki idelogia/24/1/44.
131 Romanos, *Mia Athinaiki vengera*, p. 128.
132 Evangelos Nakos, personal interview, Gardiki, 2007.
133 Raptis, *Apomnimonefmata*, p. 34.
134 Priovolos, *Mia alisida mnimes*, p. 151.
135 Kosta Vlahou, *I antistasi stin Lakka Souli 1943–1944* [The resistance in Lakka Souli 1943–1944], unpublished, Zosimaia Library Ioannina, pp. 91–2; Tsogas, *Aima kai dakria*, p. 77.
136 DIS/File 915/A/11a/Vrettakos Leonidas pros Diefthinsi Istorias Stratou. Istoria ton tagmaton asfaleias Spartis/10/1/1955, p. 23.
137 ASKI/AKKE/Box 413/File-23/6/13.
138 ASKI/AKKE/Box 413/File-23/6/13.
139 Dimitris Filakiotis, *Ethniki antistasi ananmiseis apo to Velvento* [National resistance, recollections from Velvento] (Athens: self-published, 1977), p. 112.
140 ASKI/AKKE/Box 413/File-23/6/13.
141 ASKI/AKKE/Box 413/File23/6/22.
142 ELIA/AEPK/Ethniko Apeleftherotiko Metopo (EAM) Panthessaliki epitropi/24/04/1944.
143 ELIA/AEPK/Ethniko Apeleftherotiko Metopo (EAM) Panthessaliki epitropi/24/04/1944.
144 DIS/File 915/A/11a/Vrettakos Leonidas, p. 21.
145 ELIA/AER/File 4.22/18/06/1944/pros to IIon anexartito tagma Illeias pros tin YIII taxiarxia.
146 Moutoulas, 'To EAM stin Ileia', p. 158.
147 Moutoulas, 'To EAM stin Ileia', p. 150.
148 Moutoulas, 'To EAM stin Ileia', p. 186.
149 ASKI/AKKE/Box 418/File-24/2/102.
150 ASKI/AKKE/Box 418/File-24/2/102.
151 ASKI/Arheio Nikou Moiropoulou [the Archive of Nikos Moiropoulos] [henceforth ANM]/prokirixi-Lae tis Arkadias.
152 ASKI/ANM/prokirixi-Ston Lao tis Arkadias.
153 Antonopoulos, *Ethnike Antistasi*, pp. 1135, 1137–40, 1410–16.
154 IAM/Box 141/Istoria tou Ethnikoapelefthetorikou kinimatos stin perioxi tou 30ou sintagmatos, p. 5.
155 IAM/Box 141/Istoria tou Ethnikoapelefthetorikou, p. 7.
156 IAM/Box 141/Istoria tou Ethnikoapeleftherotikou p. 8.
157 Smirni Maragou, *I Lefkada sti dine tis katohes kai tou emfiliou* [Lefkada in the maelstrom of the resistance and the civil war] (Athens: Elliniki Evroekdotiki, 1989), pp. 267–8.
158 Logothetis, *To hreos*, p. 99.
159 Maragou, *I Lefkada*, pp. 278–80, 292–9.
160 Vagias, *I Arta tis kahotes*, p. 227.

161 Romanos, *Mia Athinaiki vengera*, p. 169.
162 Kremmos, *Hroniko*, p. 120.
163 GES/DIS/File 914/ST/14/Ethnikes Omades Antarton/Koino Geniko Stratigeio/Apofasi up'arithmon 17/26-8-1943; GES/DIS/File 914/ST/15/ Ethnikes Omades Antarton/Koino Geniko Stratigeio/Apofasi up'arithmon 18/29-8-1943.
164 GES/DIS/KMA/File.1-101/Diatagi peri efodiasmou.
165 ASKI/ANM/Eparhia Mantineias/Eparhiako simivoulio aftodioikisis, prokirixi pros tous proedrous koinotiton/23/08/1944.
166 ASKI/AKKE/Box-412/File-23/5/177/5.8.1944.
167 ASKI/AKKE/Box-412/File-23/5/177/5.8.1944.
168 Kremmos, *Hroniko*, p. 115.
169 ELIA/AVK/Diafora ipomnemata ektheseis ton apo tis katareuseos mexri simera diadramatisthedon en to nomo Kastorias kai Voiou Gegonota, p. 20.
170 Papananos, *To Anti-iroiko imerologio*, p. 83.
171 Dimitri Soutzou, *Imerologio Enos Antarti* [A guerrilla's diary] (Athens, 1989).
172 ASKI/AKKE/Box 493/File-30/1/108.
173 ELIA/Arheio Napoleon Zerva [The archive of Napoleon Zervas]/File 1/ Epistoli sto Geniko Arhigeio tou EDES, Politiki Grafeio-07/01/1945.
174 LHCMA/The Dobrski Papers/Dobrski 35 in Dobrski 29-35/SOE Operations in Greece and the Aegean, p. 10.
175 TNA/HS 5/697/Report by Capt. D.T.H. Nicholson on Past activities etc. in Greece, p. 9.
176 LHCMA/Woodhouse Papers/Woodhouse 5/1/1/in Woodhouse 2/7-9, 3,4 & 5/1/1.History of the Allied, p. 38.
177 TNA/HS 5/697/Report by Capt. D.T.H. Nicholson on Past activities etc. in Greece, p. 9.
178 TNA/HS5/J.B. Ponder/Report on Economic Conditions in Greece, p. 1.
179 Nigel Clive, *A Greek Experience, 1943–1948* (Salisbury: Michael Russell, 1987), p. 91.
180 LHCMA/Woodhouse Papers/Woodhouse 2/2/ in Woodhouse 2/Resistance Diary, p. 91.
181 Tasoula Vervenioti, 'Antartises tou ELAS kai Mahitries tou DSE' [Women fighters in ELAS and in the DSE], *Kleio* 3 (2006), pp. 163–87.
182 The PEEA was a provisional government established by EAM in April 1944. Its main role was to act as a counterweight to the government in exile. However, it remained a figurehead, as true power rested with the KKE.
183 ASKI Digital Archive/http://62.103.28.111/neolaia/rec.asp?id=53058&no foto=0 (accessed 10 January 2015)
184 ELIA Press archive/Laiki Drasi 9/25/03/1944.
185 ELIA Press archive/Roumeliotisa/30/07/1944.
186 ASKI Digital Archive/http://62.103.28.111/neolaia/rec.asp?id=50953& nofoto=0 (accessed 10 January 2015).

187 Ponder, *Patriots and Scoundrels*, p. 167.
188 ELIA Press archive/Drasi/25/08/1944.
189 DIS/ADN/File B/4/Polemiki Ekthesi gia tin drasi ton EOEA, pp. 1–3.
190 E.J. Wood, 'The social processes of civil war: the wartime transformation of social networks', *Annual Review of Political Science* 11 (2008), p. 550.
191 Riki Van Boeschoten, *Perasame polles mpores koritsi mou* [We went through many storms] (Athens: Plethron, 1998), pp. 76, 113–14.
192 Markos Golias, *Paradosiako dikaio kai oikonomia tou tseliggatou* [Custom law and the pastoral economy] (Athens: Poreia, 2004), p. 144; Stefanos Filos, *Ta Tzoumerkohoria* [The Tzoumerka villages] (Athens: self-published, 2000), p. 44.
193 Filos, *Ta Tzoumerkohoria*, p. 379.
194 Kostas Baroutas, *Mesohora, istoria, oikonomia, koinonia* [Mesohora, history, economy, society] (Athens: Erodotos, 1998), pp. 121–2.
195 Giorgos Georgiou, personal interview, Arta, 2011.
196 Imperial War Museum/Thomas Raymond Mason/Oral Interview.
197 Stavros Papagiannis, *Ta Paidia tis likainas, oi epigonoi tis 5hs Romaikis legeonas kata tin diarkeia tis katohis* [The children of the she-wolf, the descendants of the fifth Roman legion during the occupation] (Athens: Sokolis, 2004), pp. 375–7.
198 Ntousias, *EAM Zalogou*, p. 217.
199 Ioannes Bougas, *Matomenes mnimes 1940–1945* [Bloodstained memories 1940–1945] (Athens: Pelasgos, 2009), p. 211.
200 Kosviras, *Apo to vouno*, pp. 116–17.
201 Labros Tatsopoulos, *Nihtologio, 1940–1949* (Ioannina: self-published, 1998), pp. 96–7.
202 Kremmos, *Hroniko*, p. 120.
203 Papagiannis, *Ta Paidia tis likainas*, p. 37.
204 Kostas Sarantopoulos, *Valtetsi 1944 martiria* [Valtetsi 1944, a testimony] (Athens: Armos, 2003), p. 107.
205 Papagiannis, *Ta Paidia tis likainas*, p. 212.
206 Papagiannis, *Ta Paidia tis likainas*, pp. 229–30.
207 Christopher Woodhouse, *Apple of Discord: A Survey of Recent Greek Politics in their International Setting* (London: Hutchinson, 1948), p. 147.
208 DIS/File 922/Z/4/Grammateas ipotmimatikis E, ekthesi gia to Peloponnisiako sinedrio tou EAM, pp. 2–3.
209 ASKI Digital Archive/http://62.103.28.111/neolaia/rec.asp?id=53092&no foto=0 (accessed 10 January 2015).
210 ASKI Digital Archive/http://62.103.28.111/neolaia/rec.asp?id=53092&no foto=0 (accessed 10 January 2015).
211 DIS/AGA/Agoros, Diary, pp. 80–8.
212 DIS/AGA/Agoros, Diary, p. 86.
213 DIS/AIK/File 2/Ekthesi epi tis katastaseos periohis Pargas, p. 2.

214 DIS/KMA Archive/File1/468-572/peri tis emfanisthiseis simmorias/23/05/1944.
215 DIS/KMA Archive/File1/468-572/peri tis emfanisthiseis simmorias/23/05/1944.
216 Giorgos Lefkaditis, *Anadromes, enas proin eponitis thimatai* [Recollections, an EPON veteran remembers] (Lamia, 1998), pp. 91–3.
217 ELIA/GDA/File 16/diafores diatages/ekthesi tou sin.Ipsilanti.
218 ELIA/GDA/File 16/diafores diatages/ekthesi tou sin.Ipsilanti.
219 ASKI/AKKE/Box 410/File-23/2/27.
220 DIS/KMA/File 1/702-844/2/8/44/Diatagi G.A peri EEA.
221 DIS/KMA/File 1/702-844/diatagi genikou arhigeiou peri sheseon EEA kai stratou/1/08/44.
222 ASKI/AKKE/Box 496/File-30/4/147.31.3.44, p. 15.
223 ASKI/AKKE/Box 496/File-30/4/147.31.3.44, p. 17.
224 ASKI/AKKE/Box 496/File-30/4/147.31.3.44, p. 14.
225 ASKI/AKKE/Box 496/File-30/4/147.31.3.44, p. 17.
226 ASKI/AKKE/Box 496/File-30/4/147.31.3.44, p. 14.
227 Mazower, *Inside Hitler's Greece*, pp. 267–73.
228 ELIA/AEPK/Pros to Thessaliko Grafeio tou KKE/03/02/1944.
229 ASKI/AKKE/Box 418/File-24/2/91.
230 ELIA/AEPK/Ekthesi Epitropis Mesenikola pros tin Panthessaliki Epitropi tou EAM/16/04/1944.
231 ELIA/AEPK/Ekthesi Epitropis Mesenikola pros tin Panthessaliki Epitropi tou EAM/17/06/1944.
232 ELIA/AEPK/Kommounistiko Kommas Elladas/Perifereiaki Epitropi Karditsis/23/3/44.
233 ELIA/AEPK/pros tin Panthessaliki Epitropi tou EAM/01/05/44.
234 Arseniou, *I Thessalia*, vol. 2, p. 286.
235 ELIA/GDA/File 14.2/afaireseis apo viografies kai apo martiries/martiria Mimi Maragou/p. 2.
236 Arseniou, *I Thessalia*, vol. 2, p. 287.
237 ASKI/AKKE/Box 412/File-23/5/170.
238 IWM/Ward, Report on visit to Greece, p. 4.
239 ELIA/AEPK/Ethniko Apeleftherotiko Metopo/24/04/1944/pros tin eparhiaki epitropi farsalon.
240 ASKI/AKKE/Box 418/File-24/2/71B.
241 LHCMA/Prentice Wickstead papers/19/1 in 5/Drive into Pindus, p. 5. The words 'quote and unquote' indicate the military assessment of the disdain with which the peasants viewed their protectors.
242 TNA/HS/5/701/Report by Captain W. Killick, p. 8.
243 TNA/HS/5/701 Report on Kaimaxala area by T.J. Johnson, p. 48.
244 Baerentzen (ed.), *British Reports from Greece*, p. 77.

Conclusion

'Varkiza is over' proclaimed one of the countless pieces of graffiti painted on the walls of downtown Athens during the violent riots of 2008.¹ Such references to the resistance period are far from unique; literature, slogans and images of the occupation period were casually and extensively used by protestors who strove to situate their actions in a broader genealogy of resistance in which the ELAS guerrillas played a pivotal role. However, the memory of the resistance does not linger only among rebellious youths. The images and jargon of the resistance have permeated public discourses and are used extensively by the public, politicians and media pundits in a series of polemics that shows no signs of abating.² The resilience of the resistance and its protagonist – the guerrilla – is also underlined in the prodigious production of history books, memoirs, novels and films that centre on this turbulent period and in the often heated debates that have followed the release of some of them.³

How can we explain this fascination with these men, and what does the resistance mean to the countless people who evoke its memory and activities? No doubt many identify with the patriotic image and rhetoric of the resistance and regard the guerrillas as a latter-day version of the 1821 freedom fighters. Such representations are not novel; indeed, during the occupation the guerrillas were represented as the continuators of the 1821 revolution and other struggles for freedom from antiquity onwards. These images was eagerly seized on by a host of politicians, journalists and pundits, who extolled the guerrillas as symbols of the nation's indomitable will for freedom and martial virtue, and were repudiated with equal vigour by many scholars who insisted that the guerrilla was first and foremost a political fighter, who was certainly a patriot but

A history of the Greek resistance

was also moved by a much broader vision of political and social emancipation.[4] Others were attracted by the similarities between the guerrillas and the various anti-colonial fighters from the 1960s onwards. Finally, some idealised the guerrillas as the martyrs of a defeated revolution and patron saints of the radical causes in which they believed. The appeal of the guerrilla probably lies in the ambiguity of his image, which allows him to become a hero for all causes and factions. This book constitutes an effort to move beyond these mythical reconstructions and answer several pertinent questions: who were the guerrillas, what motivated them to endure hardship and risk their lives in combat, how did they experience their participation in the war and how did they govern and interact with the people in whose name they fought?

Historians have claimed that patriotism and ideology were the foremost reasons that led men to enlist and motivated them to fight. However, for rural young men like Thomas Karakitsos, neither had any bearing. Karakitsos was the first person I interviewed for this book. A tall, gaunt man with sparkling blue eyes, he began his career as a tailor; however, the war destroyed his trade and he was barely able to make a living in the rugged mountains of his native Souli region. In the spring of 1943 Karakitsos joined ELAS. This decision was influenced by his paternal uncle, who advised him that becoming a guerrilla was the best way to brave the situation and actually accompanied him to the recruitment office. A few weeks later he defected to EDES, this time accompanied by a different relative. This change of heart was not prompted by disillusionment with ELAS, but rather by the prospect of monetary rewards and a sense of family solidarity. However, this was not the end of Karakitsos's adventures. In 1947 he joined the insurgent communist Democratic Army, and after fighting with distinction for two years he followed his comrades to political exile in the Soviet Union. Disappointed by the realities of 'existing socialism', Karakitsos managed to return to Greece a decade later with the help of a former EDES comrade, who after the war rose to become a minister in the Karamanlis administration.[5]

Men such as Karakitsos were far from rare in rural Greece. Yet their stories remain obscure, as most scholars persist in seeing this turbulent period through ideological lenses. However, for the rank and file of the resistance, enlisting and defecting was seldom dictated by ideology; as Karakitsos pointed out, choices were dictated by *anagi*, want, and *fovos*, fear.[6] Kinship played an equally important role since it enabled the resistance organisations to put down roots in the insular peasant societies and gain the trust of the notoriously xenophobic peasantry. It is doubtful

Conclusion

whether Karakitsos would have been able to defect without the help of his uncle, who vouched for him to the local EDES commander.

Men like Karakitsos presented the resistance with a formidable problem; turning raw and often unwilling recruits into fighters who would be willing to withstand hardship and lay down their lives for a cause about which they had little understanding. The resistance organisations strove to achieve this through a rigorous programme of indoctrination. However, these efforts had a very limited impact on the recruits. So, why did the guerrillas fight? The majority of Karakitsos's comrades came from adjoining hamlets in the Souli province, and most had known each other from before the war. These ties, which were further strengthened by common experiences of hardship and loss, endowed the guerrilla bands with remarkable solidarity.

Leadership played an equally significant role, as did ideas of honour and masculinity. However, the persistence of such ties also created a host of problems that neither ELAS nor EDES were able to overcome, such as insubordination, an aversion to discipline and a refusal to fight outside the local district, which became more and more pronounced after the onset of the civil war. The lack of ideology was also no doubt responsible for the defections between the various organisations. Historians have often overlooked side-changing; however, during the war hundreds of men changed sides, often more than once, prompted by want, fear, greed or a sense of personal and regional loyalty. Such problems were also very much present in the civilian realm as EAM and EDES political cadres used their positions to settle family feuds, enrich themselves and advance their social position. Despite their efforts, the resistance organisations were unable to transform the ardently individualist attitudes of peasants or provide an alternative to the clientelist model of politics.

Kinship and regional ties were not able to bridge the growing gap between civilians and guerrillas in Free Greece. Hardship and the experience of combat not only augmented comradely solidarity but also progressively led the guerrillas to sever their ties with civilian society and develop an exalted perception of themselves and their task. Guerrillas believed that their sacrifices gave them the moral high ground *vis-à-vis* civilians and entitled them to their unlimited help. Conversely, civilians who had seen their properties time and again destroyed by Axis troops, and witnessed the guerrillas' inability to protect them, increasingly came to resent such attitudes, especially after the onset of the civil war. Violence was often an issue between the two groups, and became increasingly vicious as the occupation dragged on.

A history of the Greek resistance

However, violence should not be seen as a by-product of guerrilla frustration. The threat of violence loomed large in guerrilla–civilian relations from early on and played an instrumental role in the creation and sustenance of the resistance organisations. The emergence of the first guerrilla groups was accompanied by a terrific outbreak of violence against real and alleged traitors, moral 'deviants', community leaders, gendarmes and simple peasants. The purpose of this violence was twofold: to gain the sympathy of the peasantry through the punishment of marginal individuals, robbers and thieves, and at the same time to discourage potential dissenters and demonstrate to the peasants that lack of cooperation was not an option. Violence accelerated rapidly during and after the civil war as the resistance organisations tried to stem civilian disenchantment in Free Greece and deal with the various collaborationist militias that in many cases threatened its very existence. However, violence was not always dictated or implemented from above. The presence of the guerrillas provided local communities with an unprecedented opportunity to settle scores; such cleavages were often masked and are still seen by many as essentially political. However, the truth is that members and adversaries of the resistance were ultimately moved by personal and regional concerns above all else.

What are we to make of such attitudes? I believe that we will not be able to fully understand the character and nature of the Greek resistance unless we situate it in a broader European context and compare the experiences of the People's Armies with those of other armed resistance groups in south-eastern Europe and beyond. The resistance was not a Greek phenomenon; indeed, both EAM/ELAS and EDES were a part of a much greater movement that emerged under different circumstances but more often than not sought to address similar issues, employing methods that sometimes differed little from one country to another.

The men who composed the various 'People's Armies' in Europe came from varying backgrounds. The majority of French and Italian resistance fighters were workers, students and middle-class activists. Yugoslav partisans and Greek andartes, on the other hand, were predominantly peasants. Despite these differences, the experiences and motivation of the guerrillas in occupied Europe presented remarkable similarities. A study of occupied Yugoslavia noted that peasants 'changed colours according to time, location and whom they met … the poor would join the resistance in periods of high tide, and otherwise gravitated towards collaborationist formations which offered better conditions'.[7] Such attitudes were no less prominent in western Europe; a scholar of the French resistance noted that 'proximity or chance usually determined an individual's choice of group'.[8]

The French Maquis, like the Greek andartes, were highly territorial and even though most groups adhered nominally to the political tenets of the parent organisation, the majority of the rank and file more often than not identified with the primary group and their commander rather than with a particular political ideology. This outlook was further strengthened by the regional character of many of these groups, which like their Greek counterparts were raised and operated in a highly regional way. These attitudes had a significant impact both on the character and the nature of the guerrilla movements. Partisans, Maquis and andartes gradually developed a *condottiero* attitude; they viewed the people in whose name they fought with contempt, were prone to violence and seldom shied from changing sides when a more affluent or powerful patron appeared in their area:

> in the Lot, the leader of the Maquis was a trade unionist called Jean-Jacques Chapoy, who was admired on all sides. Suddenly, in February 1944, he announced that he was changing his allegiance from the AS to the FTP, but his group remained loyal to him. His Maquis remained the same except for the name.[9]

Such attitudes were no doubt influenced by recruitment patterns. Kinship and regional networks played a particularly important role in the formation of the armed bands across Europe, especially in Yugoslavia and Albania and in parts of northern Italy, where armed groups were often structured around the extended families of activists. However, family solidarity was not the only factor that led peasants to side with a particular resistance faction; personal, local and religious allegiances had an equally important influence and often played a pivotal role in the outbreak of factional violence. This was particularly true in areas such as Montenegro and parts of Albania, where clashes between the various resistance organisations were merely the continuation of pre-war feuds between rival peasant families.[10]

Attitudes towards both discipline and civilians presented equally impressive similarities. Yugoslav and Soviet partisans, French Maquis and Albanian Chetas often 'eschewed discipline … as being antithetical to the romance and elan embodied in the persona of the partisan'[11] an attitude that was in no small part responsible for the often abysmal military performance of guerrilla formations across occupied Europe. Relations between partisans and civilians also followed similar patterns.

Justice and requisitioning were the two foremost points of contention between guerrillas and civilians. Partisans believed that their sacrifices entitled them to the assistance and gratitude of the peasantry, who often had a very different opinion. However, attitudes varied considerably between different countries and groups. For instance, violence against the peasantry was relatively rare in France but not in the Soviet Union. Such attitudes were due largely to the political and social culture of the various guerrilla groups. Many Maquis were townsmen; however, a very large number of them had roots in the countryside and even though the peasants were often viewed with suspicion by the French left, the French Communist Party never espoused the anti-peasant rhetoric that was so common in the Soviet Union. Conversely, few Soviet partisans had ties to the rural areas; most were workers, Komsomols and intellectuals who saw the peasant as essentially backward and anti-Soviet. Such perceptions led partisans to regard all peasants as potential spies and traitors, and prompted them to adopt ruthless punitive measures to pre-empt dissent.[12]

Attitudes were much more benevolent among 'traditional' guerrilla groups, such as the Yugoslav Chetniks and EDES. Unlike their left-wing counterparts, both organisations operated in a highly decentralised manner and even though both received considerable outside backing, they ultimately relied on the goodwill of the peasantry. Therefore, violence was kept to a minimum, as they were wary of alienating their basis of support. The decentralised model of command adopted by the two organisations and the lack of a powerful unifying ideology (the Chetnik ideology was a vague combination of royalism and Serbian irredentism) also hindered their efforts as state-builders and encouraged dissent among regional commanders:

> Chetnik commanders often had a proprietary attitude to their respective districts. They were loath to operate outside their patch, difficult to remove, insubordinate and at loggerheads … the further they were from Mikhailovich headquarters, the more local commanders became warlords who paid lip service to the King's representative, but took orders only when it suited them.[13]

Differences in culture were also reflected in the deployment and use of violence. Traditional guerrilla organisations were much less keen on violence against their countrymen; however, they showed fewer scruples when dealing with ethnic minorities. ELAS used violence much more extensively than EDES both in Epirus and in the rest of Greece. What

Conclusion

was the reason for this difference? The persistence of traditional attitudes within EDES certainly played an important role. EDES band leaders and guerrillas viewed themselves as the guardians of their districts and compatriots, and often disobeyed orders to commit violence against civilians. Perhaps the most important difference lay in the character and the goals of the groups. Left-wing movements across Europe had as their aim the radical transformation of society along socialist lines; violence was therefore seen as a legitimate means of transforming and reshaping civilian society. However, this answer is inadequate; violence was not dictated simply by political outlook but was also shaped by culture and the social structures of particular areas. Clashes between the partisans and their rivals were much more violent in Montenegro than in Macedonia, while more killings took place in the Emilia Romagna than in other area of Italy during the occupation.[14] Historians have gone a long way towards uncovering and discussing the patterns and causes of violence, but a much broader scope is needed.

These observations merely touch the surface of the resistance phenomenon in occupied Europe. Resistance historians have focused largely on issues such as ideology and memory, and have often overlooked the experiences of the protagonist of the period – the guerrilla. Recent studies have sought to address this discrepancy by discussing a number of important issues, including violence, civil–military relations and reprisals; however, considerable work remains to be done in these areas. Future research must move beyond narrow national confines and consider these issues from a trans-national perspective. Such studies will facilitate a much better understanding of the resistance phenomenon and everyday life in Hitler's Europe during the Second World War, as well as the struggles and upheavals that persist in many of the areas in which the 'People's Armies' made their stand against Axis rule.

Notes

1 The Varkiza accord put an end to the clashes between government forces, the British and ELAS that took place in Athens during the winter of 1944–45.
2 Stathis N. Kalyvas and Nikos Marantzidis, 'To Istoriko parelthon os ergaleio propagandas' [The historical past as propaganda tool], *Kathimerini*, 21 July 2013.
3 Kostis Kornetis, 'From reconciliation to vengeance: the Greek Civil War on screen in Pantelis Voulgaris's *A Soul so Deep* and Kostas Charalambous's *Tied Red Thread*', *FILMICON: Journal of Greek Film Studies* 2 (2014), pp. 93–116;

E.R. Kosmidou, *European Civil War Films: Memory, Conflict, and Nostalgia* (New York: Routledge, 2013), pp. 117–46.
4 Mazower, 'The Cold War', p. 229.
5 Thomas Karakitsos, personal interview, Paramithia, 2008.
6 Thomas Karakitsos, personal interview, Paramithia, 2008.
7 Stevan Pavlowitch, *Hitler's New Disorder: The Second World War in Yugoslavia* (New York: Oxford University Press, 2008), p. 95.
8 Julian Jackson, *France: The Dark Years, 1940–1944* (Oxford: Oxford University Press, 2003), p. 485.
9 Jackson, *France: The Dark Years*, p. 485.
10 Milovan Djilas, *Wartime* (New York: Harcourt Brace, 1977), p. 136.
11 Slepyan, *Stalin's Guerrillas*, p. 91.
12 Karel Berkhoff, *Harvest of Despair: Life and Death in the Ukraine under Nazi Rule* (Cambridge, MA: Harvard University Press, 2004), p. 280.
13 Pavlowitch, *Hitler's New Disorder*, p. 94.
14 Sarah Morgan, 'The Schio killings: a case study of partisan violence in post-war Italy', *Modern Italy* 5.2 (2000), pp. 147–60.

Select bibliography

The bibliography contains only a sample of the sources used in the book; for a comprehensive list the reader should consult the notes that accompany each chapter.

Archival Sources/Greece

ASKI (Arheia Sinrhonis Koinonikis Istorias, Athens)
Ntoukakis Archive
KKE Archive
Moiropoulos Archive
Vranousis Archive

EDIA (Etairia Diasosis Istorikon Arheion Athens)
Tsamantakis Archive

ELIA (Elliniko Logotehniko kai Istoriko Arheio, Athens)
12th ELAS Regiment Archive
Douatzis Archive
EAM-Palama/Karditsas Archive
ERT Oral Testimonies Archive
Triantafillakou Archive
Zavitsanou Archive
Zervas Archive

ELIA (Elliniko Logotehniko kai Istoriko Arheio, Thessalonica)
Oral Testimonies Archive
Clandestine Press Archive

GAK (Genika Arheia tou Kratous, Athens)
Giannoulis Archive
Miridakis Archive
Tsouderos Archive

Select bibliography

GES/DIS (Geniko Epiteleio Stratou/Diefthinsi Istorias Stratou Athens)
Agoros Archive
Katsadimas Archive
Mavroskotis Archive
Miridakis Archive
Nikolopoulos Archive

IAM (Istoriko Arheio Makedonias)
Files 140–141/Documents, dispatches and reports of the 16th and 30th ELAS regiments

Archival Sources/Britain

Cambridge University Archives
T.E.M. McKitterick Papers

Imperial War Museum, London
K.F.C. Scott Archive
J.E. Lawson Archive
M. Ward Archive
D. Ciclitiras Archive
Oral Testimonies Archive

King's College London
Dobrski Archive
Evans Archive
Lind Archive
Lingen Archive
Myers Archive
Prentice/Wickstead Archive
Woodhouse Archive

National Archives, Kew
FO 371/General Correspondence
HS 5/SOE Balkans
WO 204/War of 1939–1945, Military HQ Papers: Allied Forces HQ

Secondary sources

Arseniou, Lazaros, *I Thessalia stin Antistasi* [Thessaly during the resistance], 2 vols (Larisa: ELLA, 1999).
Baerentzen, Lars (ed.), *British Reports on Greece* (Copenhagen: Museum Tusculanum Press, 1982).

Select bibliography

Beratis, Giannis, *Odoiporiko tou 43* [A chronicle of 1943] (Athens: Ermis, 2000).
Bourke, Joanna, *An Intimate History of Killing: Face-to-Face Killing in Twentieth-Century Warfare* (London: Granta, 2000).
Campbell, John K., *Honour, Family and Patronage: A Study of Institutions and Moral Values in a Greek Mountain Community* (Oxford: Oxford University Press, 1974).
Campbell, John K., 'Honour and the Devil', in J.G. Peristinay (ed.), *Honour and Shame: The Values of Mediterranean Society* (London: Weidenfeld and Nicolson, 1965), pp. 139–70.
Clive, Nigel, *A Greek Experience: 1943–1948* (Salisbury: Michael Russell Publishing, 1987).
Diamantis, Kostantinos, *Mnimes, polemos kai katohe: Papigo 1940–1944* [Memories, resistance and civil war: Papigo] (Ioannina: self-published, 2006).
Dimakos, Germanos, *Sto vouno me to stavro konta ston Are* [In the mountain with the cross fighting next to Ares] (Trikala: Protipes Thessalikes Ekdoseis, 2004).
Dimitriou, Dimitris, *Antartis sta vouna tis Roumelis* [Guerrilla in the mountains of Roumeli], 3 vols (Athens: self-published, 1965).
Douatzis, Giannis K., *Imerologio kapetan Othri* [The diary of Kapetan Othri] (Athens: Aixmi, 1983).
Fakis, Ioannis, *Enthimimata zois* [Recollections of a lifetime] (Athens: self-published, 2012).
Hamson, Denys, *We Fell Among Greeks* (London: Jonathan Cape, 1946).
Hatzinikolaou, Nikos, *Taragmena hronia sto Nesto* [Troubled years in Nestos] (Thasos: self-published, 2008).
Herzfeld, Michael, *The Poetics of Manhood* (Princeton, NJ: Princeton University Press, 1985).
Houtas, Stylianos, *I ethniki antistasi ton Ellinon* [The national resistance of the Greeks] (Athens: self-published, 1961).
Hristoforidis, Hristos (Garefis), 'Apo to Heirografo Imerologio tou' [From his unpublished diary], *Ethniki Adistasi* 104 (1999), pp. 72–5.
Kalyvas, Stathis, 'Leftist violence during the Occupation', in Mark Mazower (ed.), *After the War was Over: Reconstructing Family, State, and Nation in Greece, 1944–1960* (Princeton, NJ: Princeton University Press, 2000), pp. 142–83.
Katsantonis, Giannis, *Polemontas tous kataktites* [Fighting the occupiers] (Athens: Sinhrone Epohe, 1980).
Koliopoulos, Ioannis S., *Plundered Loyalties: Axis Occupation and Civil Strife in Greek West Macedonia, 1941–1949* (London: C. Hurst, 1999).
Kossevakis, Nikiforos, *I triti alitheia* [The third truth] (Athens: Aggira, 2001).
Kostoulas, Kostantinos, *Katohikes istories tou Pogoniou* [Stories from Pogoni during the occupation] (Athens: Elikranon, 2013).
Kosviras, Mihalis, *Apo to vouno ston amvona* [From the mountain to the pulpit] (Athens: Taxideftis, 2009).

Select bibliography

Kotzioulas, Giorgos, *Otan imoun me ton Ari* [The days I was with Ares] (Athens: Themelio, 1965).

Kremmos, Dimitris, *Hroniko, 1941-1944* [Chronicle, 1941-1944] (Athens: Politis, 2001).

Lainakis, Antonis. *Anamniseis apo tin ethniki antistasi* [Memories of the national resistance] (Chania: self-published, 1984).

Lazanis, Alexandros, *Anamniseis apo to metopo tou 1940 kai tis katohes* [Recollections from the 1940 war and the occupation] (Ioannina: Dodoni, 2007).

Logothetis, Poseidonas, *To hreos, mnimes kai martiries, 1940-45* [The debt, memories and testimonies] (Athens: Stohastis, 1992).

Lynn, John A. *Bayonets of the Republic* (Urbana and Chicago: University of Illinois Press, 1984).

Maidonis, Faidon, 'To Imerologio tou Fiadona Maidoni (24.6-10.9.1944)' [The diary of Faidon Maidonis], *Mnimon* 9 (1984), pp. 33-156.

Makrakis, Stavros, *Istories tou vounou* [Stories from the mountain] (Athens: Ermis, 1995).

Manolitsis, Tasos, 'I mahi tis Amfilohias' [The battle of Amphilohia], *Ethniki Adistasi* 25 (1980), pp. 39-53.

Marantzidis, Nikos (ed.), *Oi Alloi Kapetanioi, Antikomounistes enoploi sta hronia tis katohis kai tou emfiliou* [The other kapetanioi, anti-communist fighters during the occupation] (Athens: Estia, 2006).

Mazower, Mark, *Inside Hitler's Greece: The Experience of the Occupation, 1941-1944* (New Haven, CT: Yale University Press, 1993).

Mazower, Mark, 'The Cold War and the appropriation of memory: Greece after liberation', in Istvan Deak, Jan T. Gross and Tony Judt (eds), *The Politics of Retribution in Europe* (Princeton, NJ: Princeton University Press, 2000), pp. 212-33.

McPherson, James, *For Cause and Comrades: Why Men Fought in the Civil War* (New York: Oxford University Press, 1997).

Merridale, Catherine, 'Culture, ideology and combat in the Red Army, 1939-45', *Journal of Contemporary History* 41 (2006), pp. 305-24.

Mitchell, Reid, *The Vacant Chair: The Northern Soldier Leaves Home* (New York and Oxford: Oxford University Press, 1993).

Mitsopoulos, Thanasis, *Ananminiseis agoniston tou Vermiou kai tou Kaimaktsalan tou Paikou kai tou Kilkis* [Recollections of fighters from Vermio, Kaimktsalan, Paikon and Kilkis] (Athens: self-published, 1995).

Moutoulas, Pantelis, *Peloponnisos 1940-1945* [Peloponnesus] (Athens: Vivliorama, 2004).

Moutoulas, Pantelis, 'To EAM stin Ileia, I sigrotisi tis laikis igemonias 1941-1944' [EAM in Ileia, the construction of popular hegemony], PhD dissertation, Panteion University, 2012.

Nikolaides, Ioannis, *Ta hronia pou perasan, anamnseis* [The years that

Select bibliography

passed, memories], vol. 2: *1941–1967* (Ioannina: self-published, 1994).

Ntousias, Mihalis, *EAM Zalogou, ELAS Souliou* [The EAM of Zalogo province and the ELAS of Souli] (Athens: self-published, 1987).

Padoulas, Thanasis, *Flogismena hronia 1940–1945* [The flaming years] (Athens: self-published, 1982).

Papadakis, Iosif, *To Imerologio enos agonisti* [The diary of a fighter] (Chania: self-published, 2009).

Papagiannis, Vasiliki, *Kravges tis mnimes, katohe, antistasi, emfilios* [Screams of memory, occupation, resistance, civil war] (Athens: Sokolis, 2002).

Papakostadinou, Giannis, *Enthimismata potismena me aima kai dakria* [Memories drawn in tears and blood] (Athens: self-published, 1985).

Papananos, Vasilis, *To Anti-iroiko imerologio tou antartoeponiti Vasili Papananou* [The anti-heroic diary of the antarto-eponite Vasilis Papananos] (Athens: Oddyseas, 2006).

Papas, Dimitris, *To progefiroma tou Lakmona* [The bridgehead of Lakmonas] (Athens: self-published, 2000).

Papas, Giorgos, *Anamesa stous protagonistes* [Among the protagonists] (Athens: self-published, 2004).

Patsis, Vasilis, *Sta ori ta Thesprotika* [In the Thesprotika mountains] (Athens: self-published, 2009).

Ponder, John, *Patriots and Scoundrels: Behind Enemy Lines in Occupied Greece 1943–1944* (Melbourne: Hyland House Publishing, 1997).

Priovolos, Giannis, *Mia alisida mnimes, Achaea kai voreia Peloponnisos, 1940–1949* [A chain of memories, Achaea and northern Peloponnesus] (Athens: Alfeios, 2007).

Raptis, Dimitris, *Apomnimonefmata, foteines kai mavres selides mia epohes* [Recollections, dark and bright pages of an era] (Athens: self-published, 2001)

Romanos, Giorgos, *Mia Athinaiki vengera tou 1944, imerologio apo tin eleftheri oreini Ellada* [An Athenian banquet in 1944, diary from free highland Greece] (Athens: Romanos, 2008).

Roper, Michael, 'Re-remembering the soldier hero: the psychic and social construction of memory in personal narratives of the Great War', *History Workshop Journal* 50 (2000), pp. 181–204.

Roper, Michael, *The Secret Battle: Emotional Survival in the Great War* (Manchester: Manchester University Press, 2009).

Rotas, Vasilis, *O agonas sta Ellinika vouna* [The struggle in the Greek mountains] (Athens: self-published, 1982).

Roufos, Rodis, *To hroniko mias stavroforias* [The chronicle of a crusade] (Athens: Okeanida, 2004).

Sabanis, Labros, *Anamniseis apo tin ethniki antistasi kai ton emfilio* [Memories of the resistance and the civil war] (Athens: Metaihmio, 2007).

Sarafis, Stefanos, *ELAS: Greek Resistance Army* (London: Merlin Press, 1980).

Select bibliography

Shils, E.A., and Janowitz, M., 'Cohesion and disintegration in the Wehrmacht in World War II', *Public Opinion Quarterly* 12 (1948), pp. 280–315.

Skopouli, Georgia, *Sta aposkia tis istorias* [In the margins of history] (Athens: Rodakio 2013).

Slepyan, Kenneth, *Stalin's Guerrillas: Soviet Partisans in World War II* (Lawrence, KS: Kansas University Press, 2006).

Tsabiras, Sotiris, *As min vrexei pote* [Let rain never fall] (Athens: Elliniki Evroekdotiki, 2005).

Tsanaklidis, Kostas, *To 13 sintagma tou ELAS* [The 13th regiment of ELAS] (Thessalonica: self-published, 1990).

Tsiatas, Andreas, *Anamniseis apo tin antistasi 1941–1944* [Memories of the resistance] (Athens: Ziti, 2009).

Tsogas, Harilaos, *Aima kai dakria* [Blood and tears] (Ioannina: self-published, n.d.).

Vagias, Harilaos, *I Arta tis katohes* [Arta during the occupation] (Arta: self-published, 2004).

Vinen, Richard, *Unfree French: Life under the Occupation* (London: Penguin, 2006).

Watson, Alexander, 'Self-deception and survival: mental coping strategies on the Western Front, 1914–18', *Journal of Contemporary History* 41 (2006), pp. 247–68.

Watson, Alexander, and Porter, Patrick, 'Bereaved and aggrieved: combat motivation and the ideology of sacrifice in the First World War', *Historical Research* 83 (2010), pp. 146–64.

Woodhouse, C.M., *Something Ventured* (London: Harper Collins, 1982).

Ziagos, Nikolaos, *Ethniki antistase kai Aglikos Imperialismos* [National resistance and English imperialism], 2 vols (Athens: self-published, 1979).

Interviews

Anastasopoulos, Panagiotis/Zervohori 2008 [EDES guerrilla 1943–45]
Bolosis, Mihalis/Igoumenitsa 2008 [EDES guerrilla 1943–45]
Dimitriou, Giorgos/Igoumenitsa 2007, 2008 [EDES 1942–43, ELAS 1943–45]
Dimitriou, M./Kousovitsa 2007 [civilian]
Dokopoulos, Vasilis/Plataria 2008 [EDES 1943–45]
Dritsos, Dimitris/Souli 2008 [EDEE 1944–45]
Georgiou, Giorgos/Arta 2009 [EDEE 1944–45]
Haliasos, Evaneglos/Igoumenitsa 2008 [ELAS 1942–43, EDES 1943–45]
Haliatsos, Giannis/Igoumenitsa 2008 [EDES 1943–45]
Hristou, Vasilis/Igoumenitsa 2008 [civilian]
Karakitsos, Thomas/Paramithia 2008 [ELAS 1943, EDES 1943–45]
Margaritis, Dimitris/Gardiki 2008 [EPON]
Nakos, Evangelos/Gardiki 2008 [EPON]

Select bibliography

Naskas, Giorgos/Eleftheri 2008 [EDES 1943-44, ELAS 1945]
Noutsou, Aikaterini/Igoumenitsa 2008 [civilian]
Oikonomidis, Kostas/Igoumenitsa 2008 [civilian]
Sarvas, Vasilis/Filiates 2008 [EPON]
Papas, Giorgos/Igoumenitsa 2006 [EDES 1942-45]
Papatsatsis, Sotiris/Igoumenitsa 2008 [civilian]
Tseris, Hristos/Ioannina 2008 [civilian]
Tsipis, Konstadinos/Souli 2008 [EPON]
Tsodoulos, Vasilis/Igoumenitsa 2008 [civilian]
Tzakos, Nikitas/Igoumenitsa 2008 [EDES 1943, ELAS 1943-44]
Vasiliou, Giannis/Eleftheri 2008 [EDES 1943-45]
Vezdrevanis, Kostas/Igoumenitsa [civilian]
Vezdrevani, Pinelopi/Igoumenitsa 2008 [civilian]

Index

Agoros, Giorgos 28, 49, 77, 80–1
Agrapha 23, 27, 74, 87, 215, 246–7
Albania 89, 94, 100, 164, 240
   resistance 100, 106
   war 116, 123, 141, 148
   Partisan movement 148
Anogi 47, 78
Arcadia 23, 59, 224, 244
Arta vi, 25, 31, 39, 45, 50, 51, 60, 63–5,
   74–7, 95, 98, 101, 128, 153, 167,
   201, 204, 214, 217, 219, 232, 234,
   239, 248, 252
Arvanite 6, 126, 243
Athens 16–17, 20, 22, 24, 40, 58, 88–9,
   96, 129, 164, 170, 205, 207, 221,
   239

Badouvas, Manolis 43
Bakas, Thanasis 44, 80
Balkan Wars 39–40, 43, 71, 78, 132,
   184
Baloumis, Vasilis 44, 80
bandits 76–8, 83, 120, 121, 128, 140,
   165, 204
Belogiannis, Nikos 31
black market 14, 16, 22–3, 25–6, 48,
   53, 87, 91, 129, 134, 213
Blanas, Achilleas 223–4
British Liaison Officers (BLOs) 5
British Military Mission (BMM) 60,
   73, 85, 129, 212, 233

Campbell, John 139, 152, 159
Chams 67, 108, 113, 145, 241

Chetniks 262
civil war 93, 180, 187, 213, 232
Crete 21, 33, 43, 79, 84–6, 102, 166,
   173, 247

Dokopoulos, Vasilis 125
Douatzis, Giannis 45, 54, 126

EAM (Ethniko Apeleftherotiko
   Metopo) 1, 2, 7, 9, 10, 11, 14,
   17, 28, 29, 30, 31, 33, 34, 36, 40,
   41, 46
   people's courts 241–7
   ipefthinos 32, 35, 205–10, 227, 230,
   234, 237, 240, 243–6
EDA (Epitropi Diafotisis Adarti)
   180
EDES (Ethnikos Dimokratikos
   Ellinikos Sindesmos)
   oplarhigos 80, 81, 82, 97, 145
   recruitment 93–8
ELAS (Ellinikos Laikos
   Apeleftherotikos Stratos)
   kapetanios 35, 37, 42, 54, 87, 92, 94,
   126, 171, 175–9, 204, 226, 74
   olomeleia 173, 177, 185.
   omada 171, 174.
   politikos 169–72, 180
   recruitment 93–8
   stratiotikos 172
Ellinikos Stratos (ES) 213
Epirus 3, 6, 18, 21–9, 35–6, 39, 40–9,
   53, 60, 73, 75–9, 81, 87–8, 91–4,
   101, 105, 108, 120–4, 130–2,

Index

136–7, 146–7, 161, 168, 184–6, 204, 214–20, 226–8, 233, 235, 240, 242, 247, 262
EPON (Eniaia Panelladiki Organosi Neon) 56, 88, 92, 180, 210, 225
ETA (Epimeliteia tou antarti) 129
Ethniki Floga 164
Ethniki kai Koinoniki Apeleftherosi (EKKA) 213, 214, 242
Evrytania 13, 61, 93, 204, 214–15, 241, 245

Germans 99, 101, 105, 136, 138, 21
  anti-guerrilla operations 93
  army 18, 156, 248
  atrocities 138, 158, 165
  auxiliaries 145
  occupation authorities 104, 219
  officers 103
  reprisals 9, 94, 220, 235
  soldiers 14, 21, 84, 140, 142, 147, 159, 160, 182, 184, 209, 218
  zone of occupation 23
Giannota 51
Grevena 70–1, 124, 159, 238
guerrillas
  atrocities 146–7
  coercion 95, 96, 97
  combat 135–43
  daily life 115, 116
  defection 99–103
  identities 117
  ideology 86, 87
  killing 116, 146–7, 135–43.
  localism 178
  masculinity 117, 122–5, 131, 138–9, 144, 173, 176, 259
  morale 140, 155, 157
  motivation 92
  recruitment 83, 84, 87, 88, 91, 122–5
  religious beliefs 187–92
  requisitioning 135
  ritual 117–19
  self-image 116
  training 135–43

Haki, Ismail 100
Hammond, Nicholas 59
Hatzinikolaou, Nikos 115–16
Houliaras, Giorgos 74
Houtas, Stylianos 40

Igoumenitsa vi, 63, 65, 66, 69, 108, 200, 250
Ioannina, vi, 19, 26, 34, 50, 76, 87, 79, 174, 214
Italians 17, 18, 21, 23, 28, 42, 48, 57, 73, 103–4, 135, 140, 142, 147
  army 78, 83, 104, 206
  Carabinieri 16, 72
  occupation authorities 20, 24, 43–4, 55, 76
  prisoners 126, 145, 147
  soldiers 18, 21, 24, 50, 104, 146–7, 160, 201, 209
  zone of occupation 14, 23

Kalohori 99
Kalyvas, Stathis 11–12, 69, 251, 267
Karakitsos, Thomas 258–9
Katerini 51
Katsadimas, Ioannis 167, 168
Kiamos, Nikos 79, 121
KKE (Kommunistiko Komma Ellados) 36, 37, 42, 44, 56, 71
Klaras, Thanasis 13
klephts 130
Kolonikis-Karabinas, Spiros 77, 201
Komitadji 99, 104–5
Konitsa 18, 21, 178
Kossevakis family 39–41, 57, 66, 69, 77, 140, 152, 267
Koukos 221
Kounina 99
Krasanakis, Adam 43

Laconia 47, 58–9, 91, 209, 220, 244
Lakka Souli 53, 80, 97, 127, 171, 187, 228
Laokratia 163, 165
Lefkada 17, 36, 102, 231
Lidizda 204

Index

Macedonia 20, 21, 23, 25, 33, 42, 44, 50, 59, 71, 79, 83–4, 86–7, 89, 93–4, 96–102, 104–5, 119–20, 126–7, 133, 137, 147, 160–1, 179, 183, 187, 192, 206, 210, 213, 216, 220, 228, 231, 233, 235, 240, 247
Magoula 51
Maidonis, Faidon 132, 143
Makris, Apostolis 99
Makris, Vrasidas 225
Maratheas, Nikos 48
Mastoras, Tsilis 54, 79–80, 121
Mazower, Mark 10, 61, 66, 72, 107, 163, 195
Megalohari 39, 57, 77
Meskla 33, 79
Mesounta 204–5, 238
Messenia 29, 33, 58, 200, 239
Metaxas, Ioannis 107–9, 164–6, 205–6
dictatorship 76
Miridakis, Mihalis 29
Mourgana 20–1, 23, 204, 223, 240
Myers, Edmund 58, 70, 111, 142

Nikolaidis, Ioannis 26
Ntousias, Mihalis 32, 33

Odontopoulos,, Panagiotis 223
Operation Adler 214
Operation Animals 85, 142, 213
Operation Hubertus 214
Operation Panther 214
Operation Puma 214
Operation Tiger 214
Olympus 51, 71, 123

Padazis, Zois 78, 179
Paramithia 88, 109, 218–19
Paliokastro 51
Panellinia Apeleftherotiki Organosi (PAO) 41, 213, 221
Papadopoulos, Alekos 184
Papakostas, Apostolis 211
Papananos, Vasilis 88, 118, 119
Papas, Giorgos 16
peasants 18, 21–6, 29, 30, 32, 34, 41–5, 48–50, 54–7, 59, 60, 71, 73, 76–7, 79, 82, 85, 97, 100, 119, 126–8, 135–6, 139, 145–6, 156–9, 164–5, 201–4,
anti-communism 29
barter economy 95
conservatism 37
daily life 135
displacement 215–17
enlistment 85, 90–1, 93–5
illiteracy 33, 207
politics 30, 180, 206
protest 27
religious practices 188
resistance to authority 210–11
seasonal labour 28
violence 30
Paterakis, Vasilis 43
Patsis, Giorgos 140
Peloponnesus 58, 59
Petrakis, Giorgis 43
Pindus 14, 21, 23, 58, 62–3, 88, 114, 178, 215, 238, 256
Plaka Agreement 186
Pontic Greeks 44, 129, 221
Poulos, Georgios 220
Preveza 32, 60, 120, 145–6, 195, 214, 222, 242
prison camps 27, 97, 146, 224–7

Radovizi 21, 23, 39, 47, 78, 81, 88, 98
Raptis, Dimitris 205–6, 227
Red Cross 5, 28, 51, 75, 91, 214, 216, 240
refugees 18, 50, 62, 214, 218, 225, 232, 235
reprisals 215–18
Romanos, Giorgos 112, 139, 149–50, 152–3, 173–4, 196–7, 199, 250–3
Roumeli 17, 29, 44, 47, 209

Sabanis, Labros 23, 24
Sarafis, Stefanos 2, 11, 183, 197, 213
Sarakatsani 41, 48, 101, 120
security battalions 221–4
Skamnos 51
Skevis, Spiros 204
Slavophones 105, 222

~ 274 ~

Index

Souli 36, 80, 258–9
Sparta 18, 23, 218, 224, 228–9
Special Operations Executive 58, 59, 70, 85, 101, 132, 137, 146, 168, 171, 175
Stalin, Joseph 104
Stalinism 193

Thessaly 18, 21, 23, 25, 27–9, 34, 41–2, 47, 51, 57, 73–4, 75, 83, 86–7, 92, 94, 104, 117, 136, 168, 179, 184, 205–6, 213–17, 223–5, 238–40, 245, 247
Tsakas, Fanis 75, 107, 197, 204
Tsakas, Nikos 75
Tsamantakis, Nikolaos 79
Tsamantas 20, 89, 106
Tsolakoglou, Georgios 19, 20
Tsouknidas, Spiros 33, 75
Tsoumanis, Apostolis 204
Tsoumanis, Giorgos 101
Turcophones 84, 222
Tzallas, Thimios 53
Tzoumerka 21, 27–8, 29, 95, 98, 102, 167, 204, 207, 239

Valtos 21, 28–9, 40, 56, 77, 215
Varkiza 257
Vasileiou, Miltiadis 44
Velouhiotes, Ares 13, 213
Venizelos, Eleftherios 61

Vidras, Nikos 51, 71
violence
 against civilians 15–16, 18, 53–5, 97, 99, 104–6, 126–8, 141, 186–7, 210–12, 215, 218, 220, 223, 225, 227–9, 231–6.
 debates 2–3
 ethnic 47
 masculinity 138–40, 147
 mobilisation 41, 49–52, 75, 87
 occupation authorities 18, 21, 42, 60
 socialisation 115–16, 138
Vitsi 105
Vlach 6, 22, 32, 44, 48, 50, 120–1, 220, 222
Vlach Legion 51, 68, 104
Voion 20–1, 25

Woodhouse, Christopher 85–6

Xerovouni 78, 95, 184
Xinos, Nikos 56, 71, 72, 83
Xiromero 21, 75, 239

Yugoslavia 22, 105, 240
 Partisans 14, 99, 105, 232, 260–1

Zagori 18, 22, 26, 55, 100, 102, 146,
Zervas, Napoleon 16, 29, 37, 38, 39, 41, 57, 76, 77

EU authorised representative for GPSR:
Easy Access System Europe, Mustamäe tee 50,
10621 Tallinn, Estonia
gpsr.requests@easproject.com